THE
VIEW
FROM
ABOVE

THE VIEW FROM ABOVE

AN EXPOSITION OF
GOD'S REVELATION
TO JOHN

JAN DEGELDER

Library and Archives Canada Cataloguing in Publication

Title: The view from above : an exposition of God's Revelation to John / Jan DeGelder.
Names: DeGelder, Jan, author.
Identifiers: Canadiana 20210152745 | ISBN 9780886661267 (softcover)
Subjects: LCSH: Bible. Revelation—Commentaries.
Classification: LCC BS2825.53 .D44 2021 | DDC 228/.07—dc23

Copyright © 2020 Jan DeGelder

All rights reserved. No part of this publication may be reproduced, transmitted, or stored in any form or by any means without the prior written permission of the publisher.

ISBN 978-0-88666-126-7

Published by:

 The Study

Box 445
Fergus, Ontario N1M 3E2

Unless otherwise indicated, all Scripture quotations are from the ESV® Bible (The Holy Bible, English Standard Version®), copyright © 2001 by Crossway, a publishing ministry of Good News Publishers. Used by permission. All rights reserved.

*To Rita,
delight of my eyes
and loyal companion*

CONTENTS

Preface			ix
Introduction			xi
1.	God introduces the final phase of history	Rev. 1: 1 – 8	1
2.	The exalted Christ cares for his church	Rev. 1: 9 – 20	13
3.	Ephesus: pure in doctrine, but lacking in love	Rev. 2: 1 – 7	25
4.	Smyrna: Poor and persecuted, but rich	Rev. 2: 8 – 11	37
5.	Pergamum: Faithful, but compromising	Rev. 2: 12 – 17	49
6.	Thyatira: Loyal, but open to false teaching	Rev. 2: 18 – 29	61
7.	Sardis: Dead, but not without hope	Rev. 3: 1 – 6	73
8.	Philadelphia: Faithful and enduring	Rev. 3: 7 – 13	85
9.	Laodicea: Self-confident, but useless	Rev. 3: 14 – 22	97
10.	Our God is an awesome God	Rev. 4	109
11.	Christ – our hope for the future of the world	Rev. 5	121
12.	God's judgements begin to unfold. Round 1	Rev. 6	133
13.	The church is sealed to survive the tribulation	Rev. 7 – 8: 5	145
14.	God's judgements continue to unfold. Round 2	Rev. 8: 6 – 13	157
15.	The real hell's angels are coming	Rev. 9	169
16.	In the last days the Gospel proclamation continues	Rev. 10	181
17.	A prophesying church in a hostile world	Rev. 11: 1 – 14	193
18.	God comes to judge as glorious king	Rev. 11: 15 – 19	205
19.	Watch out for the angry dragon	Rev. 12	217

20. Christ exposes the deceptive nature of evil ..Rev. 13 229
21. God will resolve the conflict between
    good and evil ....Rev. 14: 1 – 13 241
22. When the harvest is ripe, God wraps up
    our history ....Rev. 14: 14 – 20 253
23. God prepares us for the completion of
    his wrath ....Rev. 15 265
24. God's judgements enter the final stage.
    Round 3 ....Rev. 16 277
25. Babylon is ripening for God's judgement ....Rev. 17 289
26. We witness Babylon's funeral ....Rev. 18 301
27. The day of Babylon's fall is the day of
    God's victory ....Rev. 19: 1 – 10 313
28. Jesus returns as warrior to begin his
    final clean-up ....Rev. 19: 11 – 21 325
29. Jesus returns as king to continue
    his final clean-up ....Rev. 20: 1 – 10 337
30. Jesus returns as judge to complete
    his final clean-up ....Rev. 20: 11 – 15 349
31. Watch the dawn of a new world ....Rev. 21: 1 – 8 361
32. Admire the architecture of the
    New Jerusalem ....Rev. 21: 9 – 21 373
33. Live the good life in the New Jerusalem ....Rev. 21: 22 – 22: 5 ...387
34. Remember Christ's urgent message:
    I am coming soon ....Rev. 22: 6 – 21 399
Bibliography 411
Study suggestions and questions 413
Liturgical suggestions 431

PREFACE

"Why do you never preach from Revelation, pastor? It's such an interesting book". For many years the question came from young and old. Well, it may be 'interesting', but for a long time I was not quite ready for it.

Then – less than a year before I retired from the ministry I began the sermon series, which meant that I had to continue after retirement to finish it. And more and more it did indeed become a fascinating journey.

Many resources have contributed to my understanding of Revelation, but a few stand out that I found particularly helpful. The more than 1100 pages of G.K. Beale's commentary (NIGTC) are an inexhaustible source of information. I also enjoyed working through the insightful Dutch commentary of H.R. van de Kamp (CNT), as well as *The Returning King* by Vern S. Poythress. But especially James Resseguie's narrative commentary has shaped my thinking about this unique part of God's revelation.

This book is not a commentary in the usual sense of the word. It is an exposition that has grown out of the above-mentioned series of sermons, and I am sure that many will still recognize the structure and flavour of sermons. Additional liturgical suggestions are available so that the chapters can still be used for preaching, if so desired.

However, I have adapted the material somewhat and it is my hope that in this way it has also become useful for personal devotional reading and group Bible study. With that in mind I have added study questions for each chapter.

Altogether it has taken a fairly long time to get to this point and I am very grateful for all the support given on the way.

I want to thank all who over the years have challenged me to preach on Revelation, as well as those who gave feedback and encouraged me to publish the results, in particular the members of Redemption Canadian Reformed Church in Flamborough, Ontario.

I thank the publishers for their support and cooperation, the tedious work of editing the manuscript, and typesetting the book.

When Jason Bouwman agreed to design the cover, I was excited. Thanks Jay. The result is exceptional.

To Rita, my dear wife – thank you so much for always encouraging me, supporting me and lovingly correcting me – not only during this project, but while walking by my side throughout more than 40 years of serving in the ministry.

Finally – all praise and thanks to God for allowing me the privilege to teach and preach for many years the gospel of salvation, the grand message that *Christ came into the world to save sinners* (1 Timothy 1:15), and for giving health and energy to finalize this book.

It is my wish that readers may be encouraged by what they find here. In this confusing world many feel uncertain about the future, because of alarming news reports and scary doomsday scenarios. But what you find online is only the view from here, from below.

However – the view from above, in Revelation, shows the unfolding of God's steady course towards the fulfilment of His promises: Jesus Christ is coming and all wrongs will be made right. His victory is secure.

Jan DeGelder
December, 2020
Waterdown, Ontario.

INTRODUCTION

For more thorough and detailed introductions concerning the date, author, purpose and interpretation of Revelation I refer to the commentaries listed in the bibliography, and in particular the ones I mentioned in the preface. Another great source for this is Cornelis P. Venema's *The Promise of the Future*.

But it may be helpful by way of this brief introduction to clarify where the author of this book stands in some of these matters.

I. Author and Date

Although there is a minority of dissenters, most scholars are of the opinion that Revelation was written by the apostle John, Jesus' disciple who is also the author of the 4th gospel, and of three small epistles in the New Testament. It is also generally considered to be the youngest book of the New Testament, written around the year 95 or 96 after Christ.

II. Four Ways of Interpretation

In the history of the interpretation of Revelation basically four schools of interpretation have developed.

1. *Preterism*

In the preterist view the visions in Revelation (or at least most of those) have been fulfilled in the time of the author, before and during the fall of Jerusalem in the year 70 after Christ. The book does not speak about a future eschatology. The pre-requisite for this view is that Revelation must be dated before 70 AD, which is questionable. Also – the global scale and dimensions of John's prophetic visions make it very difficult to restrict the impact to events in Palestine in the first century.

2. *Idealism*

The idealist approach considers all the visions entirely symbolic. They do not relate to any historical events at all. In a symbolic format Revelation pictures only the ongoing struggle between good and evil in this world, until Jesus returns. This is contrary to what it says in 1:1; 4:1 and 22:6 that the book is about things *that must soon take place.*

3. *Historicism*

   The historicist view believes that the visions John describes in Revelation must be identified with actual events or persons of significance in human (or Christian) history. This approach assumes a chronological chain of visions in Revelation to mirror a chronological chain of events between Jesus 1st and 2nd coming. In this way the interpretation becomes highly speculative and subjective, and the outcome depends on when and where the interpreter lives.

4. *Futurism*

   Those who choose the futuristic method believe that the visions must be interpreted as literally as possible, and picture future events, most of which will occur shortly before the end of history. In the details the views of those who defend the futuristic interpretation vary significantly.

III. The Millennium

Connected with especially the futuristic approach, Revelation 20:1-10 has become one of the most controversial chapters in the book. The controversies focus on the interpretation of the expression *a thousand years*, or 'the millennium'. There are basically three millennial views, although they come in several varieties.

1. *Premillennialism*

   Christ will return before (pre) the millennium. In this view Christ's return will happen after the great tribulation, a time of opposition to the gospel and persecution of the church. His return will then usher in a literal period of 1000 years, bringing universal peace and prosperity on earth, when he will be bodily present and govern the nations from the earthly Jerusalem. Many premillennialists include 'the rapture' at the beginning of the great tribulation. Some believe that the earthly temple will be rebuilt and that the temple sacrifices will be restored. The Last Judgment will come after the millennium.

2. *Postmillennialism*

    Christ will return after (post) the millennium. In this view the millennium will be a future golden age in history, before Christ's 2nd coming, either literally 1000 years, or just a long period of time. After a time of persecution for the church, the nations will turn to Christ, Biblical principles and Christian morals will dominate all areas of life, till Christ's return and the Last Judgment.

3. *Amillennialism*

    In this view the 1000 years are a symbolic representation for the entire period between Christ's 1st and 2nd coming, the complete time that Christ reigns as King from heaven through his Word and Spirit. It starts with his ascension into heaven and ends with his return from there to judge the living and the dead, and to usher in the new heaven and the new earth.

IV. When it comes to the four ways to approach Revelation as a whole, the author of this book takes a somewhat eclectic approach: Idealism combined with aspects of historicism. The visions are all seen as symbolic, but they do refer to real events in our earthly history. However – not in the sense that a particular vision can be identified with one particular event or person in history, but the visions help us to connect similar events and developments throughout history. There is also a futuristic element: some events are still to come. At this time in history the return of Christ, the last Judgment and the new heaven and earth, with the New Jerusalem are still in the future.

V. Although 'amillennialism' is technically a misnomer, since no one denies that the millennium is real, this book reflects the amillennial position in that it interprets the 1000 years as the entire period between Christ's ascension into heaven and his return in glory. This view has been dominant since Augustine (4th century), and is reflected in the Reformed confessions.

1

REVELATION 1: 1 – 8

GOD INTRODUCES THE FINAL PHASE OF HISTORY

It has taken me a long time to come to grips with the intention of this last book of the Bible – the Book of God's Revelation to John. The difficulties to understand the structure of Revelation, and then to explain the details, so that they would fit in the overall structure, were pretty daunting. So now you have this book in your hands, you may think: "He must have figured it all out".

The answer is 'no'! As a matter of fact, I have sort of given up on finding the final answers in the many confusing discussions about Revelation. But I have also become convinced that the message of this book is too important to let that stop me.

Many people look around in this world and wonder: where is God in this world full of wars, violence, famine, disasters, and you name it?

Well - Revelation gives directions when it comes to this.

But can Revelation be understood then? Yes, it can, even without having all the answers!

1 • Revelation 1:1-8

One author tells about some senior Seminary students who noticed one of the cleaning-staff reading a book.

> "What are you reading?" they asked.
> "The Bible", he said.
> "What part of the Bible?"
> "I'm reading Revelation", was the answer. The students thought they would help this poor man, who was probably all confused.
> "Do you understand what you are reading?" they asked.
> "O, yes!" he replied. They were astonished.
> "What does it mean?"
> "Jesus is going to win....!" he said.[1]

I have thought sometimes that for children and young people Revelation might be easier to understand than for adults. Read it as fantasy-literature, full of magic, mystery, and bizarre creatures. With this important difference: Revelation is real! God rules history and brings it to consummation in Jesus' return and victory.

In the time between Jesus' first coming in Bethlehem and his second coming at the end of times, Satan will attack the church. But Revelation shows us the victory of Jesus Christ. Here is our encouragement and comfort: God is in control. As his people we may find ourselves travelling through the wilderness, but we will find our way home, to the new Promised Land, the new earth and heaven, when the final phase of history is completed. This is what this book is all about.

In Rev. 1:1–8 God introduces this. And the beginning anticipates the end. Rev. 22:6–21 echoes many of the sayings of the beginning. Within this framework the pictures are moving toward the final victory.

---

[1] Anecdote told by Vern S. Poythress in his commentary The Returning King, P&R Publishing Company, Phillipsburg, NJ, 2000, page 14

A TRUSTWORTHY REVELATION

When you like reading, you will know that book-titles are important. When an author can find a catchy title for his book, he can draw the attention of potential readers.

A good book-title will help you anticipate what you can expect. It can trigger your curiosity as to what you may encounter when you pick up the book, open it, and start reading.

This is what the apostle John does with the book we are opening here. He gives his book an extensive title in the v.1-3. Or perhaps you could say that the title is *Revelation of Jesus Christ*, and then he gives us, in the rest of the v.1-3, an extensive subtitle. This subtitle gives a brief but important characteristic of the book we have in front of us.

The first thing that strikes us is that it comes to us as *the revelation of Jesus Christ, which God gave him*. So this book is not, as it is sometimes called, "The Revelation of John". No, from the first word John makes it very clear: "Yes, I wrote it; I put it on paper, but there should be no misunderstanding: what you have in your hand is not from me. It was given to me. Or better even: it was shown to me. The things you will read may sound fantastic. But it was not my fantasy. It was not my imagination."

No, what we have here comes directly from the Holy God himself! This is really amazing. This whole book comes as a direct communication from God to all of us. That makes it crucially important that we come to know what it is all about; that we understand the message God has for us.

This should be possible because it is called "revelation" and that means "uncovering". Many people think that, in this book, secret and mysterious matters are hidden in dark symbolism, like symbolic monsters and symbolic numbers. But that is not the case. This book is not hiding things. It is called "revelation". We may need to do some work to understand it, but it does mean that God is disclosing, revealing things to us.

That may not sound so special. As Christians we believe that the whole Bible is God's Word, God's revelation. It gives us the truth and it has divine

1 • Revelation 1:1-8

authority. That is true. And yet – here is something special going on. God himself is revealing his plan for the history of the church and the world.

We all look at what has been going on throughout the ages and what is going on today in the church and in the world. Sometimes we try to imagine how things will develop in the future. Most of the time it looks pretty chaotic, or outright scary. It is often confusing, and it is hard to make sense of the things you see on this earth.

Are we going anywhere? Is there any rhyme or reason to what we are observing?

Now remember – we believe that God is the direct author of the Book of Revelation in the strict sense of the word. This makes Revelation indeed a unique book. Not so much because of the bizarre creatures we hear about, but because it gives you a unique point of view. We will look at the history of the church and the world – but from above.

Our everyday earthly point of view is very restricted. It is very much hindered by our limited perspective. We only have a narrow window on time and on space. That makes it impossible for any individual to connect all the dots.

In contrast with that angle we will learn things, we will see connections in Revelation that can only be seen and recognized from above, from a heavenly point of view. That is, from God's point of view. And you can trust this – not only because we get it directly from God, but also because of the involvement of Jesus Christ. And we know this Jesus as the One who made us familiar with God the Father.

We hear in v.1 that God gave the message to him to pass it on.

In other words, what John sees in his visions was the Word of God, testified to be true by the Son of God. That makes for a trustworthy message. It is quite amazing to think of this. This revelation from God comes to John, and via him it reaches us, here, our churches, our congregations. It comes here and enters our worship.

If this is how God is introducing the final phase of history, you can trust that it will help you to make sense of what you see and hear in this life on earth. And you can trust that it will be full of encouragement and hope in this confusing world.

Look at the marvellous chain of transmission of this trustworthy revelation. It starts with God – he is the origin. Then it goes to Jesus, who in turn gives it to an angel, who passes it on to John. John was told to write it down, and then the book ended up in the hands of a reader. And now you can hear it, read it, and take it to heart.

Do we get the point? We are hearing trustworthy revelation. God takes care of this "transmission process" by which "the Word of God and the testimony of Jesus Christ" (v.2) are moving through the chain. And in his grace he puts us at the receiving end of it. So now we may know that what is coming to us is a reliable message from above. You can trust the origin.

In this concise subtitle, the apostle John tells us more about this "trustworthy revelation". It is something, he says, that God gave to Jesus, to "show to his servants". There is a lot to see and hear in this book. Revelation is not just a picture book; it is a noisy picture book. It is full of visions. It is full of moving pictures, video-clips as it where, that tell us more than words can express.

We will find out how often John says: "I looked . . . , I watched . . . , I saw . . ." It says in v.2 that John "bore witness even to all that he saw." In this way he urges us to trust his book. He wants us to believe him and to find strength and courage in what he saw. It is true – all these fascinating pictures are full of symbolism. That sounds complicated, and yet you can understand.

After all, this revelation is for "his servants". In other words, this message is not for theological professors only. It is not for a scholarly elite. It is not for specialized insiders. It is for God's servants. It is for the people that serve God every day. That is for all believers. This book is for common folk like you and me.

This gives it a lot of suspense. What are we going to see when we watch these pictures? *The things that must soon take place*, it says. "What must take place" is the unfolding of God's plan for the church and for this world. What began with Jesus' first coming *must* be completed with his second coming. God's promises will be fulfilled. It is going to happen! You are going to see what is coming.

1 • REVELATION 1:1-8

And make no mistake: it is coming *soon,* it says. You may wonder whether that still make sense today, 2000 years after it was written – this word "soon". No, not from where we are, here on earth. We may not see much progress. But the word "soon" reflects what you see from above, from heaven. It makes sense when you see God's big picture.

As church of Jesus Christ, you will soon begin to experience the things you will see, says John. And then it must and will go on, uninterrupted. No one can stop it. Jesus **is** coming. Evil **is** going to be destroyed. A new heaven and new earth **is** going to be ushered in.

Then the question is not: when will it be completed, somewhere on our calendars? But rather, we know: Since Jesus' resurrection, we are in the final phase of his victorious warfare. It will be completed. And you and I better be ready for it, whenever the moment is there! These are "the last days" says the Bible. The pictures in this book show that these 'last days' are times of intense conflict. And we are right in the middle of it.

That is why God encourages us not to shy away from this book, but to read it or listen to it, and apply it. It is *prophecy*, it says. In the Bible, "prophecy" always speaks about what God is doing or what he is going to do. But "prophecy" also comes with the urgent and inevitable call to be faithful, to repent and believe, to trust and obey. In other words – the message of Revelation wants to reach the heart and lives of God's people. God wants to reach your heart and my heart. Because he wants to comfort you and give you hope in the time in which we live.

That is why John adds in v.3 that *blessed is the one who reads aloud the words of this prophecy, and blessed are those who hear, and who keep what is written in it.*

Listeners gather around one who reads God's Word. It shows a congregation gathered for worship. This is where God calls us. This is where he addresses us. This is where we hear the sounds of his revelation and where this revelation will bring a blessing. Take to heart what you see and hear. It will impact your life. You will learn to rejoice together in what God is doing and what he is going to do.

God introduces the final phase of history

Don't miss out on this blessing. *The time is near*. Stay focussed on what is coming.

The count-down has started.

N ENCOURAGING GREETING

We continue to read our passage. We have read the sub-title of John's book, and when we turn the page, so to speak, we find out that it is actually a letter (v.4). We know about the seven letters we will come across in Rev. 2 and 3, but the whole thing is basically one letter, to be shared by all the addressees.

Just as in almost all the epistles in the New Testament, the author introduces himself. Men like Paul, Peter, and others, usually add something like "an apostle of Jesus Christ" or: "a servant of Jesus Christ". But this author simply says "John" – no particulars added. How vague and how non-specific can you get?

It is a pretty common name, and since the 19th century theologians have speculated wildly as to who this mysterious 'John' might be. However, just "John" must have been sufficient for the first readers. They did not need more details. They knew right away: this 'John' must be the John they all knew as their pastor.

That is why we hold to the traditional view that this author was the apostle John, the same who wrote the Gospel and three letters in the New Testament. It makes sense, for this John lived and worked for many years in Ephesus and beyond. He knew the people to whom he wrote, and they knew him.

Well then, this John is addressing his letter *to the seven churches in Asia*, it says. In Revelation 2 and 3 we hope to learn more about these churches. For now it's good to know that we are talking about a number of local congregations, located in what is today the western part of Turkey – at that time a province of the Roman Empire called "Asia Minor".

1 • Revelation 1:1-8

Here we find for the first time the number "seven". It will not be the last time. The number 'seven' is everywhere. It appears fifty-five times in Revelation. We know that numbers play a significant role in this book, and always, or at least most of the time, with a symbolic meaning. Seven is only one of them. You also come across three, four, ten, twelve, or some combinations of these.

Seven is very prominent in this book. It is the number of completeness, fullness, perfection. As such it is often connected with God. Here it means that you cannot say: "Oh, he also could have picked six or eight churches. No, these seven churches represent the fullness of the universal church; the entire church which Jesus Christ is gathering out of the whole human race from the beginning of the world to its end.

The purpose is that John's letter had to be read and heard in those seven churches. But then also in all the churches in John's time. And then also in all the churches of all times and places. In fact, the apostle John – or actually God himself – wants this book to be read and heard everywhere.

Why is this so urgent, also for us, today? Well, remember what we said earlier: We have this trustworthy revelation, coming directly from God himself, about his plans for the final phase of history. And now we learn that the entire Christian church is heavily involved in this. That is why we need to know. We need to be alert as to what is going on. We need the comfort of the view from above. We need the courage to persevere in the time in which we live – the last days!

This is what God provides in this book. And he does so in a marvellous way, right from the start. For when we begin to read and listen, as we were encouraged to do in v.3, John greets us on behalf of God with a most encouraging greeting, a most heartwarming and compassionate welcome to his visionary world.

This greeting in the v.4 and 5 is quite familiar to many Christians. It is often used as an opening greeting in Sunday worship services. But do you really hear it? Do you really pay attention to what God says to you there? Do you hear the comfort and encouragement with which God Almighty comes to you and addresses you in this often so confusing and frightening world? Do you hear the deep compassion with which God reaches out to you?

God introduces the final phase of history

Life can be pretty overwhelming. This affects your personal circumstances and your relationships. But it can also hit you when you look around in this world and try to get a handle on the big picture of everything that is going on. And in this book we are about to see and hear many new things. Is it going to help us? Or is it going to confuse us? You may wonder about that.

Well, whatever happens, whatever goes on, keep in mind always: *My grace and my peace will be for you*, says God. "Grace" is God's love and mercy, God's forgiveness and eternal life in Jesus Christ. And the result of this is "Peace". It gives you 'peace' with God. God's grace is the basis for a new relationship with him that will give you 'peace of mind'. By his grace, God sets this confused and chaotic world straight, and the result is breath-taking: true and indestructible peace for you, in Jesus Christ.

It says that this comes from God. But who is this God? How does he present himself as he enters your life with his grace and peace? It comes *from him who is, and who was and who is to come* (or: 'who is coming'). He is the God who controls the present, the past, and the future; the God who keeps his Word. He is and remains faithful.

He is the same God who met Moses at the burning bush (Exodus 3:14), where he said about himself *I am who I am*. That means the same. He has not changed, and he will never change. This is our God, also today, as he brings history to its consummation. "You can trust me," he says. "I do what I have promised."

"Grace and peace" also come *from the seven spirits before God's throne*. Again, think of the 'seven'! It stands for the full and invincible power of the Holy Spirit. He distributes God's grace among God's children, and he fills our hearts with God's peace.

Finally, in the third place, "grace and peace" also come *from Jesus Christ* (v.5). But then his power unfolds in another three-some. It is amazing – the glory of this three-fold office of "the Christ", your prophet, priest, and king!

As Prophet, he is *the faithful witness*. He testifies about God's love for you.

As Priest, he is *the firstborn from the dead*. He shows God's love when he died for you; when he conquered the power of death and arose.

And as King, he is also *the ruler of the kings of the earth*. He shows God's love when he protects you and takes care of you. He is above every power on earth.

This is the most encouraging greeting ever. It is almost too much to wrap your head around. Where does true grace and peace come from in your life? It is the holy and almighty Triune God, with all the abundance of his awesome power, majesty, love and compassion. He makes you share in his grace and peace. These are his gifts for his children.

Trust that his grace and peace are always close by, always – no matter how frightening, how confusing things may become as the final phase of God's plan unfolds.

A GLORIOUS EXPECTATION

All this leads to praising and worshipping Jesus Christ as the coming King. As God introduces the final phase of history, it comes with the glorious expectation that our victorious Saviour is on his way. *To him be glory and dominion for ever and ever.* Here is the first of the many doxologies in this book. Men, angels, other creatures, again and again they all make abundantly clear that all glory and praise is to the Triune God, and not to man – never!

This is the emphasis in the last part of this passage. Whatever you will see or hear, whatever is coming that might scare you – *all glory and power for ever and ever is to him who loves us so much, that he has set us free from sin by his blood*. Nothing expresses the love of God, as the redeeming work of Jesus does.

In him is your security and hope in the midst of the trials and disasters we encounter as God's revelation unfolds. Persecution or temptation might threaten to overwhelm us, but God's love in Jesus' victory over sin will help you persevere. For he is the One who *made us a kingdom, priests to serve his God and Father.*

The expression comes from Exodus 19:6. Here the Lord instructs Moses to tell the Israelites, just freed from slavery in Egypt, *you will be for me a king-*

dom of priests and a holy nation. And the apostle Peter shows that in Jesus Christ people from all nations may share in this unique privilege of Israel. *You are a chosen people*, he says to his readers, *a royal priesthood, a holy nation* (1 Peter 2:9).

These were Christians from Jews and Gentiles. But together they were renewed to serve and worship God. And that is what continues today. A new kingdom of priests is growing and growing. It is the awesome result in this world of the great church-gathering project of our victorious God and Saviour Jesus Christ.

This is so exciting! And even more so, because it fills us with the glorious expectation of Jesus' return, the source of your hope and comfort. It is this Saviour who is coming. This is the major theme in this book.

Look, God says through John, 'pay attention, keep this perspective and don't get caught up in distractions, so that it may take you by surprise. Continue to be alert'.

Behold, he is coming with the clouds. These clouds are a sign of his divine majesty. He is coming in glory. As Jesus himself puts it in Matthew 24:30 (referring back to Daniel 7:13): *They will see the Son of Man coming on the clouds of heaven with power and great glory.*

Is this our longing? Are you looking forward to seeing him come in glory? Is the longing for Jesus' return really alive among us? Are you and I ready for it? We tend to forget sometimes that we live in the last days!

But he is on his way, *and every eye will see him*, including those who have killed him. This is what everyone and everything is headed for – Jesus is coming to bring to fulfilment the final phase of history, everything in this book. Suddenly he will be there, for everyone to see. No one will be uncertain or in doubt about it. Everyone: those who believe in Jesus as the Saviour AND those who reject him. They will all recognize him as the crucified one.

And all tribes of the earth will wail on account of him. No, not because they are sorry and repent. But Christ's enemies will express their hopelessness and despair.

1 • Revelation 1:1-8

At the same time, as God's children you may look forward with confidence. *Amen. So shall it be!* Are you thrilled with this glorious expectation?

Or do you wonder sometimes: Is this really going to happen?

Listen to your God in v.8 and listen carefully. This is one of the very few times in this book that you will literally hear God's own voice.

I am the Alpha and the Omega. Those are the first and last letter of the Greek alphabet. "I am first and I am last. I began and I will complete. I have the first word and I have the last word. I am the beginning and I am the end. And you can trust my faithfulness. Remember: I am the One who is, who was and who is coming. I am the Almighty!"

And that's enough. With him you can move forward through the final phase of history. He is the only one who controls all of history.

In his hands your future is secure.

2

REVELATION 1: 9 – 20

THE EXALTED CHRIST CARES FOR HIS CHURCH

As we continue to read through Revelation 1, we hear about John's first vision. He meets the exalted Christ. And through John's report we meet the exalted Christ. Well – we read about him. But he is real! Try to imagine what it would be like to experience this. Would it be scary? John is totally overwhelmed. Should it frighten us to meet Jesus Christ?

But why should it? Jesus loves you and he is your friend, right?

Sure, but there is another side to him. C.S. Lewis captured this in a passage from *The Lion, the Witch and the Wardrobe*. Aslan, the lion, represents the Christ figure, and the children Peter, Susan, Edmund and Lucy, who are visiting Mr. and Mrs. Beaver, want to know more about him. Here is the conversation:

> "Who is Aslan?" asked Susan.
>
> "Aslan", said Mr. Beaver. "Why, don't you know?" He's the King. He's the Lord of the whole wood"...
>
> "Is – is he a man?" asked Lucy.

> "Aslan a man!" said Mr. Beaver sternly. "Certainly not. I tell you he is the King of the wood and the son of the great Emperor-beyond-the-Sea. Don't you know who is the King of Beasts? Aslan is a lion – the Lion, the Great Lion."
>
> "Ooh!" said Susan, "I'd thought he was a man. Is he – quite safe? I shall feel rather nervous about meeting a lion."
>
> "That you will, dearie, and no mistake," said Mrs. Beaver; "if there's anyone who can appear before Aslan without their knees knocking, they're either braver than most, or else just silly."
>
> "Then he is not safe?" said Lucy.
>
> "Safe?" said Mr. Beaver; "don't you hear what Mrs. Beaver tells you? Who said anything about safe? Course he isn't safe. But he's good. He's the King, I tell you."
>
> "I'm longing to see him," said Peter, "even if I do feel frightened when it comes to the point." [2]

Indeed – the exalted Christ is not safe. He is dangerous. But he is also good. And so, what do you do? You approach him with respect, as John does.

When Christ appears to John in this vision, John is between 90 and 95 years old. By that time, it had been about 60 years that he had last seen Jesus. That was when Jesus ascended into heaven. Now he meets him again and this beginning of what appears to be a one-day meeting turns out to be enormously important.

Not in the first place for John, but especially for the church – the church then and the church today.

This first vision shows that there is a strong and direct connection between Jesus Christ and his church. We may think sometimes that the Christian church is finished. It's all going downhill, and the future looks bleak. But we must remember that we have the risen and exalted Christ in our midst. His

---

[2] C.S.Lewis, The Lion, the Witch and the Wardrobe, Harper Collins 1950, First American Edition 2001, 146

work continues throughout the world, for the benefit of his church. Because he cares for his church.

CHRIST'S INSTRUCTION

When John begins to tell the story of what he has seen, he does so in the first person, quite emphatically: *I, John.....* As a matter of fact, throughout the book he puts a lot of emphasis on this "...I...". In this chapter alone: *I was in the Spirit; I heard; I saw; I turned around; etc.*

That is not because he thinks he is so important. But it does give Revelation authenticity and authority. This comes back in 22:8, when he says: *I, John, am the one who heard and saw these things.* That is like a signature at the end to reinforce the trustworthiness of this book as direct revelation of Jesus Christ. And it makes for a fascinating personal and lively report of what is happening, a story that captivates the reader.

No, John does not brag about himself. He does not stress his authority. He does not even call himself an apostle or a prophet. On the contrary, he identifies himself with the people that will read and hear what he has to tell. *I am your brother and partner*, he says. John has the unique office of 'apostle', but he is not a distant saint who cannot relate to the hardships and struggles of his fellow believers.

In this way he comes also close to us, today. "I am your brother in the faith," he says. "I am one of you and, despite the distance in time, I share in what is going on in your lives as God's children. And that's why I ask you to trust me when I am going to tell you in my book what I have seen."

I am your partner in the tribulation and the kingdom and the patient endurance that are in Jesus. As our brother in the faith, John was experiencing what all Christians can expect: the painful reality of suffering! In the last days, the days between Jesus' first and second coming, the world is often a hostile place for those who believe in Jesus. The New Testament is pretty blunt about that. And Revelation is full of it.

But then, in the midst of suffering we may also experience the comfort of belonging to God's kingdom, the comfort of living in God's presence and under the rule of Jesus Christ, our King. And because of that, even in the midst of suffering, we may know that we will be victorious. Revelation is full of that, too.

"And that's why we can also be partners," says John, *in patient endurance*. When your suffering makes life unbearable, you can hang in there, because of what is coming. Remain faithful and obedient. Resist the powers of sin and evil and do so consistently. Revelation issues this urgent call as well.

So, when John says these things about him and you, his purpose is to stress that you are personally involved in what is coming. "Make no mistake," he says. "This book, with all the things that I have seen, is about you. It is about your life, your suffering, your patient endurance and the kingdom that is for you."

Well then, he continues, *I was on the island called Patmos on account of the word of God and the testimony of Jesus*. Patmos is a small island off the coast of Asia Minor. And although it does not say so, in so many words, he was most likely exiled as the result of his love for Jesus, for his preaching and leadership. By banning him to Patmos the authorities tried to silence him and stop his influence.

But look what happens. The exalted Christ comes and amplifies John's voice. He makes him witness of visions that will be proclaimed all over the world. He makes his message sound louder and reach further than ever. And he does so, because the exalted Christ cares for his church everywhere with deep love and compassion.

And so, one day John meets Jesus Christ. That was amazing. We know that he had met him before. As a matter of fact, he had spent about three years of his life with Jesus. But that is a long time ago and this is totally different. This was just an incredible experience, as he tells about it in our text.

He remembers exactly what day it was. It happened on a Sunday. *On the Lord's Day*, he says. Some think that John means "the day of the Lord" as in "the day of judgement". But that day is still to come. No, it is the same construction that Paul uses when he talks in 1 Corinthians 11:20 about "the Lord's Supper".

The exalted Christ cares for his church

And just as this supper in 1 Corinthians 11 belongs to the Lord, so here it is about the day that belongs to the Lord, the day that was dedicated to Jesus Christ. That is the first day of the week. For the Christian church, the day of Jesus' resurrection had become a day of praise and worship, a day of celebration, and also a day filled with hope and encouragement. For on this day the church would rejoice in the anticipation of God's final victory.

In our time we do not use this expression "the Lord's Day" very often. Most of the time we use the more secular name "Sunday". We all know what we are talking about, but perhaps we are missing something. We are worshipping on the Sunday, but if you go by the name, you could ask: why not on the Tuesday or the Friday? Some Christian churches in the Middle East worship on the Friday, because that's the day off in a Muslim country. Is there anything wrong with that?

And how does this affect the way in which we experience our day of worship? It would be good to think of ways to enhance the awareness among us that the first day of the week is the day that literally belongs to the Lord – the whole day!

At least, Christ himself found it important enough to meet John on that particular day. After all, Jesus' resurrection was also a day of new beginnings, new hope, new life. And thus, the exalted Christ chooses this day to do new things and to show John new things. On this day he would see things never seen before.

It happened while *I was in the Spirit*, he explains. That was a unique experience. The Holy Spirit of God disconnects John from the physical world around him. He can see – but not with his physical eyes. He can hear – but not with his physical ears. No, the Spirit opens wide his ears and eyes for direct communication with God, for direct spiritual contact with the exalted Christ.

And then, in this condition, John is suddenly startled by *a loud voice behind him*. As I mentioned in the previous chapter, Revelation is not only a picture book, it is also a noisy book with lots of loud sounds. Here it begins already: *an unexpected loud voice like a trumpet*. And then from behind. You can imagine that John nearly jumped out of his skin.

2 • Revelation 1:9-20

The sound of trumpets was often a signal that would come with the announcement of an important message or instruction. That is what it is here. The loud voice instructs John: *Write what you see in a book and send it to the seven churches....* The bewildered apostle doesn't see anything yet, but the instruction is clear: "you are about to see things and you'll have to write an accurate report on it. Get ready!"

In other words, what John is about to see on that Lord's Day is not just for himself. He will have to pass it on to others, to his brothers and sisters, his partners in the suffering and kingdom and patient endurance: his fellow believers in Jesus Christ.

"Send this document, with all its colourful and sometimes bizarre pictures, the description of what you have seen. Send it to the seven churches in the province of Asia. These churches need to read and hear what you have seen today. They will need to be alert and aware of what is really going on in this world".

And why is that? Because the exalted Christ loves them and cares for them. That is why he wants to warn and encourage and comfort his churches.

The seven that are listed here – Ephesus, Smyrna, Pergamum, Thyatira, Sardis, Philadelphia and Laodicea – were not the only churches in Asia Minor. This order reflects a commercial travel-route from one to the next, a loop that returned to Ephesus. This was, of course, easy for delivering a copy to each church.

But there is more to it. Remember what we have seen before: in Revelation the number seven is the number of fullness. This means that these seven churches represent all the churches, the whole universal church of all times and places.

In other words: from these seven, John's picture-book will go to all the churches, all over the world, because the exalted Christ cares for all of them. In this way this unique book came also here, to you, because the exalted Christ cares just as much for you, in the church where you belong today, as he does for all his churches.

CHRIST'S APPEARANCE

As the loud voice from behind him indicated, John not only gets to hear things, he also gets to see things. And so, startled as he must have been by this voice like a sudden trumpet blast, in his vision the apostle turned around to find out who was speaking to him, and what there was to see.

Now, that was quite a sight to behold. The scene before his eyes is totally awesome! The overwhelming glory is nothing short of spectacular. John sees the first of three major appearances of Jesus Christ we find in Revelation. The other two are in Rev. 5, where Jesus is pictured as *a Lamb, standing as though it had been slain*, and in Rev. 19, where we meet him as the *Rider on the White Horse*.

Despite John's obvious shock because of what he sees, he does give us a detailed description of this amazing vision in the v.12–16. Although, if you read carefully, it turns out to be difficult to give an exact description. The whole picture is just too overwhelming, too much. He is trying to find the accurate words, but he ends up turning to similes to come as close to what it really is. And then you get expressions like: "his eyes were like..., his voice was like..., his face was like..."

And yet, what John is seeing, and the way he describes what he is seeing, looks and sounds remarkably familiar if you know the Old Testament. When you read what the prophets Ezekiel and Daniel were seeing in their visions you will notice the similarities. What Ezekiel is trying to describe (Ezekiel 1:22 – 2:2) is the appearance of the Holy and Almighty God. And in Daniel's vision (Daniel 10:1-11) we meet a Man who can be no one else but the Glorified Christ.

Here, in the final phase of history, the exalted Christ shows himself to be both.

John's description is fascinating. He begins at the periphery, and then he moves to the centre of the vision. It is as if we look through a camera with a zoom-lens, which is slowly zooming in on what is most important.

First, he sees a circle of *seven golden lampstands*. That reminds us of the lampstand that was standing in the Tabernacle (Exodus 25) or the lampstands that were placed in the Temple (1 Kings 7). Those lampstands would symbolize the presence of God's people before the Holy God.

Then, in the centre of that circle, John sees *one like a son of man*. Or: "someone like a human being". Did John know right away who he was looking at? We do not know. But we do remember, and so would John, that when Jesus lived on earth, he often spoke about himself as "the Son of Man".

Here again we hear the echo of Daniel's prophecy. In Daniel 7:13,14 the prophet tells us: *I saw in the night visions, and behold, with the clouds of heaven, there came one like a son of man.... And to him was given dominion and glory and a kingdom, that all peoples, nations and languages should serve him; his dominion is an everlasting dominion, which shall not pass away, and his kingdom one that shall not be destroyed.*

In the distant future Daniel sees this mysterious, exalted human figure, *a son of man*, who will bring an end to all pagan kingdoms.

Well, this has become reality in Jesus' death and resurrection. Just before he ascended into heaven Jesus declared: *All authority in heaven and on earth has been given to me* (Matthew 28:18). Here he is: meet the exalted Christ in his glory. The effects of all this are still being worked out in the final phase of our history. And today we find ourselves right in the middle of this, as pictured in John's book of War & Victory.

The camera then focuses on the clothes and the physical features, things that display someone's status, position, or qualities. There is the *long robe and golden sash*. They show the royal status of Christ. There is the *hair white as snow*. It symbolizes his purity or wisdom. There are the *eyes like a flame of fire*. They give him the ability to see through the pretences of this world, to expose superficial faith in the church, and to penetrate in hidden corners and see the secrets of every human heart.

There are the feet *like burnished bronze, refined in a furnace*. He is ready to march to war, and to do justice with incomparable strength and energy, trampling down the evil powers.

There is the voice *like the roar of many waters*. His voice is drowning out all other sounds, the lies and deceptive rhetoric of the voices we hear every day in the world in which we live.

Then the camera zooms in on the props, and we see some odd combinations.

Seven stars in his right hand. In the Bible the 'right hand' is the hand of powerful protection. The exalted Christ controls the powers that be, but with the specific purpose to care for his people, to protect his church.

And then there is this *sharp, two-edged sword, coming out of Christ's mouth.* That is a weird picture. You would expect a sword in someone's hand, to slay the enemy and defend the innocent. That is what a sword is for, is it not? Yes it is, and this one too. This Son of Man is ready for battle. He is ready to slay his enemies and protect his church. But the battle that unfolds in Revelation is no ordinary battle.

The sword, coming out of Christ's mouth, shows the manner in which he will conquer. His weapon is his powerful Word. *God's Word is living and active*, says the author of Hebrews (4:12), *sharper than any two-edged sword, piercing to the division of soul and of spirit.... discerning the thoughts and intentions of the heart.* Everything is exposed to the eyes of him to whom we must give account.

This sword of God's Word is what we need to be prepared for the great battles we find ourselves in, as described on the pages of Revelation. Know the Word and train yourself in handling it. For the defeat of God's enemies will be realized by the truth of the gospel, the testimony of the crucified and risen Christ.

Finally, as John zooms in on the very centre of the vision, the light increases and its brilliance intensifies to the point that it is impossible to look at. The face of this Son of Man *shines like the sun in full strength.* God's pure character as "light" is shown in the exalted Christ. The dazzling majesty of his appearance is nothing but God's heavenly glory. He came into this world as the true light of God to drive out the darkness of sin and evil.

The exalted Christ appears in this vision as our glorious Judge and the powerful Ruler over the church and the world. He is coming, clothed with power and majesty. He is coming to purge his church and to burn away sin. He is also coming to pour out his wrath on the evil and the wicked. Let the world tremble! Who can stand before him?

2 • Revelation 1:9-20

The exalted Christ appears in this vision also to wake us up and shake us up, because he cares for his church. Be filled with awe and rejoice in your exalted King.

Christ's Majesty

The effect this vision had on John was dramatic. He falls down as if he is dead – totally overwhelmed by the holy majesty of this 'son of man'. And you can understand that. It is just too much for a weak and sinful creature, this confrontation with God's heavenly glory in the exalted Christ.

However, the purpose of this vision is not to terrify John, but to comfort and encourage him. And not only him, also the seven churches, and the church today. Yes, the vision of the exalted Christ is to comfort and encourage you and me. Here is our majestic King, our Lord-protector, in all the strife of this mortal life.

And so the majestic son of man comes and places his right hand on John with the words: *Fear not*. This is fantastic! This is wonderful, this tender gesture of love and encouragement from this fierce warrior. We all know how much good it does to feel a hand on your shoulder when you're afraid, anxious or nervous. You feel: here is someone who cares for me, someone who has compassion. Perhaps we do not do this enough – just a hand on the shoulder and an encouraging word.

But then the exalted Christ continues to clarify who he is, just to underline that John does not have to be afraid in his holy presence. And if you are John's brother or sister in the faith you do not have to be afraid either. *I am the first and the last*, says Christ. "I control the beginning of everything and the end of everything and all things in between." Do you recognize this? Indeed, Jesus Christ says the same as God the Father said about himself in v.8: *I am the Alpha and the Omega*.

The exalted Christ identifies himself entirely with Almighty God. He is God! In this way he says to John, and to the church, and to you: "Trust that nothing, absolutely nothing is beyond my power. Do not be intimidated or frightened by other powers, as so many people are in this world. Nothing and no one beats my glorious majesty. And I care for my church. I care for you. And I will bring you safely home."

"I am the Living One. I am the Living God. Yes, I have been dead. I died on the cross – for you. But look at me: I arose from the dead – for you. And now I am alive. And that will never change – never!"

Through his death and resurrection your Saviour defeated the powers of death. O, it is true: if there is one power in this world that seems invincible, it is the power of death. But the exalted Christ broke it. He went in the grave and came out again. Not just for himself, but for his church, for you and I who belong to him.

How does that work then? "Do not worry," says Jesus. *I have the keys of death and Hades.* Hades follows death as the state you enter when life ends. It is like a prison from which no one can get out. You die, you go, and the door is locked behind you. That is it! But praise be to the exalted Christ, the Living God. He has the keys. He is authorized to get you out. His victory opens the dark dungeon of Hades.

This is such an enormous comfort. It is such a great source of strong hope – today already. If you die in faith, you will join the exalted Christ in heaven. But there is more to come. At the very end of history death will be no more.

A lot of frightening things will happen before we get there. But feel the right hand of the exalted Christ on your shoulder and hear his voice. "Fear not! The new world is coming and the triumph is mine. Today the book, written by John, is as relevant for you, as it was for the church in his days because I care for my church. And I promise you that one day my church will cross the final finish-line victoriously."

How do we know?

"Listen," says Jesus, "I will explain the mystery. Remember that you saw the seven stars in my right hand and the seven lampstands around me? These are *the churches* and *the angels of the churches.*" There are a lot of different ideas as to what these 'angels' are. But this is the point Jesus is making with this breathtaking vision of the exalted Christ: "with my glorious majesty and invincible power I will be in the midst of my church; in your midst – always. And I will carry you as my church – always."

Despite the hostilities and persecution, despite our own weaknesses and our inclination to assimilate with the secular world, in the ongoing battle *the Lord Almighty, great and glorious, is on our side and goes before us.*

3

REVELATION 2: 1 – 7

EPHESUS – PURE IN DOCTRINE, BUT LACKING IN LOVE

In the previous passage we looked at (Rev. 1:9-20) we noticed that, two times, the exalted Christ instructed John to write what he was about to see (v.11 and 19), and then send it to the seven churches in the province of Asia. But before we get to what John has seen in his visions, we find Rev. 2 and 3.

Here we have seven separate messages, dictated by Jesus Christ himself. They form a set of 'cover letters', so to speak, in which Christ addresses each church separately, although they are all part of the total package to be sent to each of those churches. And therefore, each one of these letters is relevant for all the churches, including us, today.

A close look at these letters shows again that Revelation really is a work of literary art. There are many connections and allusions to other parts in this book. For instance, you cannot understand the opening-sentences without the vision in Rev. 1. And the promises at the end reflect passages and pictures in later chapters.

The main content of these letters gives us insight in a variety of specific problems in the various churches. It is like a mini catalogue of the sort of issues you can expect to find in all the churches throughout history. There are lots of good things to be thankful for, but also many dangers, challenges, and temptations to be aware of.

At the same time, when you pull it all together, the pattern shows one collective problem for the whole church. That is the temptation to compromise with the world, to settle down in the great city of Babylon. We will hear more about this city later. Here it refers to the temptation to assimilate with the contemporary culture, instead of persevering in the journey toward the new Promised Land, the new heaven and new earth.

This takes different shapes and forms in different times. But not conforming to the values and beliefs of the world in which the church lives between Jesus first and second coming will be a constant challenge.

When you go through these letters it is clear that – from Christ's point of view, with the perspective from above, so to speak – not all the churches are equally healthy. And so, he is going to address each one of them according to his concerns for that particular church. At the same time, he addresses all the churches, the entire church.

This is how it comes to us. Confronted with these examples, we all must develop Christian discernment to look into this mirror, evaluate our own church-life, and respond with faithful obedience. In this light we will look at the letter to Ephesus as the first one.

The modern visitor to Ephesus, on the west-coast of Turkey, finds only ruins that have been unearthed in many decades of archeological research. But the remnants of its ancient history are still impressive. My wife and I have had the privilege of walking down the marble streets where once the apostle Paul and his companions were walking. We stood in the theatre we read about in Acts 19. It seats about 25,000 people.

Despite its ruined state you can still picture Ephesus as a once wealthy, prosperous, and magnificent city. It was famous for its enormous temple of Artemis, one of the wonders of the ancient world. The angry chorus of the confused crowd that kept shouting for about two hours "Great is Artemis of the Ephesians" (Acts 19) didn't achieve much, contrary to the results of Paul's activities. In 262 AD the temple burned down and was never rebuilt.

Today all that is left is one pillar, whereas the gospel they were opposing is still bearing fruit!

At the time the exalted Christ dictated this letter, the city of Ephesus was booming. It had a busy harbour for large ships coming from the west, and from there well-travelled trading routes went eastward, deep into Asia.

For a long-time it was a major trade-centre in that part of the world that saw many merchants and other travellers come and go. As a result of all those contacts it also became a cultural and religious melting-pot in Asia Minor.

This was the city where the apostle Paul worked for three years during his third missionary journey. We read about his time in Ephesus in Acts 19. And the preaching of the gospel was greatly blessed. From Ephesus the good news of Jesus spread to the country-side where, in a large area around the city, more churches were established.

Well, some 40 years after all this was happening, John sits down to write what Christ tells him to write, beginning with the letter we are looking at.

John is instructed to *write to the angels of the churches*. I mentioned before that there are many different ideas as to what these "angels" are. Traditionally they were often seen as the 'bishops' or 'ministers' of these churches.

But nowhere does the Bible use the name 'angel' for such a function. Others think that these are literal angels, so that every church had its own 'guardian angel', so to speak. But it is hard to write a book and send it to an angel.

There is no easy answer, but a possible solution could be that both, the stars (or angels) AND lampstands, are images of the churches. Angels would then refer to the churches as the exalted Christ sees them. That is the perspective from above. Lampstands would then be the churches as we see them. That is the perspective from below.

In other words, we may have our assessment of a church based on what we see, from below. But the glorified Christ opens our eyes for realities in the church that we do not see, from above. One example to illustrate this: to the church in Laodicea Christ says: *You say* [from your earthly perspective], *'I am rich, I have prospered and I need nothing, not realizing that you are* [from my heavenly perspective] *wretched, pitiable, poor, blind and naked*

3 • Revelation 2:1-7

(Rev. 3:17). We will find something similar in this letter to the Ephesus congregation.

Jesus Christ always begins by presenting himself – in this case as the one *who holds the seven stars in his right hand and walks among the seven golden lampstands*. This self-designation is full of encouragement for the church. There will be severe criticism and there will be a lot to deal with, but the church is church of Jesus Christ. Frightening events may confuse or scare us, but the church of Jesus Christ is never on its own in this hostile world.

The church can be suffering or persecuted. The church can be filled with arrogant self-confidence or deeply divided by internal conflict, and yet, the exalted Christ is in her midst. He "walks", so at all times he is actively present among us. And with the power of his right hand he protects, preserves, and governs the church, because he loves her as his bride, chosen to everlasting life.

And now you can also understand that he says *I know your works*. He knows everything about his churches, about the one in Ephesus, but also about the ones you and I belong to today. "I know what's going on among you, in your church-life," he says. "I know what you are busy with as congregation, what your priorities are. And I know about the daily walk and talk, the regular lifestyle of everyone in the church."

Then he goes into the local specifics of the church in Ephesus. And it must be said, there are lots of good things to mention. There are many things the exalted Christ can praise them for. And that is what he does. He praises them. "You're doing really great," he says. "You are working very hard for the church. And your perseverance in doing what is right is exemplary."

Yes, the church in Ephesus was making good progress on its journey toward the new Promised Land. And they could do so because they were not willing to trust just anybody. No, the congregation was following only reliable guides for leading them in the right direction.

The brothers and sisters in Ephesus were working hard for the church. There is always lots to do in the church. But in Ephesus many people pitched in to keep everything going. On top of that, exposing false doctrine and resisting false teachers (as they did, according to v.2) is also hard work. And it is not the kind of work that everyone always appreciates either.

But they did not slack off and give up. *I know your toil and your patient endurance*, says Christ. Endurance is important in the spiritual battle you are involved in as believers. That is why you will find it mentioned throughout Revelation. It is your active resistance against what is wrong, and your persistent refusal to accept it, even if you have to go against what everyone else thinks, believes, or says.

Christ is fully aware that they are pretty strong at this in Ephesus. *I know you cannot bear with those who are evil*, he continues. They stuck to a zero-tolerance rule in the church for people who resist God's truth. If you promote evil, wrong ideas and wicked things among the believers, you are out! And Jesus Christ commends them for that. "That's good," he says. "Keep that up."

They also had to deal with people who showed up and *who called themselves apostles*. You had men who came to the church and who claimed to be authorized by God or by Christ to bring God's messages. That sounds pretty intimidating. How can you argue with that? If you are not too sure of the gospel as God's message, it is easy to fall for such impostors.

But the Ephesians were not so gullible. They were not impressed, and they did not just believe what some eloquent speakers were saying. Always remember: you can be good in using all the pious words and all the right Christian expressions, but that doesn't mean you are right and tell the truth.

And so the Christian believers in Ephesus tested those preachers. And when they did that, they found out what kind of people these so-called "apostles" really were.

How did they do that? Well, there is in the church only one way to find these things out. You listen carefully to the claims and the messages of those men, and then you check it carefully and prayerfully with what you have heard in God's Word, the Bible. In Ephesus it meant that they had to check it with what they had heard in the past from men like Paul and Timothy and John.

And the result? *You have found them to be false*, says Christ. These folks turned out to be false preachers, fake apostles. God's Word, as they had heard it before, exposed these men as liars. And when that became clear, the

3 • Revelation 2:1-7

Ephesians did not want to have anything to do with them anymore. They refused to listen to them. They were full of zeal to preserve the true and pure doctrine. They wanted sound teaching and had no use for false doctrine and false teaching.

How is that with us, today? We all have easy access to so many different ideas, views, and opinions. And many of those ideas claim to be Christian. But how do you know? How alert are we when it comes to these things?

To begin with, if you want to do this kind of testing, you must be familiar with what sound teaching according to the Bible is all about. You have to be able to discern what you hear and then recognize false teaching. It is important enough.

The New Testament is full of this. In his first letter, chapter 4:1, the apostle John urges us: *Beloved, do not believe every spirit, but test the spirits to see whether they are from God, for many false prophets have gone out into the world.*

How alert are we? Are we ready to apply the zero-tolerance rule when it comes to false doctrine, wrong ideas, teaching that does not pass the test of God's Word? Or are we too easy-going sometimes? You hear somebody speak, you read a book or an article or a blog; you find something on some Christian website and you think: "Hey, that doesn't sound so bad. It should be alright."

Or we think or say to each other: 'Now this man is such a popular speaker or author. And he seems a nice man, a fine Christian person. Whatever he says or writes, it must be okay!' This can be especially the case when you have reliable people telling you: you should listen to this man or read this or that book by him or her.

Are you willing to put them all to the test? You may be capable of doing this. That is one thing. But are you willing to do that? Are you willing to discern unreliable guides when you listen to speakers or read stuff? And are you ready to say 'no'? Are you ready to go by the zero-tolerance rule of the Ephesians?

The question is important because we may think that it is offensive and negative to be so critical all the time. You listen to this speaker or you read this book, and you think: "perhaps it's not entirely kosher, but why make a problem of it? All this nitpicking! He is a Christian and you can always learn something".

We do not know anything about the identity of those "false apostles" in Ephesus, but the whole scenario reflects the main conflict that continues to come up in the church – the conflict between falsehood and truth. And as God's children, as God's church, we should not be afraid or ashamed to make this distinction between falsehood and truth.

The point is that two opposite and mutually exclusive claims or statements cannot be true at the same time. God created the world, or he did not. Jesus arose from the dead, or he did not. Jesus is God, or he is not.

This is pretty controversial today. People get upset when you take this approach. For many people there is no such thing as 'an absolute truth'. It is all a matter of opinion or preference. What is true for you is as good as what is true for me and it is unacceptable to be judgmental or intolerant. You are not allowed to say to people: "what you are saying there is not true. It is false. You are wrong".

Count on it: making such a distinction between falsehood and truth will not make you popular with people. But here is your comfort: Jesus Christ will praise you when you refuse to tolerate false teaching in his church.

This refusal to tolerate false teachers and this desire to defend the true faith is not only difficult today – it was just as difficult then already. But Christ knows that they *have not grown weary* during the hardships they have endured for his name. They did not give up. These Ephesians were standing firm in their conviction. They were sticking up for the truth of God's Word. They were pure in doctrine.

And there was more. In v.6 Christ says: *You hate the works of the Nicolaitans, which I also hate*. We do not know much about these Nicolaitans other than what we find in this chapter. You get the impression that they were promoting ideas that led to bad moral choices and practices. For them accepting the values of the pagan culture and living the lifestyle of the pagan world was not a big deal.

3 • Revelation 2:1-7

Why make your life so difficult? Why be such a narrow-minded, negative and critical stick-in-the-mud? You can compromise with the worldly lifestyle all around you. It should be okay to have some fun. Those "Nicolaitans" didn't have a problem with this.

This is a big challenge in the church, also today, especially in combination with a lack of discernment when it comes to pure doctrine! If you are not sure what you believe, or you do not care, you will not be sure, or you will not care either, how you should live your life. Wrong thinking leads to wrong living.

But the Ephesians want nothing of this! And Christ is happy about that.

All of this sounds pretty good, does it not? The Ephesus congregation has much going for them. We would say that this is a strong and rock-solid church. And sure, that is all true and good. But it is not sufficient! Something is missing.

But....., says Christ in v.4. This indicates a sharp contrast.

Jesus Christ's view from above discovers, underneath the strong and solid layer of pure doctrine, the weak, brittle, and crumbling layer of love. That is a disastrous flaw. It is so disastrous that it will hinder the church's pilgrimage to the New Jerusalem!

But I have this against you, says the exalted Christ, *you have abandoned the love you had first*. Jesus' words have the tone of the disappointed Bridegroom, who loves his Bride, but who has lost her love.

Like the LORD said to Israel in Jeremiah 2:2, *I remember the devotion of your youth, your love as a bride, how you loved me and followed me in the wilderness*. This is what Christ sees when he looks at his church in Ephesus. It hurts him.

What is this love? Is it love for God and for Jesus Christ or is it love for others? It is both. Your love for God will show itself in your love for others. And on the other hand, when your love for God diminishes, your love for others will also suffer.

At that time, the church of Ephesus was over 40 years old. Outwardly, little has changed in those years, or so it seems. Another generation has grown up. They stand for orthodoxy. They are willing to defend the truth, resist false teaching, and to work hard for those goals.

But the children did not feel the same intense excitement and deep love for Jesus as their parents did when they first came to faith. And perhaps even for some of these parents themselves the first love for Jesus Christ has diminished.

It sounds a bit weird does it not? How can you be so faithful and loyal to the truth that you have zero tolerance for false teaching in the church, and at the same time your heart is cold and not full of deep and warm love for the God of the church?

But think of a marriage. A husband and wife can be very faithful and loyal to each other; they can be busy taking care of each other, but more because they have this sense of duty, than driven by their first love, which was so strong on their wedding day. And that makes what looks like a strong relationship very vulnerable.

In the same way you can, as a church-member, faithfully attend all the worship-services, be involved in all kinds of activities, feel a strong loyalty to the truth of God's Word, do all the right Christian things, but more because you have this sense of duty than driven by a deep love for God. Such love can peter out. Then you are no longer devoted to Christ as you should be, and excited about loving him as you used to be.

This turns out to be an important question. What drives us? What drives you? What drives me in the church? Do you do what you do in the church because it is your duty? Because you have your own agenda? Because it makes you feel good? Because people admire you for it? Because you like to be in control? How do the things that I do betray my motivation?

Ask yourself. Examine yourself. Is it my love for God that drives me? And does that show in the things I do and how I do them? Is it not fair to say that sometimes we are not driven by a deep and heartfelt love for God? Perhaps that love motivated me in the past, but somehow it has died, and I have become apathetic, or even cynical.

The point is that for the exalted Christ this is the most crucial issue. If this first love is lacking, the church is in danger! For then all your efforts and hard work in the service of God are not worth much. Then all the good things Christ has seen in Ephesus are in jeopardy.

Remember Paul's words in 1 Corinthians 13:1–3: *If I speak in the tongues of men and of angels, but have not love, I am a noisy gong or a clanging symbol. If I have prophetic powers, and understand all mysteries and all knowledge, and I have all faith so as to remove mountains, but have not love, I am nothing. If I give away all I have and if I deliver up my body to be burned, but have not love, I gain nothing.*

This is why Christ so strongly appeals to his church in Ephesus. Do not keep going this way, but take steps to revive your first love. "Remember how wonderful, how exciting it was," he says, "when you were so filled with love for me. How deep have you fallen! Where did this deep love for God go? Repent. Change. Turn around. Make a U-turn in your thinking and in the way you live. Turn away from your complacency, or apathy, or whatever it is that drives you, and return to the deep and self-sacrificing love you started with when you first came to love me."

"And then make it a daily priority to do the things you did at first, when you were driven by your love for me. Show you love for me in your actions and choices; in what you do in the church and how you live in the world."

How can you do this? And why would you do this? Always remember God's deep love for you, as it came to you at first in Jesus Christ.

But if you do not "then your future as my church is at stake," says Christ. His warning is chilling, frightening, but clear. *I will come to you and remove your lampstand from its place.* There is no future for the church that has no love.

This warning reflects the tone of the whole book of Revelation. Jesus is on his way as the Judge. He is coming soon! The time is near. On that day, the Judge will exclude, from the circle of churches, the congregation that has abandoned its first love.

That is how serious this is, also today. Will we be there when the multitude no one can count will gather before the throne of God and of the Lamb? Will we be there on the day that Jesus will return in glory to judge the living and

Ephesus: pure in doctrine, but lacking in love

the dead and to separate the goats from the sheep (Matthew 25:31-46)? The question is urgent enough.

At the same time, there is this wonderful perspective of the promise of the exalted Christ: *To the one who conquers I will grant to eat of the tree of life, which is in the paradise of God.*

When, by God's grace, you fight against your sin and against your lack of love, you continue to resist evil and you fill your life with things that show how much you love your God and your Saviour Jesus – then your future is bright; then the joy and glory of God's eternal kingdom will be yours.

You may remember that God had planted this 'tree of life' in the Garden of Eden. But it is long gone. Because of our disobedience we lost the right to eat from this tree.

But God's amazing grace in Jesus Christ will bring it back. The 'tree of life' appears again in Revelation 22 as a permanent feature in the New Jerusalem. And the abundance of its fruit – twelve crops per year – will feed the citizens of the new heaven and the new earth for ever and ever.

Love him who loved you first. Then your life will be good, and your joy will be abundant in the paradise of your God.

4

REVELATION 2: 8 – 11

SMYRNA – POOR AND PERSECUTED, BUT RICH

Some of you may remember the name Polycarp. You may have some faint memories of church history lessons, a long time ago. Polycarp was bishop of the church in Smyrna in the beginning of the second century, perhaps already at the time that John wrote Revelation. We know that in his younger years Polycarp was a student of John.

From the book *Martyrium Polycarpi* we know that he died as a martyr in Smyrna. He was burned at the stake in 155 or 156 AD. At that time, he was close to 90 years old.

He had been asked to declare "Caesar is Lord", but he refused. When he was brought to the crowded stadium, the Roman proconsul urged him: "Swear to deny Christ and I will set you free immediately". But Polycarp answered: "For more than 86 years I have served him, and he never did me any wrong or harm. How then can I blaspheme my King and my Saviour?"

When the proconsul pressed on again, the old man answered: "Since you keep urging me to worship the emperor, and since you pretend not to know who and what I am, let it be clear to you: I am a Christian." The proconsul then continued: "I have wild animals. I will throw you to the lions if you do not repent."

"Call them", Polycarp said. "For us to repent from what is good to what is bad is impossible." The proconsul replied: "Since you don't fear the wild animals, I will let you be consumed by fire, if you do not repent."

But Polycarp said: "you threaten me with fire that will burn for a short time and then will die out. But you are ignorant of the fire of the coming judgment and of eternal punishment, reserved for the ungodly. But why do you hesitate – come up with what you want!"

Then the proconsul sent his herald in the middle of the arena, to announce with a loud voice: "Polycarp declares of himself that he is a Christian". At that moment the large crowd began to shout that Polycarp should be burned at the stake. Soon afterwards the people began to gather wood and branches, eagerly assisting the officials with the preparations. They stripped the old man of all his clothes and tied him on the pile. Thus Polycarp was burned at the stake.

This story of the persecution and the martyrdom of Polycarp happened in Smyrna. It illustrates the circumstances God's congregation in Smyrna was facing in those days. And we see an accurate reflection of those conditions in Smyrna, as the exalted Christ addresses this church in his second letter of the seven.

Smyrna is one of the oldest cities in Asia Minor. Unlike some of the other places mentioned, Smyrna still exists. Today, in modern-day Turkey, it is called Izmir. It is located about 70 km north of the place where Ephesus was. It is also a city on the coast, with a good size natural harbour, and it is partly built on the slopes of the Pagos hill. The citadel on top of this hill was called "the crown of Smyrna".

From the very beginning of Rome's rise-to-power, the city of Smyrna had been a loyal ally of the Romans. The Roman rulers recognized this and awarded the city for its faithfulness. Smyrna's loyalty to Rome became proverbial in the ancient world, to the point that the city was known by its nickname: "the faithful one".

Smyrna was also a very prosperous city in those days. It was famous for its athletic games and competitions, its gladiator-fights and other entertainment in the theatre, the stadium, or arena. The city folks enjoyed the good life.

One more detail is necessary to help us get a background picture of the situation and of the circumstances the Christian church was facing there - that is that there was also a significant concentration of Jews living in Smyrna. It was apparently a popular place to settle for Jewish refugees after the fall of Jerusalem in 70 AD.

Well then here, in this city, a Christian church was established, most likely by the apostle Paul or one of his companions, when Paul spent a few years in Ephesus on his third missionary journey. In Acts 19:10 we learn that at that time *all the residents of Asia heard the word of the Lord, both Jews and Greeks.*

When you read this letter, you will notice that the exalted Christ does not rebuke or criticize the church in Smyrna. He does not mention any dominant flaws or weaknesses that threaten the life of the congregation. That is remarkable. All he does is encourage and comfort them. That does not mean that everything was perfect in Smyrna, but this was obviously what they needed most.

The Christian church in a pagan society will face lots of challenges, and Smyrna is a perfect example of this. There is some serious persecution going on. And this can be very discouraging. You become a Christian believer, a follower of Jesus Christ, and you expect your life to be better, happier, and more joyful. But it is not! It is trouble, and over time it gets even worse. That is disappointing and it could easily make the believers in Smyrna abandon the journey to the New Jerusalem, unless they remain faithful!

And Christ knows this. He is fully aware of what they are going through. They are suffering. And it is not only the persecution from the authorities. There is also the hostile attitude in society. It can come from your co-workers or your neighbours, even from your family. And on top of that you have to deal with the slanderous attacks of others who claim to worship God.

That is why Christ chooses to present himself to the Smyrna congregation with this self-designation: *him who is the First and the Last, who died and came to life.* In this way he connects with this congregation. They see themselves under deadly attacks from all sides, but their exalted Christ understands that. And he gives hope.

As *the First and the Last,* Jesus Christ stresses his sovereign control over all of history. He emphasizes that, from the beginning to the end, everything is in his hand, including the afflictions, the persecution the church is facing.

That *he died and came to life again* shows his victory over the power of death. And because of this victory in his own death AND resurrection, Jesus – as the one who lives forever – is now able to say, as he does here, "*be faithful unto death and I will give you the crown of life*. Look at me, and trust that because of me, death will not have the final say in your life either."

This self-presentation shows again that he can say beyond any doubt: *I know.* Yes, it comes back again and again, in all these letters: The exalted Christ knows! "I know. I know everything," says Jesus, "everything about your congregation, everything in your congregation I know. Everything in your own life I know."

This means, as we saw already when we read the letter to Ephesus, that we cannot really hide anything. You can make yourself look better, but it is no use. Christ sees it anyway. That can be daunting and outright scary. He looks right through all the pious cover-ups of how we really feel, who we really are, and what we really think.

But the fact that Christ says: *I know* can also be incredibly encouraging and comforting, even relaxing. You do not have to present yourself stronger and more confident than your really feel. "Be yourself," says Jesus Christ, "because I know already how you feel. I know what you are struggling with. I know the things you have to deal with, and worry about, from the young children to the parents and to the seniors. And also here in Smyrna – I know everything. Nothing escapes me. And I don't overlook the suffering of my people."

Then, when we zero in on the specific circumstances the church in Smyrna found itself in, the exalted Christ says: I know these three things about you, the three things that make your life miserable: *your tribulation, your poverty, and the slander of those that hate you,* although they claim to love God. Now especially the latter, that slander from those who claim to love God, – that's a stab in the back, that hurts.

It sounds like they are having a rough time up in Smyrna.

Is this not often the experience when you openly express your faith in Jesus Christ and try to live it? You can get a wide range of reactions, and often, but not always, it is negative. To be a Christian and to be open about it is not so easy all the time.

Let us take a closer look.

I know your tribulation, says Christ. It is true, of course, that Christ knows all of the afflictions you are dealing with in your life. But in this context, in this situation, the word "tribulation" or "persecution" is telling. Revelation uses the word 'tribulation' more often, whenever it speaks about the distress of the church in the last days, the final phase of history, between Jesus' first and second coming.

It is still very much a terrible reality in our world today. Reports tell us that the Christian faith is the most persecuted religion in the world today when it comes to the number of countries and the number of people affected by it. It is not something that you and I experience so directly in a western country like Canada. But let us not forget that this is a daily reality for your brothers and sisters in the faith in North Korea, Pakistan, Somalia, Iran, or many other countries.

What's going on in Smyrna? Because of its loyalty to Rome and to the Roman Empire, 'emperor worship' was a big deal in Smyrna. We have noticed it in the story of Polycarp's martyrdom. The city was a centre of this kind of worship in Asia.

If you would refuse to worship the Roman emperor you would be accused of political disloyalty. If you were a Christian this would land you in jail, with the demand: "deny Jesus as Lord, worship the emperor as your Lord, with just a tiny bit of incense, then you'll be free." They made it really easy to deny Jesus. Such was Satan's strategy, luring people into denying Christ by just a minimal participation in emperor worship.

But if you did not, you would be killed. In this city full of worship devoted to the emperor, worshipping and honouring Jesus Christ as Lord of all earthly powers and doing so in public, triggered not only a lot of hatred and resistance, but also oppressive measures from the authorities.

Here in Canada we do not do emperor worship. But the resistance against the Christian faith, and sometimes even specific measures from the authorities to restrict the church in its freedom to express our Christian faith in public, is here too. Even if it comes out in what many would call 'minor things'. One example could be a municipal decision that, in new suburban developments, no properties will be made available to build churches.

Or think of the ongoing concern for restrictive measures to limit the freedom of churches and ministers not to officiate at same-sex marriages. Or some Parliamentarian floats the idea that it is time to put an end to the financial privileges of churches, such as tax exemption, or tax-deductible donations. Do we call these things "persecution"? That sounds like a big word for those unpleasant experiences.

But the question is and will be: Are we willing and ready in our comfortable church communities to obey God more than any human authority, even if that means saying 'no' to what authorities, legislators, or courts decide?

I also know your poverty, says Christ. That is real poverty he is talking about. Smyrna was a prosperous city, but apparently Christian believers did not share in this wealth. They had little material possessions. From an earthly point of view, when you look at the possibility to enjoy the good things in life, becoming a Christian in Smyrna was a real sacrifice. And that is not easy.

Now, they were probably pretty poor already to begin with when it came to earthly possessions. As is so often the case, also today, usually a new church plant does not attract the rich and famous in society, but more often the poor and struggling.

But on top of that, because they became Christians, they were facing more problems. Some lost their job. Others saw their business go down-hill because the customers did not come back, or their suppliers no longer wanted their business. And then the social intimidation: co-workers who would pester them; neighbours who would shun them or ridicule them.

Today you can run into similar attitudes at work or in school. Or think of the way in which the media, TV, magazines, and websites ridicule and criticize religion in general, but often the Christian faith and the Bible in particular.

But it does not only come from the authorities or from your hostile neighbours. There is more going on in Smyrna. *I know the slander of those who say they are Jews and are not*, says Christ.

Who is he talking about? Some see it as a conflict between the Christians and the Jews as an ethnic group. But that is too simple. Many of those ethnic Jews would have accepted Jesus as Saviour and joined the church. In addition, about ethnic Jews you cannot really say, *they are not Jews*.

No, it is about 'Jews' as the name for God's people, 'spiritual Jews', the "synagogue of God", so to speak. In a similar way the apostle Paul speaks about Christians as 'Abraham's descendants' (Galatians 3:7-9, 29). And in Revelation the Christian Church is the new Israel, with all faithful Christian believers presented and listed as 144,000 members of the twelve tribes of Israel (Rev. 7).

Well, because of this claim, those among the ethnic Jews that rejected Jesus as the Saviour became really hostile. Throughout the Book of Acts, you see the same pattern in reaction to Paul's preaching of the gospel. Antichristian Jews respond very strongly to the gospel, stressing that they alone are God's covenant people.

But this is a false claim, says Christ. *They are not*. The true Israelites, the true Jews, in the sense of "God's people", are those that follow Jesus, the Lamb of God, who came to take away our sin. The true "synagogue of the Lord" is the congregation that worships the Saviour Jesus Christ, made up of Jews AND Greeks.

Now, here is the issue. Perhaps in a city like Smyrna, full of aggressive paganism and emperor worship, Christians and Jews could have sort of supported each other as minority groups. They were both facing confrontation with the pagan pressure to cave in and assimilate.

But no, on the contrary, these antichristian Jews *slander* God's people. In Rev. 13 the same word is translated as "blaspheming" and in Rev. 16 as "cursing God".

It is a strong word that pictures fanatic and malicious opposition to Jesus Christ and to the gospel of salvation. They did what they could to give the church a bad reputation in town and to make life for Christian believers as miserable as possible.

And here again, our situation is different today. But in our secular world of aggressive atheism you will hear stories that slanderously twist the gospel, that give a false image of God. Books, articles and blogs describe Christians as a bunch of hypocrites, the Christian faith as a scam, and the church as a club that wants your money but does not care for your needs. Read 1 Peter 4. This kind of suffering, this being insulted for the name of Christ, as described by the apostle Peter, is still happening.

In Smyrna these (antichristian) Jews claimed to serve the one true God. But they are the opposite, says Christ: *they are a synagogue of Satan*. Now that's a harsh and offensive way of putting it. But remember – this does not come from some bitter Christian, but from Jesus Christ himself! And he says this because we must recognize who is behind all this hostility. That is Satan, the devil. As Paul puts it in 2 Corinthians 4:4, *the god of this world has blinded the minds of unbelievers, to keep them from seeing the light of the gospel of the glory of Christ.*

Indeed, Satan's power is behind the attitude, words, and actions of those who reject Jesus Christ as Saviour and persecute his followers. He will use whatever means he can find to oppose the gospel and destroy the church. Throughout Revelation this comes out again and again.

All this sounds pretty threatening and discouraging. What are we up against? But that is not the whole picture of the church in Smyrna. True, there is poverty and lots of other trouble and misery; they have many reasons to give up.

BUT, says the exalted Christ, *you are rich.* What does he mean – rich in the midst of poverty? This is his point: despite your poverty you do have possessions no one can take away from you. You have treasures that cannot be confiscated. You can call these "spiritual possessions" if you want, but they are very real. We talk about the life-changing fruits of the grace of God in Jesus Christ: contentment with what God gives, true peace of mind, hands-on love for others.

In 2 Corinthians 8:9 Paul points out that Jesus *became poor to make us rich*.

And in Romans 8:17 he explains that as God's children we are *heirs of God and co-heirs with Christ*. Now that sounds promising.

That is why in 2 Corinthians 6:10 the same apostle can describe Christian believers as *having nothing, and yet possessing everything*.

Here is the question for us: Do we still recognize what makes us rich today, as a middle-class well-to-do church in this super-materialistic world? What is our heart filled with? And what are our lives filled with, as a result of that?

Are we rich in Jesus Christ, or are we as Christians also caught up, just as others around us, in the consumerism and sense of entitlement that drives our society? Some have more earthly possessions than others and some are struggling to make ends meet, but regardless of those circumstances – do we feel that we are rich with possessions no one can take away?

Look around in this world. Some people are so poor – all they have is money. If you do not look to Jesus, you may be as rich as can be, but you do not have much hope for the future. One day whatever you have now will all be gone. But look to Jesus and be content. Your future looks bright, a future filled with joy and without evil or injustice. That is why your exalted Saviour can say this: *You are rich.*

Sounds great. And it is great. But in the meantime, it is still hard to deal with persecution, poverty, and slander. And it will get worse, says Jesus. The hate-campaign is only going to intensify in the final phase of our history. It will not be easy. However, *do not fear what you are about to suffer*. Trust in me as the First and the Last, the One who has everything in his hands, every moment of it!

This is what is going to happen: The devil will give you a hard time. He will attack you with all the hostile powers he can find – the slander of these so-called "Jews", the hatred of the pagan emperor worshippers – and some of you will end up in prison. That is scary, for the devil is testing you, to see if he can get you to deny Jesus as Lord. But here is the question: should I make compromises to save my skin? And will you compromise and cave in under the pressure?

"Don't be frightened," says Christ. "I will be with you, so that the test of your faith and faithfulness will bring to light your commitment to me. And take courage, it won't last forever. *You will have this tribulation for 10 days*". That again is a symbolic number. "10 days" is a complete, but limited timeframe. Christ lets us know that even in times of suffering and persecution he remains in control, not Satan.

"Do not be discouraged," says Christ, "but *be faithful*. Do not give up, even if you have to pay with your life. Yes – that might happen. But hang in there. Stay the course, whatever happens." Jesus says this, not because we are so strong. We are not.

No, he can say this, because he is strong. And he will hold on to those who belong to him and are loyal to him.

The city of Smyrna was well-known for its faithfulness to Rome, and was actually quite proud of this loyalty. But the church should always remember that in the end the only loyalty that really matters is loyalty to Jesus Christ, even if this requires the highest price – the price of your life. After all, death is a defeated enemy.

Remain faithful to your Saviour in all circumstances because such faithfulness leads to victory. Jesus died and came to life. In this way he "models", so to speak, the way to the victory of life for people that are facing hatred, persecution, and death.

This victory comes by what seems to be defeat, like Jesus' death on the cross.

But he arose victoriously. And so, as Christian believers you do not win the victory of life by violence or power, but only by *being faithful unto death*. That is the pattern of the crucified, risen and exalted Christ. For, says Jesus, then *I will give you the crown of life*. That means: the crown that is true life – life that will never deteriorate or disappear, but will be enjoyed forever.

Jesus promises the victory of life to his persecuted and suffering people as they die for their faith – at that time in the stadiums and arenas of the Roman Empire, today in the dungeons and slave-camps of countries in Asia and Africa. As the One who died and came to life, and so conquered the power of death himself – no one but Christ alone can assure us of this victory. He alone is the ultimate source of true life.

That is why he can also encourage his church then and today with the comforting promise: *The one who conquers will not be hurt by the second death.*

When you do not give up, do not cave in, but overcome the frightening and discouraging experiences in your life as God's child, and you remain faithful, you may still have to pay with the price of your life. "But don't worry," says Jesus. "That's only the first death. This will separate body and soul. But it is temporary and will bring you beyond the reach of the second death."

This second death is mentioned in Revelation 20 and 21, and is described there as the spiritual death, the eternal death. It says in Rev. 20:14 that on the great day of Jesus' glorious return *death and Hades will be thrown into the lake of fire. This lake of fire is the second death.* This is the horrible destination of all who will not enter the new Promised Land. As it says in Rev. 21:8 of those who have rejected Jesus – *their portion will be in the lake that burns with fire and sulphur, which is the second death.*

This is the death that will separate God and man. And that is forever!

What is the worst? Not persecution. Not your physical death. You will get through those hardships, as Jesus himself did and came to life again.

No, the worst is to reject Jesus and become unfaithful. For that makes you die the second death. And no one will ever get through that.

Trust that the exalted Christ will fulfil his promise of life. Not by getting you out of trouble, misery, or persecution. He might or he might not. But by encouraging you to remain faithful to him as you are going through those experiences.

Through many dangers, toils and snares, we have already come,

Tis grace that brought us safe thus far, and grace will lead us home.

5

Revelation 2: 12 – 17

PERGAMUM – FAITHFUL, BUT COMPROMISING

On the 11th of November we celebrate 'Remembrance Day' in Canada. We remember those who gave their lives to protect and safeguard our freedoms. Freedom is extremely precious. Many people in this world do not enjoy the basic freedoms we are used to in our country. And so, yes, we remember those sacrifices with gratitude.

But we cannot leave it at that. If we are thankful for freedom, we also have a responsibility as to what we do with this freedom; how we use it. This shows how we value the sacrifices that were made. I can say that I am thankful for freedom, but what does that mean when I turn around and abuse it, or squander it?

This leads of course, to the question: 'what is freedom?' And as it turns out, freedom does not mean the same for everybody. It all depends on how you look at life, what you value in life, what your priorities are in life, etc.

You get a better understanding of this when you have the opportunity to talk about these things with Christian believers from countries where people, often Christians, do not enjoy many of the freedoms we have here: freedom of religion; freedom of speech; freedom of education, and things like that.

5 • Revelation 2:12-17

So we ask again: what is freedom? The modern state of Israel built the infamous wall between them and the Palestinian territories to keep suicide-bombers out. That sounds reasonable, does it not? But then Palestinian Christians tell us: This wall restricts our freedom to visit family or the freedom of farmers to go their fields.

And it gets even more confusing when the so-called freedom-fighters in Syria are the ones that are destroying the freedom of Christian believers in that country.

At the same time, these various situations help us understand what true freedom is all about for God's people. Regardless of the circumstances the church finds itself in, our true freedom is our freedom in Jesus Christ. He sets us free from sin and evil. This is the freedom the church must hold and proclaim.

For Christians then, whether we enjoy political freedom or suffer persecution, the question is: what do we do with this freedom in Christ? Do we squander it? Do we compromise it? Or do we hold on to it?

Here is the paradox: Holding on to your freedom in Jesus Christ may take away your freedom in our secular society, or the other way round. So the question we have to ask ourselves is: are you going to compromise your freedom in Jesus Christ, to protect your freedom in this world?

This was the question the church at Pergamum was confronted with.

When we travel from Smyrna to Pergamum, we go about 70 km slightly to the north east in present-day Turkey. In the time of the Romans, Pergamum was a beautiful city, spectacularly located on the top and slopes of a high hill. It was also a powerful city. The Romans made it the capital of the province of Asia. It was the residence of the Roman governor, and the administrative and judicial centre of the province.

Pergamum was not so much a trading centre, like Ephesus and Smyrna, where the addressees of the previous messages lived, but more of a cultural centre, where the arts and sciences were flourishing. It also had a famous library. With all this came a great variety of religious influences. While emperor worship was significant, the top of the hill the city was built on had many temples for the worship of various Eastern and Western pagan gods and goddesses, too.

It is this idolatrous background of a mix of pagan religious power, political power, and cultural power that made Pergamum a dangerous place to live for the local Christian church. It was dangerous because of persecution. But also because of the many temptations. And the exalted Christ knows this. *I know where you dwell*, he says, *where Satan's throne is*.

That sounds scary. The word "throne" occurs forty-seven times in the Book of Revelation. And the vast majority of these references to a 'throne' are about God's throne. It is mentioned for the first time in Rev. 1:6, and we get a lively description of the throne of God in Rev. 4. But there are also a few rival thrones.

This political imagery is important because it helps us to identify, now already, what will turn out to be one of the major conflicts in Revelation. Who sits on the throne? Who rules the world, the universe? Who is in control?

We know "Satan" as God's fierce enemy. And God's people need to know this. His name is mentioned five times in these messages. Followed by the Beast and Babylon – symbolic figures we will come across later on in the Book – Satan is the main rival contender. He competes for people's loyalty to him. As God's enemy he is actively opposing God's rule and authority, in everything.

He does so by establishing his own counter-kingdom. He sets up his throne as the counter-part to God's throne, claiming and proclaiming that he rules; that he is in control. And the church of Jesus Christ in Pergamum is facing the frightening reality that it is located in the same city that is the heart of this counter-kingdom.

Here is the church, and Satan's headquarters is just around the corner, so to speak.

But this is not just about Pergamum. Remember that in these seven messages Jesus addresses the whole church, the universal church. So, also when Christ gives this scary picture to Pergamum, he is speaking to us. Until Jesus Christ will return in glory, until the coming of the new heaven and the new earth, God's holy throne is found above, in heaven while Satan's counterfeit

5 • Revelation 2:12-17

throne is found below, here on earth, in this world! Even after Jesus' resurrection and ascension, it is still here.

In other words, Christ says – not just to Pergamum, but to us as well – Never forget that today you, the church, are located where Satan has his throne. Indeed, we live in the midst of this hostile counter-kingdom, exposed to its hostilities.

And Christ knows this. *I know where you live*, he says to his church throughout the world in the 21st century. *You live where Satan's throne is.* "I know the great risks you are taking by being faithful to me".

"But do not be afraid. You live under the protective power of my sword. You live under the authority of the Word from my mouth."

Do not be afraid – not even if the sword of persecution kills faithful witnesses, like our brother Antipas who was killed in Pergamum.

That is why Christ presents himself here as the one *who has the sharp, two-edged sword*. The sword is a weapon to defend yourself and to attack your enemies. The picture shows that Jesus is at war – not only with all these different religions and powers in Pergamum, but with the satanic power behind all these – his arch-enemy Satan, the Devil himself! This is the same enemy you and I are facing every day.

O sure, Satan was defeated when Jesus died and rose again. But now our Saviour is getting ready to complete the job. He is getting ready for the final act with the sword of his mouth. He is coming to rule and judge with his Word and Spirit. And this final phase of history is not a time for compromise.

And yet, despite the threatening circumstances, although they live where Satan rules, the exalted Christ has good things to say about his church in Pergamum. *You hold fast my name*, he says. The believers in Pergamum remained true to their faith in Jesus. And Christ praises them for this loyalty, this faithfulness.

Even when brother Antipas was killed, my faithful witness – you did not deny your faith in me, he says. This murder must have been a shock for the congregation. But they did not forsake Jesus. They did not give up their faith. We do not know anything about Antipas, other than that he was not ashamed to confess Jesus Christ as his Lord and Saviour. He refused to compromise his faith, and he did not beat about the bush when it came to that. For this he paid with his life.

What do we do when confessing Jesus as Saviour is getting one of us into trouble? Perhaps we think: "he should have kept his mouth shut. Now he gets all of us in trouble. Who is going to be next?"

But despite the dangerous and critical circumstances in Pergamum, the congregation has been persistently faithful. The members of the church remained true to the only name by which we can be saved. For they know: No other religion or power in the world can save, but Jesus alone; the Son of God, who died on the cross and rose again – he alone is the Saviour of the world.

This is a great and encouraging testimony from the exalted Christ about his people in Pergamum. You would have loved to be part of such a strong and faithful community. However, not everyone is so uncompromising.

Christ knows more. He also knows that they were making some serious mistakes in the church at Pergamum. They neglected discipline. There were some false teachers around that seriously mutilated the gospel. And they were big time promoters of compromise with the contemporary culture. In Ephesus they did not want to have anything to do with folks like that. But in Pergamum the church failed to reject and get rid of these people.

But, says Christ, *I have a few things against you.* You have some among you, who hold on to other teachings, other ideas. Their teachings, their ideas compromise the truth of the Scriptures. They compromise the radical nature of total dedication of the gospel of Jesus Christ.

Some church-members had participated in pagan festivals, celebrations, or other social activities. But in those days that came unavoidably with idol-worship. Some may have been involved even in the immoral practices that often characterized such occasions. Others were perhaps simply enticed by the contemporary easy-going and pleasure-seeking lifestyle.

5 • Revelation 2:12-17

"And in your church you don't do anything about it," says Christ. "Believers in Pergamum, this I have against you," he says, "that you allow these people in your congregation."

You have some there, who hold the teaching of Balaam. Now this Balaam was not a real teacher in Pergamum. Balaam was some sort of magician in the Old Testament. Here Balaam is mentioned as a model, to illustrate what they were dealing with in Pergamum and what the possible consequences could be.

What the church in Pergamum was also facing was the influence of *those who hold the teaching of the Nicolaitans*! We have met them before. They were also mentioned in the message to the church in Ephesus. You may remember that the Ephesians hated their practices and so did Christ. Then you will understand why Christ is so indignant here. Believe it or not, the congregation in Pergamum was okay with having those Nicolaitans around in the church.

What do we know about this group? Not much. But we do know they promoted the idea of compromise with the pagan world in which they were living, the contemporary culture of their days. Christians should get rid of a suspicious and antagonistic attitude towards the pagan or secular society in which they live, they suggested. If you would like to participate in some of the social activities of your pagan neighbours or friends – and those were usually also religious activities – go ahead, they said! It is not a big deal.

The boundaries between the church and the world are not that important. You do not have to give up being a Christian, but you can combine your Christian faith with some of the values and beliefs of the anti-Christian culture. Some of those things are not all that bad. Not everything is always black or white.

Do not be a stickler. It makes your life much easier and safer in this world. Your pagan neighbours are actually going to appreciate you more. And it is more fun, too.

After all, you live and work here, in this world! You go to school, you have a job, you have a profession, or you run a business. That means that you have to get along and you will have to participate in the lifestyle, and sometimes

Pergamum: Faithful, but compromising

even in the religious rituals, of your colleagues and business partners. In those days, this implied eating food sacrificed to idols and joining in sexually immoral entertainment.

Compromising your faith in this way may not seem too big of a deal.

But according to Christ this is serious business. How serious? "Well," he says, "look at the story of Balaam and at his teaching." We can find it in Numbers 22 – 25.

Balak, king of Moab wanted to destroy the people of Israel. But he figured that military violence would not work. The Israelites had just defeated some powerful enemies. And so he summoned Balaam, a well-known diviner, and paid him big bucks to lay a curse on God's people. We know that this did not work either. Then Balaam came up with another plan. According to Numbers 31:16 he gave Balak the advice that led to what we see happen in Numbers 25:1, 2. Men of Israel enjoyed sex with Moabite women. These women in turn invited them to attend sacrifices to their gods and worship those gods.

No, these Israelites were not giving up worshipping the Lord, the God of Israel. But they compromised. At least that is what they were thinking. It makes sense, does it not? You can fight the enemy, but you can also try to get along as good neighbours. Then you can even enjoy the pleasures the pagans are offering.

And Balaam's strategy was successful. God's people compromised their trust in God alone, by turning to false gods. Why not both? And the feasts they were invited to, were a blast, with lots of food, sacrificed to idols and lots of beautiful Moabite girls. They really enjoyed themselves. But Balaam knew very well that in the end this would completely ruin God's people.

Well, this is what is happening in Pergamum, says Christ. In line with Balaam's suggestions, the Nicolaitans among you encourage people to cross the boundaries between the church and the world. They may claim that you do not leave your Christian identity behind when you are blending your Christian faith with whatever false teaching, worldly lifestyle, or ungodliness you are confronted with, as long as it looks interesting or attractive. But in the end it is all just disobeying God!

5 • Revelation 2:12-17

Now, it is important to note that not the whole congregation in Pergamum was infected by this. Not everybody in the church acted this way. But the problem was that the church did not resist the members that did. They did not take any action. They did not put them under discipline. They just let them carry on. That is why Jesus Christ was holding the congregation as a whole responsible.

Perhaps they were putting more emphasis on their own individual salvation, at the expense of the well-being and purity of the church as a whole. This is actually an even more urgent issue for us today, than it was in the time of the Apostles.

We know that the church is important, but in our post-modern individualistic mindset it is often first of all about my personal salvation, my own relationship with God and Jesus Christ. With such thinking the church is there for my benefit. She becomes my personal SSP (Spiritual Service Provider).

The result is that we feel less responsible for the choices others in the church are making, and for the effect it has on the purity of the church. You do things differently than I do. I would never do what you do. You would not feel comfortable doing what I do. But we both believe in Jesus as the Saviour, so we will all be fine.

But Christ says: "No – you are not fine. We are talking about my church. And about the purity of my church, my bride!"

In Pergamum some argued: "if we refuse to participate in those pagan festivals, we effectively withdraw ourselves from all social life in this city. We could lose our job. It could ruin our business. It would make me a social outcast."

And so these Nicolaitans said: "Don't worry about it. Attend those feasts, even if they are dedicated to pagan gods. Enjoy yourself, as long as you keep in mind that such an idol is nothing."

But the church in Pergamum underestimated the dangers of a compromising attitude towards the world. When you cross those boundaries and you accommodate the values and beliefs of the antichristian culture, your commitment to the Holy God is in danger. Even if there are only some in the church who promote this compromise with the world – the pagan world of Pergamum or the secular world today – it is unacceptable!

And thus, the exalted Christ issues this urgent call: *Therefore, repent.* Break with this! Turn around! He does not say this only to those who had compromised their faith. He also addresses the ones who would not make compromises themselves, but who accept these Nicolaitans, and allow this to go on. They are also guilty of compromise.

There is a lot at stake here. For 'if you do not repent', he adds, *I will come to you soon and war against them with the sword of my mouth.* Remember what Jesus had said before: "I am coming soon. The time is near." Jesus Christ himself is coming to take action against those who persist in worldly practices and so compromise their Christian life, because of friendship with the world.

And he will do so with "the sword of his mouth", that is his holy Word. "I will come to judge," he says. "I will expose their sins and publicly declare them guilty, worthy of condemnation, because their hearts were not fully dedicated to me. They gave up the freedom I gave them, for the so-called freedom the world offers".

You may start to wonder now: Is the second coming of Jesus not going to be a joyful event then, something to look forward to? That depends. The world in the final phase of history is a warzone. And Jesus is coming as Judge. He will use his sword to separate those who follow him from those who refuse to do that. He comes to fight, he says. The battle lines are drawn.

But the most important question is: where are you in this picture? Those who compromise their faith, those who assimilate to the modern world, to the expectations of the modern culture – they will find themselves on the wrong side of the battle, unless they repent. So, what do you do? Join the Winner! Jesus Christ your King. This is not the time for compromise.

Here is a strong warning for us, the church today. What do we do with the gospel of Jesus Christ today? How do we live it in today's world?

The true gospel of Jesus and his sacrifice for all our sins is offensive to many people in our modern world. We can try to sugar-coat it to avoid controversy and make it more acceptable. We can try to compromise the gospel, by

5 • Revelation 2:12-17

taking the offensive parts out. Perhaps we hope in this way to find friendship with the world. And who knows – we might even be able to be a positive influence in the world.

There is, of course, nothing wrong with trying to be a positive influence in the world, but consider the price you might have to pay for this.

Think of what John wrote in 1 John 2:15: *Do not love the world or the things in the world. If anyone loves the world, the love of the Father is not in him.*

And James issues this warning (James 4:4): *Do you not know that friendship with the world is enmity with God?*

Those who pursue such friendship with the world, he calls "adulterous people".

The gospel of Jesus Christ is offensive. We better get used to it. As Paul wrote to Timothy in 2 Timothy 3:12: *Indeed, all who desire to live a godly life in Christ Jesus will be persecuted.*

Compromising the gospel of salvation in the hope to win friends, to make it easier to influence people, to avoid controversy and escape hostility – all these things make the message of the church meaningless and leave the church powerless.

Jesus Christ does not call us as his church to be one of the many subcultures in this world. He wants us to present what we stand for as a clear counterculture. This may trigger controversy, hatred, scorn, or ridicule from the world. But that is to be expected and should not surprise us, says the Bible.

Here is the problem. If we live our Christian lives in such a compromising way that it is difficult to distinguish it from the lives of others who do not follow Jesus Christ, then the church will not attract persecution. But it will also not gain any respect, and worse, it will make the gospel irrelevant.

However, if we remain true to the name of Jesus Christ, if we preach the true gospel, if we live the Christian life without watering down or compromising the biblical message, we may trigger hatred, suffering or persecution. We might also attract the attention of some who want to follow Christ. But the most important thing is that we praise, honour. and glorify God.

Pergamum: Faithful, but compromising

But the warning is not the end. In this message the exalted Christ has another promise for his faithful church, the church that listens with an open heart to the Word of the Holy Spirit.

To the one who conquers... if you have repented and have resisted the temptation to compromise your Christian faith, to blend it with some attractive false teaching, if you have remained true to the name of Jesus Christ – here is your promise. Actually, it's a double promise this time. Christ promises two things.

First, he says, *I will give some of the hidden manna*. After Balaam and Balak we have here another reference to the Old Testament. You may remember how God fed his people in the wilderness with the manna that fell from heaven (Exodus 16). By God's grace Israel's food supply was taken care of during the journey toward the Promised Land – every day again.

In the same way God promises to feed his faithful church with the bread from heaven. This manna is Jesus Christ himself. In John 6 we read that Jesus says about himself: "I am the bread of life. He who comes to me will never go hungry. If anyone eats of this bread, he will live forever." As the journey continues through this world where Satan has his throne, our Saviour sustains us with his grace and mercy, every day, until he will appear in glory and usher in the new heaven and the new earth.

Stay the course. Reject everything that will lead you astray, that will slow you down or that will make you lose your sense of direction. "I will take care of you," says Jesus.

All this is 'hidden' for the world. But for those who are in Jesus it is very real and full of comfort and encouragement.

But there is more: *I will also give him a white stone with a new name written on the stone*. 'White' is always a symbol of purity, holiness and 'stone' is durable. Also, in the Greek courts a 'white stone' was given to mark someone as innocent and free.

In other words, here your Saviour says to you with the symbolic image of this "white stone with a new name": if you remain faithful to my name, I will give you the assurance of your imperishable freedom from sin and guilt.

5 • Revelation 2:12-17

I am making everything new, also your name. By God's grace you will be given a new identity in Jesus Christ. You belong to him. It is written in stone, so that it cannot be undone or deleted, ever!

And no one will know your new name. Only you know the intimate relationship you have with your Saviour. He knows you as no one else knows you.

This white stone with your new name is your assurance, so to speak, that he will welcome you into the perfect communion with him in his eternal kingdom of peace.

Just do not compromise your faith and your faithfulness.

6

REVELATION 2: 18 – 29

THYATIRA – LOYAL, BUT OPEN TO FALSE TEACHING

When we turn to the next one of the seven churches the exalted Christ is addressing in the book of Revelation, the church at Thyatira, we begin the second half of the roundtrip that the messenger had to make, who had to deliver John's letter to the seven churches in Asia Minor. We go from Pergamum, about 60 km South East, to Thyatira. It is on the road to Sardis, which comes next.

Thyatira was much farther away from the coast, and was located in a low valley, surrounded by hills. It was quite a bit smaller than the previous cities, more a town than a city, we would say today. Under Persian, Greek, and Roman rule it had often been a garrison town, and so a relatively large number of veterans had settled there.

Thyatira was not a powerful political centre, like Pergamum, or a busy port with a strong international flavour, like Ephesus. It was a centre of trade and manufacturing goods, with craftsmen, like weavers, tailors, dyers, leather-workers, bronze-smiths, potters. And it was famous for its purple cloth.

In Acts 16, we read about Lydia from Thyatira who was *a seller of purple goods*. When Paul met her in Philippi, she may have been on a business-trip, or she may have settled there and imported the purple goods from her hometown.

This gives some background here, because these craftsmen were organized in some kind of unions – the trade-guilds. And these trade-guilds were, as was everything in that society, associated with idols. Every guild had its own "guardian god", so to speak. Such a god was always worshipped in their meetings and at their festivals.

For pagans, the area of industry, trade, and business was not spiritually neutral. As a member you were expected to participate in everything and to eat the food sacrificed to idols. And when it turned into sexually immoral entertainment, you could not just walk out. You would be ridiculed, or worse, given a hard time.

In other words, if you wanted to make a living as a potter or a weaver, and you wanted your business to flourish, you had to be a member of such a trade-guild. If not, you would lose your position in society, you would be shunned, lose jobs, lose work, and the result: no food on the table.

This would be your dilemma as a Christian in Thyatira. Satan would challenge you and attack you, in particular, in your daily work. What do you do? On the one hand, if you participate in these trade-guild activities you are in trouble, because you deny Jesus Christ. And on the other hand, if you do not participate you are also in trouble. You might as well close shop because you cannot provide for your family. That is a gloomy and discouraging perspective.

Today, in a different time and a different culture, it can also be difficult for us. How does Satan challenge and attack your faith today in your daily work, when you go to the office or the jobsite, or when you meet with customers, or when you're on a business trip? Do you ever face this dilemma that it would be good for business to do a certain thing, but you know that God does not want you to do it?

Well, there is one lady in the church in Thyatira who claims to know the answer. But we will learn that her teaching will have scary consequences. It is not without reason that Christ's message to the Thyatira congregation is the longest one of the seven, and that from the beginning the tone is utterly serious.

This is reflected already in the way in which the exalted Christ introduces himself here. It fits again the situation in this particular church, but that does not make it less relevant for all the other churches, as well as for the whole church today.

Jesus presents himself with emphasis as "the Son of God". That is unique in Revelation, and so this self-designation really stresses his divine and royal power. Later on (v.27) we find a quotation from Psalm 2, but there are more allusions to this psalm in this message to the church in Thyatira.

Psalm 2 is a powerfully prophetic message about the coming of God's glorious kingdom. It is about Jesus Christ that God says: *You are my Son, today I have begotten you*. And God also says, about Christ, that he is, *the Anointed One, my King, set on Zion, my holy hill*. Well, "here I am", says the exalted Christ to his church, "the Son of God, your messianic king as promised in Psalm 2". Jesus Christ claims royal power and royal control over all of life, also in Thyatira.

Jesus' distinguishing traits here are his eyes and his feet. *His eyes are like a flame of fire*. Nothing is hidden from his searing gaze. No one can deceive him. He sees and knows everything. His penetrating eyes see right through our pious facades in the church. For him, the hidden motives that make people follow false teaching are like an open book. As he says in v.23, *I search hearts and minds…*

And *his feet are like burnished bronze*. He is burning with holy zeal that will consume all evil. He has powerful feet no one can withstand as he goes forward and tramples on the wicked and the impure.

There are also good things in Thyatira. Christ praises them for their loyalty. *I know your works*, he says. I know *your love* – your deep devotion to me, your Lord. I know *your faith* – your trust in God's grace; your faithfulness in holding on to me as your Saviour. I know *your service* – you are always willing to help others. I know *your patient endurance* – you remain faithful, despite the pressure from the culture in which you live.

6 • Revelation 2:18-29

And not only are these things all there, they continue to grow in this. *Your latter works exceed the first*; you are now doing more than you did in the beginning, says Christ. That is fantastic. That is the kind of growth you like to see in the church. In their journey towards the New Jerusalem, they are actually making good progress.

So, yes, there are lots of good things going on in Thyatira.

However, they are not too strict on doctrine.

In some aspects Thyatira is the opposite of Ephesus. You may remember this from one of the previous chapters in this book, the one on Revelation 2:1–7. In Ephesus they were big on pure doctrine but lacking in love. Here in Thyatira they are strong in love, but pretty careless when it comes to doctrine.

We can get stuck in this dilemma too. You have probably heard it, or even thought it yourself sometimes: "Doctrine is dry and boring. It is nothing to be excited about. No, for me it's about a warm, loving, and joyful relationship with Jesus."

But that is a wrong dilemma. As soon as you talk about your faith, about your relationship with Jesus, and why this is so important for you, you talk 'doctrine'.

Think of a conversation like this.

> "I don't do doctrine. I love Jesus!"
> "That's great. Who is Jesus and why do you love him?"
> "He is my Saviour and died on the cross for my sins".
> "Hey – that is doctrine!"

So, actually the real contrast is not rational, dry doctrine versus emotional excitement, but rather, good doctrine versus poor doctrine.

Well, here is the danger in Thyatira Jesus is concerned about. When you get poor doctrine, poor teaching, lots of things go wrong in the church! Indeed, as we saw, many good things are going on in Thyatira. *But*, says Christ, *I have this against you, that you tolerate that woman Jezebel.*

He is probably talking about a real person, a particular dominant individual that had a lot of influence in that congregation. We mentioned her earlier already, but she was not all alone. Later on, we find out that she had her followers, her supporters in Thyatira. According to them it was time to do away with some of the old and narrow-minded views that were only causing trouble for the Christians.

Christ calls her "Jezebel". This was most likely not her real name. But he uses the name of a woman with a bad reputation in Israel's history to shock the congregation. From the Old Testament we know the 'real' Jezebel as the wife of king Ahab. She was the evil queen, who seduced the Israelites to worship the Canaanite gods Baal and Asherah.[3] The Bible condemns this as 'religious adultery', which led to serious persecution of faithful believers.

Well, this woman here in Thyatira plays the same disastrous and destructive role in the church, as Ahab's wife did in Israel back in the Old Testament. The name 'Jezebel' characterizes what this woman is doing. It shows the satanic nature of her activities. She seduces the people to sexual immorality, to walk away from worshipping the true God, to eat food sacrificed to idols. She promotes 'religious adultery'.

It is actually quite similar to what we have seen before, when we talked about the activities of the Nicolaitans in Ephesus and in Pergamum. But here it is more serious, because this woman *calls herself a prophetess*. She claims that God reveals himself through her, that her teaching comes straight from heaven. She goes around in the congregation and says to people, "God told me this and so you better listen to me. You don't want to disobey God, do you?"

That is pretty intimidating. And the church allowed her to carry on and gave room for her teaching. After all, you never know! God can do anything. Perhaps you should give her the benefit of the doubt. Have you ever had people say this to you: "I know for sure that God wants me (or you) to do this or that?"

But Christ is not intimidated. "She is a liar," he says. "She is a false prophet. And what she is teaching is false doctrine. She is seducing, or misleading, my servants." The word "misleading" shows the deceptive character of this evil. Although it is bad, it sounds good. That is why people go for it. But the

---

[3] The story of King Ahab and Jezebel is told in 1 Kings 16 and following chapters

eyes of the exalted Christ are like blazing fire, and he sees right through this facade.

You can hear how indignant Christ is because of this attack on his church. That is why he gets into this harsh name-calling with the name 'Jezebel'. The folks in Thyatira need to wake up. They need to see that with such false teaching the church is heading for disaster. And the church needs to do something about this, like they did in Ephesus with those who claimed to be apostles (Rev. 2:2). They tested them, and when they found out they were false, these guys were out.

Of course, a real prophet or prophetess would be a blessing for the church. That would be one who says things that are in agreement with the true gospel.

But this woman is promoting infidelity toward God, spiritual adultery. She suggests that you can turn away from the Lord as the only true God, and from Jesus Christ as your only Saviour. Just go out and explore other exciting things, and merge as you see fit, whatever religious or spiritual experience you like.

When you look at v.24 you get a bit of an idea about the way she talked people into this. "If you want to conquer Satan", she argued, "you need to experience him and how he operates. As a Christian you should not withdraw from Satan's realm, but you should become familiar with his 'deep secrets', whatever they are. If you have this deep spiritual knowledge you will know that you can worship any idol. It is nothing. And you will also realize that it does not matter what you do with your body."

So, do not hesitate to participate in the trade-guilds, including idol-worship and sexual immorality. Get involved in whatever is out there. You belong to Jesus anyway, and in the end you will be a better, wiser, and more experienced Christian.

How careful are we when it comes to this? How careful are you, young people? You might think: Am I not in the covenant? I have been baptized. I have professed my faith. I love Jesus as my Saviour. Am I not born again? Is it not true that in Christ I am a new creation? Does Paul not say in Romans 8 (vs. 37 and 39) that in everything *we are more than conquerors through him who*

Thyatira: Loyal, but open to false teaching

loved us? And that nothing in all creation will be able to separate us from the love of God in Christ Jesus?

And if those things are true, can we not be a bit more easy-going in the things we do and the choices we make? Is it then really such a big deal to get yourself into activities your unbelieving neighbours and friends are excited about, although these may challenge your faith? Why would it be wrong for you, as a Christian teenager, to experiment with, let's say, drugs or casual sex? Everybody else does.

Sin can always come up with excuses to do what it wants, to do what is convenient, to do what is comfortable, to do what makes us acceptable to the world and the culture in which we live. And as believers we can be persuaded that all this makes sense, as long as we forget that our God is a holy God, that he is a God who hates sin and a God who wants us to hate sin.

"Do what you want", said Jezebel. "You will be ok. You will learn and survive Satan's 'deep things'". But Christ says: "You will not be ok! You will not survive. And the church will not survive either. Jezebel is lying". The church in Thyatira is tolerating her. They allow her to teach – but Jesus Christ hates it.

It is clear that the situation in Thyatira is quite serious. And the response of the exalted Christ shows that if you are not alert, if you do not wake up, if you do not nip it in the bud, a bad situation will only get worse.

There were actually some people who came to believe that disobeying God and experiencing for yourself the power of sin and evil would make you immune to Satan's efforts to separate you from God's love in Jesus Christ. In this way you can learn to make up your own mind as to what is right and wrong, what is good and bad. By nature, this idea suits us mighty fine.

But it is false doctrine. This is not what Jesus is teaching. He told us to pray: *Lead us not into temptation.*

So yes, Christ warns earnestly against the destructive influence of this woman.

But he does not leave it at that. In the messages to the other churches Christ issues warnings as he calls them to repentance. And if they refuse to repent there will be consequences. But here he goes a step further. Here the exalted

6 • Revelation 2:18-29

Christ says something remarkable; something unique that shows again how serious this is. He comes to punish directly.

This woman is a church member, and so she should know better. But Jesus Christ has been gracious and patient. He had given her ample time to repent from her religious adultery. But she refused. She did not want to. Despite the Saviour's patience, she is hardening herself in her sin. And now she will experience the consequences.

And this time it is not a warning for what is coming at the last judgment. No, here and now *I will throw her onto a sickbed*, says Christ. "I love my church in Thyatira so much that I will stop her destructive influence in the congregation. She will be bed-ridden with a disease or a serious illness."

And it is not only her. "I will also punish her followers, her supporters," he says. Did you notice that he distinguishes between two categories of followers? First there are those *who commit adultery together with her*. Adultery is here again a metaphor for being unfaithful toward God, turning away from him. Those are the followers that are spiritually misled. But the door of repentance is still open. *I will throw them into great tribulation, unless they repent of her works*, he says. He does not explain what kind of tribulation this is going to be.

The other category is called, in v.23, *her children*. Those are most likely not her real, physical children. He is talking about those followers that are really hardcore and totally devoted to her teaching. They have become like her, hardened in sin and unwilling to repent. *Those I will strike dead*, he says. He will kill them.

Again, the language of the exalted Christ is harsh and shocking. It is going to be a very upsetting and painful experience for the congregation in Thyatira. You can compare it with the effect that the death of Ananias and Sapphira must have had in the church in Jerusalem (Acts 5:1-11).

But that is the intention. That is how urgent it is to alert the congregations, to wake up the churches from the disastrous consequences of wrong ideas, false teaching, and false doctrine, promoted by people that claim to know the will of God, but do not.

Christ wants us to take this to heart. For the church in the last days it remains important that we do not ignore the urgent call to remain faithful, and that we repent when captivated by false teaching and involved in practices that are the result of those ideas. Let us talk about these things in our Bible studies in the church, but also as families, as parents and children. How alert are we? And are we able to discern? Can we tell good doctrine from poor or false doctrine?

This is indeed not only relevant for Thyatira. When these things happen, says Christ, *all the churches* – also the church where it is being proclaimed today, in the 21st century – *will know that I am he who searches mind and heart*. Whatever we hold on to when it comes to our doctrine; whatever we support when it comes to our teachings; whatever we are getting ourselves into when it comes to our practices in this world, Christ knows. Nothing remains hidden from him.

Again, it is a serious wake-up call for all the churches, also for us here, today! With his eyes like blazing fire Jesus Christ alone sees right through all the things we think, say, and do. He knows what drives us. He recognizes the ugly reality that is often hiding below the pious surface in our lives.

He claims me for himself with everything that is hidden in the deepest depth of my heart. You and I are accountable to him, as to what we do with our lives. Do not take this accountability with a grain of salt. He takes you seriously. So, we better take him seriously when he promises *to repay each of you as your works deserve*.

But this is not the end of this message from the exalted Christ, to his church in Thyatira. The good things, mentioned in v.19, show that not everyone in this congregation had followed this influential woman. Not everyone was intimidated by her teaching and had accepted her ideas as true and valuable. Not everyone had embraced the so-called "deep things of Satan". There were people in Thyatira who wanted to have nothing to do with this Jezebel and her teaching.

That does not mean that it was easy for those brothers and sisters. As mentioned in the beginning, they had a tough time with all the hostility in town and in the church. But Jesus assures them that he will not make it more difficult for those that are struggling in those circumstances. *I do not lay on you any other burden. Only hold fast what you have, until I come.*

In Acts 15 we read that the "Council in Jerusalem" discussed what could be asked of Christians from the Gentiles as requirements for a Christian lifestyle in the midst of a pagan society. They agreed to draft four rules – just four! 1. *You are to abstain from food sacrificed to idols*; 2. *abstain from blood*; 3. *abstain from the meat of strangled animals*; and 4. *abstain from sexual immorality.*

You will notice that two of these instructions played a big role in the church in Thyatira. That makes it quite likely that Christ refers to these rules when he says that he will not add another burden. If you want to deal with the threat of false teaching in the church, the response is not to make more rules. Do not try to rein it in by coming up with more and new regulations and burdens.

No, just stick with what you have. Remain faithful to Jesus Christ. Remember what he said in Matthew 11:30 - *My yoke is easy and my burden is light.* Hold on to the true gospel of salvation by grace alone. As Christ puts it, *hold fast what you have, until I come.*

What do you have? Remember what Jesus said in the beginning (v.19). Continue to show love. Continue to live by faith. Continue to serve one another. Continue to persevere patiently.

Resist the temptation of false teaching, false doctrine when people claim to have a message from God for you. It may sound good but put them to the test. And learn to say 'no' to every teaching, every doctrine that would take away your Christian freedom. In Christ you are free from sin and Satan, free to serve God.

Then, in the end, the exalted Christ will also fulfill his promise in your life.

The one who conquers and who keeps my works, he says. You who repent and do God's will; you who by grace alone remain faithful to the end; you who reject Jezebel and her teachings – you may have it difficult today, but things will change.

Thyatira: Loyal, but open to false teaching

The promise of the glorified Christ is so encouraging and comforting for the poor craftsmen in Thyatira. Outside of the powerful trade-guilds they must have felt helpless, powerless, little, and insignificant in many ways. What could they expect from the future? What could they do to change things?

But following Jesus Christ comes with a marvellous perspective. As God's people you are on your way to the Promised Land and everything will change. Today, the powers in this world often ridicule and oppress the believers who want to keep their conscience clear. But in the future, God's faithful believers will, with the exalted Christ, rule over the world and over the nations.

That is an amazing turn-around. But that is his promise. *Even as I myself have received authority from my Father*, says Christ, *so I will give you authority over the nations*. That is incredible. God's promise in Psalm 2:8 – *I will make the nations your inheritance, the ends of the earth your possession* – given to the Son of God, is now going to the tanners, bronze-workers, potters, and weavers in Thyatira – yes, to all who suffer persecution, ridicule, and humiliation because of their love for Jesus.

This promise includes the destruction of God's enemies. "In me," says Jesus, "my Father in heaven will also fulfill his plan in Ps. 2:9 for you." *You will rule them with a rod of iron, as when earthen pots are broken in pieces*. The human rebellion against Christ as King will face God's wrath. There will be nothing left to be afraid of.

To this end I will also give you the morning star, says Christ. The morning star is one of the brightest stars in the sky, and the last one to disappear from sight before sunrise. It marks the beginning of a new day.

This morning star is Jesus Christ himself. Balaam prophesied about him, when he said: *A star will come out of Jacob* (Numbers 24:17). And in Rev. 22:16 Christ calls himself *the bright morning star*.

In him, your risen and glorified Saviour, you have bright hope for the glory that is coming. In him the new day dawns, the great day of salvation that will usher in the Kingdom in which you may live in eternal communion with Jesus Christ.

7

REVELATION 3: 1 – 6

SARDIS – DEAD, BUT NOT WITHOUT HOPE

What would be a good reason to give up on the church? And when I say "the church" I am talking about your own local church where you belong and where you have committed yourself as member. Or, to put it more accurately, the church where God has given you a place, and where he has called you to be faithful to him. When do you give up on the church?

If the church does not live up to your expectations? If you feel disappointed in how the church takes care of your spiritual needs? If you are not satisfied with the programs your church is offering? Perhaps you have shopped somewhere else, and in the other church you enjoyed worship a lot more, you felt more spiritually alive and active. And all of these things may be true, but does it make sense to switch, or not? What are you doing with those feelings and experiences? Are you going to give up on your church?

Today, more than in any other time in history, the ecclesiastical world, the church-world, has become a marketplace of competing businesses. What are we doing with that?

We are all part of this modern western society, so to a great extent we are all infected by the contemporary consumerism-bug. We need something, so we go on the internet and find ten grocery-stores, ten car-dealers, ten restaurants or even ten churches. And then we compare. You have websites that will do the comparison for you. We try to match what they have to offer with what our needs are.

That is a great idea when it comes to grocery-stores or restaurants but what about the church?

Sometimes we tend to treat the church as a spiritual franchise, like coffee shops. You can get your coffee here, or there, or elsewhere. We have personal preferences when it comes to these options, and over time you may develop some loyalty to one place, but in the end it doesn't really matter where you go. They all sell coffee.

However, the church is different. The Bible speaks about the church as the body of Christ, the Bride of Christ, and he himself made you part of her. He bought her, he loves her, and has great things in store for her. That is why he wants you to love her.

Jesus Christ does not give up on his church, his bride. He remains loyal; he remains faithful. No, that does not mean that anything goes. His message to the church in Sardis makes this abundantly clear. There was a lot wrong in Sardis, and Christ rebukes her severely. But he does not give up on her.

Throughout the history of the church there have been many revivals. You may have heard about the famous Great Awakening in 18th century North America.

This is what the exalted Christ is looking for in Sardis.

To the South East of Thyatira, and about 80 km east of Smyrna, we find the city of Sardis. It was established more than 1000 years before Christ. That makes it very old. It was a city that was built on top of a hill, which made it nearly inaccessible. On three sides there were steep slopes and the only access was on one side, over a narrow strip of land.

This location made it easy to defend, and the people in Sardis were known as proud and self-confident. They were convinced that no one could conquer their city. They did not have any reason to worry about that. They were safe.

And yet, two times enemies were successful in getting in, with a surprise attack at night, when the guards were not very watchful.

Throughout the ancient world Sardis was well-known as a wealthy and strong city. This was also due to the fact that gold had been found in the area, as well as precious stones, jewels. In addition, there was always lots of traffic coming through since Sardis was located at an important intersection of highways.

A few decades before John wrote Revelation, Sardis had been destroyed by an earthquake, but with the help of the Romans, and the emperors who favoured Sardis, it was re-built as a large and flourishing city with beautiful buildings. Not much is left of it. Today it is just a small, poor Turkish village.

In this message the author, the exalted Christ, presents himself again in a way that fits the situation in the church he is addressing – the church in Sardis. There is a connection between the circumstances of this congregation, and the manner in which Christ identifies himself.

These are the words of him who has the seven spirits of God and the seven stars.

In 1:4 we heard about the "seven spirits before God's throne". The expression stresses the fullness of the Holy Spirit of God in all its power. He is, we confess in the Nicene Creed, *The Lord and Giver of life*. God's Holy Spirit is the true source of life that is perfect and complete. Here we learn that it is the glorified Jesus Christ who holds and controls the Holy Spirit and his power-of-life.

And Christ will deploy this enormous spiritual power in and for his church. He is "holding the seven stars". That means he is also the Lord of the church and indicates his sovereign control over his whole church.

This is how he comes to the Christian congregation in Sardis, and Sardis is dead (v.1). But there is still hope, says Christ, because I am in control of the Holy Spirit. Yes – only the Holy Spirit can bring new life. Only the Holy Spirit is able to revive a dead church or wake up a sleeping church.

But look at me, says Jesus Christ. And he reminds them of the fact that he has, that he gives, and that he sends the Holy Spirit of God. He has the

7 • Revelation 3:1-6

power to make the church alive and keep her awake by his Spirit. And that is ongoing in the church, because the Holy Spirit works through the Word proclaimed, the Word about salvation by grace.

This is also how God governs his church, even today. Only through the Holy Spirit do we receive true faith, life in God, and fellowship with our risen Saviour. Sometimes people get confused as to what we can expect the Holy Spirit to do and what the typical works of the Holy Spirit are supposed to look like. But it is not that complicated. The Holy Spirit fills the church and the hearts of God's people with the salvation of Jesus Christ. Think of what happens in Acts 2.

Well, that is what they need most in Sardis, just as this good news of Jesus Christ is urgently needed in all the churches of all times.

It is striking that, from the beginning, the tone of Christ's message to the church in Sardis is so critical. This is different from what we have seen in the other messages where the exalted Christ had always something good to say first. There was always something in the congregation to praise God for.

But not here. There is nothing commendable to say. And Christ knows what he is talking about. He is familiar with the situation of the church in Sardis: *I know your works*, he says. And then he goes straight at it. He comes straight to the point, and simply breaks through the pattern in the other messages.

Without calling anything "good" or "praise-worthy" in the church, not even the slightest little thing, he comes immediately with his condemning observation, his serious complaint and judgment that the congregation at Sardis is alive, in name only.

That sounds pretty outrageous and right in your face. If you would be a church member in Sardis, you would be pretty upset about it.

After all, the church in Sardis seems like a very nice, and almost ideal congregation. They are well-organized and there are lots of activities going on. They have no problems and no issues. There are no Nicolaitans or other troublemakers.

And yet, they are facing a huge crisis, and they do not even see it!

Sardis: Dead, but not without hope

As a matter of fact, the situation is dangerous, even life-threatening. But the Christians in Sardis are not concerned at all. They are deceived about their true state. But in his grace the exalted Christ shows them the tragic flaw that identifies them. *You have the reputation of being alive*, he says, *but you are dead.*

From where we are, from our earthly point of view, the church appears very much alive. It seems to be doing just fine. But from the point of view of the risen Christ, from the exalted point of view, it looks totally different. She is dead.

On the outside everything looks good. The church seems to be flourishing and full of life. They enjoy a good reputation among the other churches. "Have you been to Sardis? It is such a nice and lively congregation. It seems like some of the trouble the other churches are dealing with does not affect the folks in Sardis."

But they do not deserve this reputation. The glorious Christ penetrates the good-looking outside and he knows that the reality is different from the outward appearance. As you read through the Book of Revelation you find that this is a major conflict in the story-line of the book: outward appearances and inner realities often clash. The way things appear in this world may not be the way things are.

When you have a name or a reputation you would hope that this would indeed reflect how you really are, your true identity, also when it comes to the church. But that is not always true. And it is not true in Sardis either. Although this church has the reputation of being alive, she is dead; she is spiritually dead. She is 'dead' in the sense that she is overcome by spiritual sleepiness, apathy, lethargy.

We do not read anything about persecution or hostilities in Sardis. There was a large Jewish community in the city, but we get the impression that neither the Jews nor the Gentiles gave them a hard time. Outsiders left them alone without any trouble.

On top of that, there is no indication that within the church they were divided about heresies or worried about false doctrine creeping in. There is nothing like that.

7 • Revelation 3:1-6

How did they do this? Apparently this church had adapted her character and message so much, that it no longer triggered any opposition, any resistance in society or among followers of other religions.

They had watered down the confession of the name and the work of Jesus because they did not want to offend anybody. Messages about sin and punishment, the need for forgiveness and repentance, the need to believe in Jesus as the only Saviour may upset some people. So the congregation had come to ignore what is important, and had given all the attention to what is less important.

Yes, there was indeed peace in the church in Sardis! But it was the peace of the cemetery. And in the process the church had failed and died.

It must have been a shock when this message was read in Sardis. Especially if you enjoy such a good reputation in town. *You are dead.....* Wow! Wait a minute. Dead?

> *We just started this new program.*
> *We just had a successful fundraiser to expand our facilities.*
> *Everyone loves our senior pastor.*
> *Our music director does a great job.*

But the assessment of the glorified Christ is crystal-clear: *You are dead.* You have become irrelevant.

And this was not only shocking for the brothers and sisters in Sardis. This is also shocking for us, today. Remember, in addressing these seven churches, Christ is addressing the whole church. He is addressing us. That makes what he says here devastatingly relevant. Again, Christ holds up the mirror and he wants us to look. What are we, dead or alive? Spiritual decline is a real possibility, then and now.

All kinds of groups can call themselves "church". And they can have the good and attractive reputation of being alive and vibrant, for instance in worship, fellowship, and outreach. But are they 'truly' living churches, as God wants them to be?

That leads to an important question: what makes the church a living 'church'? What is the essence of being church of Jesus Christ?

> *Well, it is not the building that is essential.*
> *It is not the programs the church is offering.*
> *It is not the growth in numbers.*
> *It is not the great achievements of the past.*
> *It is not the ambitious plans for the future.*
> *It is not the smooth organization.*
> *It is not the reputation in society.*
> *It is not the annual church-picnic, or the annual community breakfast, or the annual Christmas concert.*

Make no mistake, there is nothing wrong with any of these things. It is all great. However, essential for being 'church' is its spiritual life, and thus the spiritual life of its members. It is the true relationship with God, which only comes in the way of true fellowship with Jesus Christ, the living Saviour, by faith through the power of the Holy Spirit. And this shows in the seriousness with which the church deals with matters of repentance, forgiveness, and obedience.

But this is not the end of the story about Sardis. Christ does not leave it at that. He does not give up on his church. We might be inclined to do that. You do not find what you are looking for in your church, so you are done with it and you move on. Why would you stick around? Who wants to be part of a dead church? But Jesus Christ does not do that. How could he? This is his church. He bought her with his own precious blood. He loves her and remains faithful to her.

So he continues to address her, telling her to re-kindle the fire. All is not lost. There is still hope. There is still a chance to revive life. That is what he wants. The glorified Christ counters the tragic flaws in Sardis with the call for spiritual awakening. And he outlines a number of steps to come to this.

His warning is urgent. In the v.2 and 3 we have a series of five imperatives, five commands: wake up – strengthen – remember – keep – repent. It is the strongest warning in all of these seven messages. In other words, make drastic changes by paying attention to what is really important and by ignoring what is unimportant.

7 • Revelation 3:1-6

In Sardis, they kept themselves busy with lots of things. But that does not fix the spiritual inertia in the congregation, because these were the wrong things. That is the serious crisis Jesus is pointing at.

Wake up and stay awake, he says to these dead or sleeping church members in Sardis. Revive what is left. He who has the seven spirits of God comes to his Bride because he loves her and by the power of the Holy Spirit he wants to wake her up from the sleep of death. Wake up and pray that the fire of the Spirit keeps burning in the church of Jesus Christ.

The good things that are still there are far and few between, and the flame of the burning zeal for God's love and grace in Jesus has become very small. This makes it so urgent: *Strengthen what remains and is about to die.* The last remnants of a living faith may almost be gone, but do not let it disappear.

It is urgent. *For I have not found your works complete in the sight of my God*, says Christ. Oh sure, the outward forms were there, the ceremonies, the rituals, the religious customs and traditions. And she thought she was doing well. But it was all empty. Everything fell short in God's eyes. She did not live up to God's expectations, not by far. What is most essential was missing, there was no living faith.

Do we hear the warning? Yes, and we keep things going. There are no lack of activities in the church. But what about your living faith? What about your deep joy in Jesus and your excitement in the Lord and in his grace? What about hearts filled with genuine faith, hope, and love? Or are we just going through the motions?

People may think that everything is going well and that the church is full of life. But what does Jesus Christ know, the one who has the view from above?

Remember, then, what you have received and heard. Remember the past. Not to glorify the past, but to embrace again what you have lost. Remember your excitement when the gospel-message of grace in Jesus Christ first arrived. Remember the joy and enthusiasm with which you once embraced the goods news of the forgiveness of all your sins. Yes, at one point the church in Sardis did have true life.

Keep this gospel and repent. This is it. If you want to bring new life into a dead church, what do you do? Develop new, creative ideas? Introduce different music, new rituals and set up new programs? You can do all that, and that might be okay, but do not expect those things to revive the church! They will not. Nothing but the gospel of Jesus Christ needs to warm the hearts and to change lives: obey and repent.

Repent and return to life, a life filled with thankful and joyful obedience.

If you do not, *I will come like a thief, and you will not know at what hour I will come against you.* That is threatening language. The expression "coming like a thief in the night" is a familiar warning from other passages in the New Testament. It stresses the need to be at all times prepared for Jesus' second coming.

"I will come as Judge, and that will then be at a moment that you do not expect me," says Christ. "When that moment will surprise you unprepared, you won't escape destruction." The fortress of Sardis had been captured twice by surprise, probably at night, when the guards were not very watchful. Christ warns that, unless they wake up and repent, something similar will happen to the church.

Several times Christ urged his disciples to "keep watch" and "be ready" in the time between Jesus' ascension and return in glory. Think of Jesus' teaching in Luke 12:35–56. We know that we should be watchful, all the time, like the 'faithful and wise servant' in Luke 12, whom the master finds waiting and doing what he was told to do at his master's return. Wakefulness is urgently needed on the journey to the Promised Land.

But how watchful are we really? Quite often we are easily distracted by other things, things that are not so important.

And yet, there is still a little bit more to say about Sardis, than what we've heard so far. *You have a few names in Sardis, people who have not soiled their garments.* "Soiling garments or clothes" is a general image of unholy living. And so, yes, there are still a few who are clean before God.

That is encouraging. No, it does not change Christ's assessment that the church in Sardis is dead. As a matter of fact, the emphasis is here on "few". It is a very small number. That shows again how bad the situation in Sardis is. Almost the whole congregation is affected by it. Almost all of them have dirty clothes.

7 • Revelation 3:1-6

But Christ does not want to see his holy bride drab and dirty. He wants to see her bright and shining. And in Sardis that is only true for a very few people. Only a very few did not give in to the powers that had turned the church into a dead church. The exalted Christ knows them all and he praises them.

At the same time, as the few living members of a dead church, it must not have been easy to go against the majority and to remain faithful in those circumstances, to resist the claims and expectations of the dominant culture, and to keep clean clothes.

But Christ will not forget those who belong to him. *They will walk with me in white*, he says. "White clothes" represent holiness, purity, and perfection. And such outer clothing is often referred to as something that shows someone's inner character. The 'spotless garments' represent the people in Sardis who kept themselves 'spiritually pure', who did not compromise their faith.

Here is the marvellous perspective: as God's faithful followers you may go for a walk in the wonderful company of Christ himself, to celebrate his victory in heavenly joy and glory. Why is that? *For they are worthy*, says Jesus.

Now, that sounds remarkable. Is eternal life not a gift of God's grace? Are we not unworthy, because of our sins? Yes, we are. We are justified by grace alone, through faith. But then you must be able to see the fruits of faith too. Here is your link between your future destination and the pattern of your Christian life today. Yes, we are worthy indeed, not because of what we do, but only by God's grace in Jesus Christ. The white clothes we will be wearing were bleached in the powerful blood of Christ.

Christ then goes on to extend the same promise to *the one who conquers*. In other words, the white clothes are not just for the few people mentioned before. Indeed, to everyone who wakes up, strengthens, remembers, obeys, and repents, life is returning in all its fullness and glory. This begins here and now. Today already, you may wear your garments of grace. But it will be completed when the glorified Christ will return and hand out the bright white wedding clothes for the grand celebration that is coming.

Is that really true? Yes, says Christ. *I will never blot out his name out of the book of life. I will confess his name before my Father and before his angels.* The 'book of life' is mentioned several times in Revelation as the Register of those destined to receive new life, the citizens of the heavenly kingdom. This registration in heaven guarantees glorious and eternal life for those who live by grace and are truly alive in this world.

Think of the situation in Sardis. People thought, 'as long as I am on the membership list of this church, with its reputation of being alive, I should be okay'. But that is a mistake. The fact that your name is in the church directory or in the computer of the administrator does not automatically mean that you are registered in God's book of life.

Wake up, strengthen, remember, obey, and repent. Then you may know that, even if you die here and your name will be removed from the church directory, the name of him who conquers will never be removed from the registers in heaven.

On the contrary, the eternal Judge will publicly verify and confirm at the heavenly court of God the Father, and in the presence of the angels as witnesses:

"Here they are, Father, all who belong to me and walk with me, dressed in white."

"Here she is – my strong, pure, spotless bride – my church."

And therefore, do not give up on the church. Even if you think that she is half-dead do not abandon her. Do not walk away, but wake up, strengthen what remains. Pray for her that the power of the Holy Spirit brings back new life.

Love her because Christ loves her as his bride and has great promises for her.

Then, one day, we will find ourselves dancing on the streets that are golden, the glorious bride and her bridegroom, the great Son of Man.

8

Revelation 3: 7 – 13

PHILADELPHIA – FAITHFUL AND ENDURING

In the previous chapter we were in Sardis and we were looking at a dead church. Not that it looked like a dead church. We would never have thought it a dead church if Christ would not have told us so. There were lots of things going on. Everything looked great and lively. No wonder they had a reputation of being alive.

But Jesus Christ had nothing good to say about her. *You are dead*, he said. Whatever was driving people in their activities in the church, it was not a living and saving faith in Jesus as the only Saviour. And then we talked a bit about what is really essential for being a living church.

As we move on and enter the city of Philadelphia, we find the opposite. Christ tells us that in the Christian congregation in Philadelphia we have a prime example of a living church. There is no criticism in this message. He has only good things to say about her.

That is not because they are so strong and powerful and influential. It is not because they are so well-respected in town. It is not because they have an impressive cathedral with a big organ. The church in Philadelphia is not a successful mega-church. No, they *have only little power*, says Christ.

And on top of that – in the antichristian Jews, and in the Hellenistic Gentiles they had powerful enemies. The opposition and resistance was strong.

And yet, *you have kept my word*, says Jesus. *And you have not denied my name*. Under mounting pressure this small band of believers has been faithful and enduring, hanging on to the Word of God's love in Jesus Christ. Here is our example, our role-model among these churches, so to speak.

They may have been insignificant in human eyes, but they were great in God's eyes. The exalted Christ has only words of praise for them.

When we travel from Sardis to Laodicea we go a little bit to the south, but mostly eastward, deeper into the interior of the Roman province of Asia, which is today western Turkey. About 45 km on the way, about one-third of the distance from Sardis to Laodicea, we come to the city of Philadelphia. Philadelphia was founded in the second century before Christ by the Greek king Attalus II. This makes it the youngest of the seven cities where the churches listed in Revelation 2 and 3 are located.

The city was established as the centre for spreading the Greek culture, language, and lifestyle further into Asia. Over time, in the next centuries, this turned out to be a successful endeavour. Sometimes Philadelphia was called 'little Athens', and in the time of the Romans it was a prosperous city, although it was often damaged by regular earthquakes. There were always buildings that needed to be fixed or were under repair.

The fertile soil north of the city made the area suitable for growing grapes, and so there were lots of vineyards and wineries. That was the reason that, when it comes to the religious life, Dionysus, the god of wine and unrestrained sensuality, was one of the most important Greek gods to be worshipped in Philadelphia.

This is the context, the background that helps us to understand what the Christian congregation in Philadelphia was struggling with. Indeed, Jesus Christ had gathered his church also in Philadelphia. And it is to this church that the exalted Christ presents himself now as *the holy one* and *the true one*.

He is "the Holy One". In the Old Testament, this is the name of God Almighty, the LORD. He is unique, glorious, and highly exalted. The same can be said about the other name: "the True One", or "the Trustworthy One".

This name indicates that God's works and words are true, reliable, and absolutely trustworthy.

Well, with both those names, which were exclusively used for the Almighty God in the Old Testament, Christ Jesus presents himself to his small and helpless church in Philadelphia. To encourage his people, he stresses his power and majesty as the only One who is the true and authentic Messiah, the Son of God.

And he also *has the key of David*, he says. The symbolism is simple and clear. The one who has keys has the authority and the power, but also the responsibility, to open doors or to shut and lock doors; to allow access or to deny access; to let some people in and to let other people out, whatever it is such doors would be leading to.

In Rev. 1:18 the glorified Christ says about himself that he *has the keys of death and Hades*. You cannot identify this with "the key of David" in our text, but the analogy is clear. With the "key of death and Hades" Christ has the power to unlock death's door and to set prisoners free from the realm of death, or Hades. This key opens the door that leads to life. And Christ is the only one who can do this.

Here, it is *the key of David. What he opens no one will shut, and what he shuts no one opens*. He is in absolute control! The expression goes back to Isaiah 22:15–25. Through the prophet Isaiah the LORD Almighty expresses his indignation and anger about the unfaithfulness of Jerusalem, the city of David.

But then his anger concentrates on Shebna, the official who was in charge of the royal palace. Apparently this Shebna had misused his powerful position. And then the LORD says, "I will punish you for this, and I will appoint a replacement in Eliakim. *I will place on his shoulder the key of the house of David. He shall open, and none shall shut; and He shall shut, and none shall open*" (Isaiah 22:22).

This was a huge responsibility for this Eliakim. No one would be able to get in or out of the royal palace without his permission and even without him knowing it. The question is: would this Eliakim be able to handle this responsibility perfectly? Isaiah 22:25 shows that the answer is 'no'.

So how does this prophecy in Isaiah 22 relate to Christ? The point is that Jesus Christ came to fulfill these words about Eliakim. He presents himself as the heir of David's royal house and kingdom. And what neither David himself, nor Eliakim, nor anyone else in the Old Testament could do, Christ has done. He opened God's kingdom.

By his death on the cross, and his resurrection, he took away what prevented us from entering. He opened the door and now the access is free for all who believe in him.

Jesus Christ was given this unique authority, *the key of David*, which opens the door to the eternal destiny of God's redeemed people, to the gates of the city of David, the New Jerusalem. He alone can do this: "When he opens – no one can shut". And the opposite is true, too. Without Jesus there will be no access to God or God's kingdom, for any one! "When he shuts – no one can open."

This self-presentation of the glorified Christ is so comforting and encouraging, especially when the Christian church is small and helpless, and finds many doors shut in this world, controlled by powerful enemies of the faith. The One with the power of the holy and true God knows exactly what is going on in Philadelphia.

I know your works, he says. "I know the difficult circumstances you find yourself in. I know the hostilities you are facing, and I am fully aware how you have handled these." In the prosperous and culturally advanced city of Philadelphia not many people were very impressed by this small and weak group of Christians. But Christ looked at this church with love and respect.

I have set before you an open door which no one is able to shut. What does Christ mean by this image? You can think of a number of different things. But remember, Christ is the key-bearer. With this power and authority, he controls your future and destination as God's people, God's church. And as we journey toward the kingdom of heaven, he takes care of his church and he provides for her, despite the fierce opposition she may be facing.

He gives open minds and eager hearts that listen to the gospel and embrace its message. He guarantees your freedom to approach God through Jesus' sacrifice. And by the power of his Holy Spirit he opens up outreach possibilities for his church that we would not even think of.

And all this comes with the permanent access Christ opens for us, giving access to God and to his kingdom. Permanent, in the sense that no one can take it away or block it. It is a door *that no one is able to shut,* no matter how difficult they make it for the church. The trials and hardships can be many for God's children. They can shut many doors for you. But no one can slam the door in your face that leads to the glorious victory in Christ's eternal kingdom. This "open door" tells you that God's plan will be realized.

You could see this first of all in the faithfulness of the congregation in Philadelphia. *I know that you have but little power*, says Christ. It was not much, this church. It was a small group, only a few members, weak and vulnerable. They did not have much wealth or members with significant influence or social status. Nothing like that! And then the opposition – it can easily become disappointing and discouraging.

And yet, despite this outward weakness, *you have kept my word and have not denied my name*, says Christ. Despite the pressure, they have persistently confessed the one name by which we can be saved, the name of Jesus. They have remained faithful and loyal to Jesus Christ and to his Word. They have believed that Christ kept the door to God open, and so they have even grown in faith and developed spiritually. And they have resisted the lure and temptations of Babylon, the attractive norms and values of the contemporary culture.

Is this your congregation? Is this your church? Do you recognize this picture? Do not say too quickly: "sure, this is us!" Is it indeed your faithfulness and loyalty to Jesus Christ and to his Word that fills your heart and drives you to stick persistently to confessing the only name by which we can be saved? And do you at all times just as persistently refuse to deny this name?

Another result of "the open door" that Christ has set before his people in Philadelphia is the surprising promise in v.9. Just as the congregation in Smyrna (Rev. 2:8–11), the church in Philadelphia had to deal with people *who say that they are Jews, and are not, but lie.* The point is again, as we saw before, that the true seed of Abraham, the true Jews, are the Christians.

But the people Christ talks about here are the antichristian Jews. They call themselves God's people, but it is the opposite, they reject Jesus Christ. And Satan leads them to slander and attack the church. They form the *synagogue of Satan*. That is scary and intimidating. Those hostilities could easily discourage this small congregation and make them feel insecure. What do you do?

Well, here is the surprise! *I will make them come*, says Christ. No, not to attack you or ridicule you or humiliate you, but *to bow down before your feet and learn that I have loved you*. This is amazing! Some of the most dangerous enemies of the church will come, turn to this small and insignificant Christian church, and repent. They will acknowledge Christ's love for his church as his Bride.

No, this is not an announcement of a general conversion of all Jews to the Christian faith. But here is our incredible encouragement, also today. Look through the open door that no one can shut. See God's glory as he fulfils his plan. And therefore, do not be intimidated, do not be frightened, do not be discouraged by hostilities, by ridicule or hatred. But continue to trust in God's victory. Christ has opened this door that no one can shut, and he will continue to do surprising things as the church journeys on, regardless of the circumstances.

This whole message to Philadelphia is so full of encouragement for God's faithful churches everywhere. The exalted Christ is so happy when his church remains faithful and shows steadfast endurance in holding on to the true gospel, even when this church is, humanly speaking, small, weak, and insignificant; when she is faced with scoffing, false accusations, and oppression. He will continue to provide security, even in the most threatening circumstances.

Because you have kept my word about patient endurance, he says, now you may trust, that *I will keep you from the hour of trial that is coming on the whole world*. "The hour of trial" refers to the trials and punishments that God will send into this world, as we will hear about it in the rest of this book. And this will be ongoing, a constant reality, during the last days. The entire time before Jesus' return is characterized by such trials, then here and then there.

Philadelphia: Faithful and enduring

It will be a time of testing. It will be a sifting process to show who Christ's enemies are and who his followers are. Will you choose to follow the Lamb of God on the journey to the New Jerusalem or will you settle down in Babylon and make your permanent home in this world? Will you side with the one true God and worship him or will you side with the false gods and worship them? Watch out! Satan will do his utmost to make you deny the name of your Saviour and forget his Word.

This time before the establishment of God's eternal kingdom will be a time of trial for the strengthening of the believers and for the hardening of the wicked. As it says in Daniel 12: *There shall be a time of trouble such as never has been since there was a nation till that time* (vs.1). *Many shall purify themselves and make themselves white and be refined, but the wicked shall act wickedly* (vs.10).

So, who are those facing this "trial"? Christ says that it is *to try those who dwell on the earth*. Or: "the inhabitants of the earth". Now that expression is often used in Revelation to refer to people who do not follow Jesus Christ, enemies of God and the church. Those are earthbound people, so to speak. Earth is where their citizenship is, as opposed to those whose citizenship is in heaven (Philippians 3:20).

However, when Jesus says to his church, *I will keep you from the hour of trial*, he does not mean that God's church will escape the tribulation and trials. It does not mean that this sifting process will not affect you and me as believers. It is going to be a difficult and dangerous time, also for God's children. You will also be tested as to your commitment to persevere and to resist the temptation to settle in Babylon.

No, Christ does not promise to rapture the believers out of this world, before the tribulation begins, but to provide the spiritual protection they will need in the midst of this. He will keep his faithful church safe. When all hell breaks loose, you will be protected in your Father's hands, since *nothing in all creation will be able to separate us from the love of God that is in Christ Jesus our Lord* (Romans 8:39).

God knows those who are his own. He knows them all and he will seal them and protect them. By his grace you will not perish.

8 • Revelation 3:7-13

Oh, it's true, "the hour of trial" will be frightening in many ways. "But don't be afraid. I have the key to give you access to God's glorious victory," says Christ. "And *I will keep you*. Trust in me when things get scary. And trust my promise: *I am coming soon*." Here is your comfort and encouragement: your trials and temptations will not last. That would be so discouraging and depressing. But no, it will all come to an end. The coming of Jesus Christ will be the end of 'the hour of trial'.

This perspective gives even more urgency to the call to remain strong. There is light at the end of the tunnel, the light of the coming Christ in glory. And in the meantime, hang in there and *hold fast what you have, so that no one may seize your crown*.

But what do you have to hold fast? Well, your faith in God's Word, and your desire to obey this word, your loyalty to Jesus Christ, your confession of the name of Christ, and your trust in the powerful victory of God's love.

Do not let go of these things when trials come and when times get tough. Do not cave in under pressure. When darkness creeps in and when Satan uses opposition, trials, persecution, and whatever he can find to make it really hard for you, turn to him who is holy and true, and who holds the key of David. Trust that what he opens in your life no one can shut, *so that no one may seize your crown*.

Yes, you have a 'crown'. This is the image of your final victory, your communion with Jesus Christ, that you may enjoy in full in the completed kingdom of God, your Father in heaven. Believe in Jesus Christ, and this 'crown of victory' is yours already. It is ready to be handed out – whether that will be on the day of your death or the day of Jesus' return – whichever comes first.

Think of what Paul wrote to Timothy: *I have fought the good fight, I have finished the race, I have kept the faith. Now there is laid up for me the crown of righteousness, which the Lord, the righteous Judge, will award to me on that day* (2 Timothy 4:7-8).

"Yes, it's yours," says Christ to the church in Philadelphia. "You have kept my word and have not denied my name. Hold on to that. Let no one take it away from you. It is urgent! Let no one distract you from focussing on me

Philadelphia: Faithful and enduring

in your life, so that you would miss out on the glorious coronation that is waiting for you."

"Continue to confess my name, and I will keep the door open for you to access the great future in store for you."

It is worth it. It really is! At the end of his message to the church in Philadelphia the exalted Christ has again marvellous promises for *the one who conquers*. That is the one who holds fast what God gave him; the one who endures in the hour of trial; the one who suffers because of his faithfulness to Jesus Christ, but wins the victory in the good fight of faith. *I will make him a pillar in the temple of my God.*

Some pillars were freestanding. Think of the two bronze pillars that were standing on both sides of the entrance of Solomon's temple. We read about those in 1 Kings 7. The one was called *Jakin*, which means "he established". The other one had the name *Boaz* and that means "in him is strength". With these names those pillars symbolized that Israel was entirely dependent on God's power.

But most pillars were part of a large building – a temple, a palace, or a mansion. And they were important. They were supporting the structure so that the building would not collapse. Those pillars could never be removed. They were a necessary and significant permanent presence in such a building. Such pillars became symbols of security and stability.

This image would speak to the congregation in Philadelphia. The believers would be pillars in God's temple, a building more stable and more secure than anything ever built in Philadelphia with its regular earthquakes.

What does Christ mean with "the temple of my God"? A temple is a place of worship. But, as we know, the New Jerusalem will have no temple. It says in Rev. 21:22, *I saw no temple in the city, for its temple is the Lord God Almighty and the Lamb.*

So, this will happen: if you overcome all the trials and temptations, and you remain faithful to your Saviour Jesus Christ, you will be given a permanent place in the perfect and triumphant church and in God's holy presence to worship him for ever and ever. United in living communion with Jesus

Christ you will receive a supporting role in the completed church as God's eternal building.

And *never shall he go out of it*. In Jesus Christ, your place in God's temple and your joyful participation in the eternal worship will be secure. For with your own eyes you will see what David is longing for in Ps. 27:4 - *One thing have I asked of the LORD, that will I seek after: that I may dwell in the house of the LORD all the days of my life, to gaze upon the beauty of the LORD and to meditate in his temple.*

To confirm the security of this marvellous future, Christ adds that he will mark you with three names, just to emphasize and assure you beyond any doubt who you are, where you're going, and who makes you ready for this.

The first is *the name of my God*, he says. You have something similar in the Old Testament already. In Numbers 6:27 we read that the LORD says, when the priests will bless God's people, *they will put my name on the Israelites*. God claims them to belong to him. And it is the same here as elsewhere in Revelation where we hear about 'seals' or 'the Father's name' on the foreheads of God's children. With this name God the Father claims his ownership. You belong to him, as his possession. This comes with the promise that he will always take care of you and protect you.

The second is *the name of the city of my God, the New Jerusalem, which comes down out of heaven from my God*. This name confirms that you have been registered as a citizen of the New Jerusalem. And with this name written on you, you know for sure that this is your destination; this is what you are heading for, the New Jerusalem or the new heaven and the new earth.

The third is the name of him who makes all this possible by the victorious power of his grace – *I will also write on him my own new name*, says Christ. We may still be somewhat puzzled by this "new name". It may refer to what Paul says in Philippians 2:9, that when Jesus Christ completed his work of reconciliation, *God gave him the name that is above every name*. Somehow this name expresses the identity of our Saviour in a way that is more glorious and more powerful than we can imagine today.

So yes, that is you as a child of God holding on to Jesus Christ and to his word. You live in this dark and broken world. And as you face the hour of trial, the challenges and temptations, the struggles and hardships, are many.

But you are marked with these three names. It is almost like a package with an address label that says that you are ready to be shipped out.

The label has the name of your Owner: God the Father, who claims you and is ready to receive you.

It has the address: your destination is the New Jerusalem, the New Earth.

And it has the name of the Sender: the glorified Jesus Christ, who by his grace makes you ready for shipping.

This is how you may go through life. Look at the names on your shipping-label and praise God for the abundant assurance that the victory will be yours.

9

REVELATION 3: 14 – 22

LAODICEA – SELF-CONFIDENT, BUT USELESS!

The letter to the church in Laodicea is the last one of the seven letters that the exalted Christ directed to the churches in Asia that were to receive his book with these visions.

Later on, we will also hear about seven seals, seven trumpets and seven bowls, with always the last one, number seven, presenting the climax of each cycle.

In a similar way this message to the congregation in Laodicea presents the culmination of this cycle of messages. It sort of sums up, or collates, the seriousness of the dangers in the churches, as well as the responses of Christ and God's promises for the faithful, who overcome these threats and dangers.

It shows Laodicea as a church in deep trouble.

But it shows, at the same time, the great depth of God's love and tender mercy.

The cities where the seven churches were located formed a half circle with Ephesus at the one end, and at the other end, Laodicea. That is again more

9 • Revelation 3:14-22

to the South East. Laodicea was a bit older than Philadelphia and had been established in the third century before Christ.

It was built in a valley that was used intensively as a natural travelling route from Ephesus, on the coast, to the Anatolian Highlands in eastern Turkey. But this was not the only highway that ran through Laodicea. There were actually three major highways that came together at that point.

Because of this strategic location, Laodicea flourished, and it grew rapidly into an important commercial and financial centre. It was a city of bankers and millionaires and was quite famous in the ancient world for its wealth.

As we read through this letter and hear how the exalted Christ is addressing the church in Laodicea, we find out that he does not have much good to say. It actually sounds remarkably like the situation we came across in the church at Sardis – that was the dead church, remember?

Christ Jesus' analysis, or his diagnosis, of what is going on in this congregation must have been quite shocking and hard to swallow for the good folks in Laodicea. It is hard to believe! They had it so good.

That is why Christ's self-presentation is so relevant for those Christian believers. "Don't dismiss my words," says Christ. "Always remember who I am." And to underline that he knows exactly what he is talking about, when he addresses what is going on in the hearts of these people, he tells them three things about himself.

"I come to you as *the faithful and true witness*," he says. This comes from God's greeting to the churches, as John gave it in Rev. 1:5. In this way Jesus Christ makes clear: "what I say is true and reliable – always. The way I describe the facts is accurate. Even if what I have to say is unpleasant, or perhaps shocking and painful, I will always be *the way, the truth and the life*" (John 14:6).

"That's why I am also called *the Amen*." In the Old Testament God is sometimes called "the Amen", but this is the only time that Christ calls himself "the Amen". It stresses his authority and trustworthiness. Never question my words.

And then: "I am also *the beginning of God's creation*". In John 1:3 we read that *through him all things were made and that without him not anything was made that was made*. Jesus Christ was actively involved in the creation of everything.

The apostle Paul confirms this in Colossians 1:16 and 17, and then he calls Christ, in v.18, *the beginning, the firstborn from the dead, that in everything he might be preeminent*. In other words, Christ was not only the beginning of the old creation – through his resurrection he also became the beginning of the new creation.

Altogether, Christ impresses on the people in Laodicea, and in the church today, how important it is to listen carefully to what he is saying. His words carry more weight than anything else. You can trust him when he analyzes the situation in Laodicea. He is not fooled by just outward appearances. He smells falsehood and deception, so to speak. You cannot pull the wool over his eyes.

And so, we better listen carefully when the glorified Christ qualifies the life of the congregation in Laodicea. That is a pretty dramatic image. He who knows everything comes with a strong judgment of this church. He begins his evaluation by saying, *you are neither cold nor hot... you are lukewarm*!

We all know this expression. This is how we know the church at Laodicea: it is "the lukewarm church". It is amazing how such a label sticks and becomes so familiar. But what is Christ saying with this image?

The people in Laodicea must have recognized the allusions. They were able to relate to this metaphor. The city was proud of its abundant wealth, but they had a problem with their drinking water. Why was that?

Well, Laodicea was pretty close to two other cities: Hierapolis and Colossae. Now Hierapolis was famous for its hot springs. The water was actually said to have healing qualities. Colossae on the other hand had ample supply of cold water via streams that came from high up in the mountains.

But Laodicea did not have any natural sources of drinking water. Their water had to come from farther away, transported by an aqueduct and pipes. By the time it arrived in the city, the water was lukewarm. You would not want to drink it. It tasted awful.

9 • Revelation 3:14-22

This shows that you cannot say that this image refers to a scale of personal commitment to God, like 'cold' is bad, 'hot' is good, and 'lukewarm' is in between. Some people explain it this way. You are cold when you do not have faith, when you reject Jesus in unbelief. You are hot when you are full of excitement, full of enthusiasm and on fire for the Lord. And when you are hanging in between, you would be lukewarm.

But then Christ would not have said: *I wish you were either one or the other – cold or hot*. And that is what he says: cold and hot are both good, whereas lukewarm is bad.

Now, how can 'cold' be good if it refers to unbelief? You don't expect Jesus to say, "I prefer you to be an unbeliever who rejects me as his Saviour, rather than a half-hearted believer. That does not make sense!

No, he is talking about the attitude and actions of the church. With this image he urges the church to be either hot or cold, but not lukewarm! Think again of the water.

Cold water is refreshing. It is useful for drinking, for quenching your thirst, especially in a hot climate. Hot water is useful for cleaning, cooking, and bathing. But lukewarm water is good for nothing.

The water in Laodicea may look okay, but when you drink it, you say "yuk". You spit it out because it is disgusting. It is an image of uselessness. And this is the image that Christ is using for a church that is proud and self-confident but does not have a clue what it really means to be church of Jesus Christ.

"Look at us! We are 'well-to-do' and fine Christians here in Laodicea, you know." But Christ says, "You are useless for my service, for the glory of my name. You are disgusting. You make me nauseous. That's why I am about to spit you out of my mouth."

Now that is an outrageous way of putting it. But really, Jesus Christ cannot stand the smug self-confident attitude, the uselessness of the spiritual complacency that was so dominant in Laodicea.

And only in Laodicea? What does it mean for you and me; for us here to be lukewarm and become useless for the service of God?

Laodicea: Self-confident, but useless

You become lukewarm when we are so focussed on material things or on the attractions of the world, that serving God is restricted to a religious activity on the Sunday. Then you become spiritually complacent and your faith becomes a superficial formality. Although, you may not think so.

You can become lukewarm towards your brothers and sisters in Jesus. You prefer to hang out with the select group of friends you feel comfortable with. Then initially you forget, but after a while you will no longer care for your commitment, your loyalty towards others who also belong to Jesus.

You can become lukewarm towards the church. What the church does has to meet your expectations and has to fit your schedule or has to suit your ideas. And if it does not, well, you might want to say: "forget about the whole business. Who cares?"

Or you try to find something that does meet your expectations or fit your schedule or suit your ideas. And this includes the worship services. O sure, you want to worship on a regular basis. But if for some reason you do not like certain things, or you just do not feel like it, or time and place of worship are inconvenient, it can become easy to stay home or do something else.

Let us talk about these things. Let us not avoid or ignore these questions, but let us challenge each other as we dig into the Bible and our reformed confessions. Let us learn more and more how we can battle spiritual complacency and spiritual uselessness. Let us help each other to avoid a lukewarm attitude toward God, toward the church, or toward each other.

So, what is actually going on in Laodicea that makes Christ say to this congregation: "you are lukewarm – you are disgusting"? What is Jesus' strong aversion based on? Why does he say these things?

Well, the citizens of Laodicea were rich. And they knew it. They were actually quite proud of it. The wealth they had accumulated made them arrogant and careless. And this self-confident attitude that was characteristic for the city of Laodicea, spilled over in the church. They were an affluent city, and you would find the same attitude among the Christian congregation, too.

This is what Jesus confronts them with. And he really wants to drive it home with this three-fold emphasis on the self-sufficiency they claim. *You say, "I*

9 • Revelation 3:14-22

am rich; I have prospered, and I need nothing!" Indeed, church-people are boasting in their economic successes, just like anyone else.

The material wealth, the riches they had accumulated, led them to look at themselves with smug self-confidence. Perhaps they saw their abundant prosperity as God's special blessing, God's special favour towards them.

And so, there was nothing to worry about. Their sins no longer trouble them. They did not see any need to change, or to look critically at themselves. "No, no. We, here in Laodicea, we made it and we are doing mighty fine, thank you very much."

Business-wise, financially, and materially they have arrived. They do not have any needs to worry about. Everything is taken care of. Everything is under control.

Does that not sound attractive? You do not have to be a Laodicean millionaire, to like the idea that you have your life under control. We all like that. It can make you pretty self-confident when everything goes according to your plan. Look at me. I can pull this off. I can make this work. And we can be jealous of people that are successful and who do have everything under control. Or so it seems.

But appearances are deceptive. A big success story can impress us. Abundant wealth, lots of money can intimidate us. And yes, we know that it all can be put to good use. But it can also cover up spiritual poverty. That is a real danger. And this is what is happening in the church in Laodicea. Their material and financial self-confidence had led them also to spiritual self-confidence or self-satisfaction.

They were so proud of their wealth. They were so absorbed in it that they did not even realize that they did not experience a living relationship, the living communion with Jesus Christ. They did not even miss it.

But the exalted Christ is going to expose this as self-deception. "You are so self-confident; you are so full of yourself as you brag about all the wealth and possessions you have collected, but you are fooling yourself. You are useless, like lukewarm water that no one wants to drink."

"Look", says Jesus Christ, "you say that you are rich and self-sufficient. And that is indeed what it looks like from your earthly viewpoint, from below. But I invite you to have a look at yourself from here, from my viewpoint, from above. From here you look totally different. You are the very opposite of what you think you are. You do not know in how bad of a shape you really are."

You are wretched and pitiable. You are poor, blind, and naked. You are just full of misery. And again, you do not even realize it. You have no clue. This is so pathetic! Nothing is more pitiable than someone who thinks that he is a fine Christian, and yet, in reality, Christ is disgusted with him and ready to spit him out.

These five words give a terrible picture of the church in Laodicea. The inner condition of this congregation is a mess. It is a spiritual disaster. It is a church that does not really need Jesus. They live without God and without Jesus Christ. They are *poor* – they do not live out of the riches of God's grace. They are *blind* – they do not see their misery. They are *naked* – they do not have the faith that covers their sin.

It is true, appearances can indeed be deceptive in this world. But also in the church. They can hide the reality. Only when we get the above point-of-view; only when we get the view of him who is the faithful and true witness – only then we will see the truth; only then we will get the true diagnosis of what is really going on. And this diagnosis cuts deep, very deep. With his words, Christ shocks them into reality. But that is needed to get to the remedy.

Indeed, the remedy. Because this is not the end for Laodicea. Christ does not stop after he has exposed the terrible spiritual disaster in that congregation. He does not say: *I spit you out*, but: *I will spit you out*. Or more accurate even: *I am about to spit you out*. He is waiting. He wants to drive out the lukewarm spirit and renew the first love. There is still hope for this church because he loves her. Great is his faithfulness.

"Here is my solution for you," says Christ. *I counsel you to buy from me......* Do you hear his tender love in how he says it? It is not: "I command" or "I demand"! No, "I counsel you; I strongly advise you." Oh, it is urgent enough. But it is the compassion with which he reaches out to his people.

9 • Revelation 3:14-22

So then, what does he have to help them reverse the downward direction this church is going? He offers three products for sale: gold, white garments, and eye-salve. And these are not just random deals but each one has been selected to fix the problems the congregation is facing. You are poor – I have gold for you. You are naked – I have white clothes for you. You are blind – I have eye-salve for you.

Of course, these products are symbolic. "You thought you were rich with all your wealth? Look at this... my pure gold... the refined gold of my payment for all your sins. This will make you really rich." The wealth Jesus Christ offers has eternal value.

One of the local products Laodicea was famous for, was its black wool. "But," says Christ, "forget about the fancy garments in the stores. Look at these white clothes – only these can cover the shameful nakedness of your sin and guilt. Fool yourself no longer, but clothe yourself with my righteousness and purity, the spotless garments that I alone provide. Get dressed for the great wedding banquet that is coming."

Laodicea was also well-known for its pharmaceutical products. "But," says Christ, "I have the healing power that really matters. You think there is nothing wrong with your eye-sight. You think that you are perfectly capable to see clearly what matters; to discern between right and wrong, good and bad.

But use my salve to put on your eyes, and you will find out how blind you were. The salve of my love will allow you to see what is wrong. It will open your eyes for the spiritual poverty hidden under your material prosperity. It will expose your sin, but it will also let you see what real holiness is all about".

"Turn to me," says Jesus Christ. He came into this world, born in Bethlehem, to provide for you what you need to fix the real problem in your life. These are the real Christmas deals. Turn to him and buy the only remedies that can meet the needs of the church, as well as our individual needs. Turn to him, who was and is *the beginning of God's creation* and find your eternal spiritual well-being.

But what about this idea of "buying" what Christ is offering here? How does that work? How can we ever buy anything from him, poor, naked, and blind as we are? We have nothing to pay with.

That is correct. But then think, for instance, of what we read in Isaiah 55. Here the LORD unfolds the great perspective of his glorious plan of salvation as it will be accomplished in Jesus Christ. And this begins by saying: *Come, everyone who thirsts, come to the waters; and he who has no money, come, buy, and eat! Come, buy wine and milk without money and without price.*

Yes, you are invited to buy without paying anything, because Jesus Christ himself paid for all of it. God's gifts are free of charge because they are priceless. God's salvation is by grace alone, because it is too precious for any of us to pay for.

Just hold out your empty hands and your Father in heaven will fill them.

You can imagine that some of this was quite shocking for the Christians in Laodicea. When Christ rebuked them it really rattled their self-confidence! But he did not say these things to beat them over the head, slap them in the face, or humiliate them. Yes, he rebukes and disciplines, but what drives him is his deep love for them. His love for his church had not become lukewarm.

And so, he does not want to alienate them. He wants to shake them up. They must understand how serious this is, so that they may turn around and renew their fellowship with him. Is it not wonderful how Jesus' love reaches out to these lukewarm people, with whom he is so disgusted, that he is almost ready to spit them out?

Do we do this? When we get frustrated by lukewarm people in the church, when we see others who become indifferent toward God and the church, do we reach out in tender mercy? Or do we rather distance ourselves? Do we encourage each other to "buy" stuff from Jesus and so to become rich and whole in him?

Always remember that Jesus Christ himself continues to reach out and call out to people, even if they have locked him out. That is your Saviour!

Behold, I stand at the door and knock, he says to the church in Laodicea.

9 • Revelation 3:14-22

Here is another beautiful image of Jesus' persistent love. He does not give up. "Don't ignore me but listen carefully. I am so close by! I know that you hear me."

Some people like to use these words in v.20 to boost evangelism activities. They suggest that Jesus is knocking on the door of the hearts of unbelievers. They go around and urge people to open the door of their hearts and let Jesus in. "He is standing at the door and he knocks," they say. "He is waiting for you to let him in".

But that is not what it says here. This is not the door of the heart, and it does not talk about unbelievers. Although it is a popular idea, an unbeliever would not be able to open the door of his heart to invite Jesus in. That is the work of the Holy Spirit.

No, this is about the door of the church, Christ's own church. And that this door is closed, shows you how serious, how dangerous the situation has become in Laodicea. The congregation seems to have excluded Christ from its fellowship. Here is a Bride who has closed the door for her Bridegroom. Christ knocks persistently, again and again, for he longs to be welcome in his church.

This makes it actually an unsettling and even bizarre picture. The church belongs to Christ. It is his home. She is his Bride. But he is outside! He is standing on the porch. And he asks for permission to enter his own church. Is that not weird?

And yet, Christ does not force his way in. He could have, but he chose not to. With a love-filled heart he keeps calling, knocking, and reaching out. During the last days before his return, his coming is not threatening, but promising. There is still the promise of new fellowship. There is still time for lukewarm, complacent Christians to renew the relationship with their Master.

Think of this. Christ stands at the door of the church, every local church! He is eager to get in. He wants very much to be part of what is going on there. He very much desires to be part of the faith-life of those in the church. Not as a religious idea, not as a far-away power, not as a symbol. No, as a real person to trust and relate to, a man to have a meal with, a man to enjoy communion with.

Do not lock him out. The church that keeps itself busy with all sorts of things people consider important, but leaves Jesus Christ outside, will become lukewarm. Such a church will eventually be spat out.

You can also do this in your personal faith-life. Do not lock Jesus out. It is not so difficult to do this. Just keep yourself so busy with whatever it is, that you do not have any attention left for him. Hang out with people that do not have much use for Jesus. And before you know it, you have worked him out of your life. It is easy enough. But it is dangerous and potentially life-threatening.

However – he lets you know: *Behold! I stand at the door and knock.* In this life he keeps knocking. And his faithfulness comes with a lovely promise. *If anyone hears my voice and opens the door, I will come in and eat with him, and he with me.*

These last few words are not just a superfluous repetition. When you welcome Christ as guest at your table, he will also welcome you as guests at his table.

Sharing a meal is a festive opportunity for intimate fellowship and celebration. And Jesus Christ is looking forward to this fellowship, to celebrating the communion, the relationship between him and us, poor, wretched, and pitiable people, when we listen to his voice and open the door to have him fill our needs.

This table-fellowship with Christ begins here in this life already. It becomes visible when we gather around the Lord's Supper table to share in the body and blood of Christ. In the Holy Supper, Christ comes and feeds us with himself to strengthen our faith.

We may do this in anticipation of the great feast at the end of time. Then this table-fellowship will be completed and perfected at the eternal banquet, *when Christ will drink the wine new with us in the kingdom of his Father* (Mat. 26:29). The wedding feast of the Lamb of God is coming.

9 • Revelation 3:14-22

And because of this renewed fellowship with Jesus Christ, the end will be glorious and victorious for all those who conquer the dangers that threaten their faith.

The glorified Christ will give you the right to sit on the throne with God.

And he will share his victorious ruling-power and awesome glory with all those that open the door for him. Do not make him wait.

10

Revelation 4

OUR GOD IS AN AWESOME GOD – HE REIGNS FROM HEAVEN ABOVE

In the previous chapters we looked at the different introductory or cover-letters, written to each of the seven churches in Asia. With these 'personalized' letters, so to speak, they were all to receive the same main letter. That is the part that starts in Rev. 4.

As Christ confronts these churches with themselves, with the weaknesses, struggles, challenges, and dangers they were dealing with, he is holding up a mirror for his whole church, also for us today! The question is repeatedly: What do we learn about ourselves? What are the warnings we must take to heart?

We also heard about the great promises Christ has for "those who conquer the dangers and difficulties". There are not only warnings, but there is also encouragement as we travel to the New Jerusalem.

And we need that because we are not there yet. That is why Christ adds in all these letters: *He who has an ear, let him hear what the Spirit says to the churches* (2:7,11,17,29; 3:6,13,22). With these words "what the Spirit says to the churches", he alerts us to what is coming in the rest of the book: Rev. 4 – 22.

In other words, Christ stresses seven times: "listen carefully to what follows, and learn how God is going to fulfil his promises. Let it warn, comfort, and encourage you."

As Christians we suffer, along with everyone else, the consequences of sin in sickness, disease, war, and disasters. And as God's children we are always again in need of forgiveness and renewal. On top of that, the faithful Christian church will often face persecution in this world.

Those are disappointing experiences in life. Yes, we confess that in all things God works for the good of those who love him (see Romans 8:28). But do we really believe this? Does it not often look as if the history and destiny of our world is controlled by evil powers?

Well, Revelation 4 and 5 help us to understand what is above and beyond our earthly reality. And what we come to see here will actually turn out to be the key to understanding the whole book of Revelation. Even in the midst of trials and temptations, in the midst of suffering and persecution, God is the Ruler who controls everything. It is all about him and about his greatness. We will first have a closer look at Rev. 4

A HEAVENLY THRONE

Does heaven exist? Many folks may claim that they have some idea that there is an after-life. But in practice most people live in a closed world. Only what you see is reality. The rest is fantasy. We have this earth and we see what happens here, but that's all we really know. You can dream up all kinds of stuff, but we do not have access to another world. There is no 'above'. There is no "old man up in the attic", as mocking blasphemers like to assure us. There is no heaven from where a God keeps an eye on us and from where he rules. We are stuck here, alone!

In this narrow-minded climate it is truly liberating to see *a door standing open in heaven*. Look: there is more then what we can see here! This is the first thing that John is seeing *after this*, he says. That means, after he has seen the exalted Christ (1:9–20) and perhaps after he has written the seven letters (Rev. 2 and 3).

It does not say how much time there was in between, but probably not much. He may even have completed those seven cover letters later on, when the main manuscript was almost ready to be sent out. Rev.1:10 suggests that John saw all his visions on the same day, the Lord's Day.

"An open door" indicates the opportunity to cross a boundary, to go to a place not normally accessible. This open door allows John to cross the threshold between earth and heaven. That is unique, and only if you have been invited will you have the privilege of seeing what is behind this door. Now John was invited, but via his eyes we also have the opportunity to cross the threshold and look at the realities beyond what we see here. That is exciting.

So, yes, John is invited. He hears the same voice he had heard in Rev. 1:10 and 12. The exalted Christ invites him to enter through this open door and find out what is behind it. *Come up here*, says Jesus, *and I will show you what must take place after this*.

This expression means the same as what we read in Rev. 1:1 and 1:19.

It sums up all that has happened already, all that is happening today, and all that is going to happen in the future. It covers the last days, the final phase of history before Jesus' return. It is about everything leading up to Jesus' second coming. It is about the whole of what we will find in Rev. 4 – 22.

Immediately John is, what he calls, *in the Spirit*. The Holy Spirit completely overpowers him and controls him, also physically. He is not hallucinating, but the Holy Spirit enables him to see and hear things that cannot be seen and heard by others.

He no longer sees with his physical eyes and hears with his physical ears. He has a vision. But that does not mean that what he sees and hears is not real. It is very real, including the location from where he will see this vision.

Well, what John is seeing is simply magnificent and spectacular. His report reflects this. It is full of awe and deep reverence. The first thing he sees is *a throne in heaven with one seated on the throne*. This is what catches his eye first. John does not say it here, but the same expression throughout the Bible makes clear, this is God's throne. And this throne is so important, that everything else is arranged around it.

God's throne appears forty-seven times in Revelation, and seventeen times in chapters 4 and 5. This makes God's throne the central reality of the whole book. But Revelation also tells us about rival thrones that compete with God's throne. In Rev. 2:13 we heard about "Satan's throne" and in Rev. 13:2 we will read about "the Dragon's throne". And Rev. 6:10 mentions "the throne of the beast". Thrones represent authority, ruling power. So, here is the question Revelation is going to answer: who rules? Who is in control? Who has the authority as the true king of the world?

From here, from below, from where we are in this dark, broken and suffering world, Satan and all his evil companions appear to be sovereign.

But when you look from above, from the perspective of the heavenly throne-room, it is clear that God rules. Here is the spiritual power-centre of the universe. The Biblical universe is not man-centered, or earth-centered. It is entirely theocentric, God-centered. Our God is an awesome God. He reigns from heaven above.

And only when you look at everything that happens in this world and in your life from the perspective of God's throne, only then you can begin to understand what is happening in this world and in your life.

John's vision is a bit like a visit to an airport control-tower. The casual observer at ground-level of a large International Airport sees planes, trucks, other vehicles, luggage-carts, etc. going everywhere. It looks pretty chaotic.

But when you are high up in the control-tower, it becomes evident that what is going on down below makes more sense. You see the overall plan and you hear the instructions.

To put it differently, through John's vision we are transported to the "control-tower" of the entire universe. In this way John, and with John we also, get the point-of-view from above that helps us interpret what happens here on earth. We will learn to recognize the big picture of what is happening in this world, and in our lives.

High above all the turmoil in this world God Almighty is "seated on his throne". That is an encouraging picture. God is not nervous. God is not frantically pacing around, shocked and upset, because of all the social unrest, political tension, wars, economic upheaval, injustice, and other terrible things going on in this world. 'He is seated.' That is an image of rest and stability. It shows his sovereign majesty and power.

All things are governed by the Lord on the throne, and everything is under control. O, it's true, the plans of the one in control often escape our comprehension. We do not always get it. Sometimes we panic. But know and trust that he comprehends everything and that his plans will not fail.

John knows whom he is talking about when he says that *'one' was seated on the throne in heaven*. But he does not try to describe God. No one can describe God. That is just impossible. His glorious greatness will always exceed our grasp. We do not have adequate words to describe the holy and almighty God. We can only use symbols and symbolic terms to come as close to the reality as possible.

John pictures the overwhelming impression he has of the glorious radiance, the shining brilliance of the One seated on the throne as the bright and brilliant shine of precious stones, gems, jewels. The appearance is as the flashing, sparkling lustre of the crystal-clear jasper or diamond. And of the deep-red carnelian or ruby.

It is difficult to connect specific properties of these gems with specific attributes of God. Today's scholars do not always know what the ancient names of these minerals stand for. But that is ok. It is about the total picture of indescribable splendour, marvellous glory, and majesty. God himself is the ultimate source of all splendour and beauty.

However, God's heavenly throne is not only a place of tranquility. We hear in v.5 that *from the throne came flashes of lightning, rumblings, and peals of thunder*. It reminds us of the Lord's appearance on Mount Sinai (Exodus 19:16-20). As I have said before, Revelation is not only a picture-book, it is also a noisy book! And here it begins. We get a frightening light-and-sound show, a manifestation of God's power and holiness as a warning that his judgments are coming.

God rules over a world in the devastating grip of sin. But he cannot tolerate sin. And he will not hesitate using the destructive powers he has at his disposal. God is high voltage! And that will be dangerous if you turn against him.

But he is not coming only to destroy the world. John also sees *around the throne a rainbow that had the appearance of an emerald*. We remember the rainbow as the sign of God's covenant with the earth, with his creation. That is in Genesis 9, after the Flood. This rainbow around the throne in heaven tells us something similar. God remains faithful. In the midst of unfolding judgments, he guarantees his people life, hope, and comfort. There will not be total annihilation.

John sees two more things that highlight the awesome majesty of God's throne in heaven. Burning before the throne he sees seven torches of fire. This alludes to the lampstand with the seven lights that were burning day and night in the tabernacle and the temple.

When you think of it, this whole heavenly throne-room is like a huge sanctuary, reflected in the tabernacle and temple in the Old Testament. As a matter of fact, that is how the author of the letter to the Hebrews talks about it. In Heb. 9:24 he talks about a man-made sanctuary that was only a copy of the true one, of heaven itself.

Well, these seven blazing torches *are the seven spirits of God*, says John. You can also say, *the seven-fold Spirit of God*. Either way, here is God's Holy Spirit in all the fullness of his power. He is full of fire to destroy the wicked. Our God is a consuming fire, says the Bible, and so is his Spirit. Be careful. At the same time, the Holy Spirit is also full of fire for the sanctification, the renewal of God's people.

The other remarkable thing John is seeing before the throne is something that looked like *a sea of glass, like crystal*.

There are many different interpretations of this sea of glass. But perhaps it is best to stay with the resemblance of the earthly tabernacle or temple. Among the temple's furnishings there was what is called in 1 Kings 7:23 *a sea of cast metal*. This was basically a basin for ceremonial washing and cleansing. And so, when John sees what resembles a *crystal-clear sea of glass*, it symbolizes the washing and cleansing power of the blood of Jesus Christ.

Have a good look at the magnificent throne in heaven and see our awesome Triune God. He governs the world. He governs your life and my life. Perhaps you do not understand everything that is going on and why. Perhaps you are confused or nervous or fearful. Or you struggle with lots of questions about poverty, hunger, violence, and destruction in this brutal world.

We do not get answers. But come, look through the open door and meet the holy and almighty God, sitting on his throne, the Ruler Supreme who controls everything. That is the best remedy when you are struggling with these things. It really is.

Therefore, in all that is going on, live as children of the Father, your sins washed away in the sea of Jesus' blood, renewed by the fire of the Holy Spirit.

HEAVENLY ATTENDANTS

As astounding as it is already, there is more in heaven than just the throne of God. John's vision shows ever-widening concentric circles around the throne. The One seated on the throne is and remains in the very centre. It is all about him and his glory. The four living creatures form the innermost circle, which then expands to the next with twenty-four elders on twenty-four thrones. Then, in Rev. 5:11 the circle widens to include a multitude of angels. And finally, in 5:13 we see the outermost circle of all of God's creatures.

Here in Rev. 4 John sees the two innermost circles of the heavenly attendants to the throne of God. His attention goes first to the wider circle. *Around the throne were twenty-four other thrones, and seated on these thrones were twenty-four elders.*

Here again you can find many different interpretations. Who are these elders? Some see them as 'angel-like' beings. But in Rev. 5:11 and 7:11 they are distinguished from angels. On top of that, in the Bible the word "elders" is never used for angels.

So we are probably talking about glorified humans, but then not just a random group of people. The word "elders" marks them as a group that represents the church. And then it makes sense to think of the entire church of the Old and New Testaments.

But why twenty-four? It could be an allusion to the twenty-four divisions of the Old Testament priests, as structured by David, although these elders on thrones do not seem to have any priestly function here.

Others have thought about the twelve patriarchs and the twelve apostles, since, according to Revelation 21, those names were written on the gates and foundations of the New Jerusalem. That seems pretty straightforward, but a written name is not the same as a live person. And in this case the apostle John would be watching himself sitting on one of these thrones. That would be kind of weird.

So, we should think more generally, most likely of wise, spiritual leaders. After all, throughout the Bible that's what 'elders' are. And as they sit on their thrones, they play an active role as rulers, who govern with God as his counsellors, his advisers.

Two significant details are also that *they were clothed in white garments* and had *golden crowns on their heads*. Their spotless garments show their spiritual purity, and their crowns show that they won the victory. In the letters to the churches in Sardis and Philadelphia we found these things as gifts of Christ, gifts of God's grace for his faithful followers. Here is another argument that in these twenty-four elders we have glorified humans, representing God's people.

In other words, the presence of these elders is a testimony of God's grace. As representatives of the church, they are who they are because of the wonderful gift of grace through the saving work of Jesus Christ. Is that not what the church is all about, the evidence of God's saving grace? And so here they are, as attendants to the heavenly throne to serve the glory of the One seated on the throne.

Then, in the centre, forming the inner circle around God's throne, are these mysterious and impressive *four living creatures*. Older translations say "animals" or "beasts", but they are not just animals. They are like animals it says in v. 7. They give an animal-like impression, but they are remarkable and very unusual creatures.

To begin with, they are covered with eyes all around, all over. This exceptional eyesight symbolizes how alert and watchful they are, all the time.

They can see in every direction. Nothing escapes their attention. It also allows them to see entirely unhindered the holiness, omnipotence, and awesome glory of the One on the throne.

But they are not identical. One looks like a lion, another one like an ox and a third one like an eagle. Now, a lion has the reputation of being the fiercest and most powerful of all the wild animals. An ox was known as the strongest of all the domesticated animals. A flying eagle is the most majestic of all the birds. John does not describe what the last one was like, other than that it *had the face of a man*. Together these fascinating creatures represent God's entire creation, including mankind.

All this equips them in an absolutely unique way to be heavenly attendants that reflect or represent something of the glory of God. After all, that was God's purpose when he made this world and all living creatures in it, that all the works of his hand would serve him and show some of his majesty.

There is also a close connection here with what we read in Ezekiel 1. There we also come across four majestic living creatures. They are not identical, though. Ezekiel saw four of the same, with each having four different faces, whereas John sees four different ones, each with one of these faces.

There is also a difference in the number of wings: the creatures in Ezekiel have four, but these creatures here in Revelation each have six. And this is exactly what the prophet Isaiah saw in his vision of the seraphim around God's throne in Isaiah 6:1–3: Each of them had six wings.

So, we recognize in these mysterious creatures the features of two very high-ranking orders of angels: the cherubim of Ezekiel 1 and the seraphim in Isaiah 6, powerful guardians of God's throne and holiness, ready to obey and serve the almighty God, anytime and anywhere. Our God is an awesome God, surrounded by heavenly attendants that represent his church and his creation.

HEAVENLY WORSHIP

As mentioned, there is a great variety of interpretations when it comes to those 'elders' and 'living creatures' as heavenly attendants. But one thing is clear: the purpose is worshipping him who sits on the throne and who lives for ever and ever.

It is important to stress again that it is all about him; it is all about serving and celebrating God's sovereign glory and power as he directs and controls all things.

That is the heart and centre of the whole vision.

Heavenly worship is the main activity of the four living creatures. They are completely dedicated. *Day and night they never cease to say*, it says. They dwell in God's immediate presence. They marvel at his glory and wisdom. They recognize the history of our world as the unfolding and realization of his will. And all this triggers non-stop praise and worship that fills the heavenly sanctuary, where the acoustics are perfect.

Holy, holy, holy, is the Lord God Almighty, who was, and is, and is to come....

This eternal quartet leads the heavenly worship of the Triune God, with a beautifully balanced song: three times 'holy' for the One on the throne with the three names Lord, God, and Almighty, of whom we hear three things: *who was, who is, and who is to come*. With this three-by-three structure – three times the divine number three – this song of glorious exultation of our Triune God reaches the highest and ultimate climax of heavenly beauty.

God is supremely holy, which is why here on earth his dwelling-place in the tabernacle and temple was called the "Holy-of-holies" or "Most holy place". And as the Lord God Almighty he alone is worthy of all praise and worship all the time. The powers and structures in our dominant culture do not control all things. They claim they do! And sometimes we think they do. But they do not. Praise our awesome God!

His sovereign Lordship is from eternity to eternity, and it overarches the past, the present and the future. He is the same yesterday, today, and tomorrow. And he leads his world from beginning to end. People can say "God doesn't exist" and "heaven is nothing but a fantasy". People can say whatever they want. But that does not stop creation's majestic praise and worship before the throne of the Almighty God.

It is the first singing that we hear in this book, with so much more to come.

And whenever they hear the song of glory, honour, and thanks of the living creatures, the twenty-four elders join in worship as an antiphonal choir. And so it goes, back and forth. The song of the church of all ages in response to, and simultaneously with, the song of all creation filling the holy throne-hall with marvellous and wonderful sounds.

God gathers his people so that they may forever praise and glorify him. Despite persecution, despite trials and temptations, despite internal strife, division, and lukewarm complacency – in the end the church of Jesus Christ will be victorious.

Praise God for the power of his grace in Jesus Christ.

That's why the twenty-four elders, who represent the church, *fall down before him who is seated on the throne* when they engage in worship. They worship the Holy God in deep humility and they are filled with great awe and reverence. They are who they are, only because of his amazing grace. That is also why *they cast their crowns before the throne*. Their victory is nothing but the victory of his grace.

And then their song blends in with the *'holy, holy, holy'* of the living creatures.... *Worthy are you, our Lord and God, to receive glory, and honour and power.*

And why is that? *You created all things, and by your will they existed, and were created.*

Recognize again a three-fold honour. "You are worthy, because of your active presence in this world as Maker and Ruler of all things. No one else could have done this. And you continue to govern and uphold all that your hands have made."

This is our God. His will alone is the real and ultimate reason for the existence of all things. And therefore, he alone is the ultimate refuge for each one of you, when you are stuck in distress, discouraged by your circumstances, or desperate in your misery.

He alone has absolute mastery, ownership, and control. His triumph is absolute. His power and wisdom are unfathomable. The universe belongs to the One who sits on the throne. And through Jesus Christ he will bring his order to our chaos.

That is why the elders join the living creatures. The God of creation is the God of the church. And so, it becomes this marvellous, coordinated, and harmonious act of worship, glorifying the holy God as Creator and Ruler – simultaneous praise of creation and church: holy, holy, holy.....!

Through John we may witness this heavenly liturgy, this heavenly worship.

When we sing our psalms and hymns today we are not alone.

Oh, sometimes our voices are weak. Sometimes we sing with tears in our eyes.

But by God's grace in Jesus Christ our voices may join the voices in heaven.

Let therefore the power of the heavenly worship empower our worship here on earth.

For it is true – in Christ *our God is an awesome God.*

11

REVELATION 5

CHRIST – OUR HOPE FOR THE FUTURE OF THE WORLD

In the Middle Ages 'visual art' was often 'biblical art' or 'religious art'. Paintings would show scenes based on Bible stories. And especially scenes from the book of Revelation were remarkably popular. One such well-known piece is "the Lamb of God", or "The Adoration of the Lamb of God". It is a famous altar-piece, painted in 1432 by Jan van Eyk, and can be seen in the St. Bavo Cathedral in Ghent, Belgium.

It is called a polyptych, because it is painted on several panels, connected by hinges. When you have three panels, you call it a triptych, and with two panels you have a diptych. The fascinating thing is that you can look at the panels as separate paintings, but when it is unfolded the panels together show one painting.

You can look at Revelation 4 and 5 as a visionary diptych – two parts of one single magnificent vision of God's glory. The first half of this diptych (Rev. 4) reveals God and praises him as the Creator and Ruler of the universe. The second half reveals God and praises him as the Redeemer, the Rescuer of his creation.

So when we shift our focus from the first to the second panel, we move from God's power in creation to his power in re-creation. But always remember that what we see in Rev. 5 is one vision with what we have seen in Rev. 4. It is still about the One who sits on the throne and who lives for ever and ever.

But there is also a difference. There is something new here. We come to see the key-role of Jesus Christ. His death and resurrection is the decisive event that brings about and will complete the redemption, the re-creation. God's work makes progress.

In our own time we may see how the Holy God continues to gather the church of Jesus Christ, with this perspective on its way to the New Jerusalem.

This happens here and in many other countries, in different cultures and under a great variety of circumstances. But what unites God's children throughout the world is the same perspective from above, the encouraging perspective of John's vision: God's work in the world makes progress. It will be completed and reach the goal of eternal and universal worship.

A MYSTERIOUS SCROLL

Scientists tell us that in our galaxy, the Milky Way, there are at least 100 billion planets. And many of these are said to be quite similar to our planet, which would suggest that our earth might be not as unique as we often think it is. This is, of course, a big boost for the search for life elsewhere in the universe, perhaps similar to our human life – who knows?! So far it is only wild speculation.

But there is also another side to this. When I read about those amazing discoveries, I cannot help but thinking how great our God is, how amazing is he, the Holy One, Creator of everything, this God whom we met in Revelation 4 as the Ruler of the universe, whose magnificent throne is in the centre of the heavenly sanctuary. Holy, holy, holy is the Lord God Almighty, who was and is and is to come.

The apostle John must have been overwhelmed. But then he sees something he had not noticed before, something small and inconspicuous that could easily be overlooked in the incredibly colourful brilliance and the abundant praise and worship that filled this huge heavenly sanctuary. He sees a scroll.

Why does this scroll catch his attention? Because he saw it *in the right hand of him who was seated on the throne*, God's right hand! Throughout the Bible God's right hand is the hand with which he does his powerful deeds. In Exodus 15 we read that "the LORD stretched out his right hand to shatter the enemy and deliver his people". And so it becomes a metaphor for God's just judgement and saving power.

But it is not only the location. As soon as John sees this scroll he notices two other details that make it even more mysterious. There was *writing within and on the back*, on both sides. This was unusual in the ancient world, but it tells us that all the writing-space was completely filled.

However, John could not read it. It says that this scroll was *sealed with seven seals*. Think again of the number seven. The scroll was completely sealed off. The content was classified, top-secret. Entirely hidden and not accessible!

And yet, that is not just it. It appears that God does not want to leave it like that. Most translations say that the scroll was "**in** God's right hand". But literally it says that the scroll was "**on** God's right hand". It looks like the Holy God, the Ruler on the throne in heaven, presents the scroll with an open hand. He offers it with the intention to reveal and activate what is written in it. It must be important.

This piques our interest, our curiosity, does it not? What is written on this mysterious scroll that makes it so important, that it gets all this attention?

As with many other details in this book, there is a great variety of ideas and opinions here. Some suggest that it contains God's covenant-promises or God's law or God's plan for the whole history of the world. Others like to identify this scroll with 'the book of life', mentioned in Rev. 3:5 and 20:12,15. Now, of course, at this moment in what is unfolding here, the scroll is still heavily sealed, so we do not know yet.

But the context can give us some idea. Remember where it is: "God's right hand". So somehow it must have to do with God's rule, God's strategy. But we can narrow this down. Remember also that the exalted Christ had said to John, *Come up here, and I will show you what must take place after this.* That is in Rev. 4:1.

11 • Revelation 5

Well, here it is, the outline of God's judgements and whatever else will be needed to complete his victory over this rebellious world, to establish his glorious kingdom and to bring about the fulfilment of his promise of salvation, as he leads his liberated people to their final destiny, the New Jerusalem.

Yes, all this is in the scroll! But it is sealed. We do not know the details. And we cannot control the developments. It is out of our hands. We cannot fathom God's mysteries. Oh, we have heard about the final destination. But you and I, we don't know yet what it will be like on the journey to get there. We are just staring at these solid, unbreakable seals, and we feel like Daniel.

In the book of the prophet Daniel we read in chapter 12 that Daniel gets a message about the end times. But then he is told to *shut up the words and seal the book (or the scroll) until the time of the end.* And when he asks, *My Lord, what shall be the outcome of these things,* he hears, *Go your way, Daniel, for the words are shut up and sealed until the time of the end* (Daniel 12:4,8-9).

With this in the background, we feel the growing suspense with the reader (or listener) of Revelation. We have entered the final phase of history. Is this the "time of the end" Daniel was talking about? What is going to happen? The One seated on the throne, with this scroll on his right hand, what is he looking for?

Then John sees *a strong angel*, a powerful messenger from God. And he hears him call out with a loud voice. So loud, so strong that everyone in heaven, on earth and beyond could hear him. Through this angel God himself issues an urgent call: *Who is worthy, who qualifies, to open the scroll and break its seals.*

This is kind of backwards, of course. You will have to break the seals first, before you can open the scroll. But the point is here to focus our expectation first on what is most important. This scroll needs to be opened. God wants to show us what must happen, and he also wants to make it happen.

This is urgent. God had created man to rule his creation, to make his will happen on earth. But we refused. The power of sin disabled us. We are no longer capable of making God's will happen in this world. We rather did (and do…) our own thing. And it turned into a huge mess. Then, in his grace and mercy, God wrote his plan of salvation. But the scroll can only be opened, that is, God's plan of salvation can only be activated and completed by someone who is qualified to do so. Otherwise there will be nothing left but God's eternal wrath.

And thus the holy God, who is a God of justice and mercy, is looking for someone who is "worthy". That is someone who fully identifies with you and me, a human, but who is at the same time stronger than the powers of sin and evil. We need an agent of God's amazing grace for a world lost in sin.

But the result of the search is disappointing. *No one in heaven or on earth or under the earth was able to open the scroll or look into it.* No one stepped forward. There is no response from anywhere in the whole universe. Oh, people have their dreams and ideals. Political leaders produce rousing speeches about peace and justice. We think that one day we will be able to eradicate hatred, war, racism, violence. But it does not work. We cannot make the world a better place. We are powerless. We are stuck. We cannot create a new world-order.

As it turns out, no one seems to have the required qualifications to reveal and execute God's plan of salvation. Do you feel the tension mounting? What if the scroll remains closed? Will the whole plan be abandoned?

The silence in v.3 is dramatic, frightening, and distressful!

When he realizes this, John is deeply affected by it. *I began to weep loudly,* he says. You might wonder why. He had known Jesus, and for decades he has been preaching the gospel of salvation. That is true of course. But now he has this point of view from above and he is wondering: is it going to work or is it going to fail?

John longs for God's purpose of redemption to be realized. John longs to see the world ruled for the glory of God. And he understands that for this to happen and to be completed this scroll must be opened. If not, there will be no just judgment for the wicked and there will be no hope and no future for God's children.

John had been invited (in Rev. 4:1) to witness *what must take place after this*, but it seems like nothing is going to happen. And he cannot help but thinking what is going to come of this world without Jesus Christ. It breaks his heart to realize that the destiny of the church and the world hangs in the balance over the question whether someone will be able to open the scroll. He weeps.

And yet, the hope is not demolished! One of the elders, one of the twenty-four we have seen in Rev. 4, comes up to John and addresses him to break the despair. *Weep no more*, he says. There is no reason to be sad and weep.

You can have this feeling sometimes that God's promises do not seem to work out, not in the world, not in your own life. "God has a plan for you and me," we say, "and it's a good plan." That sounds good, but then you experience the one disappointment after the other, and you do not see a way out. And you weep!

Do not weep, says the elder. Do not get stuck in your distress, misery, and hopelessness. Open your eyes and look around for someone who has thus far escaped your attention. Look and see the one who qualifies, because he has triumphed and has defeated the evil powers of sin and death.

And then he explains what John is supposed to see: *The Lion of the tribe of Judah*, who is also *the Root of David*. These are two titles that refer to Old Testament promises of the Messiah, the promised Saviour Jesus Christ.

The first one alludes to the patriarch Jacob's prophecy about the ruler who will come from Judah and who will be like a powerful Lion, triumphant and full of strength (Genesis 49:8-10).

The other one alludes to the Son of David, who is at the same time the victorious Son of God and thus also the origin, the root of David's kingdom (2 Samuel 7:12-13; Psalm 110:1; Matthew 1:1; Revelation 22:16).

The point is that both titles suggest a militant conquest, a powerful victory that qualifies Christ to open this mysterious scroll and its seals, take control of God's plan of salvation, and bring it all to a glorious completion.

A POWERFUL LAMB

But then, what John is seeing when he looks up is confusing for him, and definitely for the reader's (or listener's) expectations. He expected to see a Lion, a fierce and mighty warrior. But he does not. He sees a Lamb. That is the opposite. Here is nothing fierce and powerful. A Lamb is weak and vulnerable.

This alternation between "hearing" and "seeing" turns out to be an important element to understand Revelation. Several times John 'hears' and 'sees' things that are connected, but different. And then the one interprets the other one.

For now, just one example. In Rev. 7:4 John hears the number 144,000, but according to v.9 he sees a great multitude. What he hears explains the spiritual reality of what he is seeing.

Now look at Rev. 5 again. John hears: it's a Lion. And that promises a powerful and triumphant victory. But then he sees a Lamb. And that explains that Christ won this victory, not with military force, like the powers of this world, but with a power that shows his love and grace; his willingness to become weak and vulnerable, to give himself in his suffering and death on the cross for the sake of God's children.

This is emphasized by two remarkable details. The Lamb John is seeing *looks as though it had been slain*. "Like a Lamb our Saviour was led to the slaughter", says the prophet Isaiah (Isaiah 53). And in Israel the Passover Lamb shed its blood to save God's people from slavery and death (Exodus 12). This Lamb is 'slain', slaughtered. Christ should be dead. However, *this Lamb is standing*. It is alive. Christ arose from the dead.

Look at this unique and powerful picture: "a slain lamb that is standing." And recognize its glory as the result of its sacrifice.

This Lamb, who is at the same time the Lion, is a powerful Lamb. He is our victorious Saviour, our Lord Jesus Christ. In his suffering, death, and resurrection he shows characteristics of both. He is majestic and vulnerable. He is strong and helpless.

11 • Revelation 5

Here is the mystery, the paradox of our Christian faith, as we read about it in 1 Corinthians 1: God achieved his triumphant victory, he set us free from Satan's power, not by military might and violence, but through the weakness and foolishness of the gospel of the cross. The power of Jesus Christ is the power of self-sacrificing love. For worldly thinking this way of salvation is either offensive or ludicrous. But do not be intimidated by that, says Paul. *To those who are being saved the message of the cross is the power of God and the wisdom of God* (1 Corinthians 1:18, 24).

This also sets the pattern for you and me as God's children. We are to fight our spiritual battles, not with physical power or with political strength, but with purity of faith and with enduring love for God, with faithful dedication to Jesus Christ – even to the point of death, if needed. 'Martyrdom' looks like a defeat. But it is not! It is a victory that makes you share in the final victory of the powerful Lamb of God.

John can see how powerful this Lamb is. First of all, it stands in the centre of the throne. As it is surrounded by the same heavenly throne-attendants we have seen in Rev. 4, it shares in the power of the Lord God Almighty.

Then he also sees that it has seven horns and seven eyes. The 'horn' is an image of power, and again the number seven stresses how complete and perfect his power is. As Jesus said to his disciples just before he ascended into heaven, *all authority in heaven and on earth has been given to me* (Matthew 28:18).

And with the seven eyes as the seven-fold Spirit, he is also filled with this Spirit of God who fills all the earth with the gospel of salvation.

All this allows the Lamb with the power of the Lion to come and take the scroll. Everything had to wait for the cross, the resurrection and the ascension of Jesus Christ, our Mediator. Now he was given the authority to complete the history of our world according to God's plan. Now the seals can be broken by the only One worthy to bring God's justice and righteousness, God's grace and mercy to a glorious end, when from everywhere God's people come home to the New Jerusalem.

Now the throne of God the Father becomes also the throne of the Lamb. Here is our comfort as we continue to read Revelation, whatever will be going on.

The effect of this dramatic moment is breathtaking. Already before the Lamb has done anything, just because he takes the scroll, there is in heaven a great outburst of exuberant joy. *The four living creatures and the twenty-four elders* – the circles closest to the throne of God, as we have seen before – they all *fall down before the Lamb*, united in humble adoration, praise, and worship.

In Rev. 4 they never stopped worshipping God Almighty: holy, holy, holy...!

And now they also worship the Lamb as the only One worthy to open the scroll and break the deadlock. They had harps, in Revelation always associated with songs of deliverance. And they had golden bowls full of incense, lifting up the prayers of the church on earth in perfect unison with the heavenly worship to the glory of God and the Lamb.

UNIVERSAL WORSHIP

What John then hears conveys the deep meaning of what he sees. He hears *a new song*. Indeed, the worship-song of the elders and the living creatures is a new song. For the One who sits on the throne and the Lamb have done new, wonderful things. Something unique, something new has happened. Never before has there been such a great and glorious deliverance.

It is a heart-warming song of freedom and redemption, a soul-stirring song of salvation from Satan, sin, and death. The Lamb of God has died and is alive. The triumphant Lion of the tribe of Judah ushers in a new age.

Here is the glorious answer to the urgent question in v.2: "Who is worthy?"

Worthy are you to take the scroll and to open its seals. You qualify *because you were slain*. The self-sacrificing love of the Lamb in his suffering, death, and resurrection, is the basis for his victory and redemption.

And what is the result? "With the price of your blood you purchased people, to set them free from Satan's power and present them to God the Father as his children." No, Jesus Christ did not purchase every individual person in the whole world. But the scope of his salvation is universal, world-wide. They come *from every tribe, language, people and nation*. They represent every ethnic and linguistic group, every political and social category everywhere.

Whoever you are, wherever you come from, it does not matter. Believe that with his blood Jesus Christ bought you. You belong to him and to God the Father. He alone set you free from the deadly powers of sin and evil.

Jesus Christ, the Lamb of God, breaks through all our boundaries and unites people from everywhere and every background into one people of God, the holy church of all times and places, the full population of the new earth, the magnificent fulfilment of God's promise to Abraham: *all families of the earth shall be blessed in you* (Gen. 12:3).

You have made them a kingdom and priests to our God, and they shall reign on the earth, united and fully dedicated to serve the Almighty Ruler of the universe in his glorious kingdom.

But then the circle of praise widens. The concentric circles that surround the circle of the twenty-four elders expand dramatically to include angels. *Then I looked and heard the voice of many angels*, says John. "Many" is an understatement. The numbers are just staggering. When he says, *myriads of myriads and thousands of thousands,* he just means it was an enormous, huge mass, beyond counting! It was astounding: angels, angels, angels and more angels, as far as the eye can see.

They all sang, and in a loud voice. They sang the glory of the slain Lamb. That must have been incredibly overwhelming to listen to. They follow what is happening and they burst out in abundant praise, antiphonal harmony with the song in v.9 and 10.

In the song of the angels we hear seven attributes the Lamb is worthy to receive (v.12). The perfect and complete fullness of all virtues in the universe belong to him. It does not get any better and more magnificent than this in the heavenly worship service.

And yet, it is not enough. A still wider circle is needed to give full praise to the significance of the work of Christ. Finally, all of God's creation joins in universal worship. Every creature everywhere is participating, it says in v.13.

The circle becomes so enormous that John can no longer see them. He only hears all the voices, praising the Holy God and the Lamb, Jesus Christ.

Here is the grand finale, the perfect harmony of all voices, in the very climax of everything we have seen and heard in the diptych of Rev. 4 and 5. The marvellous fulfilment of Psalm 150 – *Let everything that has breath praise the LORD.*

In most exuberant songs of praise and glory all the universe worships the Almighty God and Jesus Christ his Son for their powerful work in creation and redemption.

And with the constant refrain of the four living creatures in a resounding 'Amen' as a permanent, never-ending approval of this grandiose doxology the universal worship comes full circle from where it began in Rev. 4:9.

Oh, it is true: at this point in the plot of Revelation the world is still in rebellion. God's judgments are coming. But here is a glimpse of how it was intended to be and how it will be again in the future.

Rejoice! Ultimately all things will come to glorify him who sits on the throne and the Lamb for ever and ever.

12

REVELATION 6

GOD'S JUDGMENTS BEGIN TO UNFOLD – ROUND 1.

In Revelation 4 and 5 with John's vision of the heavenly sanctuary, with the throne of God Almighty in the very centre, we have learned that the One on the throne is always in control. We have also learned that the Lamb of God, Jesus Christ, turns out to be the only one worthy to activate the content of the mysterious scroll on the hand of the One seated on the throne.

For that to happen he would have to break the seven seals with which the scroll was sealed. In other words, Jesus Christ alone is able to work out God's master-plan for this world, the plan that leads to punishment for the wicked and redemption for God's people.

Well then, here, in Rev. 6, it begins. All of a sudden the events pick up considerable speed. As the Lamb begins to open the seven seals one by one, we see and hear judgements being issued from God's throne. We see and hear from above things that explain our experiences here below, as we are on our way toward the final victory of Jesus Christ, and the New Jerusalem.

The vision of the seven seals is divided into a block of four, then two that are connected, and then the last one. In this chapter we will look at the four and the two, the first six seals. Between the opening of the sixth and the seventh seal another story is embedded. We will hear about that in Rev. 7. This will slow down the fast pace of Rev.6, to add a significant view, especially for the church, the believers.

In the meantime, the opening of the first six seals describe events that characterize our world as we move towards the fulfilment, the final unravelling of the purpose of the book. Terrible things are happening. We will see and hear bizarre things in our noisy picture book, that we call Revelation.

But the perspective is that all these things are controlled by the One who sits on the throne, and the Lamb. Behind all this turmoil the Almighty and Holy God is fulfilling and completing his plan of salvation. That is why we don't need to fear in times of trouble, tribulation, anguish and persecution.

Devastating horses

It is true, we don't have to fear trouble and persecution. At the same time, what happens when the Lamb of God opens the seals of the scroll, shows us with all kinds of symbols that such times of trouble and tribulation are coming. What John is going to hear must have reminded him of some of the things he had heard from Jesus already. Think, for instance, of what we find in Luke 21.

I watched when the Lamb opened one of the seven seals. That must have been a moment full of suspense for the apostle. We do not use a lot of scrolls nowadays, but usually the contents of a sealed scroll would only be accessible after all the seals were opened. But the drama in our vision is that God's plan begins to unfold immediately with the opening of the first seal.

It is clear that the first four of these seals belong together. The process is the same, and the results show a lot of similarities. They form one block, a devastating quartet that in close cooperation makes the world a scary place to live in. It is not the same for every individual, but we all know it's a broken world full of painful suffering, a world that is groaning under the consequences of sin.

When the first four seals are opened, we are shown four horses and their riders. The group reminds us of Zechariah's first vision. The prophet sees three groups of horsemen returning from a scouting-expedition throughout the earth (Zechariah 1:7-13). Here it is again God who sends out the horses and their riders to do his work. In Zechariah 1 they reported that *the whole world was at rest and in peace*. Later on, we have to come back to this in connection with the fifth seal.

You may have noticed, when you read Rev. 6, that John alternates again between what he sees and what he hears. He sees seals being opened, and then he hears the four living creatures taking turns in calling up a horse and dispatching it with its rider. They do so in a booming voice as loud as a thunderclap. It is only mentioned with the first one, but there is no reason to believe that the others were whispering.

Four times we hear this loud and powerful command COME! And then we see destruction and disorder, with the four horsemen wreaking havoc on this earth. But the word "come" also connects the opening of the seals with the end of Revelation. There we hear a similar call: *"Come.... Come, Lord Jesus.* That is in Rev. 22.

Within this framework, between these brackets of the word "come", we may trust that all evil, woes and judgment we encounter today, will be undone in the future, at Christ's second coming. God will turn it around. The power of these devastating horsemen comes from him. But here already we look forward to the reversal of this disorder when Jesus will come to usher in new heavens and a new earth.

The first horse is white, with its rider holding a bow, a weapon-of-war. He is also wearing a crown, or better, a victory-wreath, that was given to him. His purpose is to conquer, to submit by force. He is *bent on conquest,* says the NIV. The question "who is this rider?" is one of the controversial issues in Revelation. There are different ideas about this, and it seems that one is as good as the other.

Many believe that this rider on the white horse is Christ. They have a number of arguments for this, but the main point is the similarity with another rider on a white horse in Rev. 19. Now, that one is indeed Jesus Christ. The description in 19:11-13 makes that quite obvious.

But one of the differences with 6:2 is that he has a different weapon. The rider in Rev. 19 has *a sharp sword coming out of his mouth* and that we remember from the vision in Rev. 1:16. His conquest, his victory comes through the power of his Word, the testimony of the cross. This rider has a bow.

But the main issue is that the four horsemen really belong together as four devastating powers to execute God's judgments. That is why others state the opposite. They say that this rider is the Antichrist, a devilish parody or caricature of Christ, evil masquerading as good. Does the Bible not warn us that *even Satan disguises himself as an angel of light* (2 Corinthians 11:14)? And he forces submission with his weapon-of-war.

The question is, of course, do we really need to know who this rider is? Do we have to give him a name? We do not do this with the second and third horseman either. They represent certain powers, but as such they are anonymous. Only the fourth one has a name. But we do not have to argue about that, because it's in the text.

I believe that the rider on the white horse represents the aggressive political forces in this world that claim to rule without God, the powers that want to be in control. They want to *conquer*.

Sometimes these powers looks pretty benevolent, but when resisted, or criticized, such a power can quickly turn oppressive, and become a dictatorship that takes away our freedom. It can do so with bloodshed, but also by enforcing an ideology.

In our time you can think of secularism. Such a power will often resist the gospel of Christ, outlaw the Christian faith, and persecute Christians.

The second horse John is seeing is a fiery red one. It has the colour of blood. The rider on this horse was given the power to destroy human harmony, to make people hate each other, to take away peaceful order from the earth. People keep trying, but time and again the human dream of 'world-peace' fails. People keep hoping that eventually we will all get along better and make the world a better and peaceful place. But that also will continue to be a pipedream.

And in personal relationships it is not any better – bitter disagreements, conflicts, angry feuds and fights, it's all too familiar, then here, then there. We can make each other's lives pretty miserable. You would not expect this among God's children and in the church, but the influence of the rider on the red horse is everywhere!

This horseman has the power *to make men slay one another*. To that end he was also given *a great sword*. He represents the powers of war and warfare. You can think of all kinds of violence and hostilities, or terrorism, or civil war. And when you look around in the world, you will notice that in many of the armed conflicts in this world, Christian believers are often the victims, crushed between the fighting parties.

When Christ opens the third seal, John sees his third horse. It is black, which is, according to some, the colour of hunger. That its rider is holding *a pair of scales* points at the need to carefully distribute the scarce food. John hears a voice explaining the dire consequences of the power of this horseman. *A quart of wheat for a denarius and three quarts of barley for a denarius*. A denarius was a day's wages.

The world will suffer from a terrible scarcity of food. What Ezekiel 4:16 tells us about the situation in Jerusalem, John sees happening all over the world. The average wage of a labourer is barely enough to feed one person. How do you support your family when it becomes so tough to make ends meet? And the prices are outrageous. Wheat would be eight times the normal price, and barley five times.

What about the addition *do not harm the oil and wine*? Some have said that it means there will an abundant supply of stuff the poor cannot afford. So, only the poor will suffer, while the rich will have plenty to enjoy. But oil and wine were not luxury items in the ancient eastern society, oil was used for cooking and wine was a common drink, in those days much healthier than water.

No, everyone will suffer from the hardships when the economy collapses, often in the wake of oppression, warfare, pandemics, or other disasters. The purpose of the instruction to spare the oil and wine is to tell us in a symbolic way that, for now, God is going to limit what could easily turn into terrible famine. Again, the Holy and Almighty God remains in control of the events.

Then, when the Lamb opens the fourth seal, the fourth living creature summons a fourth horse. Now that is a horrifying sight. It has a gruesome, sickly colour: pale greenish or greyish. And its rider is the most terrifying of all. This one has a name: *Death*. And his ugly companion *Hades* is trotting right behind him. 'Death' kills and cuts down, and 'Hades' collects the victims and swallows them up.

The grim reaper is making his deadly rounds in this world, killing people through wars, starvation, pandemic diseases, or natural disasters. It happens all the time and all over the world. Yes, he is powerful and frightening. But even the powers of Death and Hades cannot do what they want. Even the powers of Death and Hades are controlled by the One who sits on the throne in heaven.

He sets the boundary. *They were given authority over one-quarter of the earth.* Twenty-five percent is the limit. Later on in the book this will increase: one-third of the earth will be affected by the trumpets in Rev.8, and when the bowls of God's wrath are poured out in Rev.16 the devastation will be unrestricted. This is only round one.

This is our world. You and I read and hear the news every day. We see the terrible woes that plague mankind since the fall into sin. But John's vision helps you to recognize behind the disturbing headlines the power of these devastating horsemen, sent by the One who rules from heaven. Their power characterizes the whole period before Jesus' return. Such things have occurred – are occurring now – and can be expected to occur until that glorious day.

God judges a rebellious world so that people may repent and turn to him. At the same time, Jesus Christ, the Lamb of God, will use these same events in our lives to teach us to trust in him, to rely on him and to grow in holiness. In the midst of the trials in this world you are cared for, because of his plan for you.

Calling Martyrs

And that plan will unfold when the Lamb opens the fifth seal. When that happens the tempo slows down, and the scene changes. The four galloping horsemen who bring destruction and death, disappear out of sight. The scene switches to heaven, where John sees *under the altar the souls of those who had been slain for the word of God and for the witness they had borne.*

So, John sees an altar in the heavenly sanctuary. Here is the first of eight references to an 'altar' in Revelation. This altar appears to have different functions. It reminds us of both the 'altar of burnt offering' and the 'altar of incense' that stood in the Old Testament tabernacle and temple.

Here this altar is a place of refuge. Throughout the ages Christians have been thrown to the lions, burned at the stake, tortured, massacred, and more. The souls of these martyrs, killed for their faith, found shelter and safety with Christ in the sanctuary in heaven. Here they are waiting for the resurrection of the dead.

It is good not to gloss over the fact that John sees souls. Can you 'see' souls? What do they look like? We have no idea, right? Do the souls of our loved ones, who passed away to be with Christ, do they have any awareness of time or of what's going on with us, here on earth? We tend to say, 'we don't know', and leave it at that.

But here it seems like they have some visible form. They wear clothes! And John also hears them. They can *cry out with a loud voice*. And what they call out, shows that they are fully aware of time, and of what is happening on earth. They also have desires. They are longing for the end. They are looking forward to the day wherein God will do justice and bring all his children safely home.

Some people suggest that what John sees is a vision, so it's all symbolic, it's not real. It is true, of course, that in his vision John sees and hears things you cannot see and hear with physical eyes and ears. But does that mean it is not real?

The souls of the martyrs call out with a loud voice. It is urgent. Remember the report of the horsemen in Zechariah's vision: *...we found that the whole world remains at rest*. There is no sign that salvation is coming soon. Then Zechariah hears the urgent call of the angel: *O LORD of hosts, how long will you have no mercy on Jerusalem and the cities of Judah* (Zechariah 1:11-12)?

We hear the same urgent tone in the appeal of the martyrs in heaven. *O Sovereign Lord, holy and true, how long before you will judge and avenge our blood on those who dwell on the earth?* "Those who dwell on the earth" are the people that scorn and defy the holy God and oppose the work of Christ and his church.

Then, just as we hear in Zechariah 1:13 the LORD responding with kind and comforting words, here also John hears and sees, in response to the call of the martyrs, words and images that comfort, encourage, and give hope.

It is true, Jesus teaches us to love our enemies, just as in Luke 23:34 he himself prayed for those who crucified him. But these calling martyrs are not driven by a selfish desire for personal revenge. No, they are longing for the great day that God will set everything straight, eliminate evil, show his justice and reveal his majesty and holiness.

What John sees and hears are the martyrs in heaven. But they express the same desire as the faithful believers, the suffering church on earth. That makes this "How long?" a crucial question for John's whole book, and thus for us today.

How long does the church in heaven and on earth have to wait until God fully overcomes all evil and injustice in the world? How long do we have to wait before the way of the cross is vindicated in our lives, and in the eyes of those who today ridicule the way of the cross?

God's answer is twofold. *They were each given a white robe.* This is a sign of purity, righteousness, and holiness through communion with Christ in heaven. We see the same in Rev. 3:5 and 7:14. That is encouraging, but it does not answer the question.

Then they were told *to rest a little longer.* Their prayers will be heard. But not yet. The day has not yet come, but it will come in God's time. All their fellow-servants have to be brought in first. God alone knows the exact number, and it is not yet complete. That is why delaying his full wrath now, serves the complete wrap-up of the gathering of Christ's church in the time to come.

The flipside of this patience that God shows, is that there will also be more victims of persecution: *brothers who were to be killed as they themselves had been!* This is where we find ourselves today. Together with our brothers and sisters in heaven we are to wait. But as we are waiting and as the church continues to suffer, we may know this: all the things we are dealing with here and now are within God's grand plan.

This is his way of winning the victory over evil. Do not worry, eventually all injustice will be avenged and punished. And eventually all brokenness will be healed. That is a promise! In Rev. 16:5, 6 and 18:20 the outcry of the martyrs is being answered. Yes, at this point we all have to wait a little longer. But the delay is coming to an end, for, as it says in 12:12, *Satan knows that his time is short.*

FRIGHTENING CALAMITIES

God will hear the prayer of the souls in heaven. And when it comes, his wrath on those who dwell on the earth will be terrible indeed. The opening of the sixth seal triggers lots of frightening calamities. The cosmos joins the earth in disasters that shake the very fabric of the created order. John sees how the dread and horror of what is happening comes about in two ways, a crashing universe and a terrified mankind.

It starts with a great earthquake. In the Bible this is often an indication that God is coming as Judge. And here it is also the visible sign that the present world order is fractured beyond repair. In the end all human structures, all human accomplishments, all human pride that ignores God, it all comes crashing down.

And then the sun turns black, the moon turns blood red, and the stars fall out of the sky. The whole universe is out of joint. In Genesis 1:14 we read that on the fourth day of the creation-week God put the sun, the moon, and the stars in the expanse of the sky *to give light upon the earth.* But when his world, filled with moral and spiritual decay, is dissolving into chaos, God turns off the lights. Enough is enough. There will be nothing left but icy cold and frightening darkness.

And then the sky itself recedes like a scroll. It curls up like a piece of paper. Yes, even mountains and islands, emblems of what is solid and immovable, they are uprooted, just like that; moved out of place and thrown around by the enormous powers mobilized by God. The holy and almighty God begins to undo his creation. He is going to tear down and demolish his old world.

Try to visualize what John saw and you can imagine the picture of dread and despair, confusion and consternation that we have in v.15 and 16. The opening of the sixth seal shows us the terror on the day of wrath for the wicked. It shows how those who reject the sacrifice of Jesus Christ and refuse to repent will experience God's judgement. It scares the living daylight out of them, all of them!

Verse 15 lists six categories:

the kings of the earth: the supreme political rulers, prime ministers and presidents;

the great ones: other public figures and power-brokers in the world;

the generals: the military leaders;

the rich: the wealthy businessmen and economic leaders;

the powerful: the men and women, the celebrities who influence our culture through science, arts, entertainment, sports, education, the media, and you name it;

And finally *everyone* – free or slave.

In the face of God's judgment those distinctions become irrelevant. From the lofty to the lowly, no one will escape the cosmic collapse. When the whole world falls apart everyone is equal. John sees the entire godless world terror-stricken. They all recognize who is coming, and like Adam and Eve after the fall, they can only think of fleeing and hiding from the wrath of God Almighty on the throne and of the Lamb.

Is this the last Judgment? It sure looks like it, sounds like it and feels like it! And so, we think it is! However, it is not the end! Not yet! The seventh seal is still coming. And that will open up another cycle of disasters, when angels sound the seven trumpets, a second round of judgments is coming!

But for the people it sure feels like 'this is the end'. For them the fear, the panic, the despair are very real. And in one last desperate attempt to hide, they call on rocks and mountains to protect them. They would rather be crushed under rocks or mountains and nowhere to be found, than having to face the

Almighty God. They would rather be buried alive, than have Jesus set his eyes like blazing fire on them.

And in their deep despair they cry out another key-question of Revelation: Who can stand on the great day of the wrath of the Almighty God and the Lamb?

Who can stand on the day that the just anger of God turns against the evil and corruption that has spread on earth? Are we all doomed to destruction?

The apostle John will hear and see the answer.

In the meantime, in a world slated for demolition and urgently in need of messianic repair, here are the two desperate questions everyone needs to answer:

"Who can stand in the Judgment?"

And the other one, in contrast with this: "How long, O Lord, until you judge?"

Which of these questions is yours? What fills your heart when you look around?

The despair that leads you to Jesus Christ to find hope?

Or the despair that leads you to be afraid and horrified?

If you do **not** flee **to** Jesus Christ, you **will** have to flee **from** him.

But there is no place to hide.

13

REVELATION 7 – 8: 5

THE CHURCH IS SEALED TO SURVIVE THE TRIBULATION

In Revelation 6 we saw how God's wrath begins to demolish his creation, when Christ opens the sixth seal of the scroll. When that happens all the people in the world, the powerful and the lowly, the rich and the poor, they all panic. It is a horrible experience. They get so scared that in despair they call out: "Who is able to stand in the judgment of God? Who can survive this ordeal?"

In the mouth of these frightened callers it sounds like a rhetorical question, with the suggested answer: "Of course, no one can. This is just too terrible."

But that is not true. In Revelation 7 John will hear an answer. God is going to respond, so that we may know and will not despair; so that we may have hope, no matter how dark the world may become, even if the whole world comes crashing down.

God is going to respond with the vision of his redeemed, standing before the throne in heaven and in front of the Lamb Jesus Christ.

You could call this chapter an interlude; a narrative, embedded in the discourse of the scroll that was sealed with the seven seals. It is sandwiched, so to speak, between the events at the opening of the sixth seal and the opening of the seventh seal. It interrupts – and in so doing, slows down – the progress in the work of Christ to activate the content of the scroll, God's plan for the final phase of history.

This is not unique here. A similar pattern of high-speed events, followed by a slowing down of the progress, occurs between the moments that the sixth and seventh trumpets are sounded. The one is in Rev.9:13 and the next one in 11:15.

But these are not just incidents. It is God's purpose to draw our attention to things that are crucially important to be aware of at those specific moments.

When total destruction seems to be inescapable, God wants to comfort and encourage his people by showing that his faithful servants are sealed. They are protected in the midst of his judgments, no matter how great the tribulation may be.

This means a dramatic delay for the opening of the seventh seal. But we will get there!

A FIXED NUMBER

When the frightening sounds and screams of all the turmoil that came with the opening of the sixth seal are fading out, you can imagine that John is still thinking of this desperate cry: "Who can stand on the great day of the wrath of God and of the Lamb.....?"

But then a different scene unfolds in his vision. He sees four angels standing at the four corners of the earth, holding back the four winds of the earth. The earth does not have real corners, of course, but think North, East, South and West. By doing this, these angels prevent unrestricted violence from destroying the whole earth.

We have seen the terrible devastation that was the result of the powers that broke loose after the sixth seal was opened. And now we are waiting for the seventh seal. There must be more to come. What will it be like? Is the violence of God's final judgment going to break loose in full force now? If it happens, there will be no escape.

We know how much damage can be caused by violent hurricanes and tornados. We do not have a lot of experience with this in Canada, but in the US they do. Think of hurricane Katrina in the south, in 2005, and a few years later hurricane Sandy in New York. Well, here these strong, destructive winds from all directions are symbolic of God's judgments that are still coming.

And these four angels have the power, the authority to do this, to let those winds loose. But they do not. At least, not yet! It is like God Almighty has his finger on the button that will trigger the final explosion, but he does not push it. At least, not yet!

But why not? What is holding him back?

Then John sees another angel, coming up from the east, like the sun. He seems to usher in a new, bright day. That sounds hopeful. This angel has with him *the seal of the living God*. In those days, the impression of a seal in wax signified ownership and promises protection. In other words, with this particular seal of God people could be 'marked'. And this marking would suggest that you belong to the God who is life, who gives life and guarantees life. This marking would mean you do not need to worry, he will protect you.

Well, in order to do this marking, the angel with the seal needs time. And so, we hear him call out to the four angels in a loud voice: *Do not harm the earth or the sea or the trees, until we have sealed the servants of our God on their foreheads*. He is talking about all the believers of all times and places. And we find out that, because of them, the Lord shows patience. Think of what Peter says in 2 Peter 3. *The Lord is patient with you, not wanting anyone to perish*.

Indeed, God is holding back the calamities of the final judgment to safeguard the protection of his people. He is still gathering his church. This delay of his judgment gives room for the sealing of all those who are his; all those who will be able to stand on the day that the storms of his wrath will be blowing in full force.

13 • Revelation 7-8:5

It says that this seal will be *on the foreheads of God's people*. When something is on your forehead everyone can see it. In this way the "servants of God" can be distinguished from the "followers of the beast", who we meet in Rev. 13. In 13:16 (see also 19:20) these people also receive marks on their foreheads. And so, we discover that all people are marked. No one is free, either you belong to the living God, or you belong to his enemy. You bear either God's seal or the mark of the beast.

We understand that this 'seal on your forehead' will protect you, but we don't really know what it looks like. In Rev. 14:1 it says that the 144,000 *had the name of the Lamb and his Father's name written on their foreheads*. But that does not help either. Unless you think that it is a literal symbol in the form of a brand or tattoo, or something like that, on your forehead. But that is unlikely.

The best solution is to see those seals as things that become visible in your life, as things that reflect your values or beliefs. That means, if you are sealed with the 'seal of the living God' you are going to live so that others can see that you belong to God and Jesus Christ. With the seal of God, others can identify you as a Christian. This seal shows that Jesus Christ owns you, that you trust in him to protect you, and that you are willing and ready to worship him and live for him every day.

This is the seal that guarantees your protection in God's coming judgment. To be sure, we are talking about "spiritual protection". Throughout Revelation it is clear that Christians will not always escape physical harm and danger. Many have suffered and will suffer persecution. Some have to die for their faith. Indeed, believers will not escape their share of trouble and misery. But they will survive.

It is the Holy Spirit who gives this seal. In 2 Cor. 1:22 the apostle Paul connects Christ's *seal of ownership* with *the Holy Spirit in our hearts*. And Eph. 1:13 says that when you believe, *in Christ you were sealed with the promised Holy Spirit*. And this seal protects you, it says in Eph. 4:30, *for the day of redemption*.

So, yes, when you believe God's promises and you embrace Jesus as your Saviour, the Holy Spirit seals you. And then the Holy Spirit will also take care of you, so that you can keep it up, and can stand on the day of God's wrath. This is so encouraging. Sometimes we worry about these things but for those who belong to Christ, there is no need to be anxious.

Here in North America we are not persecuted, presently. But if that would come, would you be able to keep it up? Would you dare to show the seal on your forehead, or would you rather hide it? Would you trust him who has sealed you? Sometimes you wonder about that. And without persecution, you face the many attractive temptations in this world. Would you let your 'seal' determine your choices?

And what about our children in this increasingly secular and often hostile world? How are they going to handle the many temptations and challenges, and the pressure to assimilate? Keep telling yourself and your kids that in his grace the Lord has sealed you and them through the Holy Spirit with the seal of his ownership.

In Revelation 7 John does not see the sealing, but he hears the result. He hears the exact number of those who were sealed: *144,000 from every tribe of the sons of Israel*. What he sees later on (in v.9) looks different, an incalculable multitude from everywhere. The question, 'are these groups the same, or are they distinct from each other?', has triggered many different ideas and opinions.

Now remember what we have seen before. It is important to know that what John hears and what he sees may seem different, while it is actually the same thing. But then the same thing characterized from two different points-of-view that complement each other, and sometimes interpret each other. In this case, what he hears is the inner reality, the spiritual reality, and what he sees is the outward reality.

The number that John hears, 144,000, is a symbolic but fixed number that represents the full number of those who belong to God. It all starts in the Old Testament. That is why they are called "God's Israel". The basic unit is twelve, which is the number of Israel's patriarchs. But as God's saving work expands in the time of the New Testament, we also see twelve apostles. And so the entire church of Old and New Testament can be represented by 12x12=144.

However, this is multiplied by 1000. That tells us that, in the end, the spiritual reality of the church of God is a large, but perfectly harmonious and completely unified community.

This spiritual reality is also emphasized when we hear that the 144,000 are equally divided. The exact same number of sealed servants of God comes from each of the 12 tribes of Israel. This fixed structure suggests again that the numbers are symbolic and reflect the fullness and completion of God's people.

In Rev. 14:4 it says that these 144,000 *follow the Lamb wherever he goes*. So, we are talking about faithful, dedicated followers of Jesus Christ, Christian believers from everywhere, from Jews and Gentiles. The glorified Christ owns them and promises to protect them. This again makes the number 144,000 a symbolic number that represents the full and fixed number of all God's children, of all times and places.

This eliminates other views of who these 144,000 are. Some think they are believers from Jewish background only. Then they read the name 'Israel' and of the tribes as referring to the literal, physical Israel. Or they take the number literally and think of a limited spiritual elite of martyrs, separate from the 'great multitude', which John is seeing in v.9.

But in the New Testament the name 'Israel' is used more often for the whole church of Jesus Christ. God's New Testament church continues to be built on the old foundation that was laid in the Old Testament history of God's covenant with Abraham and Israel. And as the New Testament church grows and expands, God fulfills the many promises in the words of the Old Testament prophets.

In the same way, the roll call in the v.5 – 8 tells us that God's old promises of the reunion of the twelve tribes, as you find it in the prophecies of Isaiah and Ezekiel, are fulfilled in the church of Jesus Christ. All of God's believers are sealed and accounted for. Christ finishes his gathering project and reaches its fixed number. God's people are complete. They will not perish in the judgement but stand on the day of God's wrath.

The church is sealed to survive the tribulation

TOO MANY TO COUNT

Then, when John looks, he sees something different from what he just heard. He sees a huge crowd, *a great multitude that no one could number*. This is the outward reality. The complete Israel of God, symbolized by the fixed number 144,000, includes all who follow Jesus Christ from all over the entire world. God knows them all, but for us there are just too many to count.

This is not a picture of the Christian church John was familiar with in the time that this book was written. No, in his vision the apostle sees the complete fulfilment of God's promise to Abraham, when in Genesis 15:5 the LORD took Abraham outside, and said, *Look toward heaven and number the stars – if indeed you are able to number them. So shall your offspring be.* That must have been awesome to behold.

I want to emphasize again that this is the same group as the 144,000 in v.4. They are identical but seen from a different perspective. The different things John hears and sees complement each other. We have seen the same in Rev. 5: John hears 'lion' (v.5), but he sees 'a lamb' (v.6). Here we see the amazing magnitude of the final results when God gathers and seals the fixed number we have heard.

They come from *every nation, from all tribes and peoples and languages*. In other words, the total sum of all believers from all over the globe is incredibly multi-cultural. Every ethnic, cultural, and linguistic group or category in the world is present in the church. An astonishingly numerous people of God is being prepared for its final destination, a new earth.

How significant is the Christian church nowadays? Sure – worldwide Christians are still the largest religious group. But how optimistic are we about its future, especially in the West? However, the final result of all mission and evangelism, all church-planting and discipling is breath-taking. It blows you away, this glorious vision of the church as it shall dwell forever in the immediate presence of God and of his throne.

Indeed, in contrast to those who try to hide in caves and under rocks on the day of God's wrath, these Christians will *stand before the throne of God and before the Lamb*.

13 • Revelation 7-8:5

As mentioned earlier, the terrified question in Rev. 6:17, "who can stand?" sounds rhetorical. "Of course, no one can. It's just not possible!"

But here is the surprise: a huge crowd of people, standing before the throne of God. Who can stand before the almighty God? Who can face him on the day of his wrath, without being terrified? The church can. Yes, sealed on your forehead by the Holy Spirit, you will find yourself among the great multitude that by God's grace can and will survive the tribulation AND the last judgment.

How is that possible? Look! They are all *clothed in white robes and with palm branches in their hands*. We have seen those white robes before, as a display of purity and righteousness, as well as a sign of victory.

And the 'palm branches' indicate what kind of victory this is. John 12:13 is the only other time in the New Testament that we see 'palm branches' in people's hands. That is during Jesus' festive entry into Jerusalem.

In other words, the great multitude is celebrating the victory of Jesus Chris. It is his sacrifice on the cross that makes all this possible. That is also why they glorify and praise God for his wonderful deliverance...... *crying out with a loud voice* (v.10). Here is another 'loud voice'. It gets pretty noisy again.

Quite often folks from different tribes and nations that speak different languages do not trust each other and cannot get along in this world. But that is going to be different in the church. We all learn to sing in unity and harmony about our gracious salvation from sin and Satan. *Salvation belongs to our God, who sits on the throne, and to the Lamb*! Praise God as you follow the Lamb. He protects and guides you as he leads you on the new exodus, into the new Promised Land. In his grace he will safely steer you through trials and dangers.

Then all the heavenly throne-attendants we have seen in Rev. 4 & 5 join in. They are ready to worship the Holy God when they see and hear the exuberant praise of this magnificent mega church-choir. Two 'amens' in v.12 bracket a powerful six-fold glorification of the holy God. They affirm the praise of the church (v.10) for bringing the complete number of his children safely home.

Then one of the elders comes up to John with a few questions. "Tell me", he says, "this crowd that you see here, *who are they and from where have they come*?" That is not because he does not know. He is going to answer his own questions. But engaging John in this dialogue is a teaching-tool to have John focus his attention on the very heart of what is happening.

The elder then identifies this huge multitude as people *who are coming out of the great tribulation*. There are a variety of views on this 'great tribulation'. Many think of it as a final period of severe persecution, shortly before Jesus' second coming. But it is not only a future reality. The whole period of the last days, that begins with Jesus' first coming, and will continue until his return, is a time of various trials for God's people. First here, then there, believers of all times and places are faced with oppression.

God's children do not escape this tribulation, but they will pass through it, come out of it, and survive. And this comfort, this encouragement is not only for later. No, it was for God's children in the past and it is also for God's children that suffer today. In the midst of the reality of the great tribulation today, Jesus Christ encourages us by showing us the reality from his perspective, from above.

So, then, how did they survive? And how do we survive today? *They have washed their robes and made them white in the blood of the Lamb*. This is powerful symbolism. Having your sin-stained robes bleached in the blood of Christ symbolizes your freedom from sin and guilt. God's grace in Jesus' sacrifice will get you undamaged through whatever tribulation comes your way.

Christ won the victory. Believe in him, follow him, and share in his victory. Then one day you will find yourself standing before the throne of God and in front of the Lamb. Then look around and all that you will see is this great multitude that no one can count.

And, as the elder outlines, the future of this great multitude is bright. Those who place their confidence in Christ will worship before God's throne and in his temple day and night. You will enjoy uninterrupted fellowship with the holy and almighty God. He will shelter his people so that the dangers of your journey through this world will no longer threaten you (v.16). He will

13 • REVELATION 7-8:5

bring his children home, all of them, no matter how difficult the road is. Just follow the Lamb as your shepherd.

The last verses of Rev. 7, v.15–17 reflect already the new reality of your final destination, the new earth, as it is more fully pictured in Rev. 21. Under the caring love and guidance of the Lamb, life will be good, happy, prosperous, full of grace and peace. And no more tears, ever again!

What a contrast with the chaos at the end of Rev. 6.

This would be a wonderful, comforting and encouraging way to end this vision.

But we have one question left.

PRAYING FOR JUDGMENT

What about the last, the seventh seal? John is still waiting. And so are we. Waiting to get the full picture of what is written in the scroll. Just when, at the end of Rev. 6, the end seems to be around the corner, the pace slows down. As readers and listeners, we all get the opportunity to catch our breath.

But then there is the seventh seal. Suddenly, without warning, the pace accelerates again. Are we now ready for the climax of Jesus' second coming?

When the Lamb opens the seventh seal, expectations run high. This is the last one! Is this the climax? Will this be the deathblow, the final knock-out? The reader and listener are kept on edge. Is this the end?

But no, the seventh seal does not usher in the final judgment. As a matter of fact – nothing is happening. It seems like an anti-climax.

We read in Rev. 8:1 that *there was silence in heaven for about half an hour*. That is a remarkable pause in this fast-moving and noisy book. Again, one can find multiple explanations as to the meaning of this half an hour of silence, this dramatic pause in the march towards the end, which seems so close now. It is a matter of concentrating all the attention on what is coming.

Heaven is holding its breath. The united choirs fall silent. Filled with awe, everyone is waiting for what God is going to do.

During this suspenseful half hour John sees *the seven angels who stand before God*. The word "the" suggests that this is a particular group. In Luke 1:19 the archangel Gabriel says about himself that he "stands in the presence of God". So, perhaps we are seeing an identifiable group of seven archangels. *They were given seven trumpets*.

So, somehow the opening of the seventh seal marks the beginning of another series of seven. There is more to come. Tension is mounting and it heightens our anticipation of what will be next. However, the angels do not sound their trumpets, at least not right away. Everything remains silent. Something is holding them up. But what is it?

Then John sees another angel come forward to stand at the altar in heaven. We have seen this altar before (Rev. 6:9). This angel has *a golden censer*. That is a small shovel to carry burning incense. This was also part of the temple worship in the Old Testament. Apparently this angel is going to offer a lot of incense. This is a symbol of Christ's intercession, together *with the prayers of all the saints*.

In other words, the prayers of the church, of the martyrs, of the 144,000, of those being gathered to join the great multitude – and all this in one package – mixed with the ongoing intercession of Jesus Christ, reaches God on his holy throne.

And the silence continues. Everyone is watching. What is God going to do with it? Does he hear our prayers? When martyrs are tortured for their faith, they pray, but nothing seems to happen.[4] We can struggle with the apparent silence of God when we pray. And let us not even talk about the idea that our prayers could actually affect and influence the world in which we live and what is going on in this world.

And yet, despite all of this, God does hear. The prayers of his suffering and persecuted children will not go unheard or unanswered. How do you know?

---

4 In his 1966 novel *Silence* the Japanese author Shusako Endo confronts us masterfully with this theme.

Look what happens. As the silence becomes almost unbearable, the angel fills his censer with fire from the altar *and throws it on the earth*. God responds by sending his judgments on the earth. It is true, God's judgments are executed according to his own plan and instruction. But he gives the prayers of his believers an important role to play when it comes to triggering those judgments.

And then the silence breaks. With a sudden loud, ear-splitting noise. Here is God's response to the prayers of his church. *There came peals of thunder, rumblings, flashes of lightning and an earthquake*. When you compare with the similar sound-and-light show in Rev. 4:5, you will notice that "an earthquake" is added to the terror. Something new is happening. As he responds to the praying voices of his children, the holy God is coming down in judgment, to destroy all evil, injustice, and wickedness.

Today the church that is sealed to survive must also be a praying church. Are we? Do we pray persistently for justice and righteousness? Do we pray unceasingly for the freedom and liberation of God's people? Do we pray for Jesus' return and the coming of God's kingdom?

14

REVELATION 8: 6 – 13

GOD'S JUDGMENTS CONTINUE TO UNFOLD – ROUND 2

In February 2013 a large meteorite, weighing about ten tonnes entered the earth's atmosphere in Russia with a speed of about twenty kilometres per second and exploded. About eleven hundred people were injured. Some folks in the area thought that this was the end of the world.

But this was not the biggest meteorite ever. In 1908 a huge one came down in Siberia with an impact of incredible magnitude. The sound of an enormous explosion was heard thousands of kilometres away. And where this meteorite struck the earth, a pillar of fire rose to an estimated height of about twenty kilometres.

Throughout western Siberia and Europe, the meteoric dust in the atmosphere turned the daylight into a dim, reddish dusk for awhile. In a circle of about ninety kilometres all the forest was levelled to the ground, and in a circle of about twenty kilometres everything was entirely burned up. Now this really sounds like something from Revelation 8, does it not?

In fact – it is something from Revelation 8.

Dramatic things are happening when the Lamb opens the seventh seal. No, not right away. Seven trumpets are given to seven angels in 8:2. But they are going to sound only after what happens in 8:4, 5. We have looked at this in the previous chapter. These trumpet blasts are going to be God's response to the prayers of his children for Jesus' return.

But now all is ready for the next round of God's judgments, to be announced by these angels, as they sound their trumpets. That these judgments are unfolding after the trumpet blasts shows that there is still opportunity to repent.

So, yes, these trumpets set in motion seven judgments. You and I generally see trumpets as musical instruments. But they are also used, and in the Bible most of the time, to announce special events or to start a battle. Here, in Revelation 8 – as for instance in Joshua 6 – the trumpets sound alarm. They warn of imminent dangers. You could compare it to the sirens that are used for alarming people in cities, urging them to find shelter during air raids in modern warfare.

In our text, the glorified Christ is warning the world. God's judgments are unfolding. We have seen the first round in Revelation 6. Now it continues. Time and again in the history of our world the sirens are sounding. Is anybody listening?

Alarming Trumpets

As mentioned, the opening of the seventh seal in Rev. 8:1 introduces the seven angels who are getting ready to sound the seven trumpets. Now, in 8:6–13 we will only listen to the first four of those trumpets. That has a practical reason: all together it is a bit much for one chapter to look at Revelation 8 and 9, and these four trumpets will give us enough to think about for now.

But it also makes sense on a different level. It is clear that these first four trumpets belong together. They are of a somewhat different nature than the other three.

God's judgements continue to unfold – round 2

You can actually see the same when you look at the seven seals. You may remember from Rev. 6 that breaking the first four seals describes the four horses and their powers.

In this passage, 8:6–13, you can see something similar when you look at the effect of these four trumpets. They all trigger disasters, harmful calamities that have a major impact on all life, including human life, on this earth.

You could call those events "natural disasters". That is indeed what they often look like. And that is what people think they are. They will always try to find natural, scientific explanations when terrible things are wreaking havoc on this earth. And quite often scientists can do that. But remember, this is the limited view from here below, which is not able to detect what's behind it.

However, John's vision will show us the view from above, the view from where the Almighty God rules from his heavenly throne. And then we learn that in fact there is nothing natural about these frightening events. The Holy God is unfolding his judgments over this world.

Of course, the effects of the first four trumpets are not identical. They affect the earth and all life on earth in four different areas: the earth, the sea, drinking water, and the sky. But what sets them apart from the fifth and the sixth trumpet (the seventh has its own unique character again, just as the seventh seal had) is the different kind of harm, and the different target for the harm that is being caused (see Rev. 9).

What we find in 8: 6–13 is about physical harm and destruction that affects all human life in this world. Although the judgments of God's wrath are aimed at the godless and the wicked, here they affect the life of believers and unbelievers alike. God's alarming trumpets are warning all of us in this world.

When we listen to the angels sounding these trumpets, the intensity and also the speed with which all this is unfolding is overwhelming. Imagine standing there and seeing all these things. It is just breathtaking and again, so loud! The sounds are ear-splitting, deafening. You can imagine that John would hardly know where to look first, and then there is something else. Everything seems to be happening at the same time, everywhere.

When John hears the first angel sounding his trumpet, the effect is dramatic and, just as with the other trumpets, the impact is felt worldwide. *There followed hail and fire mixed with blood...* a terribly destructive mixture of hailstorms and thunderstorms with lightning flashing all over, is attacking the earth.

In connection with this passage from Revelation 8, it might be helpful to read parts from Exodus 7, 9 and 10. John describes these judgments in language that reminds us of the some of the plagues in Egypt. But now it is something that happens on a much larger, global scale. And the impact is much wider, of course. What is happening after the first trumpet recalls the seventh plague in Egypt (Exodus 9:13-25).

That all this hail and fire is mixed with blood emphasizes the horrible character of what is going on. "Blood" could indicate that there will be a large number of victims of this disaster. It could also refer to the blood-red sky that is the result of the huge razing fires, when one-third of the earth goes up in flames. Such an enormous area. It is hard to imagine! Have you ever driven through an area recently affected by forest fires? Have you ever seen pictures of a landscape wrecked, blackened, and scarred by those fires, thousands of hectares sometimes?

John points out that all this hail and terrifying lightning *was thrown down upon the earth*. You will find similar expressions in what it says about the other trumpets. And it all shows that what is happening is controlled from heaven. The Almighty God on the throne in heaven is once more the "hidden actor", so to speak, in this unfolding drama of God's judgments. Something we only recognize because John's visions show us the view from above. Christ had called him, remember: *Come up here, and I will show you what must take place after this* (Revelation 4:1).

The consequences of these ongoing frightening hail and thunderstorms are horrible and disastrous; one-third *of the earth was burned up, as well as one-third of all the trees and of all the green grass.*

This ratio, one-third, is a verbal thread throughout this passage. It is used twelve times in chapter 8, and its frequent use heightens the tension. It is no longer one-quarter that is affected, as in round one, when the seals were opened (Rev. 6:8). Now it is one-third. What is next? It gives a feeling of urgency. Two-thirds are not affected, and so there is still room to repent, but the total destruction is coming closer, and time is running out.

When all this greenery, all these agricultural products, the fruit, the herbs, vegetables, and you name it, when all these things are consumed by the roaring flames, God's judgment destroys a considerable part of the world's food supply. But it also talks about *the green grass,* the essential food for sheep and cattle. And those things affect all of us because we all live off the land.

But while all this is going on, there is already the warning sound of the second trumpet. And look what is coming. It is gigantic! It is really big! John sees something so immense, he is looking for an adequate image to describe it. It was *something like a great mountain, burning with fire,* he says. It is not a mountain, but it is "something like it". An enormous, a huge ball of fire, *thrown into the sea.*

This monstrous colossus hits the sea with an enormous bang and splash, and given the size, you can imagine the terrible consequences: huge flooding and destructive tsunamis everywhere. The terror of God's judgment is felt on the sea, but also by all the coastlands, and the people that live there.

We hear again the ratio one-third, *a third of the sea became blood.* It reminds us of the first plague in Egypt (Exodus 7:14-21). Here it can be the blood of the victims that colours the water. History tells about naval battles that killed so many, that for miles around, the sea was red because of the blood.

And one-third *of the living creatures in the sea died.* Everywhere there are dead fish, dead whales and all kinds of sea creatures. And then it also destroyed *one-third of the ships,* which includes, of course, crewmembers, passengers, cargo... All gone! And through all this God's judgment does severe damage to all international trade.

Nevertheless, two-thirds of the ships remain sea-worthy. And so, this trumpet blast is again an urgent warning to repent and turn to the living God. Throughout the centuries such maritime disasters always have this warning character. Every sailor can tell you that the power of the sea in turmoil is awe-inspiring.

But there is not much time to think. The next trumpet is sounding already. It is number three. Yes, the disasters come quickly, one after the other. The food has been affected already, now it is going to be the fresh water, the rivers and springs, the sources of drinking water for people and animals.

John sees *a great star, blazing like a torch, falling from heaven.* A star is supposed to be high in the sky. Could it be a comet? Or a meteorite? Or an asteroid? Have you seen the YouTube videos of what happened in Russia on February 15, 2013?

Well, whatever the exact identity of the burning projectile John sees dropping from above, it is like a nuclear missile from heaven, bombing *one-third of the rivers and all the springs of water.*

Indeed, God himself is acting again. His judgment moves the universe out of joint and shakes what seems like immovable structures. It is utterly devastating and ruins a large portion of the supply of drinking water. Clear drinking water sustains life and health on earth. When that is lacking life becomes difficult. Polluted, contaminated water causes sickness, diseases and sometimes death.

Well, that is exactly what happens, says John. He emphasizes how serious this impact is, by telling us that the name of this great star is *Wormwood*. That is the name of a shrub with a bitter taste. This is symbolic for the effect: *one-third of the waters became wormwood.* It means that the water turned bitter. It has an awful taste and becomes undrinkable, useless. And many people who do drink it, are dying from it.

And while all these judgments are rapidly unfolding, the fourth angel sounds his trumpet. The terrifying turmoil continues, scarier than ever. It becomes dark, not pitch-dark, as in the ninth plague in Egypt (Exodus 10:21-23), but God's judgment is dimming the lights on earth on a global scale! *One-third of the sun was struck, and one-third of the moon and the stars.* And this affects one-third of the light during the day and during the night.

Just as food and water, so also light is needed to make life flourish on earth. This gloomy darkening of the atmosphere is sinister and frightening. It is an evil omen that makes people feel uncomfortable. When the lights in the sky fail, you know you can expect catastrophic events with cosmic dimensions.

And yet, the failure of the light is still partial. The urgent call to repent remains. The Holy God employs his judgments to throw heaven and earth into chaos. In doing so he issues his warnings for this world that is heading for Jesus' second coming.

WARNED PEOPLE

What do we do with the loud warnings of these sounding trumpets? It is incredibly loud and impressive alright. But is anybody listening? And if there are people out there who are listening, is there anybody in this world who does something with it and takes these warnings to heart?

We have to admit that we do not necessarily understand everything and every detail of this overwhelming mass of visions. It can get puzzling and confusing when the dramatic events keep piling up, when God's judgments are rapidly unfolding, one after the other with no break.

Throughout the centuries people have often tried to identify specific political, economic, or military events in the time in which they lived, as the specific fulfilments of some of these visions. But that becomes very arbitrary, especially when people try to find out how what we have experienced was announced by this or that trumpet. Or when they try to calculate where we are today on the scale of judgments. But then, perhaps everything is still to come.

Let us watch out for speculation. When people get carried away by their imagination, you can get pretty bizarre interpretations.

However, that does not mean that we can do nothing with it. That does not mean that it does not refer to our reality in the world in which we live. On the contrary. Revelation does reflect our world, our reality, also the reality we see and experience today. This tells us already that God's judgments in the events of this passage cannot be restricted to a short time, just before the end of the world.

No, John pictures events that look like 'natural disasters'. More than that, God shows those to him, as cosmic calamities on a huge, worldwide scale. He does this to show that the fulfilment of these things cannot be boxed in, in one single and separate event.

The point is that these unfolding judgments will be fulfilled in a series of happenings that will occur again and again throughout this dispensation.

We all know that throughout the ages all these things have ravaged our world. And they still do - devastating hailstorms and hurricanes; threatening thunderstorms and wild-fires that are out of control; crops failing because of flooding or drought; devastating earthquakes, volcanic eruptions, and tsunamis; people starving to death or dying from disease or from drinking contaminated water.

The world has been, is and will always be full of these things. But do not shrug your shoulders. Do not say, "that's just natural misery; what else? It's terrible if you're in the middle of it, but what can you do about it?"

Do not let the view from below fool you. We live in 'the last days' of a world that more and more turns its back on God. Such a world becomes increasingly dark. And therefore, in the final stage of our history – the time between Jesus first and second coming – God's judgments are unfolding any time on any part of the globe.

That is threatening. It is also a warning. All these disasters indicate how God is going to obstruct and break down life on earth to punish the godless and the wicked. When he affects life on earth in such a destructive manner, the living God lets the world know that he is on his way to the day that all the walls will crumble, and the whole world will face his judgment and be brought to its knees.

Is the intensity of God's judgments increasing as time goes on? Will it get worse closer to the end? Perhaps, although those things are hard to measure. But even if that would be so, you can never put it on a scale with dates attached to it!

And yet, when one angel after the other comes forward to sound his trumpet, it does add a tone of increasing urgency. Many people think they will eventually be able to control what is going on in this world. They think they will be able to prevent what they call "natural disasters", or to eradicate diseases, or to control climate-change.

They will not. To be sure, to some extent they may be successful here or there. Science and technology are not without progress. But because of

God's unfolding judgments, controlled from heaven, the situation in this world will never be stable and harmonious – never! This is the world we live in today.

But with these judgments God is also constantly urging people to repent. Do we recognize his serious warnings? Do we live as warned people when we hear his trumpets and see the impact in our world? Are we willing to see, in everything, God's hand? Are we willing to alert others to see this, to show them the view from above? And do we urge them to repent and turn to Jesus Christ?

Our history, including the disasters, pandemics and other calamities that shake up our lives, is all the work of the Almighty God. These things are not just random events, or accidents. They are God's judgments. That is a hard sell nowadays. People do not want to hear that a tsunami or an earthquake or a drought comes as God's judgment and warning. And this includes many Christians.

"How can you say that God has a hand in these terrible things," they say. "So many good people are innocent victims of those disasters. How can a God who is love allow such things to happen?" Some people get upset. "This is so hurtful and judgmental," they say. "You add insult to injury when you tell the poor folks who are already suffering, that they suffer because of God's judgment."

But the point is not that God picks on certain individuals or on particular groups or categories of people. What ever happens throughout the world, it is all part of God's judgments with cosmic dimensions. But the view from here below fails to recognize this.

Mankind lives as if they control life and do not need God. But time and again the Lord reminds us in a drastic manner that he alone is God. He keeps reminding us that it is not safe to ignore him. Holy, holy, holy is his Name!

We have seen the remarkable parallels with some of the plagues in Egypt. The only true God beats up and knocks down the Egyptian gods. Why does he do that? So that people would acknowledge him and obey him. Well, here the same happens on a global scale. The only true God beats up and knocks down all man-made gods today, with the urgent call to repent and discover his love and grace in Jesus Christ.

The fact that only one-third is being destroyed, means that two-thirds is still functioning in the last days. Life is still possible. Repentance remains possible. God's trumpet blasts are clear warning signals that should strike terror in human hearts so that people may turn to Jesus Christ and find salvation and hope.

What about us? Do we hear the sound of the trumpets, calling us out of complacency and self-confidence? What about our future and the future of our children in this frightening world, groaning under God's unfolding judgments?

Let us go back for a moment to the time that Israel was in Egypt. Remember the ultimate purpose of those horrible plagues that terrorized the Egyptians (Exodus 6 – 11): liberation and freedom, freedom from slavery for God's children.

The same is true here. These trumpet blasts trigger devastating judgments. But they are at the same time the prelude to God's deliverance. The liberation of God's people is coming. He will lead his church out of the darkness of suffering and persecution, to the new Promised Land, the New Jerusalem.

Yes, just as the Israelites in Egypt, God's children today suffer from many of the same judgments as anybody else in this world. We live in this world and we are reminded that salvation is by grace alone. All we can do is trust in God's good plan. But the forecast is great. We are heading for the grand feast of Jesus' return.

In 1 Thessalonians 4 and 1 Corinthians 15 we read that one day we will hear again a loud trumpet blast. But then it will no longer be an alarming sound. Then it will be the festive announcement of the resurrection of the dead and the grandiose new beginning. Death and destruction will not have the final say, but the last word is for him who says: *I am making everything new...!*

A CALLING EAGLE

It is good to keep this hopeful perspective in the midst of all the upheaval we read about in this chapter because it is not over yet. After the fourth trumpet has sounded it is actually quiet for a moment, and so the reader or listener can relax a bit.

But the respite is very short.

In John's vision a flying eagle appears, which briefly interrupts the trumpet blasts. It could be a reference to one of the living creatures around God's throne. Remember that the fourth one was *like a flying eagle* (Rev. 4:7). In this way we can know that here we have a direct messenger from the Holy God himself.

A golden eagle is one of the largest, most impressive, and majestic birds, when it soars overhead, high up in the sky, *directly overhead*, it says. This means also that this bird can be seen and heard everywhere.

John hears this eagle crying out with a screeching, terrifying loud voice: *Woe! Woe! Woe to those who dwell on the earth.....!*

In the Bible the word "woe" is a typical introduction to ask attention for a serious prophetic message. The prophet Amos uses it in 5:18 and 6:1. And Jesus uses it in Matthew 23:13–36, *Woe to you, Scribes and Pharisees*. In the words of the eagle, the last three trumpet blasts that are still to come, are grouped together as "three woes". That sounds pretty threatening, scary even.

Here again we have an urgent, three-fold warning for the calamities that are still approaching. But there is one significant difference. The frightening disasters that follow the three trumpet blasts still to come, are targeting in particular, *those who dwell on the earth*. Now, of course, we all dwell on the earth. But in Revelation this expression always refers to the unbelievers, God's godless enemies. Think of the cry of the souls of the martyrs under the altar in Rev. 6:10.

This is also confirmed in Rev. 9:4, where we hear that the coming terror, whatever it is going to look like, will only affect *those people who do not have the seal of God on their foreheads* (see also Rev. 7:4-8; 14:1).

So yes, three more trumpets to go. And what is to come will be worse than what has happened so far. This three-fold 'woe' makes you shiver because of the doom and gloom that is coming over a decaying humanity in a rebellious world. How dreadful will it be to fall into the hands of the living God, who is a consuming fire.

But in the end, both God's children and God's enemies, all will see the great glory of the Holy and Almighty God, when he has reached the ultimate goal of all his judgments.

And everyone will acknowledge, either with joy in Jesus Christ, or with gnashing teeth and filled with hatred that the Lord is just and gracious and therefore worthy of all praise.

15

Revelation 9

THE REAL HELL'S ANGELS ARE COMING

Some Christians do not like the Book of Revelation. That has been the case throughout the history of the church. Martin Luther did not care too much about it. And it is the only book in the Bible John Calvin never wrote a commentary on.

One of the problems many people have with Revelation, is that there is so much violence in this book. Today, there is much discussion going on about the violence found in Scripture. It is often focussed on some of the graphic descriptions of violence in the Old Testament, but the book of Revelation is also under attack.

What ought we to think of this? It is true that we read about armies, war-horses, aggressive beasts, battles, and people getting killed. But Revelation does not give many graphic descriptions or bloody details.

And there is something else. You can criticize Revelation and other Bible passages because of all the violence. But what about the high demand in our society for movies with a lot of aggressive violence? Or the popularity of many violent video-games? It seems that violence is part of our culture. It is present in the world in which we live, and it always has been, whether we like it or not.

15 • REVELATION 9

In that sense Revelation is a realistic book. It describes the history of our world. This history is filled with cruelty and brutal violence. It is, therefore, no wonder that to a certain extent Revelation reflects this violent picture.

This does not mean that Revelation glorifies violence. But the Kingdom of God can only come when God's enemies are gone. That is why God warns them. But they will not go voluntarily. And he will not let the wicked get away with their evil. That is not a matter of meaningless violence. That is a matter of just judgments.

When we read Rev. 9 we feel how dark and threatening God's judgments are becoming. On his way to the end of the world God uses two more trumpet blasts to unleash powers from hell to call all nations and all people to come to their senses.

THEY POISON HUMAN MINDS

Recall, that we are still looking at John's vision of the seven angels sounding seven trumpets. We heard the first four already, and now we will listen to the next two. The difference is that the emphasis here is on devilish activities. As a matter of fact, it is the first time we hear that God is using devilish powers for his purpose, to carry out his judgments.

When the fifth angel sounds his trumpet, the vision becomes freaky. So far everything we have seen took place in heaven and on earth. But now for the first time the "Abyss", or "bottomless pit" is also involved.

John sees a star *that had fallen from the sky or from heaven to earth*. What is this 'star'? Or who is it? Is it Satan? The Bible tells us that the Devil rebelled against God and lost his position (2 Peter 2:4; Jude 6). In Rev. 12:9 we read about him as the 'great dragon' or 'ancient serpent', who *was thrown down to the earth*. Is there perhaps a connection with what Jesus says in Luke 10:18, that he *saw Satan fall like lightning from heaven*? Or is it just an unknown evil angel? Here again opinions differ.

We then hear that this star *is given the key to the shaft of the bottomless pit*. The word is also translated as *Abyss*. It refers to the place where evil spirits, demons, devils, even Satan himself, are dwelling. In Luke 8:31 many demons beg Jesus *not to command them to go into the Abyss*. In line with Revelation 20:1-3 we can say that the "Abyss" is hell before God's final judgment. Here Satan's henchmen are awaiting trial.

In this vision it is pictured as some place under the earth, somewhere deep down, from where the surface of the earth can be reached via a shaft. But do not go look for it. It is a vision. Words like "underworld", or "underground" do not suggest that you can literally find it somewhere underneath here. It is the opposite of above, of heaven. That means it is as far away from God's throne room as one can go.

However, that does not mean that God has nothing to do with this. The opposite is true. We hear that "the key was given." And that "the locusts were given power." And that "they were told." God does that. In other words: these demonic powers only operate within God's plan and under God's control.

It is comforting to know in this brutal world that the One who sits on the throne in heaven rules. And that even devils and demons can do nothing without the Almighty God allowing it. We think sometimes that evil rules, and we wonder why God does not put an end to it. Do not worry, he will! Evil does a lot of damage, but God uses even the work of Satan as his judgment and as warning for the wicked.

So, yes, the "key to the shaft of the Abyss" symbolizes the authority to let the demons out. And when that happens, the 'underworld', so to speak, wanders into this world with the purpose to torture and to kill. That sounds pretty frightening. And it is! But remember, it is only possible with God's permission.

As the history of our world unfolds and comes to completion, devils are let loose on the earth. And they are going everywhere. Satan fills the world with demons and evil influences. The inspiration from hell is spreading and being felt all over.

This is visible in John's vision, when after the opening of the shaft, black, dense clouds of filthy, stinking smoke billow upward and spread over the earth. The smoke and evil fumes are penetrating everywhere. It becomes a layer of smog that darkens the sun and the sky. Air pollution at its worst.

15 • Revelation 9

This depressing picture of gloom and doom symbolizes how the forces of evil fill our human world with the smoke of deception and delusion. Smokescreens everywhere. When people are led to believe whatever they want, except the Word of the Living God, spiritual darkness creeps in and the result is moral confusion. Satan is clever enough to work in a very subtle way, but it is penetrating everywhere in human society. If you have ever read C.S. Lewis' "Screwtape Letters" you know what I mean.

But there is more. Out of the dark smoke John sees a huge swarm of locusts coming down on the earth. In Northern Africa, Arabia, and the Middle East desert locusts are a real terror for the farmers. A locust plague is totally destructive. They devour all the green vegetation, strip the land bare, and cause a devastation you can only comprehend if you have seen it.

Think of the 8th plague in Egypt (Exodus 10:12-20). And that one was only affecting the land of Egypt. This is happening on a global scale. The prophet Joel also gives a graphic description of the impact of an enormous swarm of locusts (Joel 2:1-11).

But what we see here in Revelation 9 goes way beyond this. For these are not normal locusts. These are hellish locusts. Remember where they come from. In addition, normal locusts are voracious eaters of grass and greenery, but these are not. The demons from the world below appear in this world in the monstrous forms of locusts, armed with the weapons of scorpions, the silent killers of the desert.

Here is a horrific army of evil spirits, who were told to leave the green grass and plants alone, and to focus on torturing people. But not all the people. The attack targets God's enemies, the people who do not belong to Jesus Christ. As it says here, *only those people who do not have the seal of God on their foreheads*, referencing back to Rev. 7.

When John goes on to describe these locusts, we get a terrifying picture. It is hard to describe exactly what demonic powers look like, and you feel that John is searching for adequate words and images. In v.7-9 he uses a lot of similes: "It was like this…, or something like this…, or it resembled…"

We do not need to over analyse the details of this aggressive army of savage and almost invincible warriors, evil angels ready to attack, bound for victory, and approaching with the thundering sound of horses and chariots. It is a graphic description of an intimidating and frightening spectacle. The real hell's angels are coming!

However, these are not 'purebreds' of the underworld. They also have human features. *Their faces resemble human faces and their hair is like women's hair.* They combine characteristics of the world below and this world. The demons come with a human face. Evil can take many sinister forms, but in the end it has a human face.

We know that the evil things in this world are instigated by Satan and his demons. But evil has a fertile soil in our human nature, which is *so corrupt that we are unable to do any good and inclined to all evil.*[5] This is because in the end all evil in this world is the result of our rebellion against God's will.

So, yes, in these locusts we have some dangerous and frightening attackers. They are also well organized. They have a king. Naturally, locusts do not have a leader, but these ones are led by *the angel of the Abyss*. We cannot really confirm who this is. Satan? It is possible. The same one who in v.1 was described as "the star fallen from heaven"? That is also possible. But we do not know for sure who he was either.

We do know that the name of this king, *Abaddon* or *Apollyon*, means "Destroyer". That tells us that here we have a Dark Lord who is opposing our Lord Jesus Christ, the "Saviour".

So how are they going to do this? How do these locusts attack? V.10 tells us that *they had tails and stings like scorpions, and in their tails they had power to hurt people.* This goes back to v.3 where we read that *they were given power like the power of scorpions*, and to v.5 where *the torment the people suffered was like that of the sting of a scorpion when it stings someone.*

Scorpions are small, nocturnal animals that live in desert-areas. From a few species of scorpions the sting can be deadly. But even if it is not fatal, the poisonous sting of a scorpion causes a burning fever, painful suffering, and terrible agony.

---

5 Heidelberg Catechism, Question & Answer 8.

15 • Revelation 9

This symbolism of a plague of locusts, with scorpion-like features, points at the influential powers of hell that are operating in human hearts and minds. To be stung means to be injected with devilish ideas, theories, and deceptions in your mind. The apostle Paul warns Timothy against *departing from the faith and being devoted to deceitful spirits and teachings of demons* (1 Tim. 4:1).

God allows the powers from below to sting people who do not hold on to the truth of his Word. In other words, he allows the powers of darkness to poison human minds, to confuse human thinking, and to corrupt human society. The demons, the evil spirits on earth, are missionaries from hell, real hell's angels.

This is strong language. When we look around it does not look so bad. In our secular society many decent, well-meaning people live without God, and many of them seem perfectly happy and fine with that. They enjoy life. And quite often their thoughts, ideas, theories, moral views, and things like that, sound clever and reasonable.

But do not be fooled by the view from below. John's vision with the view from above shows the horrible reality. Joy and happiness without God are temporary and not real. People get paranoid about their material wealth, their health, or their looks. The emptiness can only be filled with more and more new stimulus all the time. And in the end, evil will not bring the fun and success people desire and expect, but suffering. And if something terrible happens unexpectedly, something they cannot control, they panic. Without God, life becomes miserable and meaningless.

Only one thing can protect you against this poisonous sting. That is the seal of God on your forehead. This seal is what identifies you as belonging to Jesus Christ and living under his protective care. When he is your Master, you do not have to fear. The seal of God's ownership is able to resist the demonic powers that try to poison your mind. They will not harm you. Repent and find God's grace and reconciliation through Jesus' death on the cross. Seek your life outside of yourself in Jesus Christ, who rose from the dead. Then you carry his seal and Satan will not get you.

If not, the sting of the scorpion-like locust will prove to be self-destructive. God's judgment will give people over to become victims of the demonic powers they have embraced. Then life will deteriorate to the point that people would rather be dead than alive. But that will not help.

And yet, the suffering is not unrestricted. It is only temporary. God sets the boundaries because his goal is repentance. These horrible locusts will be allowed to torture people for a limited time, symbolically indicated as not more than five months. Many will survive and have time to repent.

THEY KILL HUMAN LIVES

Then we hear the sixth angel sounding his trumpet. Now things get even scarier! John hears this anonymous voice coming *from the horns of the golden altar before God*. We have seen this altar before. That was in Rev. 6:9 and 8:3. And again you can find a number of speculations as to who is speaking. We do not know for certain, but one thing becomes clear, whoever's voice it is, what it says has the approval of the One who rules from the throne in heaven.

The voice from the altar instructs the sixth angel to *release the four angels who are bound at the great river Euphrates*. This sets in motion a horrible scene, an unprecedented disaster up until that point in time.

These four angels are not the same as the ones mentioned in Rev. 7:1, who were *standing at the four corners of the earth*. The ones in our text are "angels of wrath" or "angels of death". They are authorized to launch some pretty frightening developments, and they gladly do so. But note again (in v.15) that they can do nothing unless and until God commands it, exactly at his time.

The *great river Euphrates* was far to the east of Israel, and in the Old Testament that was often the direction where the enemies of God's people would come from: the Assyrians and the Babylonians. It is symbolic for the hostilities God's children are facing, because of the great conflict we are all part of in this world.

With the view from above, Revelation shows that there are two major cities in this world. The one is the *Great City of Babylon,* symbol of the evil world, which is hostile to God. In contrast with this, we see the *New City of Jerusalem,* the eternal dwelling place of the Holy God and his people.[6]

In connection with these cities, there are also two major rivers. The Euphrates belongs to Babylon and is associated with bringing death and destruction. In contrast with this, the river of life is flowing from the throne of God down Main Street of the New Jerusalem, to give life to all who live there. In other words, the name "Euphrates" alerts us that we are going to see a glimpse of the horrors that come out of Babylon.

So then, what is happening when these four angels are going at it? Now remember, as we have noted before, what John sees interprets what he hears, or the other way round.

He hears the number of the mounted troops: 200 million. That is an incredibly huge army. But what does he actually see? What John sees in the v.17 and 19 makes clear that this is not just a large human army, but a demonic cavalry. It explains that the number he heard is a symbolic number to emphasize that the evil powers have an enormous endurance, because of their huge reserves. There are always new armies available, ready for battle.

John sees an incalculable number of fearsome creatures, horses and riders that look really weird and frightening, because they have only one purpose, that is to destroy and to kill human lives. John sees a world full of violence!

It is kind of freakish to see how horse and rider blend together and become one bizarre creature. Their breastplates take on the same colours as what comes out of the mouths of the horses: the red of fire, the dark blue of smoke, and the yellow of burning sulphur that is belching forth from the mouths of these creatures, products of the underworld that reflect the suffocating atmosphere of hell.

What adds to our bewilderment is the frightening mix of body-parts. The powerful bodies of war horses have heads like the heads of lions and tails like snakes with aggressive heads. Indeed, these fire-breathing creatures can attack also with their tails.

---

6 See the contrasting descriptions in chapter 17 and 18, versus chapter 21

Different from the locusts we saw before, these bizarre monsters lack all human-like characteristics. They come straight from hell, directly from the Abyss and no one on earth can stop them. The real hell's angels are coming. And the effects are dramatic. These devilish creatures will bring hell to earth, as they go around killing one-third of mankind. This is a horrible picture.

The destructive power of these killing-machines is enormous. But you cannot identify these living beings with flame-throwers in the front and deadly poison-sprayers at the back with particular weapons. They symbolize the terrible war-tools and war-machinery of every description in any time. Today you can think of missiles with nuclear warheads, chemical weapons, or other weapons of mass-destruction.

What we see here represents war. Not one specific war but all wars throughout the centuries. Many wars have been ravaging the world during the history of mankind. For most people 'war' was often a more 'normal' situation than 'peace'. And the number of victims runs in the millions. You only have to think of the two world wars in the 20th century.

Not many people like war, but it's good to remember that, just as all other things, war is also included in God's plan, God's decree. And he can even use 'war' as a warning-voice to call the wicked to turn to him.

Sometimes one has to take up weapons for a just cause, to protect freedom and restrain greater evil. And yet, let us not glorify war. It always comes with much pain, suffering, and horrible misery. So-called "war heroes" will tell you that 'war is hell'. It does terrible things to people. In times of war men can turn into incarnate devils.

What do we do with all this, today? We live in this world, which is filled with never-ending violence. And there is always a war, or a civil war, being fought somewhere in this world, in which people commit horrible and bloody atrocities. But there is still time for repentance. With one-third being killed, two-thirds continues to live.

How do we look at this in the light of the Bible? Here is the answer. In this broken, sinful world, wars are God's judgment on evil people, on wicked mankind. In wars the God who rules from his throne in heaven unleashes hellish powers. That makes wars truly horrifying and the blood of the vic-

15 • REVELATION 9

tims cries out to heaven. But it also makes for serious warnings and very urgent calls to repent.

Is there any good news in this? Yes, there is, even when God's people become victims of terror and bloodshed. The good news is that God is just and righteous as he punishes evil and wickedness, hatred, and meaningless violence.

He comes to establish his kingdom here on earth. Hold on to your Saviour Jesus Christ, and through the dark and dangerous alleys of this world he will lead you to the safety and security of his eternal kingdom. For his kingdom is the kingdom of true justice and true righteousness. He will rule from sea to sea and to the ends of the earth.

THEY HARDEN HUMAN HEARTS

What is the result of all this? Throughout the period of the last days, the final phase of history, the exalted Christ, who rules all things in accordance with God's plan, will again and again inflict disasters as his warnings and calls to repent and be saved.

How do survivors respond to all those warning disasters between Jesus' first and second coming? Do people come around to honour God? These loud trumpet blasts are supposed to awaken stubborn mankind to see its destructive ways, to obey God and to turn to Jesus Christ. That is the purpose. God warns. Is anybody listening? Do we see massive dramatic conversions everywhere?

The big picture is clear: no, it does not happen despite all these warning voices. Sometimes, when terrible things happen, people are shocked, scared, and they panic. But when it is all over, these feelings disappear, and life goes on as if nothing has happened. After the 9/11 disaster (2001) in New York the churches were packed with shocked worshippers. But that lasted only a few weeks.

The rest of mankind did not repent of the work of their hands, says John. The survivors who have experienced these disasters had time to repent. But you can hear how deeply disappointed John is when he concludes that the lure of spiritual promiscuity by trusting in idols, false gods, is much stronger than the threats of God's judgments: torture, plagues, and Satanic monsters of the deep.

Foolish and stubborn, they continue to ignore and resist the living God by turning to powers that cannot do anything, counterfeit, useless and powerless gods. They continue to dismiss God's commands and refuse to serve the one true God. That is going on everywhere. Today, the gods of money, power, sex, sports, hedonism, self, and you name it, may be more popular than the gods of gold, bronze or wood, but it all works the same way.

God's unfolding judgements harden people in their resistance. The plagues, the terror of the real hell's angels do not soften human hearts, but instead, harden them. It is like the reaction of the Pharaoh to the plagues in Egypt. Every time he ignored the urgent call to let the Israelites go, he dug himself a deeper hole.

This is what is happening in our world today. Yes, God's church continues to be gathered. People do repent and follow Jesus Christ. But the big picture, especially in most of the western world, is one of resistance and incredible hardening in evil, despite God's judgments that show his powerful presence in the world.

This means that this world will continue to be a world without peace, a world filled with violence. For this stubborn unwillingness to repent will bring about, via the seventh trumpet, the outpouring of the bowls of God's wrath (Revelation 16), which will lead to the culmination of the final judgment. All this heightens the suspense at this moment in Revelation because it urges us to *wait for the day of God, and so hasten its coming*, as Peter puts it in 2 Peter 3:12.

What does this mean for the church today – for you and me?

First of all, it is comforting. The exodus is coming. Full freedom is on the horizon. We will reach our destination, as with joy we will enter the gates of the New Jerusalem.

Secondly, it is a warning. Yes, also for us! "Do not conform to the world". That is a real danger. The temptation of modern idol-worship, worshipping the works of our hands, is very much alive for us. It is so easy to replace

15 • Revelation 9

worshipping the living God with whatever you think will give you joy, happiness, security, hope, satisfaction, fulfilment. Ancient and modern idols look different, but they have one thing in common. *They cannot see or hear or walk* (v.20). They do nothing!

In the third place, it is also encouraging. With all these horrible judgments that ravage this evil world, we may be inclined to leave the world alone, to hide in safety, waiting for the whole thing to blow up. That is what Jonah tried to do, when in smug self-confidence he was waiting for the destruction of Nineveh (Jonah 4).

However, in this violent and unrepentant world the proclamation of the gospel of Jesus Christ becomes even more urgent.

In this darkening world ruled by evil powers from hell, spreading the gospel of the living God as a God of grace in Jesus Christ is the most pressing issue for the church.

There is still time to repent.

Let the world know that the King is coming.

16

Revelation 10

IN THE LAST DAYS THE GOSPEL PROCLAMATION CONTINUES

What have we seen so far of John's vision? In Rev. 4 the apostle John was invited to enter the heavenly throne-hall. Here the Almighty God rules in majesty and glory. Then he saw the glorified Christ, the Lamb that was slain, who takes a scroll, sealed with seven seals. Christ alone is worthy to open the scroll and break the seals, to activate God's plan of salvation (Rev. 5).

Then we witnessed what happened when the Lamb opened the seals. But you will remember that in Rev. 7 the pace of events slowed down after the sixth seal had been opened. There was an interlude, a pause, between the sixth and the seventh seal. In the midst of frightening judgments, the Lord comforts us with the vision of the 144,000, God's sealed and protected children, the great multitude no one can count.

After that the seventh seal brings in seven trumpets. And then the speed picks up again with a new series of dramatic and terrible judgments, the one after the other. That is in Rev. 8 and 9. And what was the result after the sixth trumpet? We read at the end of Rev. 9 that *the rest of mankind did not repent of the work of their hands, their idolatry, murders, and sexual immorality.* And then what?

Well, in Rev. 10 we find that the frantic pace slows down again. There is another interlude, a pause in the events, this time between the sixth and seventh trumpets. Again, the Holy and Almighty God takes the time to encourage his church not to give up, not to be discouraged, but to keep doing what the church is called to do, proclaim the gospel. The world needs to know that God's plan will be completed.

A TRUSTWORTHY MESSAGE

Just when the end seems to be around the corner, just when we get ready for the seventh trumpet to sound, bracing ourselves for something worse than the locust-scorpions and the other terrible creatures we came across in Rev. 9, just then, John's vision pauses. The exalted Christ takes a moment to empower and re-assure John, and us today, for the future in this dark, desperate, and broken world of the last days.

For that purpose, John sees *another mighty angel coming down from heaven*. We see lots of angels in Revelation. But here we see the second one, of only three, that are called "mighty angels". At crucial moments in the story these angels represent the decisive power of God.

We see and hear the first one in Rev. 5:2, posing with a loud voice the most decisive question: *Who is worthy to break the seals and open the scroll*. The third one appears in Rev. 18:21 with a powerful demonstration of the destruction of the great city of Babylon, which represents the evil antichristian world and culture.

About the second, the one here in this passage, it says that he is *coming from heaven*. That means that this mighty angel comes straight from God. The Holy God himself sends him directly with his message, a message that will be confirmed by an oath. That is how important, how trustworthy, and how urgent it is what God has to say to John and to us. The mission and message of this angel comes with direct divine authority.

You can also see this when you look at the angel. You can see it in his brilliant outward appearance. He is *wrapped in a cloud* and *his legs are like pillars of fire*. I take these two together, because they allude to Exodus 13:21. There we find that the Lord protects Israel when they leave Egypt, by leading them to the Promised Land with a *pillar of cloud by day and a pillar of fire by night.*

With *a rainbow over his head* and *a face like the sun* this angel resembles not only the exalted Jesus Christ (Rev. 1:15,16) but also the Almighty God who rules from his heavenly throne (Rev. 4:3). This is not Jesus Christ himself, but in this angel John sees an awesome reflection of the intense glory, majesty, and faithfulness of the Holy and Almighty God and the glorified Son of God. He is ready to protect and lead his new Israel out of this hostile world into the new Promised Land.

All this makes for an incredibly encouraging picture. Whatever is happening when God's devastating judgments unfold in these last days, our glorious God remains in control. And his encouraging message is a trustworthy message.

When the seventh trumpet will sound, we can expect things to happen that will be more frightening than ever. But before we are going to find out, the majestic and glorious appearance of this angel underlines that his message is God's own message. It is a message that comes with God's authority, a message full of comfort for people who love Jesus. It is a message we can trust.

But how do we know that this angel has a message for us? Well, it says that *he had a little scroll open in his hand.* The picture reminds us of what we read about the prophet Ezekiel (2: 9,10). He is given a scroll, which comes with the instruction to speak God's word to the rebellious Israelites.

When we hear about a scroll here in Rev. 10, we remember the other scroll, from Rev. 5. And then the natural question arises: could there perhaps be a connection between these scrolls? Would the content be similar, or even the same?

When you compare the two, you will find some obvious differences. To begin with, in v.2 John uses the diminutive. He talks about a 'little scroll'. But we should not make too much of this, because later on (in v.8) when he talks about the same thing, he uses the regular word for 'scroll'. Apparently these words are interchangeable here.

A more visible difference is that, in Rev. 5 the scroll was sealed in God's hand, and then given to Jesus Christ, the Lamb, because he was worthy to open the seals. Whereas in this chapter the scroll is open in the hand of an angel, to be given to John, who will be called to proclaim its message.

However, those differences have nothing to do with what is written in this scroll. And so, it makes sense to see here the same scroll with the same content. It is about God's purpose for our world, as it unfolds in our history. It his plan of salvation for his people and the judgments of his wrath for those who resist and hate him, his enemies.

The difference is this: in Rev. 5 we learn how this purpose of God is to be activated, carried out and fulfilled by our Saviour Jesus Christ. Here, we are told how this message is to be proclaimed by John first of all, and then by the church as God's trustworthy message. After all, we are talking about God's purpose for the world, for his whole creation.

This is underlined again by a remarkable detail in this picture. Look at the posture of this mighty angel. He is huge. He is an immense giant.

It says that *he set his right foot on the sea and his left foot on the land*. Now, you and I could stand on a rocky beach, with one foot on a rock and the other in the water, and say the same thing: 'my right foot is in the sea and my left on the land'. That is nothing spectacular. But this is different. Think of the angel planting his left foot on the Canadian prairie and his right foot in the middle of the Atlantic Ocean.

This is unbelievable. As an enormous skyscraper, this mighty angel is towering high above everything, above the whole globe. He is literally dominating all of God's creation. The highest mountains in the world dwarf to nothing in comparison with this mighty angel. That is pretty intimidating. Imagine how John must have felt.

All this is to emphasize the universal significance of the appearance of this angel. And it makes abundantly clear how important his message is for all of creation and everything in it. It is for everyone in this world.

When you think of the gigantic size of this angel, you can also imagine what it sounds like when he opens his mouth to give a loud shout like a roaring lion. A frightening sound, which with supernatural strength, reverberates all around the world. Everyone in heaven and on earth must hear him and his powerful message.

Then something unexpected happens. At least, unexpected for us, the unsuspecting listeners! The angel's roaring shout triggers a loud response. *When he called out, the seven thunders sounded.* "Thunder" is in these verses another aspect that reminds us of the Holy God appearing in great glory and majesty.

Actually, when you think of it, this whole passage is so cram-full of God's power, glory, and majesty. It is everywhere. It is in every detail. It is just amazing! Our God is such an awesome and marvellous God, forever worthy of all honour, praise, and worship. And that is on purpose. For this is how we need to remember the Lord and hold on to him when the world gets dark.

It reminds us of Psalm 29. In this thunderous song thunderclaps are qualified seven times as *the voice of the LORD*. In other words, in these seven thunders of Revelation 10:3 the Holy God himself speaks. Indeed, seven times we hear the majestic voice of God Almighty in all its awe-inspiring power.

There is only one problem. We would love to know what God is saying in his seven-fold message, but we do not get to. Do we have here another seven judgments, like we have them in the seven seals, the seven trumpets, and later, in the seven bowls (Rev.15 and 16)? Perhaps. We just do not know. No one knows.

Well, that's not entirely true. John knows! But he is not supposed to tell us. When he hears God's seven thunders speaking he wants to write it down. That makes sense. After all, in Rev. 1:11 and 19 he had been instructed to write down carefully what he was going to see and hear. And so far he has faithfully done so. But now he is told: "Don't do it! Keep it secret!"

It says that *he hears a voice from heaven.* Could it be the voice of the exalted Christ, or of God himself? In any case, the voice has enough authority to make him stop. *Seal up what the seven thunders have said, and do not write it down,* is the command. John knows more than we do. But he is not allowed to report the message and pass it on to us. On the contrary, he must "seal it all up" so that it will not be accessible.

We do not hear 'why', but the result is that we will never know.

Perhaps it makes you wonder why we still need to hear this. If God does not want to tell us what the seven thunders said, what can we do with the information that these thunders 'just said something'? How helpful is that?

The point is that our God wants to keep us humble. We need to depend on him and trust him. He reminds us that it is okay that we do not know everything. When God works out his plans in the history of our world, there is more going on than we know and understand or comprehend. We will never know all the factors, all the powers, and everything about the principles that are operating in this world.

In God's gospel message to be proclaimed in these last days we hear about seals, trumpets, and bowls and what these things do to establish his kingdom. But as our history moves toward completion, God has also other forces at work we do not know about. And he does not provide detailed predictions of all future events. That does not mean, however, that his message is not trustworthy.

On the contrary, you and I, we can all trust God's Word. That Word does not answer all your questions. God's message does not give you all the details of his plan of salvation. Many aspects of God's strategy to get you safely to the end, he did not disclose. But that is ok. You can trust him who rules creation, also your life, from his throne in heaven. This makes the message of his angel a trustworthy message.

Trust in the Lord. Be confident that he knows everything, and as the journey towards the New Jerusalem continues, he governs everything for your benefit.

An Urgent Message

Having said all this, what is it that makes this mighty angel come down from heaven to present this message to John and to us? What is the urge to ensure that the proclamation of the gospel continues in the last days? Well, we will find out.

As John looks on, this gigantic and glorious angel, still standing on the sea and on the land, raises his right hand to swear an oath by the Almighty God. It is a pretty elaborate formula that he uses in v.6:

He swore by him who lives for ever and ever, who created heaven and what is in it, the earth and what is in it, and the sea and what is in it.

It pictures the Lord abundantly as the eternal and powerful Creator of everything. It stresses that indeed everything, literally all things in heaven, on earth, and in the sea, without any exception, are all made by God.

This implies that he is also the God who controls all of creation and everything in it. And this in turn, shows us that God is also fully aware how his whole creation is suffering because of its bondage to sin and decay. And how his people are suffering and struggling in the increasing darkness of the last days. In Romans 8 Paul talks about "a groaning creation, eagerly waiting for its liberation".

In this swearing of the oath, the angel draws all our attention to the powerful and urgent character of his message. He announces and declares with great emphasis for everyone to hear: *There will be no more delay!* The end is coming soon.

When the prophet Daniel had his vision of the End Times, he asked in Daniel 12: 6, *How long will it be before these astonishing things are fulfilled?* Then a man who shows remarkable similarities to the mighty angel in Revelation 10 (see Daniel 10:5,6), gives him the answer, in the form of an oath, that he will have to wait for a while.

You may also remember how in Revelation 6:10 the souls of the martyrs cry out: *O Sovereign Lord, holy and true, how long before you will judge and avenge our blood on those who dwell on the earth?*

They were also told that they had to wait a little longer.

Well then, the waiting time for all who are looking forward to the end of suffering and injustice is almost over. Here is God's announcement, presented under oath by his mighty angel: "There will be no more delay". Yes, we have come to the end of the time that was indicated to Daniel in Daniel 12:7. It will soon be over!

In Daniel 12:4 and 9 the prophet was told to close up and seal the words of what he had seen and heard *until the time of the end*. Well, in Revelation 22:10, when the apostle John has seen and heard everything, he is told to *not seal up the words of the prophecy of this book, because the time is near*. God's final judgment is about to come. This is the time of the end. The God of heaven and earth is coming to avenge the blood of those who have been killed because of their faith.

That does not mean that God's disastrous judgment is going to be the end of his work. Our God maintains his plan for a new world. That is what he has promised. He will usher in our full salvation, our glorious inheritance. But this also means that God's enemies will feel his wrath. The seventh trumpet will announce the next seven-fold series of God's final judgments, the seven bowls of God's terrible wrath.

So, what is going to happen? *In the days of the trumpet call to be sounded by the seventh angel, the mystery of God will be fulfilled*. It will usher in God's final judgment. The seventh trumpet will lead directly to Jesus' second coming. God's purpose for all of us and each one of us will be accomplished.

Do you feel the excitement? This is our time! The suspense is mounting. God's angel swears an oath that the course of our history is approaching the end. The hour of completion is near. Are you looking forward to that?

The expression "the mystery of God" does not indicate something we know nothing about. But it acknowledges that we can never figure out God's plans on our own. We can only know God's will and plan for us, if and insofar God reveals it to us.

And then we also realize that there is indeed much of God's plan that we do not know. In that way it still remains a 'mystery'.

But we do know what the completion of this 'mystery' is going to look like. This is comforting and encouraging today. But it is also a warning. God will win the victory over all evil. And he will liberate his persecuted and suffering children. *Just as he announced to his servants the prophets*, adds the angel.

In other words, these are things God reveals to us. We know them from his Word, from the Bible. And through these prophetic promises and warnings in the Bible, God keeps calling us to repent and believe his Word. We know the gospel. We know the good news of Jesus Christ. The truth and urgency of this message was again confirmed by this solemn oath of God's mighty angel.

The mystery of God is going to be fulfilled without delay. The clock is ticking. Our time to repent is almost up. This makes John's message for the church, our message here today, and the church's message for the world an urgent message. There is no time to lose. Do not delay. Repent and believe.

God puts the world, the church, you and me personally, on high alert. He is about to wrap up his plan for our history. The powerful oath of the angel heightens our anticipation of what is coming. It sure fills all those who read the book of Revelation and listen to it, with growing suspense; at least it most certainly should.

And yet, we still have several chapters to go till the end. More things must happen, before the New Jerusalem will appear and all the tears will be wiped away. This is the re-occurring pattern in Revelation, to keep us on the edge of our seat: "Soon, but not yet". The end seems near. We are told that it is near, and yet postponed until all God's purposes can be accomplished.

And for this, God wants to use his church. This makes the message of the church an urgent message. We see how God's judgments ruin this world. Recognize the thunder of God's voice in what is happening all around us, and in our own lives.

But do not give up. Through the faithful testimony of his church in this world the Almighty God will complete his work and accomplish his goal to the glory of his Name. A new creation is being prepared. You will be surprised when you see it!

16 • Revelation 10

A BITTER-SWEET MESSAGE

And yet, the end is not right there. The seventh trumpet does not follow immediately after the sixth. The third 'woe' is still to come (mentioned in Rev. 8:13 and 9:12). But in John's vision God creates space to reassure his children with comfort and hope.

Even when God's judgments inflict large-scale sufferings on the wicked, we should not forget that in the midst of frightening darkness the perspective remains the victory of Jesus Christ and the survival of his church.

That's why the proclamation of this trustworthy and urgent gospel-message must continue in the last days, despite resistance and opposition. In the last part of this chapter we see John himself getting actively involved in this.

The heavenly voice he had heard before, in v.4, telling him not to communicate the words of the seven thunders, this same voice now orders him to go and take from the angel the open scroll with the gospel of God's plan of salvation in Jesus Christ.

'What I have revealed, I want you to communicate in this world', the Lord says to John. That's why the angel will hand over God's message to John. And in turn John will have to pass it on to God's servants, God's church, to be proclaimed in this world.

Then, when John does so, God's angel instructs him to *take it and eat it*. Here is again a remarkable parallel with what we read in Ezekiel 2 and 3, where the prophet is also instructed to eat a scroll. Now eating a book sounds kind of weird. You can, of course, say 'it's a vision', and in visions strange things happen.

That is true, but to understand the symbolism, think of the expression that describes an avid reader. We can say that someone like that "devours books". You get so deeply into it, that the content of the story, the message, affects you personally and becomes part of who you are, so to speak.

John has to digest and internalize completely the message he has to bring on behalf of God. This will empower him to proclaim God's gospel with passion and great urgency. There is much at stake. The Holy God calls him and us to proclaim salvation for all who turn to Jesus Christ while also proclaiming God's wrath to an unrepentant world.

That is why the angel warns him. Proclaiming God's message for this world will turn out to be a bitter-sweet experience. *Eating this scroll will make your stomach bitter, but in your mouth it will be sweet as honey*, he says. And this is exactly what John experiences when he does what the angel tells him to do (v.10).

The message of the Bible is delightful. The author of Psalm 119 says that the words of God are sweeter than honey. It is always exciting to proclaim God's grace and forgiveness for lost sinners. Nothing is sweeter and lovelier for any preacher than bringing the glorious message of the Father's deep love in Jesus Christ. Especially, because you can say that the fullness of all this is coming soon.

But the same message also gives you much pain when you think of those who reject Jesus Christ and refuse to repent. Then the result of the words of God about his deep love, grace and mercy becomes bitter. For then it becomes a message of condemnation. God's word also speaks about his destructive judgments and wrath.

Indeed, the gospel message is a good message to the glory of the Almighty God. But for John, for you and me in this dark and broken world it is at the same time a bitter-sweet message. God is love. But God is also holy. And so his Word does not only bring joy, it also causes suffering.

That is why the proclamation of the gospel must continue. *You must again prophesy*, we hear. Whether grace or wrath, forgiveness or judgment, it must go on. As long as the last days continue – no matter how dark or bad it is going to be – the church must carry on. She must proclaim to a world lost in sin and heading for destruction that there is hope in Jesus alone. Do not become discouraged by resistance. This is how God's mystery will be accomplished.

Are we ready to take this message to wherever it needs to be heard in this world? Are we ready to explain to people the implications of what they do with this message, how they respond to it?

Let us not give up. Because God does not give up!

There will be no more delay.

17

Revelation 11: 1 – 14

A PROPHESYING CHURCH IN A HOSTILE WORLD

You can read the Book of Revelation as some sort of "running commentary" on what is happening in our world. Not in the sense that you can watch the news every evening or read the headlines every morning, and then turn to Revelation to find the exact equivalent in the events described. That would be arbitrary speculation.

And yet, Revelation does give us a unique perspective of the things that are going on in this world. It tells the history of our world through the view from above, the view from heaven, the view of the Almighty God who reigns from heaven above.

We recognize this unique perspective again in Rev. 11. At the end of Rev. 10 John was told: *You must prophesy again.* This 'prophesying' becomes now the assignment of the church. And so, we hear in Rev. 11 about the "bitter" experiences the faithful church must endure and overcome, when it preaches the "sweet" gospel of Jesus Christ in this hostile world.

17 • Revelation 11:1-14

This prophecy will be secured

During the interlude between the sixth and the seventh trumpet blast the apostle John is again actively involved in his vision. It keeps him busy.

This time he is given *a measuring rod*. And with that he is told to *measure the temple of God, and the altar and the people that worship there*. But he is also instructed *not to measure the court outside the temple*.

It only says that "he was told", and so we do not know who talked to John here. But given the connection with Rev. 10 the voice could be the same as in 10:4, 8 and 11. That may have been the voice of God himself, or the exalted Christ. After all, this voice goes on, at least till the end of v.3, and talks there about "my two witnesses".

So, John sees a temple. When he received these revelations, there was no longer a temple in Jerusalem. But when he was younger he was, of course, quite familiar with the temple, and he knew how significant the temple had been for God's people.

In the Old Testament the temple was the very centre of God's presence on earth, God's dwelling place in the midst of Israel. And the Holy God could dwell with sinful people because of the altar. That was the place of reconciliation and worship, because of the sacrifices for the forgiveness of sins.

In this way the 'temple, with the altar' becomes a symbol for God's presence on earth, in the midst of the community of his people. The Holy God dwells within the living communion of those who are reconciled to him and worship him. This is the essence of what it means to be a faithful Christian church on earth. In his letter to the Ephesians (Eph. 2:21,22) the apostle Paul calls the church *a holy temple in the Lord*, and then he says to the believers: *In Jesus Christ you are also being built together into a dwelling place for God by the Spirit.*

Now, why this 'measuring'? Measuring an area is like staking out a property to separate it, claim it and secure it as yours. Then you can protect it against intruders. You build a fence around it and put up signs: "No Trespassing".

Well, here John's action to measure the temple symbolizes that God secures his claim to safeguard his faithful church.

For the congregation of Jesus Christ, for you and me, there is great comfort in this symbolism. In this hostile world we live under God's protection. As God's children you are his precious possession, bought with the blood of his Son Jesus Christ. That is why God takes care of his church when his judgements are being inflicted on the wicked world. He keeps her as "holy space".

In the Old Testament the 'outer court' belonged to the temple-complex in a broader sense, but it is outside the actual temple. John has to leave that area alone. But what is not measured will not be protected either. And that means that it will come under control of the Gentiles, the nations, God's enemies.

God's enemies come so close to the church, that they will be able to threaten and attack her. In other words, being under God's protection does not mean that the church is not vulnerable. As believers you will face suffering and death. But you will not perish. You will always be secure in God's hands, even if you have to die.

These same enemies of God will also *trample the holy city*. Elsewhere this is often a reference to Jerusalem, but Revelation reserves the name 'Jerusalem' exclusively for the 'New Jerusalem', the city of God. Revelation avoids using the name "Jerusalem" for the wider urban area around the temple, the city that rejected Jesus.

For us this represents the hostile world in which the church is present. It is the world in which we live as God's people.

You can call it 'holy' in the sense that God created it to serve and glorify him. But today human society is run as an "unholy space" by pagans who hate Jesus.

This will go on for forty-two months, the full period between Jesus' first and second coming. It is a time of intense conflict between God's people, the followers of Christ AND their opponents. It is the time of the great tribulation, the suffering and persecution of the church, as it occurs in various ways and in various places as time goes on between Jesus' ascension and return.

17 • Revelation 11:1-14

This is our time. In the sharp contrast between the church and the world, the church is facing trouble and distress. And yet, even under oppression, within the spiritual reality of God's sanctuary, in his church, faithful worshipers will be secure.

And why is that? Because God has a job for them to do in this final phase of history. In this increasingly pagan and hostile world the Lord protects and secures his faithful church for a purpose. He is sending her into this world with his prophetic message, to continue his work.

And I will grant authority to my two witnesses, and they will prophesy for 1260 days.

Here we have another symbolic image: God's two witnesses. "Witnesses" are people who testify to the facts, people who are under oath to tell the truth. In this case, the truth about Jesus Christ and the facts of salvation: that Jesus suffered and was crucified; that he died but rose again; that Jesus is the only Saviour.

The exalted Christ empowers these witnesses to be God's mouth to proclaim his Word. That there are two of them is simply because according to the Law of Moses a testimony is valid if presented by a minimum of two witnesses.

Some think of these witnesses as two specific persons in the history of the Church, or close to the end, just before Jesus' return. But the working period of 1,260 days is the same as the forty-two months of pagan oppression, the whole era between Jesus' ascension and his return.

Rather, these two witnesses represent the faithful church of Christ as it presents the testimony of Jesus in this hostile world, until the final judgment of God's wrath. These prophesying witnesses symbolize us! Today, God sends us into this hostile world to prophesy, just as long as the world is ruled, oppressed by God's enemies. That is, until the glorious day of Jesus' second coming.

The clothing of the witnesses reinforces their message. The *sackcloth* is a symbolic detail that points at the need for penance and repentance. The hostile powers that dominate the world and threaten God's church must be confronted all the time with the message of God's grace and forgiveness, with the urgent call to repent and obey God. But those powers must also be confronted with the warning of condemnation for those who in unbelief reject the message of Christ.

These two witnesses are models for all of us in the church. You and I are to be faithful to the testimony of Jesus, even in the face of violent persecution. Are you willing to face martyrdom? That may sound pretty far-fetched in our comfortable circumstances in Canada, and in most western countries. But then, you do not know what will happen when you really stand up for Jesus in public.

Always remember that through the testimony of these witnesses, through each one of us, Christ will complete his work in this world. And that in the end God himself guarantees our vindication. Indeed, persecution by God's enemies AND protection by God himself; witnessing AND facing opposition – these are all things that happen in different times and at different locations throughout the last days.

But as they happen, God will secure his prophetic message. We see this illustrated in these witnesses as *the two olive trees and the two lampstands* (v.4).

This image comes from the Old Testament, from the prophet Zechariah (Zechariah 4). There are differences, of course, but the symbolism is the same. The lampstands are spreading the light of God's power and glory. And they can do so without interruption, no matter what happens. They never lack fuel, because the trees supply the lamps with an abundance of oil that keeps the lamps burning.

The picture shows how God, through his witnesses, his whole congregation, wants the bright light of the gospel of Jesus to shine into this dark and hostile world. The testimony of the church may be threatened and under attack, God will secure its flame. He will fuel it by the power of the Holy Spirit.

Are you such a lampstand? Are you out there as a light-bearer for the Lord of the earth? Are you faithful to the testimony of Jesus Christ in this hostile world? Do others notice that the burning light of your fire for him cannot be extinguished, fuelled as it is by the power of the Holy Spirit?

But, are we not fighting for a lost cause? That is how it feels sometimes, does it not? And that can be so discouraging.

Trust that God himself will secure the prophetic message with which he sends you into this world. For that reason, he gives his two witnesses enormous powers. The v.5 and 6 show that they are invincible. Our pagan society will try to stop the church from prophesying God's Word. But whatever people try, it will be unsuccessful. People want to get rid of God's message, but God will not let it happen.

The powers of these two witnesses remind us of the authority of Elijah and Moses. Elijah was hated by most Israelites, and Moses was hated by all the Egyptians. But the Lord affirmed their authority by different powerful signs: fire (2 Kings 1; Numbers 15:35), drought (1 Kings 17), water turning to blood (Exodus 7) and other plagues.

Also today, when the church is true to God's Word, it may proclaim with authority that God's judgments will ruin our world when people refuse to repent and turn to Jesus Christ. Our message is not only the good news of salvation, it also includes that judgment against evil-doers is unavoidable. The Church's message is one of power – power to save AND power to punish.

We have seen already what happens when the seven seals were opened, and when six of the seven trumpets sounded, and there is more to come. Why is there so much hatred, misery, violence, war, economic and social turmoil in the world?

Here is the answer: when the world rejects the gospel of Jesus Christ, the testimony of the faithful church, our human society will turn into chaos and suffer God's judgments – now and in the future.

THIS PROPHECY WILL BE SILENCED

God's faithful church may have a powerful message, but it is still vulnerable to hostile attacks, to the point even that it will be silenced. We see this pictured in what happens to the two witnesses. When they have completed their job, it seems that God withdraws his protection and allows more room for other, frightening, hostile forces.

The beast that rises from the bottomless pit (or: the abyss) will make war on them and conquer them and kill them. With brutal violence it will silence the voice of the church.

It says "**the** beast", as if we have met this monster before. But here in Rev.11 we hear about it for the first time. We will learn more about this bizarre and frightening creature in Rev. 13, but the fact that it *comes up from the abyss* is significant. Because the 'abyss' we know from Rev. 9. It is the place where these scorpion-like locusts came from, remember? The 'abyss' is hell before God's final judgment, filled with evil spirits, demons, devils, including Satan himself.

And so this 'beast from the abyss' represents a concentration of antichristian power, stirred up by Satan, urged on by hell, driven by devilish hatred, to oppose the truth, to silence the church's message, to persecute and destroy the Christians and simply snuff out their testimony.

This time the action will be successful. That does not mean that this beast will kill every individual believer, but enough to ruin the organization of the church and silence her voice in this world.

And this is not enough for those enemies. This beast and its followers will be so excited about their success that *the dead bodies of these murdered witnesses* will be on public display *in the street of the great city*.

Did you notice? It is no longer called 'the holy city', as in v.2, dominated as it is by the powers from the abyss. Now it is called 'the great city'. That is an expression we find eight times in Revelation, and it always refers to 'Babylon'.

From of old 'Babylon' was Israel's powerful adversary, the arch-enemy of God's people. And so it has become symbolic for the whole antichristian world and culture, which has aggressively rejected the prophetic message of the church.

John emphasizes how evil this city is, by giving it three other symbolic names. "Sodom" stands for thorough wickedness, violence, and filthy immorality. "Egypt" stands for slavery and oppression. And "the city of the crucifixion" stands for deep hatred against Jesus Christ and his followers.

When you bring this all together, this 'great city' is the absolute antithesis of the other city in Revelation, the New Jerusalem. The city of this world is the city of man, which opposes God and rebels against him. Babylon is where the beast reigns. And his reign seems powerful and successful.

But do not be mistaken. That is the perspective, the view, from below. However, the view from above shows that where the beast reigns, humanity goes down in chaos, while the city where God reigns will flourish in peace, harmony, and joy. The war between the city of God and the city of man continues throughout history, until Babylon is destroyed[7] and the New Jerusalem comes down from heaven[8].

Remember again, that also this death of the two witnesses is not a scenario of a special end-time moment. Throughout the final phase of history, life for the church becomes impossible at different times at different locations. First here, then there, the voice of the church is brutally silenced.

In the image in our chapter it seems as if the hostile political and cultural powers have triumphed. But keep in mind the two different points of view. This is what it looks like from below. However, notice that it says in v.9 that the whole ordeal will be over in 3 ½ days. That's a symbolic number for a very brief timeframe. The perspective from above tells us that the death of his witnesses will not stop God from reaching his goal. The victory of Christ must be close.

In the meantime (v.9 and 10) the inhabitants of the earth, the hostile and wicked oppressors, are so excited that they throw a big party to celebrate this happy moment. The death of the church is a major victory. Finally, they have been successful in silencing the voice of the Christian witness in the world.

From all over the world people come for an 'unholy pilgrimage' to admire the success of the beast, and to mock the remnants of the dead church of Christ. They do not even allow the dead bodies to be buried. That is how deep the hatred is.

---

[7] This is pictured in Revelation 17 and 18
[8] This is pictured in Revelation 21 and 22

Yes, the world will be relieved and say, "Finally, they will no longer pester us with their gloom-and-doom messages". The witness of God's people is repulsive to God's enemies. They do not want to hear, and they get fed up with, the biblical testimony. A constant call to repent becomes a real pain in the neck, an annoying torment, if you want to make the world a better place on your own terms, without God.

When you come to think of it, the contrast that is symbolized here sounds pretty extreme. It is black and white. But that has a good reason. You see, when people look at what drives them in life, they usually find a mix of motives. As a believer you want to follow Christ, but your obedience is flawed. It is mixed with sin, and often inconsistent.

On the other hand, non-Christians want to rebel against God. But in practice they are also often inconsistent. They act not as evil as they could, and sometimes they can even imitate good Christian values that they really appreciate.

Now this mix of good and bad, both in you and in the non-Christians around you, has good aspects. It helps you to live in peace among each other and relate to others. It can even open the door for you to testify about your faith in Jesus Christ.

But it can also easily obscure the seriousness of the most fundamental conflict in history, the conflict between the Holy God and his enemies. And since Revelation focuses on the fact that we are all involved in this conflict, it gives a very black-and-white picture of good and evil. The two witnesses are perfectly faithful witnesses of the truth, whereas their opponents are extremely evil and hostile.

And here again Revelation gives us the view from above, to remind us of what is going on behind the scene. This is the reality of our world that is often obscured by the cover of civil and moderate strategies that we use to hide our deepest loyalties.

Look at your own life. Where are you in this deadly conflict? What does your loyalty to Jesus mean for you? And do not ignore, under the veneer of friendliness, the deadly opposition against God and Jesus evident in the lives of others.

17 • Revelation 11:1-14

This Prophecy Will Bear Fruit

When we turn to the last act of the drama that unfolds in our passage, we learn that the festive mood of v.10 is short-lived. The unholy revellers are too early, for as it turns out, the joy only lasts 3 ½ days. Then suddenly things change. God Almighty interferes in a way no one had counted on.

It says that after 3 ½ days God gives back to these two murdered witnesses *the breath of life*. It reminds us of Gen. 2:7, where it says that God *breathed into man's nostrils the breath of life*. The result is that they can stand *up on their feet* again. This is what happened in the Valley of the Dry Bones, one of the visions of the prophet Ezekiel (Ezekiel 37:1-14). In other words, the resurrection that occurs on the main street of the wicked city of Babylon is nothing less than God's miracle of a new creation.

And this is encouraging symbolism. After malicious attacks and severe persecution had wiped out the church, we will see the victory of the church's witness.

We will even see that this testimony will bear fruit, believe it or not!

It is a terrifying experience for God's enemies and for the enemies of the church. They see it happen. This is incredible. The church of Christ was dead, terminated, eliminated, annihilated. But she is back, restored and full of life. Picture them standing there: horror-struck, frozen with fear. The party is over, boys!

You see, when the perspective from above, from heaven, breaks into the perspective from here, from below, God's enemies will panic. It confuses your view and turns your world upside down. The reality is not what you thought it was.

The reality is that the church of Jesus Christ cannot be eliminated permanently from our society, from our world. That is just not possible. The prophetic witness of the church can go through difficult times. Sometimes it is forced to be silent, at least for a while. Then people think they have gotten rid of it. But time and again it comes back into this hostile world.

And the good news is that the gospel will be victorious. *A loud voice from heaven* calls them to ascend up to heaven, beyond the malicious power of their enemies. It says that *their enemies watched them* when it happened. They may hate to admit it, but the fact is that no one will be able to get rid of the church and its urgent and persistent message of salvation in Christ alone.

Then, as if all this is not frightening or astonishing enough, there is at the same time *a great earthquake*. It is a scary reminder of the urgency of the message of these two witnesses: now is the time to repent. The Holy God, who has sent his church to announce his coming, is coming soon in power and glory!

The effect of the earthquake is devastating. Ten percent of the evil world was destroyed and the symbolic number of victims is 7,000. It is significant! Although this is not the end, not yet, it is an alarming and frightening warning of what is coming: *the third woe is soon to come*, it says in v.14.

You may remember that in Rev. 8:13 a flying eagle had announced three woes. The first one appeared with the fifth trumpet blast (Rev. 9:12). The second one has passed with the sixth trumpet. And the third one is almost here. We should all realize that the opportunity to repent is rapidly drawing to a close. There is only a narrow window left.

On the day of the Final Judgment it will be over. But God still reaches out to this world. The earthquake in v.13 leaves many survivors. They are in shock and terrified, but life on earth continues, because our God does not give up. He continues to look for faith and repentance in this dark and hostile world.

And here is the miracle: *they gave glory to the God of heaven*. This is such an incredible twist in this chapter, that some scholars concluded that this cannot be a true repentance. It must be fake, in the sense that only out of fear these people acknowledge God's power. But it does not say so. As a matter of fact, whenever people refuse to repent and give glory to God, it says so in Revelation.

But throughout this final phase of history our God is full of surprises. As things are getting ready for the Final Judgment, the prophetic message of

17 • Revelation 11:1-14

the church will bear fruit in many lives. People come to glorify God as the One who rules from heaven.

Now, if God does not give up, neither should we. For you and me, for the whole church, the need remains urgent in the last days of this hostile world, to remain a faithful and witnessing church till the very end. Do not be intimidated by hostile attacks.

The Christian witness in our society will not only trigger angry reactions and persecution. It will also bear fruit. Leave that to the Lord. Just keep proclaiming the message, and by his grace people will turn to Jesus Christ and bring glory to God.

This is how God will take you and all his children along on the way to his final victory.

18

Revelation 11: 15 – 19

GOD COMES TO JUDGE AS GLORIOUS KING

Although most nations in the world have an elected president as head-of-state, some countries are still under the headship of a king or queen. Monarchies are often very old institutions. And many people in countries that do not have a monarchy see it as an outdated and irrelevant anomaly in today's modern, democratic society.

Even in countries with a king or a queen as head-of-state there is often a small, but vocal, group of republicans that wants to get rid of the monarchy.

And yet, when a crown-prince gets married, a royal baby is born, or a new king is crowned, something remarkable happens.

In nations as liberal, morally diverse, politically divided and individualized as Great Britain and The Netherlands, those occasions bring people together around their king in a remarkable unity that crosses all party boundaries.

Despite the nasty comments of hard-core republicans, for a short time at least you see the kind of harmony an elected president, as a political figure, can never achieve.

18 • Revelation 11:15-19

Well, if this is what a king can do who has no real power whatsoever, and whose function is mainly ceremonial and symbolic, imagine what a king can accomplish who has all the power and authority in the world, and is going to use this power for the benefit of his people.

For many Christians Ascension Day is an often forgotten feast-day. However, many faithful church celebrate Ascension Day and remember that the risen Saviour Jesus Christ ascended into heaven and was seated at God the Father's right hand to govern with him from his heavenly throne.

Christ went up to assume his royal power, his kingship over the world, over all the nations, to bring about new harmony; to unite people from all over the world in the glorious kingdom of his Father.

Indeed, our God is a glorious King. He is also a victorious King. And we need to remember how encouraging AND how warning this is, as our journey continues towards the day of his final judgment.

Listen

In the big picture of Revelation, we are still in the second cycle of God's judgments. The first series unfolded when the seven seals were opened. The second series unfolded when the seven angels sounded the seven trumpets. However, that is not complete yet. We are still waiting for the seventh trumpet!

After the sixth trumpet, at the end of Rev. 9, the progress in John's vision slowed down. It was interrupted by what the apostle describes in Rev. 10 and the first part of Rev. 11. But now, after the visions of 'the angel with the scroll' and 'the two witnesses', it seems we are picking up speed again when the seventh angel sounds the final trumpet (v.15).

It completes the series that began in Rev. 8:6, and at the same time it activates the last series of seven judgments. Although, we will not get there before Rev. 15 and 16.

But remember that in the story of Revelation this seventh trumpet blast marks a significant moment. In Rev. 10:7 we have heard the oath of the mighty angel with the scroll in his hand: *There will be no more delay! In the days of the trumpet call to be sounded by the seventh angel the mystery of God will be fulfilled.*

This is what is happening here. The mystery of God is going to be fulfilled. That means that now God's plan with this world will be completed. Our God is coming to reclaim his full royal authority over all the earth. This seventh trumpet blast announces the great day of the fulfilment of all God's promises.

It declares that now the hour of God's final judgment is near, at hand.

Well, in the light of Rev. 10:7 you would expect John to describe Jesus' glorious return when he hears the sound of the seventh trumpet.

But he does not. Not yet! That will come much later in the dramatic developments that are unfolding in the book of Revelation. Think of the last chapters.

Oh, the end is coming. The sound of the seventh trumpet keeps us on the edge of our seat. It is close. It is very, very close! But before that, John is going to tell us many more things to help us understand what is going on in our world, the world in which we live.

Those things are all coming in Rev. 12 – 14. We need to be reminded that the time of the last days is going to be a rough time for the church of Jesus Christ.

And then we find in Rev. 15 how the seventh trumpet triggers the seven last plagues wreaking havoc in this world.

Well then, within this framework of persecution, hardships, and judgments, we have a surprise in the passage we are listening to in the second half of Rev. 11.

Terrible things are going on. We saw it in Rev. 9 and in the first part of Rev. 11. And we will see more of it. The hatred, the hostility toward God, toward Christ and his church is fierce. This is the world in which you and I live. This is the world in which we live as church. That can be exhausting, frustrating and disappointing. And sometimes you wonder what the world is coming to.

But here we come to see what is behind all this. Here is your peace of mind. Yes, the Almighty God is coming to judge. But in the end all that is left is the great victory of our glorious King and of his Son, the exalted Christ. It is the view from above that shows us today already the awesome reality of God's royal power.

Horrible woes are coming when the seventh angel sounds his trumpet. There is no doubt about it. But the first thing to note is that John hears something. He hears singing! The trumpet blast triggers loud voices. So, let's listen.

There were loud voices in heaven, John says. First we hear a loud song of victory and praise, coming from within the throne-room of the Holy and Almighty God. But then we also hear other voices. And they respond to the first ones. We hear a responsive, an antiphonal victory song. It goes back and forth.

Now this second choir is formed by the twenty-four elders who are worshipping God. That is what it says in v.16. We have met them before, in Rev. 4, 5 and 7.

But to whom do the loud voices of the first choir belong, in v.15? It does not say, and so, as we have seen at other occasions, the scholars have different opinions and speculate about it.

Some think that John hears choirs of angels. That is not impossible, of course. We have heard those in Rev. 5 and 7. But another possibility makes more sense.

Remember what we have seen in Revelation 4 and 5. In chapter 4 we heard singing in a similar antiphonal fashion (v.9–10) where the twenty-four elders fall down and worship God after and in response to the song of praise by the four living creatures surrounding God's throne in heaven.

Well, since this is how the voices alternate in Rev. 4 it makes sense to see the same thing in this passage: the loud voices from heaven (v.15) belong to the four living creatures, God's awesome heavenly throne-attendants.

You may also remember that these four creatures represent all of God's creation. So - this is what is happening. Listen! At the piercing sound of the seventh trumpet all of God's creation bursts out in this loud victorious song of praise, this triumphant proclamation that the Almighty God has assumed his kingship:

> *The kingdom of the world has become the kingdom of our Lord and of his Christ, and he shall reign for ever and ever.*

"Kingdom" then means dominion, rule, sovereignty. You could say "kingship".

This is encouraging news. In v.14, just before this passage, it said: *the second woe has passed, the third woe is soon to come.* But this is not the third woe. As a matter of fact, the third one of the three woes, announced in Rev.8:19, is never mentioned as being passed. But regardless – what we have here is not a 'woe', but a joyful celebration of the transfer of dominion, the rule of this world to the Almighty God and his Anointed.

To be sure, that does not mean that God was not king before. No, we know that our God is the eternal King. He always reigns with sovereign majesty. Think of many psalms in the Old Testament that honour and glorify God as King.

And yet, we also know that God's power and authority are not always apparent in this world. Through our fall into sin the world fell into the enemy's hands. It became 'occupied territory'. Quite often Satan seems to be the supreme ruler, who dominates 'the kingdom of this world'. And we all experience the results. As Paul puts it in Romans 8: the creation is groaning under the consequences of sin and under God's judgments.

But here is the good news: This is coming to an end! When the first six trumpets sounded, one-third of the world was destroyed, and the rest of mankind did not repent (Rev. 9:18,20). The resistance remains strong. That is frightening. But do not worry. All hostile opposition will be abolished, and the Kingdom will be fully restored to its rightful owner and ruler. That is the glorious victory these heavenly voices sing about. That is what you and I may look forward to with joy and excitement.

Although it does not look like it from where we are here on earth, from where they are, from heaven they see already a cleansed and renewed world, a world that is fit to receive the Holy and Almighty God as its eternal King; a world that is fit to be *the kingdom of our Lord and of his Christ*. That is a breath-taking reality.

As mentioned before, God always had the power to reign. But now the wonderful effect of his active rule will come to light in this world.

Notice that those who exercise this ruling-power are mentioned in one breath: *the Lord and his Christ*, his Anointed. Jesus is 'God's Christ', God's Anointed One, to be installed as King. He arose from the dead and ascended into heaven, to be seated at God's right hand. This means that he shares in God's government.

When we listen to these voices from heaven, we hear them praise God for the day of Jesus' ascension into heaven. The day that God Almighty gave him his seat in heaven, *far above all rule and authority, power and dominion, and every title that can be given, not only in the present age, but also in the one to come* (Ephesians 1:20, 21).

When Paul writes this, he tells us that today already, you and I may know that through Jesus the Christ God governs everything, everything in this world and everything in your life. And that he will reign for ever and ever.

Again, in our experiences here below we often don't see it, do we? The bad news can be too much. The powers of evil seem so strong. But here is your comfort, here is your encouragement: when Paul talks in Romans 8 about our world as a world groaning in pain, he says these are the "pains of childbirth", the pains that lead to the birth of a renewed and cleansed world. That will be a world in which God's reign, God's dominion will never be challenged or disputed.

Do not be distracted by all the loud noises that come from this world. Listen to the voices from heaven and be encouraged. Our world is getting ready. The Day of the Lord is coming and will reveal the full royal splendour of his sovereign power. He will reign for ever and ever, and every eye will see him.

But as we noted already, there is more to listen to. John hears a second choir.

The twenty-four elders, sitting on their thrones before God – you may remember this picture from John's vision in Rev.4 – fall down on their faces to worship and glorify God, filled with deep and humble respect. And they also sing!

With abundant joy they respond to the great news, the heavenly proclamation of God's victorious kingship. They echo the jubilant declaration of the four living creatures. These twenty-four elders represent God's church in the Old and the New Testament. This is such a marvellous perspective. Filled with thanks, praise, and awe God's holy, catholic, church joins all of God's creation in unified glorification of the ruling power of Jesus Christ, ascended into heaven as the glorious King.

In wonderful harmony they reinforce for us the royal majesty of the Lord God Almighty. And as we listen to their song, we hear them acknowledge the arrival of the ascended Christ in heaven. *You have taken your great power and begun to reign*. For in him and through him the mystery of the Almighty God will be fulfilled.

You can be so absolutely sure of this, that these elders can characterize the Almighty God as *the One who is and who was*. You will remember that Rev. 1:8 and 4:8 talk about him as the God *who was, and is, and is to come*. Now this third tense is no longer needed. It can be taken out, because here we learn to celebrate that God has come. *The kingdom of the world has become the kingdom of our Lord and of his Christ* (v. 15). Christ has taken his great power and has begun to reign.

Listen carefully and hear heaven sing from this perspective. Listen carefully in the midst of trouble, misery, and persecution. Listen carefully in a world where devilish powers seem to have the last word: the glorious King has come in his great and awesome power, and he has begun to reign.

Yes, the story of our broken lives continues. The story of our dark world continues. The festive end is not there yet. But it is coming. And today you may already know that no evil power can stop your King. That is the marvellous reality of his power and majesty, as well as the power and majesty of the ascended Jesus Christ.

Oh, Satan and his evil henchmen have tried, and they will continue to try. *The nations raged,* they have rebelled against the Lord. They have attacked, conquered and killed his church, pictured in the death of the 'Two Witnesses' (Rev. 11:7,8).

But that was not the end of it, on the contrary, *your wrath came.* And so *the time has come for the dead to be judged.* In fact, the hatred and resistance against God, and the persecution of his church, is paving the way for God's judgment. Indeed, God is coming to judge as our glorious King. The time has come.

This means two things. First, it is time *for rewarding God's servants* and *for destroying God's enemies.* In the next chapters we will hear a lot more about how God is going to do this. But rejoice today. The Lord is King! Serve him, revere his name, praise and worship him, obey him, talk about him, all of you – "both small and great". It does not matter how important or how insignificant you are. God does not care. Believe in him and you will be rewarded with his gifts of grace when you enter the joy of your Lord.

Others will also be rewarded when our glorious King comes to judge. It is also time *for destroying the destroyers of the earth.* If you turn against the Almighty King, if you corrupt and pollute our human world with sin, evil, hatred, violence and immorality, you will not survive God's cleansing-operation to refit this world to be his kingdom.

Watch

John does not only hear something, he also sees something when the seventh angel sounds his trumpet. This is the second effect. "God comes to judge as our glorious King". The day of his judgement is close, extremely close. It is closer than ever. So, let us watch what is happening.

John tells us that right before his astonished eyes *God's temple in heaven was opened, and the ark of his covenant was seen within this temple.*

This must have been so amazing! We know from the Old Testament the descriptions of the temple. We also know that this earthly sanctuary was modelled after the one in heaven. As a result, when John tells us what he sees in his vision, we understand the meaning, because of what we know from the Old Testament.

The 'ark' was the most holy thing in the temple. That is why it was hidden in the 'most holy place'. No one was allowed to see it. It was called "the ark of the covenant", because God had put the 'constitution' of his covenant in it – the two stone tablets with the Law, also called "The Testimony". The cover on top of the ark was called "the atonement cover" or "mercy seat". We read about all these things in Exodus 25.

All this made the ark a powerful sign of God's covenant relationship, his real, intimate, and perfect fellowship with his people. The ark guaranteed God's active and gracious presence with people who trust and obey his Word. If people did not trust and obey the Holy God, they would find out that the ark, as sign of God's active presence, could also be a dangerous thing.

The problem was that in the Old Testament the 'most holy place' was always closed. No one had free access to God. Sacrifices went a long way, but you could not appear in God's holy presence, just like that. Only the High Priest could, once per year. And only after he had performed various rituals to protect himself.

Watch carefully and be amazed when you recognize what is happening here. You see the temple open. You see the most holy place open, and everyone can see the Ark of the Covenant, this secret and holy sign.

That means that because of the sacrifice of Jesus Christ, God has now fully revealed his glory for everyone to see. In Jesus Christ God now dwells with his people as never before. At the same time, if you reject Jesus' sacrifice, Jesus' atonement for your sins, God's presence will be more dangerous than ever before.

When the risen Christ ascended into heaven, he re-connected heaven and earth. He gives us here on earth free and direct access to God the Father in heaven. And the covenant of God's grace is no longer written on stone and hidden in an object that is a sign of this relationship. But by the life-changing power of the Holy Spirit God's covenant of grace is realized in the hearts and lives of God's children.

O children of God's love, this is the astounding reality of the last days of our history. In the darkness and brokenness, the King of glory dwells with you, to have fellowship with you. His holy presence guards you and protects you. His holy presence guarantees the marvellous renewal of all things. He acts for your benefit. He fulfils what the four living creatures and the twenty-four elders were singing.

But here is also our struggle in the final phase of our history. As time goes on we sometimes wonder about our glorious King. We do not see the mystery of God being fulfilled. And the persecution continues, first here, then there. Throughout our human history, also throughout our personal histories, the truth that God rules is often hidden for us. *The time has come to judge*. Are you sure?

Oh, yes, we do believe that God's risen Son Jesus Christ ascended into heaven, that he rules on his Father's throne and that in one way or another he is there for our benefit, our well-being. After all, through him you do have free access to the Holy God, your Father in heaven.

But from here, from below, we do not always see it. So often it is as if Satan rules, as if the powers of destruction are in control. But that is not true!

"Come here," says John, "and look carefully. Watch the vision of God's open temple. Watch the powerful sign of God's presence. Nothing remains hidden or concealed. Your Saviour rules on the throne in heaven. In him your God comes so close. In him your God is approachable, always!"

And the day is coming that everyone will see it and hear it. The day is coming that the loud voices in heaven will not sound in a vision only, but all over the world, for everyone to hear.

Then God's children will no longer doubt that God is the glorious King. They will share in the wonderful salvation for his people, as they enter the joy that never ends.

And then God's enemies can no longer deny that God is the glorious King. Frightening terror will seize those who are hostile towards the holy God and his church, as they face eternal punishment.

God's royal majesty is gracious and full of compassion. But it is also awe-inspiring. For the wicked the Ark of the Covenant, as sign of God's presence, indicates that now also God's wrath is about to be fully revealed. That is why it appears with the evidence of God's awesome power.

There were flashes of lightning, rumblings, peals of thunder, an earthquake and heavy hail. Such dramatic phenomena accompanied the appearance of the Holy and Almighty God at Mount Sinai (Exodus 19). His glorious power and majesty were terrifying and dreadful. And he is the same today.

This is the third time we hear this, but take a close look at the slight differences.

In Rev. 4:5 we hear about *flashes of lightning, rumblings and peals of thunder* – a threefold manifestation of God's frightful power.

Then, in Rev. 8:5 it was lengthened to include *an earthquake* – God's judgments reach the earth to realize his purpose.

And now here, in Rev. 11:19 it is lengthened again to include *a great hailstorm* – God's judgments unleash destructive powers.

Do you see it? The list gets longer and longer. As we come closer to the end, God's judgments intensify and become more frightening all the time. And it will get worse when the world comes to its very end. That's in chapter 16:18–21. The tension is mounting to have us prepared for the grand finale to come.

Because the question becomes more and more urgent: What side will you be on, when the seventh trumpet will unfold this grand finale? You do not know when it will be here.

But be prepared. Acknowledge and worship the Holy and Almighty God as your glorious King. If you do not, you will face his royal wrath.

No, you can never do this on your own, in the midst of all the frightening powers that are still so strong in this world.

But believe in your Saviour Jesus. He ascended into heaven. And even before the current ruler of the world has been thrown out completely, he has already established the glorious Kingdom that will never end.

Now, that is encouraging!

19

REVELATION 12

WATCH OUT FOR
THE ANGRY DRAGON

If you have read Tolkien's book "The Hobbit", you have also met the great dragon 'Smaug'. You may have seen a picture of Smaug sleeping in this huge pile of silver, gold and precious stones, in a cave deep in the mountains. He guards his stolen treasures, but as long as he sleeps he is okay.

If you have watched the second part of the movie-series "The Hobbit", called "The desolation of Smaug", you have also seen this dragon. Slowly he wakes up, an enormous, vile monster, ready to kill and destroy. But he fails to kill the hobbit Bilbo and the Dwarfs, and in a vicious mood he heads for Lake Town.

In this chapter we also meet a dragon. It is a huge, fiery, blood-red, fire-breathing powerful dragon, a frightening monster.

But this one is not sleeping and guarding his treasures. No, this one is wide awake, and he is angry, really angry. He is furious!

Let us be realistic. You would not like to run into a dragon at the best of times. They are pretty unpredictable. That is why in "The Hobbit", Bilbo Baggins is so careful. He tries not to wake up the sleeping Smaug when he sneaks into the Lonely Mountain.

19 • Revelation 12

But running into a dragon who is filled with fury and rage is definitely not a good idea. You do not want to be in his way.

Well, this furious dragon here in Revelation 12 is after you and me. He wants to kill us. He wants to kill God's people, Christian believers. He hates those *who keep the commandments of God and hold to the testimony of Jesus*, it says in v.17.

Why is that? Why is he trying to get you? We find out in John's vision in this chapter. It shows us the background history that led to the fierce and destructive anger that we are facing in this raving mad and dangerous dragon.

Today, we need to take note that three times already this dragon suffered a humiliating defeat when he tried to reach his goal. And he knows that he is running out of time.

A CHILD

You will remember that the first effect of the seventh angel sounding his trumpet was encouraging. In Rev. 11:15–18 we heard heavenly songs of praise, because of the never-ending reign of the victorious Christ. It shows that this seventh trumpet blast marks a key moment in the developments pictured in Revelation.

Now the end is really, really close.

But we are not there yet. The narrative continues. In Rev. 15 we will see how the seventh trumpet triggers the next sequence of seven: seven angels carrying seven bowls, filled with the seven plagues of God's wrath, more frightening judgments the world is facing.

But before we get there, John's visions will give us an in-depth overview of what is going on behind the scenes. We must be aware of the powers that are at work in this world behind the powers that seem to be at work in this world. We need to have a picture of this, so that we better understand the seriousness of God's judgments.

But it will also help us not to despair of the final outcome of what is going on in the world, and to know what to watch out for!

John's vision pictures Satan's fiercely aggressive activities by means of three animals: the dragon (Rev. 12), the beast out of the sea (Rev. 13a) and the beast out of the earth (Rev. 13b).

We look around in this world and we see a lot of aggression, war, civil war, cultural or religious violence, racism, oppression, and persecution. Well, the view we get here, the perspective from above, shows us that the real clash, the real war is not between world-powers or civilizations. It is between Christ and Satan. And that war spills over in the war between the church and the world.

Here we meet the first one of these powers, the dragon. And as was mentioned earlier, he is really mad, furious. Rev. 12 is kind of unique as its vision scans all of history from above, in an extremely compact way, to make clear why this dragon is so angry. At the same time, although the vision should make us careful, we learn why we shouldn't worry too much about it.

The dragon represents or symbolizes Satan, the devil. He is the one who *prowls around like a roaring lion, seeking someone to devour* (1 Peter 5:8). That also reflects his anger and frustration.

Now we know that Satan was not only present at the fall into sin (Genesis 3:1-7), but the LORD also addressed him, when he said, after the fall: *I will put enmity between you and the woman, and between your offspring and hers; he will crush your head, and you will strike his heel* (Genesis 3:15). Satan remembers this, of course. Rev. 12 demonstrates that Satan sees how the fulfilment of this promise is unfolding, and he can do nothing about it. He tries to stop it, but he cannot. It is really maddening, frustrating.

In the first part of his vision John sees three characters: a woman, a dragon and a child. The conflict or enmity is between the first two characters, the woman and the dragon. However, what is really at the centre is the child. As it turns out, this child, in the end, is the cause of the conflict, the key person in the hostilities. That is Jesus.

The main characters are linked by the word "sign". The woman is *a great sign*, whereas the dragon has a lesser status. It is merely called *another sign*. The word "sign" stresses how important it is that we look at these things as symbols that point at another reality.

The woman symbolizes the church, the one community of God's chosen people in Old and New Testament. Although, in v.5 the emphasis may be more on God's people in the Old Testament, the people of Israel, later on that shifts somewhat more to God's New Testament people.

And as we saw already, the dragon symbolizes Satan, the devil. That is even said with so many words in v.9, where he is also called *that ancient serpent*. This reminds us again of the dirty role he played in Genesis 3. In this way the dragon symbolizes the one supernatural power that is behind all evil.

Well then, the first thing John sees is *a woman*. It is a view of stunning beauty. She is wonderfully adorned with a robe that has the shining splendour of the sun. She stands on the moon as her celestial pedestal, and is crowned with a royal diadem with twelve stars. She is full of majesty. She is the glorious queen of the universe.

The brilliance of the heavenly reflection shows that she belongs to God – the Holy and Awesome One, who dwells in unapproachable light.

There is another woman in the Book of Revelation. But she is the exact opposite. The stark contrast with the purple and scarlet clothing and the glittering jewelry of that one is striking. She is also called "great". But she is "the great prostitute". We will meet her in Revelation 17 and 18. Both women appear as queens, but the one is nothing but an ugly and satanic perversion of the other.

The woman John is seeing is nine months pregnant and in labour. She is about to give birth and cries out in painful agony. Giving birth is always a vulnerable moment for a woman, sometimes filled with tension.

In this case the tension is made a lot worse by what we see when the other sign appears. We see *a great red dragon with seven heads and ten horns and on his heads seven diadems,* or crowns. That sounds like a frightening monster. Imagine running into something like that. The colour 'red' indicates its malicious and bloodthirsty character. He is so powerful that his tail is like a weapon of mass destruction; it swept one third of the stars out of the sky.

His seven crowned heads and ten horns give the impression that this dragon is a powerful ruler. But that is deceiving. He is trying to mimic God's power and God's authority, but he is really nothing but a violent and very destructive oppressor, wreaking havoc throughout the universe.

By now we know him as the devil, Satan, the one who is filled with hatred against God and against those who belong to God. With his power he is constantly opposing God's plans. In whatever way he can, he will always try to prevent God from accomplishing the salvation he has promised. And this is still his goal today in your and my life. He has not changed, other than that he becomes angrier all the time.

And then the scenario becomes extremely tense..... *The dragon stood before the woman...... so that when she bore her child he might devour it.* The closer it comes to the moment of delivery – the more intense is his hatred and hostility. It's actually a horrible picture. Think of it. A 9 months pregnant woman in labour is no match for a big dragon ready for the kill.

And there is no misunderstanding as to the intentions of this dragon. He is just waiting to kill and devour the child the moment the woman would give birth. You can feel how the tension is mounting during the dramatic stand-off between the woman and the dragon until the child is born.

For where does this fierce confrontation come from? It is rooted in God's words in Genesis 3:15, God's promise of the Messiah, Jesus Christ, the Saviour of the world. The future of heaven and earth is at stake. The future of life is at stake.

The woman, the church – and here with the focus on the Old Testament people of God – was given the role, the task to bring forth the Christ. This makes the entire history of the Old Testament the story of the conflict between the woman and the dragon, because of the child.

Here we get in a few strokes, the view, the perspective from above of what happened in Bethlehem, at Golgotha, including Jesus' resurrection and ascension into heaven, the final act in the mighty drama of Old Testament history.

The promised child, the Saviour of the universe, Jesus the Christ, who will crush the devil's head, is about to enter this world. But the dragon is determined to prevent this from happening. After all, he is this devil; he is this serpent who was told that one day the Son of the woman would destroy him. He will do whatever he can to thwart his own defeat.

Is he successful? No, he is not! As a matter of fact, he does not have a chance. God himself interferes. As soon as the woman gives birth to her child, it is immediately *caught up to God and to his throne*. Some translations say, "snatched up".

It 'was snatched up'. Who did that? God did! The holy and almighty God is the hidden actor in this drama. He seems absent. But he is there. Not only as the initiator of the plan, outlined in Gen.3:15, but also as the enactor, he remains in control of the fulfilment of his own words. This is why this whole chapter is so comforting. God's purpose can never be frustrated. He restricts the devil's rage.

When God snatches this male child up to heaven and has him *installed as king to rule all the nations with a rod of iron* (v.5), we hear the echo of Psalm 2, the victory song of the Messiah, Jesus the Christ. It is the same song where we also hear that *the One enthroned in heaven laughs. He scoffs at his enemies.....*!

In Rev. 12 we hear the triumphant laugh of God almighty, which triggers the fierce anger of the dragon. He failed to reach his goal. Oh, he hates this child that just escaped him. One day he will again have to face the Son who will destroy him.

In this conflict between the woman and the dragon God gives us this view from above to show us the real scope, the real nature of the conflict between good and evil. It also shows us the outcome of this conflict. From here, from our earthly perspective, it is hard to see. The church is more and more marginalized. The evil powers just barge ahead and no one seems to be able to stop it.

But the view from above teaches us two things. Be on your guard. An angry dragon is a dangerous enemy. But also: Be encouraged. He is not invincible.

An Angel

What happens next? The second act in this dramatic vision shows a different scene. It is a war scene. In the v.7–9 John's description of what he sees is full of violent language. We are witnessing a fierce and intense battle. Of course, we do not know what kind of weapons these armies were fighting with: missiles, fighter jets, swords, bow & arrow, who knows?

But a battlefield is always a place with lots of loud noises, shouting, clanging and banging, fire, smoke and explosions. We are again getting a view from above of what's going on, to warn and encourage us here below.

The new character in this act is Michael. We know this Michael from Daniel 10 and 12. There we read about him as God's *chief prince*, the heavenly army commander, who at that time led the fight against the evil power behind the Persian Empire. He is always ready to defend God's people in critical circumstances.

So, we see two powerful military leaders with two armies of angels facing and opposing each other. The one from heaven, the other from hell. God's arch-enemy the dragon meets God's arch-angel Michael! It is not the last battle we read about in Revelation, but it is definitely the most significant battle.

But we may wonder, what triggered this battle, where Michael and his angels are fighting against the dragon and his angels? Why does the dragon not give up after his first defeat, when he did not catch the child? He will no longer be able to get the child he was after anyway.

Well, this dragon, whom we already know as *the ancient serpent, the devil, Satan and deceiver*, he is also called: *the accuser of our brothers* (v.10). The word for "accuser" is a judicial term that is used only here in the New Testament. It is similar to what we would call a "prosecuting attorney". Where does that title come from?

You may remember from Bible chapters like Job 1 and 2, and Zechariah 3 that for a long time Satan always had access to heaven to accuse God's children of their sins before the throne of God.

But with the child in heaven, that is over! Now Satan is barred. Try to picture for yourself how General Michael with his army of angels is standing on guard to enforce this, to deny the dragon access to heaven and to block his way when he tries to storm the gates.

In the bitter battle triggered by this confrontation, the dragon loses his claim for a place in heaven, and *he is thrown down to the earth*, together will all his demons.

This expression "thrown down to the earth" reflects that it was a brutal, violent act and it is used repeatedly to emphasize the humiliation of this defeat at the hand of God's archangel. This is the moment Jesus himself refers to when he says in Luke 10: 18 *I saw Satan fall like lightning from heaven.*

But the question is: why? Why does it turn out this way? Why does Satan no longer have access to heaven and why is this the outcome of the battle?

The answer has to do with this child. Remember, after he was born, he was "caught up to God and his throne". Christ is not mentioned in v.7–9, but he still plays the decisive role. We hear about this in the song that John hears in v.10–12. After all the violent noises of the battle have died out, John *hears a loud voice in heaven.* Again – it is loud. As mentioned before, Revelation is a noisy book.

Despite all kinds of speculations, we do not know who this loud singer is. But in his song he reacts to Michael's glorious victory and it is important to listen to him because, as we have seen a few times already in this book, what John hears usually explains or interprets what he sees in his visions.

Here too, the song in v.10–12 interprets the war in heaven. And it reveals the spiritual reality that is behind the outcome of this heavenly battle. We learn that the victory of the archangel is actually a celebration of the fact that Jesus Christ has achieved his decisive victory.

Think of this. What we are seeing (through John's eyes) is a vision. And what takes years or decades in real life, can happen instantly in a vision. We hear in v.10, that *now the salvation and the power and the kingdom of our God, and the authority of his Christ have come.* It appears that the child snatched up to God is no longer a child. Now he turns out to be the powerful Ruler, Jesus, the glorious Christ, ascended into heaven and seated at the Father's right hand.

But here is the clue. We know that Jesus ascended into heaven after he died on the cross and arose from the dead. In other words, this dragon sees himself confronted, not just with a new-born child, but with Jesus' death and resurrection; with the blood of the Lamb of God, the blood that paid for all the sins of God's children!

And that is incredibly powerful because it is this blood that makes Satan's accusations null-and-void, invalid, futile. They just bounce off Jesus' sacrifice. Sure, the devil will continue to tempt you to sin and accuse you. But Jesus' reconciliation sets you free. *Who shall bring any charge against God's elect* (Romans 8:33,34)?

Here is the great turning-point. By the blood of the Lamb, Jesus Christ, and by the testimony of those who rely on this blood, the monstrous dragon suffered a terrible defeat. The arch-angel Michael did so, empowered by the victory of Jesus Christ. In other words, the victory in this cosmic battle, when the dragon storms the gates of heaven, this victory was achieved at Golgotha, on the cross.

Shout for joy because of this. Because of Jesus' death, resurrection and ascension, heaven could be swept clean. Praise the Lord! Satan has been defeated, again!

At the same time, do not forget that the full realization of this victory is waiting for the final unravelling of the plot of our history. Today we are still in occupied territory, where Satan is free to roam around, filled with fury as he is. That is dangerous! Do not underestimate him because he knows that he cannot afford to lose any time. Watch out for the angry dragon. He does not give up.

A WOMAN

The conflict intensifies as it comes closer to home. This dragon does not like being humiliated. And this is now the second time. He cannot stand it! Flung down to the earth, he hits the ground, smashes into rock or dust or dirt, or whatever it is, but he gets up again, and scrambles to his feet, raving mad, seething with anger.

He must do something. The crucified and risen Christ is out of his league. The final confrontation with him will come at the end of history. That is in

Rev.20. So, what else can he do in the time that is left? Who else can he find to vent his rage on?

Then we see that this angry dragon turns to the woman who had given birth to the child. That frustrating reminder is enough to pursue her (v.13). He hates her, the church of Jesus Christ in this world. And his goal is to get rid of her, to annihilate her. He can only be satisfied, at least to some extent, when he has entirely eliminated her.

However, it does not work. She is beyond his reach. That is a great comfort for God's people. Yes, there is persecution. Many try to silence the message of the church and to declare it irrelevant or even illegal. But God's church will survive and complete her journey. Christ will continue to gather people till the end of the ages.

So, what is happening to this woman?

In v.6 it says already that immediately after her child was born, *she fled into the wilderness, where she has a place prepared by God, in which she is to be nourished for 1260 days.* Verse 14 gives us the same picture. Here it says that *the woman was given the two wings of a great eagle, so that she might fly into the wilderness, to the place where she is to be nourished.*

This whole picture is filled with allusions to Israel's exodus out of Egypt and its journey towards the Promised Land. They were beyond the reach of the Pharaoh, taken care of, protected and nourished by God in the desert.[9] It reinforces the promise that God's church will not perish in the wilderness of this world, but will reach her eternal destination. Even the "eagle's wings" reflect what the LORD says in Exodus 19:4: *How I carried you on eagles' wings and brought you to myself.*

Trust that God will take care of his church, all the time! From our earthbound perspective the church often lives in a barren desert, at the margins of our society, a place of affliction and persecution, a struggling wilderness community. You wonder what her future is like.

---

9 The story is in Exodus, Leviticus, Numbers and Deuteronomy

But from the perspective from above she is the glorious and splendid heavenly queen.

God will continue to protect her, provide for her, and nourish her for 1260 days (v.6) or "for a time, times and half a time" (v.14). That is the same length of time. And it is also the same length of time mentioned in Rev. 11:2,4. It's the in-between time, stretching from Jesus' ascension into heaven till his return in glory, the day of the final victory, when she will be ushered into her heavenly home.

But the dragon does not give up. Out of his mouth he spews a stream of wild water, a strong, destructive torrent. It is not necessary to see this river as a metaphor of something specific. Just as God's river of life gives life, so Satan's river of death brings death and destruction.

But the dragon fails again. In a sudden and unexpected move the earth helps the woman by swallowing up all that water. Here is another allusion to Israel's exodus, when the LORD parted the water of the Red Sea, to protect his people, and drowned their hostile pursuers. Here God is again the hidden actor and powerful Saviour. He uses his creation to frustrate Satan's plans and protect his church on her way to the glorious new heaven and new earth.

It says that *the dragon became furious* when he saw what happened. He is beside himself with raging anger. This is his third defeat. Now what? He does not seem to get anywhere and he knows that the clock is ticking.

But he still does not give up. He adjusts his strategy and now he turns to you and me personally, children of the woman, Christian believers *who keep God's commandments and hold to the testimony of Jesus*. He knows each one of us. He knows when and where you and I are vulnerable. He knows our weaknesses.

This makes us all part of this story. It is the paradox of your Christian life. Jesus victory over Satan triggers his anger against you, against all those who follow Jesus.

But remember, these are the last convulsions of a monster that has been defeated three times already.

19 • Revelation 12

Yes, as long as our home is the wilderness, the power of evil is still present and affects us all. That is a threatening scenario. Take the warning to heart.

But be encouraged on your journey towards the new Promised Land: Satan will find his final destruction.

20

REVELATION 13

CHRIST EXPOSES THE DECEPTIVE NATURE OF EVIL

Have you ever heard the word "hexakosioihexekontahexaphobia"? It means "fear of 666". This number, which we find at the end of Revelation 13, is probably the most well-known and most often quoted number in the whole Bible.

It has taken on a life of its own as an occult symbol for dark, evil, spiritual powers. Just saying the number sends shivers up the spines of many people. Some have refused to accept phone numbers, license plates or credit cards with 666 on them. Once a high school student somewhere in the US refused to run in an athletic race, because she was assigned the number 666. In 2003 the US Interstate 666 was renamed by the Highway Department, because people called it the "Devil's Highway". Some were convinced that it was cursed, so that on that Highway more accidents would happen than anywhere else. On the other hand, Satan-worshippers kept stealing the highway signs.

But what does 666 actually stand for in the context of Rev.13? And what is the relationship with the beast that we see here? Many have tried to explain this with the help of gematria. "Gematria" is an ancient system to assign numbers to the letters of the alphabet, or even to a word or a phrase.

However, the wish to find a specific solution triggers many wild speculations as to what or who the number 666 stands for. Many see it as the key that unlocks the identity of the antichrist. This has led to a bizarre variety of options, depending on the imagination of the one who is decoding the number. 666 has been said to refer to the Roman emperor Nero, or the Pope, Hitler, several American presidents, and others.

But what is lacking in all these explanations are the *wisdom* and *understanding* needed, according to v.18, to see the comfort in this number. We will come back to this when we have seen the full picture of John's vision in Revelation 13.

Evil's Appearance

It might be good to refresh our memory as to where we are in the main structure of the Book of Revelation. After the introductory chapters, the Lamb of God received the scroll of redemptive history, sealed with seven seals (Rev. 4 and 5).

He opened the seals one by one, and then we found in Rev. 8 that the seventh seal initiated a new series of seven, the seven trumpet blasts. Then, in Rev. 11 we heard the sound of the seventh trumpet. This one announces seven bowls with the seven last plagues of God's wrath. After this, John's visions will lead us straight into God's final judgment.

But before all this unfolds in Rev. 15 and the following chapters, there is again an interruption in the sequence, an interruption that the glorified Christ uses to warn us, but also to comfort and encourage us. That is in Rev. 12–14. Here we find ourselves right in the middle of that section.

In a way you can say that Rev. 13 gives us an important clue that helps us to see how Revelation unlocks the history of our world. It gives the view from above that shows us how the Almighty God is dealing with the powers of sin and evil in this world.

When Satan is thrown out of heaven, and hurled down to the earth, the conflicts in this world intensify. That was Rev. 12. Then the vision continues.

We see this raving mad dragon standing on the beach, the place where land and sea meet. That does not promise any good. Remember Rev. 12:12 – *Woe to you, O earth and sea, for the devil has come down to you in great wrath, because he knows that his time is short.*

This is his mind-set when he goes off to do what it says in 12:17, to *make war on those who keep the commandments of God and hold to the testimony of Jesus,* the believers. To that end, Satan now summons his agents, his evil accomplices to assist him in his attack on God's people, God's church, on you and me.

John tells us that he sees two beasts, two symbolic animals. He sees one rising out of the sea (v.1), the other one rising out of the earth (v.11). They look quite different, but that is deceptive. In reality they form an evil coalition, like earth and sea belong together. And together they attempt to master the whole world.

It is pretty frightening what John sees slowly emerging from the water, a bizarre but fierce monster with repulsive features. It comes *out of the sea.* In Revelation "sea" is symbolic for the realm of chaos and hostility. That is why it says in Rev. 21:1 that the "new heaven and the new earth" will have *no longer any sea.* Then the proper order will be restored, no more chaos. Here the fact that this monstrous creature arises from the sea shows its intention to throw this world into chaos and disorder.

John describes in detail what this beast looks like. It is remarkably similar to the dragon (Rev.12:3). With *ten horns and seven heads* it has all the terrible features of Satan, the devil, God's fiercest enemy. "Horns" are symbols of power to destroy, and "heads" refer to ruling authority.

In other words, whatever this beast does, it operates in this world with a power and authority driven by Satan. This is reinforced by two other things.

The first is that it has diadems, or crowns, on its ten horns. These are signs of royal authority. In Revelation only three characters are wearing those: Satan (Rev. 12:3), this beast, and Christ (Rev. 19:12). But Christ has numerous crowns, while the evil characters have only a few. That is good to know!

The other detail that shows his malicious intentions, is that on each of its seven heads it has, very prominently and visibly, *a blasphemous name.* Now in the Bible your name expresses who you are, it tells something significant about you. In other words, while this ferocious monster claims divine authority, it defies at the same time the one true, living God. Its purpose is to oppose God and take his place as ruler of the world.

In a sense this beast, with its claim of being qualified to rule this world with divine power and authority, is a caricature of Christ.

Now, how and where do we see this beast show up in our world today?

Here again, what we read in the Old Testament can help us. In the book of the prophet Daniel we read that Daniel sees a vision of four scary beasts (Daniel 7). It is then explained to him that these represent four kingdoms, four hostile political powers that threaten God's people. When you compare the descriptions, this horrific monster that John is seeing, combines many of the frightening aspects of the animals in Daniel's vision into one (v.2).

That means that this beast out of the sea represents all the evil political powers in this world that turn against God, against Christ and his church throughout our history. It exposes those antichristian powers as inspired by Satan.

John's first readers would have recognized this in the hostile Roman Empire and its rulers. But we should not restrict it to that. We can expect the same anywhere and anytime between Jesus' ascension and his return.

When political power, the power of the state, becomes antichristian in its values, and it wants to force these values on all its citizens, it always turns into a cruel monster, ready to devour God's children. When human power and authority in this world demand absolute loyalty and obedience, the consequences are terrifying. For then the goal becomes to resist God's authority, destroy his work, and annihilate his people.

In the appearance of this beast you can already see that it is inspired by the power of the dragon, Satan himself, the source of all evil. And the impression that this power is invincible, is reinforced by a remarkable observation (v.3): one of the seven heads was fatally wounded. That is a serious blow to the power of this monster, or so it seems! However, here is the surprise, the mortal wound miraculously healed.

Think of the symbolism. There are times that antichristian political powers are weak and do not have much influence. Those are times of relief for the church, freedom for the gospel of Jesus. But a little later the hostile oppression will raise its ugly head again. This astonishing healing miracle tells us that this beast is just too powerful. The powers that hate God and the church will not die.

This powerful position of the first beast, and so the influence of Satan, is promoted by the second beast. And it makes clever use of this impressive healing-miracle to do so (see v.12 and 14). However, you would not expect this agenda when you only pay attention to what this second beast looks like.

John tells us that he sees this other beast come *out of the earth*. Here the word "earth" represents the human world, the breeding ground of what is sinful, evil. But this animal looks quite different. As a matter of fact, it is not frightening at all, it has only one head, no crowns, and just two horns. It has the innocent, harmless, non-threatening and trustworthy appearance of a lamb.

But that is deceiving! As soon as this beast opens its mouth, we find that out. When it starts talking, it shows its destructive evil nature, its true malicious character. *It spoke like a dragon*, says John. Here we have another henchman of the Devil, ready to promote evil and hatred towards the Holy God and his church.

This innocent appearance comes as a warning. When you want to distinguish good from evil, do not be fooled by your first impression of what you see. Do not just think to yourself, "it looks good. This person is decent, friendly, and harmless and his message seems pretty reliable. I can trust him."

No, take time to listen carefully. What you hear him say may sound alright, but is it according to God's Word, the Bible, the true gospel?

That is why this second beast is also known later on as *the false prophet*. That is in Rev. 16:13, 19:20, and 20:10. The Bible often warns against false prophets. They look innocent. They present themselves as faithful and trustworthy messengers from God. But they are not. Their words are lies dressed up as truth. And their goal is to mislead people. In Matthew 7:15 Jesus says: *Beware of false prophets, who come to you in sheep's clothing, but inwardly are ravenous wolves.*

Here too, it says in v.14 that *he deceives those who dwell on earth.* In a sense this second beast is a caricature of the Holy Spirit. As the Spirit makes you believe in Jesus Christ, so this beast wants to snatch you out of God's hand and make you worship the powerful beast from the sea. His job is to convince folks that it is beneficial and worthwhile to be loyal to beast number one.

Just as any dictatorial government in this world, so also Satan employs a ministry of propaganda. Here the appearance of beast number two suggests that he acts on God's behalf. But in reality he is Satan's Public Relations Chief, in support of the first beast.

And he has impressive and persuasive means to work with. We read that he *performs great signs*. He tries to mimic the two prophetic witnesses we met in Rev. 11, to the point that he even *makes fire come down from heaven to earth*. In that sense he is the evil counterpart of the great prophet Elijah (see 2 Kings 1). But it is all meant to deceive people. In 2 Thessalonians 2:9 Paul warns us against *the activity of Satan* which comes with *all power and false signs and wonders, and with all wicked deception*. He talks about *a strong delusion*.

This beast out of the earth represents the spiritual, philosophical, cultural and religious structures in our society. Yes, also 'religious' because he does preach worship. Although it is not the worship of the One True God. He promotes a worldview that supports and validates the antichristian political powers in the world.

It is a frightening picture, these two evil buddies that seem to run the world together, driven by Satan himself. The first is a horrific monster. But the second, although it looks harmless, turns out to be just as dangerous as the first one.

The first is Satan's hand or fist, the second is Satan's mind.

EVIL'S INFLUENCE

John's vision also shows us how effective these devilish powers co-operate with each other in our world. The influence of the evil they represent is just incredibly powerful. We read that *men worship the beast from the sea*. It is the amazing healing and survival of this monster that leaves the whole world astonished, totally mesmerized, filled with awe and ready to follow, without critical questions.

How impressed people are, shows in the rhetorical questions they ask (v.4). Think of some of the exclamations in the Old Testament. For instance, in Exodus 15:11 we hear: *Who is like you, O LORD?* The answer is obvious: "Of course no one is."

Here people exclaim: *Who is like the beast? Who can fight against it?* The obvious answer without any doubt is again: "No one is. That's just impossible." For those followers, this beast takes the place of Almighty God.

It is all around us. So many people believe that you do not need God. Our human political or economic powers are invincible. They want to run our lives in everything. They will save the world. Their claim to be like God is pretty persuasive. *Who is like the beast?* But in John's vision the exalted Christ shows us the true nature and the worldwide impact of this evil influence.

With its arrogant and blasphemous language, the beast will have the upper hand for forty-two months. This represents the whole time until Jesus' return. Blaspheming and slandering the Holy God is what he likes to do, slandering and ridiculing God's children here and in heaven is his favourite activity. God? That's ridiculous, there is no God! To think he is ruling this world and our society according to his will and work? Nonsense.

And these evil political powers are so successful in waging war against the believers, that Satan's authority and influence reaches every corner of the earth, *every tribe, people, language and nation* (v.7). The whole world is under his spell.

Or almost! There are also some *from every tribe, people, language, and nation* who refuse to worship the beast, purchased by the blood of the Lamb (v.8).

The symbolism of this beast also includes more subtle ways to influence people. In democratic countries, like ours, political powers do not demand literal worship. But we are told to look at the power of 'the State', not only to fix economic and social problems, but also as the source of moral and spiritual values. You better believe the government's claim that 'the State' knows what is good for you and for your kids.

And if you do not, you are socially unfit. But don't worry, the state has the means to make sure that you will behave like a good and well-adjusted citizen in our secular society. Things like public education, financial regulations, human rights tribunals and required sensitivity training for those who challenge politically correct views.

As Christians we may not feel the immediate threat of death in such countries but if you do not accept the godless values and assumptions of this pagan society, you can feel distrusted and not accepted.

This pressure through political power and government programs is reinforced by the influence of ideological, spiritual or philosophical evil in this world. This is symbolized by the second beast. Prompted by Satan's hatred for God, he cleverly uses his many tricks and pseudo-miracles, his *great signs*, to deceive people.

As a false prophet he ignores both the reality of sin, and salvation by grace through Jesus. He makes false promises about a world without war, hunger and poverty if we would only believe his ideas and trust him. He makes people walk away from God, from Jesus Christ, and his church. He deceives them into thinking that falsehood is truth, and that they should worship the creation instead of the Creator.

His deceit affects people's mindset and thinking. He gets them excited about new ideas and a different worldview. His arguments seem convincing enough. In the Bible we read about signs and miracles to strengthen faith in God. Think of Elijah's fire from heaven, and of the signs the Apostles performed in the New Testament.

"Well", says this false prophet, "look at me. I can do the same. Forget about God."

"And guess what – I can do even more!" The Old Testament sometimes ridicules and pokes fun at idols (Deuteronomy 4:28; Psalm 115:4-8; Psalm 135:15-18; Isaiah 44:9-17). These dumb images cannot see, hear, or speak.

"Watch me," says the false prophet, "If you make an image of the first beast, I can make it talk" (v.15). This is totally amazing.

All these astonishing things fascinate and impress people. They convince them that the spiritual and philosophical ideas of the false prophet must be correct. He makes it so obvious that life makes more sense without faith in God and without faith in Jesus Christ. And if you do not agree and you do not share such a worldview, they think you are stupid, backward, and out of touch with reality. You do not get it.

Consider the use of mass media and social media. Yes, they can be used to reach more people with the gospel of Jesus Christ than ever before and that is a blessing.

But in today's society, communication via these means and through educational institutions have also become Satan's most powerful tool to teach us the secular views of ourselves and the world we live in. A materialistic worldview considers God absent, irrelevant or non-existent. Money, health, intelligence, beauty and sexual pleasure – those are the things that give us the good life.

And this lie is so pervasive, that all this seems obvious, natural, and inevitable. Think of it. How can these ideas be wrong, when the miracles of science and technology show us how superior our modern views are? Our society has come a long way since the Dark Ages, and without God.

With missionary zeal the modern militant atheists are trying to rid the world of religion. In 2013 a philosophy professor wrote a book, called *A Manual for Creating Atheists*.[10] It is meant as a guide for talking people out of their faith. And if you argue with this and you ask critical questions, you are just ignorant. You don't think. You are not 'with it'.

---

10 Peter Boghossian, *A Manuel for Creating Atheists*, Pitchstone Publishing, 2013

The advance of these evil influences seems unstoppable. The beast from the earth seems firmly in control. It says that it *causes all.... to be marked on the right hand or the forehead*, as a way to identify that person as belonging to the beast from the sea.

This word 'mark' occurs seven times in Revelation. Heres it is some sort of ID for the loyal followers of this beast and his boss, the Devil. It is not a visible mark, like a tattoo, or something like that. No, it is your attitude as it shows in what you think and say (forehead) and how you act (right hand). And what are the consequences?

Think of your Costco membership card. You cannot shop at Costco if you are not a member. But that is not a big deal. You can shop elsewhere. Here the consequences are much more dramatic. Consider v.17. If it is not clear from what you say and how you act that you belong to this antichristian monster, if you refuse to declare that you agree with the modern antichristian values, they no longer want customers like you.

You will need this ID to survive. If you do not, you'll have no access to goods and services. You will not be able to carry out your business in any form or shape. You will be reduced to poverty, and eventually starve to death.

But here is our problem as God's children. We already have something on our foreheads remember? That is the 'seal of the Lamb'. We have heard about that in Rev. 7:3, and we will hear about it again in Rev. 14:1. And you cannot have both. It is either one or the other; you belong to the one true God and his Son Jesus Christ **OR** you belong to Satan and his malicious sidekick. There is no neutral ground here.

The 'seal of the Lamb' protects against God's judgments. That is great. That is full of comfort. But is that enough, when the evil powers makes your life miserable, because you do not have the 'mark of the beast'?

EVIL'S FAILURE

This exposition of the true nature of evil makes for a pretty scary picture of the world we live in. It is a frightening perspective for you and me, for all of God's people, for the church, to become more and more marginalized in the world, because we do not have the 'mark of the beast'.

And yet, even in severe tribulation, in the most dreadful days that precede Jesus' return, there will be faithful believers in this world, people who trust that all things remain under God's control. John's vision of these two beasts is not only a forewarning, it is also encouraging. That is right, encouraging. It encourages us to open our eyes and recognize the ultimate failure of evil.

Remember, in these visions the glorified Christ gives John, and us, the view from above, from heaven, so that we see things that we do not see from here, from below. From the perspective of its followers this frightening monster is an impressive god-like power, with unlimited authority. But the perspective from above shows that he is subject to God's plan, and that he can only operate with God's permission.

Do not be afraid! Sure, Satan can summon his helpers out of the sea and the land. But in Rev. 10 we saw God's mighty angel *standing on the sea and the land*. It looks like our world, controlled by evil, can only yield evil. But that is not true. This whole bunch will fail. God remains in control. That is why it says several times throughout this chapter, that *he* (either the first or second beast) *was given*, or, *was allowed*. (that's in the v.5, 7, 14 and 15).

This identifies the holy and almighty God as the major Actor in this story.

Yes, he alone is the only all-powerful One, despite the beast's claims. Even when *all who dwell on earth will worship the beast* (v.8), in the end all opposition against God will turn out to be futile. From his throne, the glorified Christ shows us evil's inevitable failure. Hold on to this view, this perspective, when it seems impossible to restrain the evil powers in this world.

Many will worship the monstrous evil powers that operate among us and seem to be so successful. And what will happen if you refuse? "Be encouraged," says Christ, "for your citizenship is secure in heaven" (compare Philippians 3:20,21). If you refuse to worship the evil beast, you may know, writes John, *that your names have been written before the foundation of the world in the book of life of the Lamb that was slain* (v.8). This "book of life" is mentioned six times in Revelation. It is the register of those who belong to the Lamb of God, to Jesus Christ.

Believe in him and you will never perish. Trust that the war against God's people (v.7) will only go as far as God allows. Trust that the evil powers will fail to change God's eternal plan of salvation. Don't be scared when you get to know the true nature of evil, but hold on to your comfort that *before the foundation of the world* God chose you to be saved by the blood of Jesus.

Can you be sure of that? *If anyone has an ear, let him hear*, says John in v.9. Listen carefully to God's Word and recognize the promised failure of Satan and his nasty sidekicks. In faith embrace your Saviour and remember that he alone brings eternal life and that his kingdom will last forever.

No, that does not mean that when you belong to the Lamb of God and your names are written in the 'book of life', you will escape captivity or death when the evil darkness covers the world (v.10).

Persecution will be a terrible reality. The question each one of us must ask ourselves is: what do we do in such times? Should we be intimidated? The answer is 'NO'. For the reality is also that the power of evil is limited. This calls us, as believers, to show *endurance* in resisting the values of the beast and its followers. It calls us to show *faith* in holding on to the testimony of Jesus (v.10).

It also calls for *wisdom* (v.18). We repeat, do not be intimidated by the beast. He has a number. And I want you to recognize with *spiritual wisdom*, says John, that this can be calculated, because it is just a human number, 666. This evil beast claims to be divine, but he is not. Then he would have the number seven. But he does not!

Triple six is a six, reinforced by six tens and six hundreds. So yes, this beast does represent a horrendous concentration of powerful evil. But do not be deceived. Take the look from above and know that he is not almighty and he never will be!

Let the number 666 comfort and encourage you. In the end all the evil the dragon can produce, supported by these two beasts and all their worshippers will be a huge failure!

Remain faithful to your Saviour Jesus.

He will turn out to be stronger, because he has already won the victory.

21

Revelation 14: 1 – 13

GOD WILL RESOLVE THE CONFLICT BETWEEN GOOD AND EVIL

In 2013 a gentleman with the name Ryan Bell, who used to be a pastor, was asked: "What difference does God make in your life?" He found answering that question harder than he had initially thought, and so he wanted to find out for himself. He decided to live for a year as an atheist, without God, starting January 1, 2014.

For a real Christian this is a silly experiment, of course. As if living with God is some sort of hobby that you can drop or pick up again, any time you feel like it. Today this is how many folks may look at religion. It is about your own spiritual needs.

But God exists. He really does, regardless whether Mr. Bell, you, I, or anyone else, believes it or not. And when you realize this, and that your relationship with him determines the very core of who you are, that your faith in Jesus is your very identity, you cannot even imagine keeping up for just one day pretending that he does not exist.

Nevertheless, the question, "what difference does God make in your life?" is a good one. Not because you can simply switch between living with or without God, as if that would determine God's existence.

21 • Revelation 14:1-13

However, there is this distinction in our world between those who trust in God and those who ignore God. Or, to put it in the words we hear in Revelation 13 and 14, the distinction between those who follow the Lamb and those who follow the beast.

You will remember that Rev. 13 pictures antichristian violence by the mock-trinity of the dragon (Satan) and his two monsters. The frightening beast from the sea had numerous worshippers following him (see v.3 and 4), although not everybody joined the unholy parade.

The question now becomes, how is this conflict between good and evil, as pictured in Rev. 13, going to end, and how is the church going to survive this ordeal?

The view from above in John's vision in Rev. 14:1–13 shows that God himself will resolve this conflict. And what will be the outcome for you? That depends on what side you are in this conflict. Do you live with God or without God?

GOD IS A GOD OF GRACE

The first thing John sees, when the frightening vision of Rev. 13 disappears, is a joyful and pleasant surprise – the very opposite of the threatening picture in Rev. 13. He sees *"The Lamb, standing on Mount Zion"*.

We know that "the Lamb" is Jesus Christ. In Rev. 5, John saw him standing as a Lamb, "looking as if it had been slain". He is the One who sacrificed himself, "the Lamb of God who took away the sin of the world." But he also came to life again. He is the child from Rev. 12, "caught up to God and his throne". And now when John sees him standing here, it is a victorious, triumphant image.

"Zion" is the old name of the mountain where the LORD had his temple built. Throughout the Old Testament it stands for the place where God is present, the place from where he governs his people. It was also the place where God's people came to worship.

And in the promises of the prophets, Zion becomes the place of refuge, the place where the redeemed will be gathered. In Zion God guarantees salvation and security for all who seek him and worship him.

Here, in Revelation, this 'Mount Zion' is more than a particular geographical location, like the earthly Zion. But it is not heaven either, or the New Jerusalem. We are not there yet. No, the name is symbolic, referring to every place in this world where God is worshipped by the followers of Jesus Christ, and where they are protected by his care. In a demonic world, Zion stands for the realm of safety for those who share in Jesus' victory.

And you know what is so wonderful? John sees that the believers *"with the Lamb on Zion are 144,000"*. Do you remember those people? We have met them before, in Rev. 7. It is the same group, all the people of God. The vision shows the heavenly view of God's church on earth of all times and all places, the total number of God's people, with each one of them known, numbered, and marked by God himself.

Today this church is still a work in progress. And it still needs a lot of work. Yet, in the end they will all be there, the full number, safe and secure. But today already the risen Christ Jesus guarantees our safety. O, yes, the angry dragon will continue to attack you. But worship the Lamb, place yourself under his protection, and you will have nothing to fear.

How do we know this? Remember what we also heard in Rev. 7. The 144,000 were 'sealed' on their foreheads. Well, here we find out what this 'seal' looks like. *"They had the name of the Lamb and his Father's name written on their foreheads."*

You can never hide what is on your forehead. It is your attitude in life that demonstrates to whom you belong. Let it be visible that you belong to God the Father and to Jesus Christ. They own you. But they also protect you. This mark tells you that nothing can separate you from God's love in Jesus Christ.

All this makes this glorious view of the Lamb with his 144,000 marked followers on Mount Zion a joyful surprise. The dragon and his two beasts will attack you and try to make you unfaithful to God and your Saviour. But in the fierce battle between good and evil, our God shows himself a God of grace.

21 • Revelation 14:1-13

Then John also hears something (v.2)! It is a sound from heaven, loud and lively. But he finds it hard to describe it adequately. Three times he says that it was "like this or like that." First, he compares it with *"the roar of many waters,"* majestic and impressive, as when you stand close to Niagara Falls. He then compares it with *"the sound of loud thunder,"* powerful and overwhelming. But he concludes by comparing it with *"the sound of harpists, playing on their harps,"* melodious, sweet, lovely, a wonderful mix of impressions that move heart and soul.

But after a moment John recognizes the sound as singing. He hears heavenly voices. Marvellous! But, who are these mighty singers? Many scholars suggest that the 144,000 are singing. This is not very likely. They are still in the process of learning this song, it says in v.3. On top of that, this sound comes from heaven.

So, again, who are singing here? John hears (and perhaps sees) that this chorus is singing *"before the throne and before the four living creatures and before the elders"*. That picture brings us back into God's heavenly throne-hall, described in Rev. 4 and 5. We should therefore think of the massive angel-choirs we read about in Rev. 5:11, *"numbering myriads of myriads, and thousands of thousands"*. In a most glorious manner heaven responds to the gathering of the 144,000, God's people, God's holy church redeemed by the Lamb.

We do not hear what they are singing, but it is called *"a new song"*. In Scripture we always hear about 'a new song' when God's people have reason to praise the Lord for new, powerful acts of salvation. In many of the psalms, Israel is called to 'sing a new song' to celebrate God's new victories over his enemies.

Here the heavenly voices teach the church a new song to praise the God of grace, because of Jesus' sacrifice on the cross. It is incredible, but true, that in the midst of much antichristian oppression and hostility you do not have to hunker down in fear. No, you may join the angels and learn to celebrate your salvation from sin and from the evil powers of this world with a new song to the praise and glory of God.

And *"no one could learn that song except the 144,000, who had been redeemed from the earth,"* the apostle adds. Only if you belong to Jesus Christ you will be able and learn to sing with all your heart to express your 'new' experience of God's gracious redemption.

That is not exclusive in the sense that others are not allowed to participate. But if you do not believe in Jesus as your Saviour, you just do not get it and you do not care. For folks that do not experience the love of God and the joy of salvation by grace, it doesn't make sense to join in singing about it. But for those 144,000, for the church of Jesus Christ in this world, it is the most natural thing to do. After all, as Christian believers we have seen God's amazing power as a God of grace, have we not?

The apostle John then goes on to list five reasons why it should be easy for the church to learn this new song in praise to God for his goodness and grace.

The first is that the believers *"have been redeemed from the earth"*. The 'earth' is here the realm of sin. So, by his saving grace in Jesus, God has liberated us out of there, and set us free from the evil rule of Satan.

The second is that they *"have not defiled themselves with women, for they are virgins"*. For some that is a disturbing statement. It seems to imply that the redeemed are only single men, who abstain from sexual activity, and that women are excluded from salvation, because they are unclean. But that does not make any sense.

The point is that here, as more often in the Bible, sexual imagery is used to describe our spiritual commitment. Just as adultery is often a metaphor for idolatry, turning away from the true God to serve other gods, so 'being virgins', or 'keeping pure' (as translated in the NIV) becomes a metaphor for remaining faithful to the true living God, and rejecting the values and beliefs of the antichristian culture.

In other words, John uses this strong image to emphasize that as God's church we can only learn to sing this new song of salvation, if we remain entirely, one hundred percent loyal and devoted to Jesus Christ as his pure bride.

The third reason that makes the church sing to the glory of God, is that we *"follow the Lamb wherever he goes"*. Think of the Israelites in the Old Testament. After they had left Egypt, they followed the cloud by day and the pillar of fire by night, on the journey to the Promised Land. In the same way as God's children today we may follow Jesus Christ to the new Promised Land.

It is true, that this journey is filled with trials and struggles. We experience that the way of the Lamb is the way of the cross. And yet, this is also the way to glory. Jesus calls you to hold on to him and to follow him, without being afraid of the consequences in this life. Trust that with him your future looks bright. That will make you sing!

John's fourth point is that as Christian believers we have been *"redeemed from among mankind as firstfruits for God and the Lamb"*. The symbolism of the 'firstfruits' presented to God is rooted in Old Testament harvest laws. By God's grace you have been separated from this sinful human world. "You have been bought with a price," says Paul to the Corinthians. You have been given a new purpose and a new destination, to serve and worship God and your Saviour.

And the fifth characteristic of God's children: *"in their mouth no lie was found, for they are blameless"*. This is serious. In Rev. 21 and 22 we hear that "all liars" are barred from entering the New Jerusalem. So we must resist Satan's lies, hold on to the truth, become more and more Christ-like, and find ourselves "blameless" by grace alone.

Well, here is the profile of the church of Christ, as it is singing on its way to eternal glory. No, it is not a profile that reflects our achievements. It is a profile that only reflects the glorious power of God's grace in our lives.

Do you recognize this profile as your profile? Is this your church? Rejoice, because today already, as the Holy God is on his way to resolve the conflict between good and evil, today already we may live under the protection of God the Father and the Lamb. Today already we may sing with the angels the new song of the victory we have in Jesus. Because the Holy God is a God of grace!

GOD IS A GOD OF JUSTICE

If only the 144,000 followers of Jesus can learn to sing the new song of God's grace, because they belong to the Lamb, what about the future of the rest of mankind? How will they be affected when the Holy God is going to resolve the conflict between good and evil that has plagued this world since the fall into sin? What will happen to the followers of the beast?

John's vision continues. The heavenly song fades out, and the scene changes. He then sees three angels flying in midair. That is in v.6, 8 and 9. They appear one after the other, but all three of them have the same purpose, namely, to warn the people of the coming final judgment that they may repent and turn to God in faith.

This flight high above the earth and these loud voices work together to heighten the dramatic tension in these verses. Everyone on earth must hear what these angels have to say, and no one who continues in unbelief is going to escape the consequences.

The first Angel "*has the eternal gospel to proclaim*". The gospel is always God's good news of salvation; the joyful message that God the Creator is the glorious King of the universe, and that through Christ he is going to establish his new world. And this gospel is "eternal", unchangeable, never outdated, and valid for ever.

But it is not only eternal, it is also universal. The gospel is for all "*those who dwell on earth*". Regardless of the time in history, culture, background, language or whatever, everyone, everywhere is called to fear, glorify and worship God the Creator.

This gospel message is also really urgent, because, says the angel, "*the hour of God's judgment has come*". There is no time to lose. Many in this world live as if there will never be any judgment at all. But everybody will one day come face to face with his Maker. And only the gospel of Jesus opens the way of escape. Return to God by faith in Jesus Christ before it is too late. Fear him. Worship him and not the beast. The Creator alone is worthy of all praise and worship.

What comes out of the mouth of this first angel, is nothing but the Christian missionary message of the church of all times. Is this our message in the world today? Is this our focus when we think about mission and evangelism, that all people are to worship and give glory to God the Creator? Are we addressing the chief sin of people that they refuse to worship the One who created them and sustains them? Do we let people know that God is warning the unrepentant world?

This makes the gospel proclamation urgent and serious business. For if you choose not to repent in response to its message, God will punish sin!

As he resolves the conflict between good and evil, God also demonstrates his justice.

Then the second angel appears in John's vision, and he makes a remarkable announcement. *"Fallen, fallen is Babylon the great"*. That is remarkable for two reasons.

In the first place, this is the first time we hear the name 'Babylon' so the reader or listener does not know anything about it. A detailed description comes in Rev. 17. Let me say now already that Babylon represents all the hostile threats against God's people of all times and places. It is the great anti-city to the New Jerusalem, and the centre of all false worship. It is the symbolic city of this world, the human culture and society where all antichristian worldviews come together.

Secondly, we note that it says "fallen is Babylon" – that is the past tense as if it is already accomplished. But it has not happened yet. The destruction of Babylon is still to come. We will hear about it in Rev. 18. But it drives home that it is inevitably going to happen. Babylon will surely be destroyed, that's a guarantee!

And why is that? *"She made all nations drink the wine of the passion of her sexual immorality."* In the expression "sexual immorality" or "adultery" we have the flipside of the same sexual imagery as in v.4.

Just as "keeping pure" is a metaphor for being faithful to God, so "adultery" is a metaphor for idolatry, following Satan. And this kind of 'adultery' has an intoxicating influence on people. It leads to the destructive behaviour and lifestyle that is so rampant in our society. It offends God deeply.

And therefore, in stark contrast with Zion, the city of God, as a place of redemption, Babylon, the city of Satan, will become a place of utter destruction, because God is not only a God of grace, he is also a God of justice.

And then we hear the loud, booming voice of the third angel. It is so loud that no one can claim not to be aware of the dramatic consequences when you call Babylon your "home". *If anyone worships the beast and its image and receives a mark on his forehead or on his hand, he also will drink the wine of God's wrath.* In other words: "if you refuse to repent from evil, if you refuse to turn to God, because you love to drink the intoxicating wine of Babylon, the God of justice will make you drink the wine of his anger, his wrath" (see Jeremiah 25:15-28).

If you are going to attach yourself to this evil world, you will perish with this world. You cannot stubbornly persist in sin and expect to get away with it.

Then the angel gives a graphic picture of the terrible suffering of those who follow Satan, and refuse to repent and worship God (v.10, 11). The fire, the burning sulphur and rising smoke are a grim reminder of God's punishment for Sodom and Gomorrah (Genesis 19). But here it will go on for ever and ever, without relief, day and night.

What do we do with this horrendous picture? The idea of endless torment is abhorrent for us. It troubles not only non-Christians, who believe that everybody is innocent and that all suffering is senseless and morally wrong.

Even many Christians have a hard time with the reality of hell. Is God not a God of love? And does Jesus not teach us to love even our enemies? After all, they might repent and become our brothers and sisters in Christ!

On top of that, there are many decent people who may not believe in the Holy God and who may not follow Jesus, but who still do things that reflect the power and glory of God, things we respect, things we admire them for.

However, let us be careful not to distort the biblical truth. All these considerations are true and apply today. As long as we live together in this world, we reach out to unbelievers, we pray and hope for repentance of even the most terrible sinner.

But at Jesus' second coming the possibility of repentance comes to an end. It is over. No second chance. Even Jesus himself says this. Read the Parable of the Weeds, and its explanation, in Matthew 13: 24–30 and 36–43.

21 • Revelation 14:1-13

That is radically different from today, when there is still time to repent. Then we will see undiluted wickedness; evil in all its ugliness. In wicked people, evil will then come to full fruition. Today it is hard for us to imagine how much worse evil may actually become. We begin to see glimpses of it today. That is awful.

Yet, for us today the reality of hell is beyond comprehension. But we must accept that God alone is God. He will resolve the conflict between good and evil. And he knows what he is doing when he displays grace and when he displays justice.

Today for you and me, and everyone else it is the most serious warning that only by turning to Jesus Christ we can escape the hellish agony. He is the One who drank the wine of God's wrath in our place.

This warning is especially urgent if you want to belong to Jesus and enjoy his blessings, and at the same time you enjoy living in Babylon, living according to the values and beliefs of a culture without God. This message urges you not to settle down in Babylon, but to reject such cultural and spiritual accommodation and to stay focussed on your trek to the New Jerusalem.

So, where do you want to belong: Zion OR Babylon?

GOD IS A GOD OF HOPE

Where does this leave us, today – *the saints* (v.12), the believers, *those who keep the commands of God and their faith in Jesus*? Should faithful Christians gloat over the horrible fate of those who worship the beast? Absolutely not.

It makes the call to reach out in compassion even more urgent. And we must also take the warning to heart, not to be impressed by the ways of the world. Do not be intoxicated by the beauty and grandeur of Babylon. Accommodation to a culture driven by Satan will always end in disaster.

But praise the Lord! The God of justice, the God of never-ending punishment is also a God of hope. As he is on his way to resolve the conflict between good and evil, he calls for your *endurance*, says John.

Yes, you will need "patient endurance", because God does not promise that your trouble and oppression, your trials and temptations in this world are going away before Jesus returns.

You will need "patient endurance" to resist the tempting ways of Babylon and the beast. Keep God's commands, remain faithful to Jesus Christ, and keep singing. Do not cave in to the attractions of the surrounding society and its immoral idolatries, however innocent and seductive they seem.

No, this is not always easy. In fact, it can be really difficult! But it is possible. Always remember that God is a God of justice AND hope. Do not give up. The ultimate vindication is coming when the conflict between good and evil will be resolved.

This hope is confirmed twice!

First by the exalted Christ! At the end of this vision John *hears a voice from heaven*. It does not specifically say who is talking, but it is probably Jesus himself, because he was the One who had instructed John in the same way in Rev. 1:11.

He tells John, "*write this.* What I am going to say now is so important that I explicitly want you to put it black-on-white for my people. Make sure that everyone at all times can read my words of encouragement for all my children, my words of hope in the midst of disasters and persecution, even to the point of death."

Blessed are the dead who die in the Lord from now on. The Holy God will resolve the conflict between good and evil. And this resolution will come with violent judgments and eternal punishment. But there is hope! For God's children the end of life will be radically different from what it will be for the wicked, as pictured in v.9–11.

When you die in the Lord Jesus, you are blessed, you will be happy, regardless what your life here on earth was like. Our God is a God of hope beyond this earthly life. His grace will lift you out of this dark world, where so many horrible things happen, and usher you into glory.

21 • Revelation 14:1-13

When you die in the Lord Jesus, you will see, face to face, the One who died for you, and who now lives to intercede for you. You will see his glory as the One who conquered sin, death, and Satan.

Let these words of hope comfort us when we bury our dead. God's children die in this broken world, and many of them suffer on their way to the grave. But together with them we all look forward to the day that the conflict between good and evil will be resolved permanently. It is coming.

And then the Holy Spirit confirms it again: *YES*, he says, *blessed indeed* are those who belong to the Lord. For those who follow and worship the beast, there will be no rest, day or night (v.11), but when you die in the Lord Jesus, you will find the true rest that will never end.

All the trouble in this sinful world, ripped apart by the conflict between good and evil, you may leave it all behind. The Holy God will take care of that.

But whatever you do in this life to the glory of God, will follow you and stay with you forever as the eternal evidence of God's grace in your life.

You and I may be encouraged today that the Lord is faithful to the end.

May that truth encourage us to also remain faithful to him.

22

Revelation 14: 14 – 20

WHEN THE HARVEST IS RIPE, GOD WRAPS UP OUR HISTORY

In the United States, "The Battle Hymn of the Republic" is a popular patriotic song, written at the beginning of the American Civil War. The first lines go like this: *Mine eyes have seen the glory of the coming of the Lord; He is trampling out the vintage where the grapes of wrath are stored.* The lyrics refer to Revelation 14:19–20. The poet links the American Civil War with God's judgment of the wicked in this passage.

About 80 years later the words of this song gave John Steinbeck the title of what is perhaps the most famous American novel of the 20th century: "The Grapes of Wrath". This book, published in 1939, describes the tragic fate of a poor family of tenant farmers during the Great Depression in the 1930's. Terrible drought and famine drive them from Oklahoma to California, searching for jobs and food to survive the future.

But in California they continue to suffer abuse, injustice, and poverty. The rich farmers would rather destroy their abundant crops to keep the prices high, than feeding the hungry. The title of Steinbeck's novel symbolizes its theme, namely, the oppressive circumstances of the poor, who suffer abuse and injustice, will result in terrible wrath.

The question for us is: the grapes that are trampled in the great winepress of God's wrath, as mentioned in Rev. 14, do they refer to political evils, as suggested in "The Battle Hymn of the Republic", or to social evils, as in Steinbeck's book?

Of course, we can rightly say that those things are all part of the evil in this world. At the same time, we have to realize that the text goes much deeper; this contrast between good and evil runs deep.

In the first part of Rev. 14 we saw that God is going to resolve the conflict between good and evil, the conflict between the dragon and the Lamb, between Satan and Christ, between Satan's followers and those who worship the Lamb.

In the last part of this chapter Christ shows us the results of this in John's vision of a twofold harvest, described in the v.14–16 and 17–20.

THE GRAIN-HARVEST OF HIS SALVATION

Before we get into more details, the first question we need to answer is this: does the vision that John is seeing in our text, show us a two-fold harvest – one that symbolizes the gathering of all the believers at the end of times, and another one as an image of the gathering and punishment of all the wicked at the same time?

When you read through the passage it seems obvious. But some argue that it is really about one harvest, a harvest of severe judgment. They base this on Joel 3:13. There we read: *Put in the sickle, for the harvest is ripe. Go in, tread, for the winepress is full. The vats overflow, for their evil is great.* This seems to support this idea of one harvest, in two images. He does give the impression that he only talks about God judging the wicked, although v.16 of Joel 3 gives a different picture. There he also refers to the LORD as *a refuge to his people, a stronghold to the people of Israel*.

When connected with Joel 3:13, John's vision could be pictured as one judgment in two parallel images or metaphors that refer to the same event. The purpose of such a structure would be to emphasize the seriousness of God's wrath.

However, there is strong evidence that in this vision we see images of two different harvests. You could say that the one is a positive metaphor and the other one is a negative metaphor.

The most significant difference is that the first harvest is one action, one stage – which is harvesting or gathering, probably of grain. It does not say anything about threshing or winnowing to separate the wheat from the chaff. Winnowing, in the Bible, is an image of judgment. Think of Matthew 3:12. But harvesting grain, on the other hand, is used as a positive picture of gathering God's people into glory.

In contrast, the second harvest, the grape-harvest, has two actions, two stages. After being harvested, the grapes are being trampled in the winepress of God's wrath. The latter is a picture of judgment and severe punishment.

This makes it worthwhile to have a closer look at what John is seeing. It starts with an amazing vision of a beautiful white cloud. And the surprising thing is, there is someone sitting on it. He sees *one like a son of man*, a human being.

In the Bible, a cloud is often a manifestation of God's glorious presence. Think of the cloud that led Israel when they left Egypt (Exodus 13), or the cloud that filled the tabernacle and the temple (Exodus 40; 1 Kings 8). The colour white reflects God's heavenly light, his purity and holiness.

But there is more. The person John is seeing wears *a golden crown*. That is a symbol of his majesty, his royal authority. It tells us that this person rules with the power and glory of a king. Altogether it is a triumphant view. The one on this cloud in the sky is exalted above all human powers in this world. In him the victorious glory of Almighty God himself is coming to our world.

Who is this? There are enough reasons to believe that *the one seated on this cloud* is no one less than our Lord Jesus Christ in his royal majesty, our exalted Saviour.

Some have questioned that. "He must be someone else, a lesser figure," they say. "Perhaps an angel." After all, it says in the next verse (15) that *another angel came*. And on top of that, it would be odd (as happens in v.15) that an angel would come to command or instruct the glorified Jesus Christ, would it not?

22 • Revelation 14:14-20

And yet, there can be no doubt that the expression *one like a son of man* refers to Jesus in his heavenly glory. It is this same title that comes with the description of his splendour in Revelation 1:12-16. And all this goes back to Daniel 7:13-14, where the prophet Daniel sees *one like a son of man, coming with the clouds of heaven, who was given authority, glory, sovereign power, and an everlasting kingdom.* This is a prophecy about Christ.

Another notion in the New Testament confirms this. We know how the Bible tells us that at his return Jesus will come on the clouds of heaven. This will be totally overwhelming. His glorious appearance will be seen everywhere. Everyone will recognize him as King. And *at the name of Jesus every knee will bow in heaven and on earth and under the earth* (Philippians 2:10, 11). And here he is. Despite the rebellious violence against him in this world – here he is, powerful and victorious!

The question is: What are the implications of Jesus' victory for you and me, for all of us and for all the people in this world, for those who believe in him and worship him **and** for those who resist him?

John's vision shows us the image of Christ in his role as "reaper", ready to harvest the crops. As such that sounds neutral. But the vision also makes clear that this 'reaper's role is not neutral, because the reaper is, at the same time, the judge, and his harvest is one of people. And in his role as 'reaper', Christ is going to reap people for salvation **and** he is going to reap people for judgment.

Today, we are being told that all human choices and all the various directions people choose in their lives are equally valid. But the Bible does not support that. The question that matters is: which differences and distinctions between people are relevant to separate them when Judge Jesus comes for the harvest?

We tend to separate people along the lines of their cultures, histories, backgrounds, traditions, ethnicity, political views, etc. But those things turn out to be irrelevant when the reaper comes. He has different standards. The people to be harvested are either, what the Bible calls, righteous people or wicked people. And the difference between these two is one of grace. Do you live by God's grace, through faith in Jesus, or do you refuse to repent from sin and turn to Jesus?

To be sure, on the day that God is going to wrap up our history, all human beings, all of us, without any exception, will face the same Judge. The two different images in John's vision are strongly connected by that same one Judge in the person of Jesus Christ. But the results will be different, radically different. The results will be each other's very opposite.

In the first part of his vision, the positive metaphor of the grain-harvest, the harvest of the righteous, John sees the 'one like a son of man', sitting on his cloud, with *a sharp sickle in his hand*. This is a piece of farming equipment. In the ancient agricultural world, it was used for harvesting grain. The word "sickle" is used six times in these verses. It is a verbal thread that ties both parts together, to remind us that these two harvests, although not identical, are strongly connected.

And so we see the royal Judge, equipped and prepared to go. The reaper is ready for the harvest. But he does not do anything! What is he waiting for?

He has to wait for the right time. He must wait for God's time. Indeed, right now the exalted Christ is still waiting for the signal that the Holy and Almighty God is ready to wrap up the history of our world. This is the tension of the time we live in. Christ is ready. Today already he is eagerly waiting for the signal that it is time. Are we? Are you just as eagerly waiting for this moment as your Saviour is?

In John's vision, in the view from above, it does not take long. The apostle sees *another angel coming*. That is not "another" one "like a son of man" on the cloud. That would imply that this "son of man" was actually an angel. No, it is another angel, in addition to the three mentioned earlier in this chapter (Rev. 14:6, 8, 9).

This one is coming *out of the temple*. He comes directly from before the holy throne in the sanctuary in heaven. He comes with a message straight from God Almighty, a message for the glorified Christ, who is waiting with his sickle in his hand. And what he has to say he calls out with a loud voice. He shouts the commands of the holy God, clearly, and for everyone to hear.

Such shouting is not disrespectful towards Christ. This angel is just a messenger. All he does is follow the instructions God has given him, to pass on the heavenly command: *Put in your sickle and reap, for the hour to reap has come, for the harvest of the earth is fully ripe.*

This is such an incredibly powerful moment. This is the moment Jesus has been waiting for. Now the time he has been looking forward to, has come!

In Matthew 24 Jesus is having this conversation with his disciples about signs that would indicate that the end of time is near or has come. And then he says this in v.36: *Concerning that day and hour no one knows, not even the angels of heaven, nor the Son, but the Father only.* That is remarkable. Did you realize that? Even Jesus himself does not know. He can only wait. Just as you and I can only wait.

Only God the Father knows, the almighty Creator of heaven and earth. He who began everything, he alone decides when the time has come to wrap up our history, the history of his creation. John's vision shows us what is coming when the grain-harvest is ripe. The sign is given and the glorious 'son of man' swings his sickle over the earth.

When we take Joel 3:13a and read through Matt. 13:36–43, where Jesus explains the Parable of the Weeds (*cf.* Matt. 12:24-30), we get a deeper understanding of the metaphor of the grain-harvest. It refers back to what was said in Rev. 14: 4, about the 144,000 to be offered as first-fruits to God and to the Lamb. This imagery has to do with the harvest celebrations in the Old Testament.

Jesus will be collecting all God's people from out of this world. Wherever you are in the journey of your life on earth, when Christ gets his Father's message that the harvest is ripe, he will come to collect you. And together with all God's children, all of them of all ages and from all over the world, he will bring you to your final destination. And no one will be left behind.

Do we have any idea when the harvest will be ready? Yes, we do. When the last believer in this world has turned to God and has embraced Jesus as his or her Saviour, then *the hour to reap has come.*

This puts us on the spot. It makes it urgent for the church to remain busy with making disciples, followers of Jesus, of all nations (Matt. 28:18-20). All over the world mission and evangelism remain top priorities for the church until the very end.

No, that does not mean that we know the date. But instead of looking around, shaking our head about all the bad stuff that is going on and wondering why Jesus is waiting, we better get ready by doing faithfully what the Lord calls us to do, as long as we have the opportunity.

But when the command is given by the Father, the moment Jesus has been waiting for arrives. And immediately he swings into action. *So he who sat on the cloud swung his sickle across the earth, and the earth was reaped.* Yes, indeed, Jesus is ready to go at it, any time!

And how great, how wonderful it will be to see the exciting results when the harvest is brought in, the harvest of his own church gathering work; the completion of his grand project, as it has been unfolding throughout the centuries. We will see the fruit of mission work, evangelism, and church-planting; we will see the fruit of the weekly preaching, of prayer, pastoral work, catechism-classes, youth-work, Bible-study; we will see the fruit of Christ's church gathering work in all its glory!

What a marvellous moment this is going to be for all who believe in Jesus Christ. From everywhere and from all times we will get together for the grand reunion. The dead will rise; the living will change, and we will all see each other on that great and glorious day.

I am sure you would all like to be there, so we better be ready for it. For when it is time, it all comes to its final closure. God is wrapping up our history.

THE GRAPE-HARVEST OF HIS WRATH

The second part of the vision in this passage comes under the same theme as the first part. It is the theme of the coming harvest when we will all face the same Royal Judge. And when I say "all", I mean that every human being will come to know him, whether he or she believes in him or not.

Of course, when John describes his twofold vision, he pictures the one harvest following after the other. That is the only way to describe it. But it is good to realize that both harvests actually happen simultaneously, at the same time.

However, as we've seen, the two metaphors are not identical. Here we find the image of a grape-harvest. And just as the grain-harvest turned out to be a positive metaphor, an encouraging picture, so we will learn that the grape-harvest is a negative metaphor, a frightening picture.

In other words, just as Jesus' second coming as victorious King and righteous Judge will bring salvation to God's people, so it will bring judgment and eternal punishment for the wicked.

John's vision reinforces the message that resounds throughout this book. Whoever does not heed God's warnings, whoever does not repent, whoever does not have life and hope in Jesus Christ, he can expect God's judgment.

This time the one who reaps the harvest is not Christ. He will have another role. This harvest is gathered in by an angel (v.17). He too has with him *a sharp sickle* as a harvest tool, to carry out God's wrath, God's judgement over the wicked.

Just as the image of the grain-harvest refers back to v.4, the 144,000 as the firstfruits to be presented to God and the Lamb, so the image of the ripe grapes refers back to v.10, the wine of God's fury, poured into the cup of God's wrath.

John sees this angel coming out of the temple, directly from the presence of God, and thus personally authorized and qualified by the Almighty Ruler of the universe himself. The first one with a sickle, Jesus Christ, the Son of God, does not need this authorization. All he needs is the signal when it is time.

The angel with the sickle will need the same signal. He does not know either when it is the exact right time. He also must wait for further instructions to learn when the grape-harvest is ripe, ready to be gathered in.

Here again is the tension of the time we live in. The harvest of God's wrath is coming. But today there is still time to repent. Today is still the day of grace. However, no one knows when it will be over. This makes the message of the church even more urgent: repent and believe in Jesus Christ before it is too late!

But here again, in John's vision, with his view from above, things move quickly. A third angel appears, another messenger instructed by God's command to pass on the message that it is time for the grape-harvest. Here is another loud voice, calling out with a powerful sound: *Put in your sickle and gather the clusters [of grapes] from the vine of the earth, for its grapes are ripe.*

About this angel we learn that he *has authority over the fire* and that he comes *from the altar*. What does that tell us? In Revelation we find 'the altar' also in Rev. 6: 9, 10 and in Rev. 8:3–5. The image refers to the Old Testament altar of incense, the golden altar before the throne of God. From this altar the smoke of incense would rise up as a symbol of the prayers of God's people, ascending to God himself.

Do you remember what happened in Rev. 8:3–5? There an angel stood at the altar to offer incense, with the prayer of all the saints, before God. Then he filled his censer with fire from the altar and threw it all on the earth. God's response to this offering was his judgment in the first six trumpet blasts. That is in Rev. 8:6 and Rev. 9.

Perhaps the angel here in Rev. 14:18 is the same, with authority over that fire and coming from that altar. Here is the picture: when this angel gives the signal that it is time for the grape-harvest, then, in harvesting and crushing the grapes of wrath, the Holy God hears the prayers of the believers.

Always remember that God's wrath for the wicked is not just an unreasonable outburst of furious anger. No, God's wrath is a measured response triggered by his perfect justice. Therefore, God's judgement is his final answer to the prayers of his people, the cries for justice.

When he is given the green light, *the angel swung his sickle across the earth, gathered the grape harvest and threw it into the great winepress of the wrath of God.*

He collects the entire multitude of those driven by evil, the followers of the beast, the worshippers of the dragon, all who refuse to repent, but resist and hate God and reject his love in Jesus Christ.

Usually you would not use the same tool for harvesting grain and harvesting tender fruit, like grapes. Grapes should be handled with more care. But not here! This grape-harvest gets a rough treatment with all the "throwing and trampling". And just as the grapes are crushed, so the wicked will experience severe punishment.

What we read in the second part of Joel 3:13, and also in a chapter like Isaiah 63, gives us the clues to understand the devastating seriousness of what is going to happen when the grapes of wrath are ripe. Indeed, when the time has come this frightening harvest will be inevitable. In Rev. 20 we will hear more about the Last Judgment itself. Here we are shown the horrible results of this Judgment.

And do we have any idea when those grapes will be ready? Yes, we do! Now again, we do not have a date. But when all the evil and wickedness, all the injustice and corruption in this world has reached its horrible peak, when things cannot get worse, then the fullness of God's wrath and judgment comes. Then this whole evil vine will be cut down and uprooted.

The angel with the sickle collects it all and throws everything in the winepress of God's wrath. God wraps up the history of this world, so thoroughly damaged by sin. Enough is enough.

When John then talks about these grapes being, trodden, trampled, crushed in the great winepress of God's wrath, the metaphor becomes very thin, so to speak. The graphic and gory language conveys the seriousness of God's punishment that awaits those who refuse to repent and believe in the Saviour Jesus.

Now here is a curious question. Who is doing the trampling? It is remarkable, but it does not say. Later on, in Rev. 19, we find out that it is Jesus Christ. There John describes in v.11-21 the vision of the victorious Christ as the Rider on the white horse. Of him it says (in 19:15) that *he treads the winepress of the fury of the wrath of God Almighty*. The One who saves God's creation, is also the One who will cleanse it. The Redeemer is also the Judge.

Then the picture changes dramatically. You would expect wine or grapejuice to flow out of the winepress. But what John is seeing is blood. An enormous amount of blood! The graphic imagery reflects the language of Isaiah 63. The harvest turns into a terrible carnage, a horrendous bloodbath, a huge lake of blood wherever you look, as far as you can see, so deep that horses can swim in it.

The distance of sixteen-hundred stadia, or about three hundred kilometres, portrays how terrifying the scene is. But do not overlook the symbolism of 'four by four' and 'ten by ten'. With four as the number of the earth and ten the number of completeness, the message is clear that this is a worldwide bloody massacre.

The barbaric bloodshed is shocking for our modern sensitivities. There is no way we can ignore or soften the disturbing violence of this vivid picture. Jesus Christ wants to shock us into reality. Do we see the seriousness of our choices? The intoxicating influence of the secular culture of Babylon is too dangerous to allow it to go on as if it does not matter. Spiritual sleepiness threatens our spiritual well-being. Wake up!

Whatever people tell you, whatever ideas may be promoted today, do not believe that following Jesus Christ can go together with accommodating the power of Satan. That is not a valid choice. Revelation 14 keeps sharpening the choice we all must make. You cannot bear the name of God, the seal of the Lamb **and** the mark of the beast.

But there is one encouraging detail in this last verse. Trampling the grapes of God's wrath will happen *outside the city*. This is the holy city, the city of God, the New Jerusalem, the dwelling place of God's people, saved by grace through the blood of Christ. God's children will remain unharmed in the Judgment.

Yes, the Holy God will establish his eternal Kingdom. But as his plans unfold in the time in which we live, he keeps issuing his warning signals, his urgent calls to repent, because it is not going to be a smooth and peaceful transition.

It will be realized through worldwide bloodshed of unprecedented magnitude.

Take refuge in God's love. Seek your security in Jesus' blood, and you will be safe! When God wraps up our history, the final victory of our exalted Saviour is not in doubt.

Jesus will reign from shore to shore for ever and ever.

23

REVELATION 15

GOD PREPARES US
FOR THE COMPLETION OF HIS WRATH

When we looked at John's vision in the last part of Rev. 14, we concluded that, when the harvest is ripe, God will wrap up the history of our world. We may think that everything will always continue to go on as it always has. And many people like to believe this. But the Bible tells us differently.

At the end of Rev. 14 we saw what happens when the grain-harvest of God's salvation is ripe, and what happens when the grape-harvest of God's wrath is ripe. Things are coming to a head. That is unavoidable. The question that still remains is how this is going to develop.

Here we are leaving the lengthy detour of Rev. 12, 13 and 14, and return to the main story-line of John's book. After the seventh trumpet (11:15) the storyline suddenly stopped with v.19. But we pick it up again in chapter 15:5.

And now we notice that the seventh trumpet ushers in the final series of seven: the seven bowls with the seven last plagues. This drama unfolds in Rev. 15 and 16, with the outpouring of the last bowl, number seven, unleashing the Final Judgment. This Judgment is then shown in more detail in Rev. 17 and 18.

23 • REVELATION 15

It is going to be such a horrendous and frightening experience that God does not want us to be un-prepared for this. Therefore, when John tells us in Rev. 15 what he sees, it is only the beginning, the preliminaries, so that you and I may be prepared for what is coming. This passage gives us the heads-up, so to speak.

A BRIEF SUMMARY

When the apostle John begins to describe for us the one vision that unfolds in Rev. 15 and 16, he sees what he calls *another great and amazing sign*. He has used this expression before. That was in Rev. 12: 1, 2. This verbal threat connects the "seven angels with the seven last plagues" (which he sees here) with the pregnant woman and the fiery red dragon, which he saw in Rev. 12.

These signs are so 'great', because together they point at the decisive role of the coming of Jesus Christ in this world, his first coming, when he became man, and then his second coming as the eternal Judge.

And as we move through the Book of Revelation, the visions pictured before us focus more and more on this end, the final and climactic judgments that come with the second coming of Jesus Christ. And we all need to see what is really going on in this world to be encouraged and prepared.

That is why John stresses again that he saw this 'great and amazing sign' *in heaven*. You will remember that heaven is where he was taken up when it all began in Rev. 4:1. That is where he was taken up to see for himself, and to show us, the view from heaven, the view from above.

John tells us that now he sees *seven angels with seven plagues, which are the last, for with them God's wrath is finished*. That is how he summarizes it.

Later on, we will hear more details about this. In v.6 he describes how he sees them coming out of the heavenly temple. And the actual seven plagues are to be released in Rev. 16. Then we will learn that these angels were instructed to lash out against this wicked and unrepentant world, and hit it hard, really hard, with those seven plagues. It will not be pretty when the holy God comes to punish this world.

But we are not there yet. In v.1, John begins by providing a brief summary of what is going to happen. We could see it more as a 'title', a 'heading' or a 'superscription' above the whole vision he describes for us in Rev. 15 & 16. "This is what this whole new vision is all about," says the apostle. "Seven angels will let loose seven plagues to finish off the wrath of God." You better be prepared for this. We are heading for the Final Judgment. It is inevitable.

The horrors pictured in Rev. 16 (and also 17 & 18) are many. We can easily become overwhelmed and discouraged, or even desperate, when you find yourself in the midst of all the terror and misery, all the ugliness and pain, all the horrible disasters in this broken world. What are we heading for?

But then the apostle John calls us to see what he saw. Have a look from here, he says, from above, from heaven, and recognize the burning wrath of God Almighty. But you will also learn that with these last plagues, God's wrath will be completed. Jesus returns and when the Final Judgment comes it will all be over!

The word 'plagues' we remember. It alludes to the 'plagues' with which the Lord ravaged Egypt, before Israel's exodus (Exodus ch. 7–12). He pummeled the Egyptians left, right and centre, till they no longer knew where to hide. And the whole ordeal ended with Pharaoh's crushing defeat, when he and his army drowned in the Red Sea (Exodus 14). Through all this, the Lord set his people free and onto the road to the Promised Land.

Well, the same thing is happening here. That is what is happening to the church in the history of our world, also today. When God comes with the terrifying horrors of the "seven last plagues", his purpose is the freedom of his people.

You may wonder in what sense these plagues are "the last". Some do not believe that there is any linear progress in Revelation. Then "last" means that now for the last time we hear about the same judgments we have heard about earlier in this book, when the seven seals were opened, and when the seven trumpets sounded.

But that does not really work. The storyline of Revelation is complicated and has many sidelines. But there is also progression, development. John's visions demonstrate that we progress towards the end, and that as we get closer to the final day, God's judgments become progressively heavier and more intense.

Think, for instance, of the change from afflictions that affect one fourth of the earth (in Rev. 6, at the opening of the seals), via judgments that affect one third (in Rev. 8, at the sounding of the trumpets), to plagues that affect all the earth (in Rev. 16, when the bowls are poured out).

And there is more. After six of the seals have been opened, we see an interruption. After this, the opening of the seventh seal ushers in the angels with the seven trumpets. And after six of the trumpets have sounded, we see another interruption. Then the seventh trumpet-blast (after more interruptions) gives way to the seven bowls with the plagues.

But here is the clincher: Since these are the last seven, there will be no more interruption. God goes straight from the sixth to the seventh plague, which is going to be his Final Judgment that will complete his wrath. And no more interruption also implies no more repentance. Things are really coming to a head.

Now be careful! Here below we cannot connect this linear progression with particular events and times in our history. Where we are in this journey, we do not know, so that we cannot calculate the day of the end. Jesus' own words still stand, that he will come like a thief in the night.

But the journey is real. Revelation tells and shows that we are moving in one direction. And it is all God's plan that he will fulfill and complete for your sake. As the Pharaoh's army was drowned in the Red Sea, so the total defeat of the army of Satan and his henchmen will get you into the new Promised Land.

No, the journey will not get easier when the last things come near. In previous chapters we have already seen visions of terrible judgments that are coming over this world. And the announcement that with the seven last plagues God's wrath will be completed, makes it scarier than ever. What can we still expect?

That is why, in this brief summary of v.1 God himself prepares us. Yes, terrible things will happen but remember that when the world is on fire, when civilizations collapse, when disasters strike, the One who is completing his wrath is the Holy and Almighty God, your Father in heaven. And he is not just killing good and innocent people, men, women, and children, in random acts of uncontrolled violence.

Some people want you to believe that this is the kind of God we meet in the Bible. In 2008 an atheist US Senator filed a lawsuit against God, "for making terrorist threats of grave harm against innocent people". He accused God of causing widespread death and destruction of many millions of the earth's inhabitants, through terrible floods and earthquakes, horrendous hurricanes and tornadoes, pestilential pandemics, while showing neither compassion nor remorse. God as terrorist and mass-murderer.

The suit was dismissed, but one day the blasphemer will meet his Maker, and will be made to acknowledge that God is a God of justice. His judgments are deeply passionate, and at the same time, a properly measured response to those who reject his love in Jesus Christ. Those who persistently refuse to repent and refuse to embrace his love, will find themselves in the hands of an angry God.

A GREAT VICTORY

So, yes, we better brace ourselves for the dark and horrible judgments that are coming. In that light, the first thing that John is seeing when God is preparing him and us for what is going to unfold as these last seven plagues will ravage our world, is actually surprising.

Think of it, what do you expect when you hear about the climax and completion of God's wrath? Sounds pretty awful.

But listen to what the apostle is telling us. He sees a smooth and sparkling sea. And on the seashore a large and happy crowd, a victorious multitude. And he hears them sing about the royal glory of God Almighty, about the Lord's majestic power.

No, there is nothing gloomy or scary in this picture in v.2 – 4. Surprisingly, this vision begins by showing the church as it will be after the last day, after the final judgment, after God's wrath has been completed. In the view from above we may see already the great victory before all God's terrible judgments have been completed.

This is such a tremendous encouragement in the midst of all the wreckage caused by God's judgments and in the midst of all the violent oppression in this world, a comfort and encouragement that can make you sing, even in dark days. This is how God helps you to be prepared for what is coming.

The apostle sees the splendid shine of the pavement in heaven, before God's throne. It is the same as what he saw before, in Rev. 4. There it says that in the glorious space *before the throne there was as it were a sea of glass, like crystal.*

Here we feel again how John is looking for words to describe adequately what he is seeing. *It appeared to be a sea of glass mingled with fire.* It is transparent, smooth, sparkling, somewhat mysterious, but also brilliant and beautiful.

The word 'sea' has several allusions. One of them is that it resembles the "sea of cast metal" in the earthly temple. This makes it a symbol of the washing and cleansing power of the blood of Jesus Christ. The mix with fire, adds the symbol of God's holiness as maintained in his judgements over evil. Fire is often an image of judgment.

All these aspects together make this glassy and fiery sea an awesome reflection of God's glory and righteousness, as it comes out in his acts of judgment on the wicked and his acts of grace in Jesus Christ.

In this way this 'sea' is also an allusion to the Red Sea. At that time, the Lord saved his people by having them cross the sea on dry ground, and by drowning the Pharaoh and his army (Exodus 14). The connection with the glassy sea in this passage makes sense. We find here other references to this defining moment in Israel's history.

Just as the Israelites were standing on the seashore, looking at the dead bodies of the Egyptians, and praising God with a song of victory and deliverance (Exodus 15), so John sees beside this magnificent sea, before the throne of God almighty, *those who had conquered the beast and its image, and the number of his name.* We remember this evil duo from Rev. 13.

Who are they, these joyful conquerors? When we look at the location before God's throne, we may conclude that we see the same group that we met in Rev. 7:4–10 and in Rev. 14:1. We see again the 144,000, the great multitude that no one can count. We see the total of God's redeemed children, all God's people saved by grace in Jesus Christ, all the followers of the Lamb of God, who took away their sins.

They have recognized the evil nature of the beast, as Satan's malicious helper, and resisted it. They have refused to worship the image of this awful beast. And they have understood the real meaning of the number 666. They have rejected Satan's evil temptations. They have triumphed over the political and cultural powers that are hostile to God and to his Word.

When we look around, read, and listen to what is going on in the world in which we live today, they look so strong – these powers. But they will not last. Satan will not win. How do we know? Take the view from above and see the great victory.

No, the conquerors John is seeing could not have done this on their own. They were victorious only by the power of God's grace in Jesus Christ. And it was by the power of this same grace that they have been able to endure the troubles and persecutions because of their loyalty to Jesus Christ. That is why they celebrate their victory as his great victory.

This is what John, and this is what we, are seeing and hearing. God has given them harps, and now they make music and sing to the glory of God. They praise the Lord for his awesome power and majesty. They glorify him for his deep love and mercy, but also for his justice in the great victory they are celebrating.

Is it not amazing that this is what we may see and hear in this passage, this great victory? God prepares us. The completion of his wrath is coming. The horror will be beyond description. Are you scared?

But in the midst of these dramatic visions of frightening judgments, God does show us already a glimpse of the future of his people, the future of his church, the future of a great and glorious victory over all his enemies, the future of a singing church.

23 • Revelation 15

How comforting and re-assuring is the view of this great victory, when the terrifying judgments are still looming. And this is confirmed when we hear what these conquerors are singing. It says that *they sang the song of Moses the servant of God and the song of the Lamb*. This 'lamb' is Jesus Christ, crucified and glorified.

It seems to say that they sing two different songs. But it is actually one song. These singers praise and glorify the Lord God Almighty. He alone is highly exalted because he saves his people by his marvellous and righteous acts. And by his great power he has granted victory to his people – the victory won by the exalted Christ, the Lamb. With this song the church celebrates this great victory over God's enemies.

But it is also called "the song of Moses". The real song of Moses we find in Exodus 15. With this song the Israelites celebrate their freedom and deliverance after Moses has led them out of Egypt and through the Red Sea. They praise the Lord for the plagues that had destroyed Egypt, and for the defeat of the Egyptian army. The great victory of God's grace gave safety and security on the journey to the Promised Land.

Well, this song of Moses is the 'example song', the 'model song', so to speak, for the Song of the Lamb. Just as in Exodus 15 Israel ascribed the victory to God alone, so we hear in the view from above the triumphant church sing about the great victory of God's grace through the saving work of the Lamb Jesus Christ.

In this way God prepares us for the completion of his wrath. Yes, the judgments in the seven last plagues will be horrifying. But the purpose for the destruction of God's enemies is to save those who belong to him by grace alone, just as the destruction of Israel's enemies secured Israel's safety at the Red Sea. Now, that is a great victory to look forward to and to sing about, also today.

So, listen to this song of Moses and of the Lamb over and over again, and be encouraged by its wonderful content. It is a powerful song that praises God Almighty, the glorious King for his mercy and justice, his holy and righteous acts, even when he pours out his wrath in the seven plagues. With deep awe and admiration, it expresses the confidence that, in the end, people from all nations will see the light of God's love and will turn to him to worship him.

What is coming when the seven bowls of God's wrath will be poured out, is outright frightening. But by giving his people the view from above, God prepares us for the final unravelling of the story. He shows us what is beyond the terrors of God's wrath. Have a good look at the great victory and recognize how the completion of God's wrath will usher in your glorious salvation when you follow Jesus Christ, the Lamb of God.

In Rev. 16 we will find out how bad it is going to be. And it will be really bad! But God prepares us for the worst, by showing us here the very best that is to come, everlasting praise because of his great and glorious victory.

A SOLEMN ORDINATION

God also prepares us for the completion of his wrath, by showing how he remains in absolute control as he is getting ready for the seven last plagues, including the Final Judgment.

In v.5 the apostle continues: *After this I looked...* The actual chronology is somewhat confusing here. The summarizing introduction in v.1 puts the emphasis on the angels with the last plagues. But then the attention is going elsewhere, when he pictures for us the great victory of the end, in the singing multitude of the redeemed beside the glassy sea. But now he brings us back to the great sign of *the seven angels with the seven last plagues*, to give us more details about this sign.

He describes for us a solemn ordination event in heaven. It is an important moment to watch. It tells us that, whatever is coming, is directly coming from the Holy God himself. The terrifying events in Rev. 16 are his righteous judgments, designed by him, and executed by his specially ordained and instructed servants. He prepares us, so that we will not overlook his fair and faithful care when the going gets tough.

John then sees in heaven *the sanctuary of the tent of witness*, which is also called *the tabernacle of the Testimony*. The words refer back to the Old Testament. First the tabernacle, and later on the temple, signify that the Lord God is present among his people. In the centre of the sanctuary was "the ark of the covenant", with the law of the 10 commandments. This was also called

"The Testimony" (Exodus 25:16, 21). You could call this the "Constitution" of the covenant-relationship between God and his people.

By using these images John's vision stresses that, what is happening here, happens directly in the presence of the Almighty God himself. It happens where he rules in his splendour and glory, his might and beauty, and where he rules according to his covenant-constitution.

And here is the origin of the seven last plagues. Indeed, also in the terrible things that are happening when the seven bowls of God's wrath are poured out on the earth, the Lord remains faithful to his covenant-law. His covenant promises include salvation when you turn to him in Jesus and punishment when you refuse his love.

By saying that *the tabernacle or temple was opened*, John picks up the main storyline again where it was in Rev. 11:19. And then something remarkable happens. *Out of the sanctuary came seven angels*. One by one they appear, directly from the presence of the Holy and Almighty God. It must have been an awesome, breathtaking view to behold, as they solemnly line up for the ordination ceremony to follow.

Try to imagine this. Look at them. All of them dressed identically: robes of clean, dazzling white and shining linen and brilliant golden sashes.

The attire of these angels reflects the priestly and royal glory of the exalted Christ. In Rev. 1:13 John saw Jesus Christ also in a long shining robe, and with a golden sash around his chest. In what these angels are going to do, they represent the glorified Christ himself, the eternal Judge.

Then, what happens next is even more impressive. Is it not fantastic that in John's vision we may again have a close look at what is going on in God's throne room, just as we saw in Rev. 4 & 5? Do you remember the four living creatures, God's throne-attendants? Well, one of them hands to each of these seven angels, one by one, *a golden bowl full of the wrath of God, who lives for ever and ever*.

Now consider this: in Rev. 5:8 we hear that the four living creatures are holding 'golden bowls' full of incense that represents our prayers. Now we read that the golden bowls are filled with God's wrath. And that the living creatures give them to the seven angels. What a strong re-enforcement of the message that the Lord uses our prayers, as Christian believers, to set the world straight through his just judgments.

These bowls filled with God's wrath symbolize the fierce, unmitigated, and righteous character of God's holy anger. In Rev. 16 we will face the terrible consequences of this anger, God's wrath for this wicked world.

It is an impressive and solemn ceremony. We have often noticed that Revelation is a noisy book. But you can imagine that this powerful moment, is a silent moment because it re-enforces again that in the progression of God's judgments we are approaching the point-of-no-return.

The apostle John tells us that *the sanctuary was filled with smoke from the glory and power of God and that no one could enter the sanctuary until the seven plagues were finished.* In the Bible 'smoke' is often a manifestation of God's awesome glory and power. When the Temple was dedicated we read that the priests could not enter to serve, so overwhelming was the presence of God's glory in the cloud of smoke that filled the temple (1 Kings 8:10–11).

Here, in the last verse of this passage, it happens again. And it is actually deeply disturbing. It means that during the seven final judgments God's grace is no longer accessible. The seven last plagues cannot be stopped. Time and again the wicked are being warned to repent as God's judgments affect this world only partially.

But one day this opportunity for repentance will be over. One day it will be too late!

Let God prepare you for what is coming. No matter how bad it gets, nothing will ever spiral out of God's control. When his wrath is completed, there will be wreckage and ruins, everywhere. But that will not be the end.

For then the heavenly temple will open again, and the cloud of smoke will be lifted.

We will see the throne of God and of the Lamb. And we will see his face.

24

REVELATION 16

GOD'S JUDGMENTS ENTER THE FINAL STAGE – ROUND 3

The "Institute for Economics & Peace" is a research organization for global issues. Its research is based on the idea that peace is a pre-requisite for the survival of humanity. Every year this institute publishes a report, called the "Global Peace Index". Over the last years the conclusion is quite disturbing.

Contrary to human dreams, hopes and expectations, our world is becoming less safe and less peaceful every year. In the last ten years more and more nations are involved in armed conflicts, or outright war or civil war. 500 million people live in warzones. In 2019 the number of refugees in the world was 70.8 million. Terrorism, genocide, hatred, and brutal violence are on the rise, and lead to increasing worldwide instability.

What are we headed for? What does our future look like, if we will not be able to turn this trend around? But then, who says that the future of mankind is in our hands?

John's visions in Revelation make very clear that it is not.

To be sure, there is, of course, nothing wrong with striving for peace in our human world. Jesus wants us to condemn and resist hatred and violence, terrorism, racism, and genocide. He calls us to support poor and starving refugees.

At the same time, the Holy God is on his way towards the completion of his wrath against all wickedness, injustice, evil and oppression.

In Rev. 15 we have been given the heads-up for what is coming when the last series of seven judgments will unfold. Seven bowls with the seven last plagues have been handed to seven angels.

The terrifying events we encounter in Rev. 16 are executed by God's ordained servants on his behalf. We come to the point-of-no-return. And with the end around the corner, John sees them coming in rapid pace, one disaster after another.

The Last Warnings

You may remember from the previous chapter that Revelation 15 and 16 belong together. It is one vision. Rev. 15 is an introduction to prepare us for the horrible things that are coming in 16. We will be facing "the completion of God's wrath" when the seven last plagues, God's final warnings for a wicked and unrepentant world, will be released. After John has witnessed the solemn ceremony when seven angels were given seven bowls, he tells us what happens next.

He hears *a loud voice*, coming from the temple in heaven. In light of what he has just pictured for us in Rev. 15:5–8, this must be the powerful voice of the Almighty God himself. He lets us know that all preparations have been completed. He gives the signal that the moment has come to move from preparation and instruction, to execution of his last punishments, his ultimate and final warnings.

Yes, God himself lets us know, and through the church he lets the whole world know that for him and for everybody on earth the end is rapidly approaching. He commands his execution squad to bring about the dramatic disasters of the seven bowls: *Go and pour out on the earth the seven bowls of the wrath of God.*

The word "pour out" tells us that these bowls are going to be turned upside down, so that all the content goes, entirely! The full and unrestrained wrath of the Holy and Almighty God is being unleashed without holding anything back. This will be more horrifying, terrifying, and frightening than anybody can ever imagine.

Initially, when we saw the opening of the seals, only one-quarter of the earth and mankind was affected by God's judgments. Later on, when we heard the trumpet blasts, one-third was affected. But now God's wrath is unrestrained and felt everywhere. When these bowls are poured out total destruction is unleashed on all God's enemies.

Let us take a closer look. The first bowl is poured out on the land. The effect is incurable suffering in the world. People get malignant tumors, festering open wounds, painful swellings, infectious diseases. The pandemic hits worldwide although it does not affect everybody. God's wrath specifically targets those who hate him and resist him.

In Rev. 13 we heard about the 'mark of the beast'. It is a way to identify people who are loyal followers of the beast from the sea, the powerful antichristian sidekick of Satan. Initially this 'mark-of-the-beast' seemed to come with the promise of a good, prosperous life. But in the end it turns out that this 'mark' singles you out for experiencing the awful agony of God's wrath.

When the second bowl is emptied, all the water in the sea turns into the blood of a dead person. It is dark and coagulating. It emits the foul smell of death, as all life in seas and oceans is killed. An environmental disaster as never seen before. The world is filled with a disgusting stench, everywhere.

In Revelation "the sea" is usually the symbol of the realm of evil and chaos. The first beast in Rev. 13, with its frightening, devilish power, came out of the sea. Later, in Rev. 19:20, we will hear about the destruction of this beast, but here already God makes clear that this is coming. Evil and chaos will face a horrible end.

But it is not only the water of the sea. When the third angel pours out his bowl, all the fresh water, the drinking water on earth, turns also into blood. Fresh water is one of the most essential conditions on earth to sustain life. When you travel to some countries, they tell you not to drink the tap-water because it is often contaminated and you'll get sick, but when you boil it first, or you drink only bottled water you'll be fine.

Well, here you can do nothing about it. All the water is so terribly polluted that it is absolutely undrinkable. Try to imagine it. You turn the tap, you shower, you turn on your washing-machine or dishwasher: blood, blood, and more blood. Life becomes impossible. The symbol of life on earth becomes a symbol of death.

Then the rapid succession of bowls being poured out, leading to one worldwide disaster after the other, is briefly interrupted. That is good. It has been pretty overwhelming, and we can easily lose sight of why God is doing these horrible things.

And so, before we move on to the fourth bowl, John tells us what he hears. You may remember that what John hears in his visions usually interprets what he sees. What he hears gives us the view from above.

We meet "the angel in charge of the waters". That is a significant detail. The point is that it is not just any angel, but this particular angel, who is somehow responsible for water management or for supplying drinking-water on earth. And it is this particular angel who praises the holy God as just, when he makes all water useless.

We first hear this angel re-affirm this. No matter how drastic God's final warnings are, his judgment remains fair, when *those who have shed the blood of God's people, are given blood to drink. It is what they deserve.*

And then we hear "the altar" echo this (v.7). In Rev. 6:9–12 we heard the souls of the martyrs from under the altar crying out to God for justice. Well, the end is around the corner, and here it is. Praise God for being true and just as his judgments avenge the blood of those murdered for their faith in Jesus Christ.

But after this brief intermezzo the pace of God's last warnings picks up again. And it is not getting any better in this world: pandemic diseases, environmental disasters, and now unbearable, extreme global warming. God's wrath coming out of the fourth bowl affects the sun. The fourth trumpet blast darkens the sun. But here it is the opposite. The sun burns with intense, scorching heat, and nowhere can people find protection. There is no shelter from the blazing fire.

It may look like something from a doomsday-scenario in a thick report about greenhouse gasses and carbon-footprints. But it is the Holy God who directs this. It says that *the sun was allowed to scorch people with fire*. God empowers the sun to sear people with this penetrating heat.

The fifth angel poured out his bowl on the throne of the beast, and its kingdom was plunged into darkness. In Revelation the word "throne" refers most of the time to God's throne. But it is used three times as a parody of God's throne. We can read about "Satan's throne" (Rev.2:13), or, as here in v.10, the "throne of the beast" (see also Rev. 13:2). It symbolizes the claim of the beast, and Satan, his boss, to rule the whole world with divine authority.

Indeed, the "throne of the beast", the centre of the antichristian political and cultural powers in this world, claims the loyalty of every human heart. That leads us to ask an urgent question: Who rules your heart? Who rules my heart? Where is the loyalty of your heart? Who am I committed to? Who are you following? Who is running your life?

Satan claims to be pretty successful! "Let me run your life," he says, "and you will be able to fulfil your human dreams of a better and more peaceful world". Can we not give him the benefit of the doubt? Christianity does not seem to do much good anyway, at least, so we are told.

But watch out! God's judgment is plunging everything into darkness. This refers specifically to the moral and political disappointments and confusion which in the end will characterize the kingdom of the beast, inspired by the devil. The people who believe the promises of the beast, have great dreams and high expectations. They encourage each other: 'We may be going through tough times and sometimes we will face setbacks. But don't give up the hope that together we will build a better and safer world. And we can do so without God'. They are convinced that the rule of this beast will usher in a better society, where people will have better lives.

But they are in for a rude awakening; without God, without Jesus Christ, our world will only become darker all the time. Think of the "Global Peace Index" report, mentioned earlier. Our world is filled with painful disillusions that leave people confused, frustrated, and often scared when they think of the future. What is happening to the human dream? Why does life not turn out as we had hoped for and worked for?

Altogether God's final judgments are turning into serious last warnings that underline the loud call of God's angel in Rev. 14:7: *Fear God and give him glory, because the hour of his judgment has come.*

Are people listening? Do they repent when they realize how dark their lives have become? No, they do not! On the contrary. Look at v.9 and v.11. They refuse to repent and give glory to the Holy God. They continue to blaspheme God as the One who controls all that is happening. They may chew their tongues in pain, but they dig in their heels, bitter and angry, because of their agonizing experiences.

Perhaps you wonder how people can be so stubborn. But really, as a Christian, when you share and defend your faith, you often get asked, "how can you believe in a God who controls everything?" Or people will tell you: "If there is a God who allows all the misery and suffering in this world to go on, I want nothing to do with a God like that. The idea makes me angry."

And John records this because it shows why God's final judgment is inevitable. That is not because the Lord is not gracious. Everyone who repents and turns to him for help and comfort, will experience his grace. But a world that does not seek the cause of its trouble and disasters in its own sin, but blames God, and curses him, because of what is happening, such a world is heading for destruction.

THE LAST BATTLE

When the sixth angel pours out his bowl, we see a different kind of judgment. Initially it does not even look like pouring out wrath on God's enemies!

As a matter of fact, it looks like it will make life much more dangerous for God's people. But, there is more to it.

John tells us that this bowl is poured out *on the great river Euphrates*, with the effect that *its water was dried up*. To understand the symbolism in this vision, it is good to remember a few things from the Old Testament about the Euphrates River.

In the Bible the Euphrates is important as the natural boundary that separates Israel from hostile powers in the east, like Assyria and Babylon. They were troubled by those enemies, but there was no easy access. This wide river was always an obstacle for the kings of those eastern nations.

But now we see, through John's eyes, that God removes this obstacle, the water dries up. This vision tells us that in the final stage, when God is completing his wrath, he allows the evil powers in this world to join forces against God's church. He allows them a final effort to overrun her and crush his people. You may wonder why God is going to do that. But we will see!

The vision suggests that this unified preparation for the last battle of God's enemies is going well. John sees something coming out of the mouths of the dragon, the beast and the false prophet. The first two we know. The dragon is Satan (Rev. 12) and the beast is Satan's powerful and loyal helper from the sea (Rev. 13:1). The 'false prophet' may seem new on the scene, but it is actually a new name for the other beast, the one from the earth (Rev. 13:11). He is looking after Satan's deceptive Propaganda Program in this world, his Public Relations Chief.

Well then, what comes out of these three mouths are three identical evil spirits. They look like frogs. Although frogs were unclean animals, they seem harmless. But John gives us the view from above; do not be fooled, these are evil spirits.

So what do we see? We see this huge concentration and accumulation of evil in the world. We see three powerful demonic forces rallying together in a joined effort to develop one satanic strategy. These three demonic spirits are acting as one. They send out one message to what are called here, *the kings of the whole world*. "Come out for the battle," they say. "United we stand."

The result is that all the political, economic, cultural, and spiritual powers in this world that are against the Holy God and his church, against the Lamb Jesus Chris, are going to join forces for the last battle. The war that has been going on since the fall into sin, deeply intensified since Jesus' death and resurrection, this war is coming to a head.

Together these three evil buddies will give the malicious energy in our world a strong boost. United, they go out to deceive people with miraculous signs. They get them excited for the great and last action against God Almighty and his church. "Let's get rid of the Christian faith and of the Christian believers, once and for all," they say. The non-Christian culture achieves amazing things. Who needs the God of the Christians?

It sounds like a frightening scenario if you belong to God's people. You will run into aggressive enemies everywhere.

John's vision pictures a massive, large-scale military operation. This is symbolic of fierce attacks on our faith that can take many different forms. Sometimes it comes as outright and direct violent persecution. Sometimes it comes as a subtle, almost pleasant, spiritual attack. Whatever works for the devil and his hellish buddies, he can and will make use of it to get you.

But this symbol of a huge political and military power, amassed against the church of Jesus Christ, is meant to drive home how serious this is. Do not underestimate what you are up against when God is ready to complete his wrath.

This is emphasized again in v.16, which pictures the kings of the whole world, gathered for the last battle at a place called *Armageddon*. Now there are many different ideas and interpretations as to what *Armageddon* means or what it stands for.

Let's look at just two examples:

Some see the "battle of Armageddon" as a worldwide war between military superpowers in our world, like, for instance, Europe and the US, versus China and/or Russia. The problem with that interpretation is, of course, that it all depends on the political situation at a given time in history.

Others see the "battle of Armageddon" as a literal battle at the end of times, just before Jesus' return. Then all the nations on earth will march against the earthly city of Jerusalem. Those are the people who carefully follow the conflicts in the Middle East with the idea that here God is now fulfilling his prophetic visions.

But we need to remember that in John's visions we are given the view from above on what happens here below. And so, we should not look for 'Armageddon' as a location you can find on a map. The name is a symbolic reference to "Megiddo" in the Old Testament. In the time of the Israelite Judges and Kings the plains of 'Megiddo' was the site of a number of decisive battles between Israel and its enemies.

In other words, the name 'Armageddon' calls us to be alert. The last battle of the antichristian world and culture against God and against the church of Jesus Christ will be decisive for your future as God's people.

The question must be asked, should we be scared? The answer is: NO!

In v.15 we hear the voice of the exalted Christ all of a sudden. The interruption is kind of unexpected. It seems almost out of place here. But in the midst of all this frightening sabre-rattling of the evil world-powers, Jesus wants to encourage us. *Behold, I am coming like a thief.* "Do not be afraid or intimidated when all this scary stuff is going on but be ready for me to appear at any time".

And now we understand that emptying the sixth bowl does indeed pour out God's terrible wrath over his enemies. It is true, the powers against God and against the Christian faith seem to become stronger, as they get ready for the last battle. But remember, in v.14 the day of the battle is called "the great day", not "of the dragon or the beast"; No, it is "the great day of God Almighty".

God Almighty, he makes room for his enemies to join forces. He allows them to flex their spiritual muscles. But only with the purpose to destroy them all in one blow. We will hear more about that in Rev. 19:19–20 and 20:9.

However, the call to "be ready for this coming victory" also includes the call to "remain watchful in the spiritual battle that is going on". Spiritual complacency is always a danger for the believers. But the end is rushing in! *Blessed is the one who stays awake, keeping his garments on,* says Jesus. Be ready to oppose Babylon. Be prepared to resist the deceiving voices of the antichristian culture, to withstand the temptation to compromise between good and evil in your own life.

The final battle will be fought in our lives as an individual spiritual battle.

THE LAST JUDGMENT

Then John immediately sees the seventh angel pouring out his bowl. This is kind of surprising. Between the opening of the sixth and the seventh seal other visions interrupt and slow down the progress. And the same happens between the sixth and the seventh trumpet blast. But not anymore!

When God's wrath enters its final stage, there will be no more interruptions. With the end around the corner the rapid pace of what John sees happening does not slow down. The oath of the angel standing on the sea and the land (Rev. 10:6) will be fulfilled: *There will be no more delay*. When, with emptying the seventh bowl God's wrath is completed (Rev.15:1), the end of the world has come.

The Holy and Almighty God himself, from his throne in the heavenly temple, proclaims loud and clear: *It is done!* His instructions, given in v.1, have been carried out. But it says more. He also announces that, what John was told when it all started in Rev. 4:1, *Come up here, and I will show you what must take place after this*, this also has been completed.

It is done. With the seventh bowl, God's grand plan of salvation and of judgment has been accomplished. The history of this world comes to a closure. And that is good. The wicked show no sign of repentance, and for God's children it has been long enough.

Of course, we know that the narrative does not stop with Rev.16. But the visions in the next chapters are basically showing in more detail what John's vision shows very briefly here already in v.19, the destruction of Babylon.

In Rev. 17–20 we will see what this destruction of Babylon means for God's enemies, while in Rev. 21 and 22 we will see what it means for God's church, God's children, for all Christian believers.

John's view from above shows what happens when Judgment Day will be here. The seventh bowl is *poured out into the air*, the atmosphere that surrounds the whole earth. In other words, whatever the effect, it will impact everything in all creation.

To confirm this, God's loud voice triggers enormous cosmic disruptions, powerful signs of his awesome presence. We have already seen and heard the great sound and light show that accompanies God's majestic appearance. But the closer we come to the end, the more overwhelming it gets.

In Rev. 4:5 we read about lightning, rumblings, and peals of thunder. These things come back in 8:5, but then an earthquake is added. We see and hear the same again in 11:9, but then it comes also with a great hailstorm. Well, in this picture of the last judgment all this is so hugely intensified that it is without precedent in the history of mankind.

No one has ever felt such a tremendous earthquake, and no one has ever seen such enormous hailstones. Boulders of over forty kilograms come down as ravaging missiles.

Whatever seemed immovable in this world, such as islands and mountains, is uprooted and disappears. The whole creation gets out-of-joint and falls apart when the wrath of the Almighty God explodes.

And what is the result for our human world?

John first sees *the great city split into three parts*. With figurative names like Sodom and Egypt (Rev. 11:8), or Babylon, this 'great city' is a symbol of the antichristian political power in the world, representing Satan's hatred towards God and his people. Well, when the last judgment comes all this impressive power will fall apart, break into pieces, and become utterly powerless.

Following this, the apostle sees *the cities of the nations fall*. Big cities are symbols of human strength, pride, and self-confidence. The first city after the fall into sin was built by Cain, and the first city after the Flood was Babel. Well, when the last judgment comes all human pride and self-confidence will crumble, and the structures of human society will turn into total chaos.

And why is that? Why do these things happen? Because God remembers what was said about Babylon the Great by the angels in Rev. 14. It is time for Babylon to drink the wine of the fury of God's wrath. Even in the midst of these horrible experiences the cursing and blaspheming of God's name goes on and on (v.21). Enough is enough!

Are you looking forward to this? Should we? It does not sound like something you would look forward to, does it?

And yet, in God's message, "destruction" is never the last word.

The completion of God's wrath gives way to the complete liberation of those who cling to his grace in Jesus as the only Saviour.

That is why even a dark chapter like this, ends with strong hope and encouragement.

For by means of his last judgment, your God comes to create his new heaven and his new earth for you, who believe in Jesus Christ.

In God's loud exclamation in v.17, *it is done,* we also hear the echo of Jesus' powerful and victorious word on the cross: *It is finished*! (John 19:30).

This makes the vision of the Last Judgment "true gospel", believe it or not!

It is the good news of Jesus' victory over sin and death.

Through him God's grace and forgiveness overcome the darkness of God's judgments.

25

REVELATION 17

BABYLON IS RIPENING FOR GOD'S JUDGMENT

With Rev.17 we are entering into the last section of the Book of Revelation. At the end of John's vision in Rev. 16 the seventh angel poured out the last of the seven bowls of God's wrath. And then we heard in v.17 the loud voice of God Almighty, from the throne in heaven saying, *It Is Done*! God's wrath has been completed. God's Final Judgment is here.

Rev. 16:18–21 gives a brief summary of the events on Judgment Day. From here on we are given more detailed visions and explanations as to the events that are rapidly unfolding on that day. We will come to see the implications of this climax in the final chapters of Revelation. In chapters 17–20 we'll see the implications for God's enemies, the powers of evil, and in chapters 21–22 the implications for God's people, God's church.

The first part focusses on the fall, the destruction of Babylon. But this clean-up is not an isolated event. It also involves the destruction of Satan's helpers, the Beast and the False Prophet (19:11–21) and the destruction of Satan himself (20:7–10).

We are shown these things, as if they happen in chronological order, but in fact these are parallel events on the great day of God's judgment. This is also the case with the rest of these chapters. We will see some flashbacks, but the events are all connected and come together, punishment and renewal.

This is how we will also meet two women in these chapters. They are introduced in an identical manner, but they are each other's opposite. In both cases, one of the seven angels of the seven bowls invites John. *Come, and I will show you*, he says (Rev.17:1 and 21:9). But what John sees is totally different. As a matter of fact, the contrast is stark and intentional. In Rev. 17 he sees an ugly prostitute, identified as the city of Babylon, and in Rev.21 he sees the lovely Bride of Christ, identified as the New Jerusalem.

So here is the choice you and I have to make, knowing that the day of God's Final Judgment can be here anytime: Do we follow Jesus Christ to the new Promised Land, the New Jerusalem, portrayed as the Bride of Christ. Or do we settle down in Babylon, portrayed as an immoral prostitute?

What John sees and hears in Rev. 17 shows us Babylon's true colours, as well as her final destination. Do not make a mistake here.

BABYLON'S TRUE NATURE

To help us understand what is happening in the eruption of events on the great day of God's final judgment, John is given an interpretive guide. It is one of the seven angels that were involved with the terrible judgments in Rev. 16, when the seven bowls of God's wrath were poured out. This tells us already that in this chapter (and the next) we are having a closer look at what is happening on the Day of Judgment, in this case it is about the great city of Babylon falling apart.

Come, he says, *I will show you the judgment of the great prostitute, who is seated on many waters*. We find out, though, that the actual punishment comes only at the very end of this chapter, and in more detail in Rev. 18.

We are going to see first how well-deserved this punishment is. We are going to see first how the world is getting ripe and ready for God's wrath.

Carried by the power of the Holy Spirit, John is transferred *into a wilderness*, a desert. In Revelation the wilderness, or desert is either a sanctuary that provides safety (as in Rev. 12), or it is a desolate wasteland, where life is impossible. That is the case here.

What are we seeing, through John's eyes, in this desert? It is kind of unique, in the sense that we do not see or hear much action in this vision. What the apostle describes is a pretty static picture, like a painting, or a sculpture.

He sees *a woman sitting on a scarlet beast that was full of blasphemous names and had seven heads and ten horns*. We will hear more about this woman and this beast but note now already that this "desert-setting" signals what is coming. It symbolizes that her destruction is unavoidable. She is called "Babylon" and we will hear more about that, but whatever "Babylon" stands for, it will be laid waste and will come to nothing. This comes back in Rev. 18:2, where Babylon becomes a habitat of frightening desert creatures. So, yes, the desert is a fitting backdrop here.

But let us take a closer look. By now this beast is an old acquaintance of ours. You recognize him, do you not? Indeed, it is the beast from the sea that we met for the first time in Rev. 13. With his bright red colour, his seven heads and ten horns, he is the spitting image of his boss, Satan. His numerous blasphemous names show that he hates God. And he represents the political powers that hate God's church.

But this woman is new for us. We have heard her name, but we have not met her before. It is clear that the woman and the beast enjoy close cooperation. They are very much in tune with each other. That tells you already something about her.

Next the apostle gives a vivid picture of what she looks like. He describes her flashy, super-expensive outfit of purple and scarlet. In the ancient Near East only the very wealthy could afford such clothes. And then we see her excessive adornment with gold, jewels, and pearls; the way she shows off is really over the top.

Her brazen self-presentation, which is meant to impress and seduce people, radiates an obscene and devilish spirit. All this reflects her true nature as a prostitute. She combines the lure of sexual pleasure with the lure of wealth and luxury. "Come to me," she says, "I will make you happy and all your dreams will come true." According to v.2 many political leaders and numerous other folks in the world have been deeply influenced by the immoral ideas and practices of this prostitute.

There is some offensive language here. The metaphor in this passage is controlled by porn-words. But it is symbolic, and so this is not only about sexual relations. Think of Old Testament prophets like Hosea, Isaiah, and Ezekiel. They used images of immoral sexual behaviour to picture the seriousness of Israel's religious, social, political, and cultural mix-up with the pagans in those days.

In other words, in Rev. 17, sexual boundary-crossing is a metaphor for accommodating to the antichristian culture, and indulging in its idolatry, its quasi-religious activities, evil desires, luxuries and sensual pleasures.

And let us be alert! This antichristian culture can present itself as impressive and attractive. The woman holds a golden cup in her hand and when the outside looks so beautiful, surely, the content must be delightful. A precious goblet with fine wine, presented with the promise that what she is offering will make the world a much happier place.

But if you trust her, the consequences will be the opposite. What is inside her cup is just horrible, disgusting, and poisonous. It is what the angel called *the wine of her sexual immorality* (v.2). When you drink from it, you will be polluted with the abominable filth of her immorality, her perverse idolatrous practices and selfish evils that lure you away from God. It will poison you and eventually kill you.

Who is this woman? Where do we place her in the whole context of Revelation? John then tells us what it says on her forehead: *Babylon the Great, the mother of prostitutes, and of the abominations of the earth.*

It is called "a mystery" because it needs an explanation.

The woman is identified as "Babylon", as the angel puts it in v.18, *the great city that has dominion over the kings of the earth*. But what does the name "Babylon" tell us? The first Babylon was the city of the tower (Genesis 11). The second Babylon was the great city of king Nebuchadnezzar (2 Kings 25:1-21; Daniel 1 and 4:29, 30). Do you recognize the principle of hostile rebellion against the Holy God that wants to control the whole world? This is the Babylon-principle that pops up throughout our history, also today, in different forms and shapes.

We have heard the name "Babylon" before, in Revelation 14:8 and 16:19, but that was almost in passing. Here we find out what "Babylon" stands for.

It is the strong and influential antichristian culture, with its promiscuous and adulterous lifestyle. It is the power that lures people away from God and Jesus Christ by controlling their moral choices. "Babylon" stands for everything God hates in this world, the arrogant idolatry, and the aggression against his church, which provokes him to anger. It is the place of the ultimate concentration of depravity.

All this makes Babylon the very opposite of the other city we will see appear in this part of the book, the New Jerusalem, just as the great prostitute is the very opposite of the other woman, the glorious and lovely bride of Christ.

But, yes, at first sight Babylon may look impressive and attractive. She promises wealth, luxuries, satisfaction, sexual pleasure, a fulfilled life, and happiness, and all of this without God. And many people who do not care about worshipping God will tell you that this is exactly why Babylon is such a fun place to live.

For John's first readers the city of Rome was the source of those evil attractions. But this culture of idolatry, greed, materialism, selfishness, and immorality was and is everywhere. Our modern society with its focus on material wealth, sexual freedom, tolerance for false religions, and a fun-filled, selfish lifestyle is Babylon today.

Advertisements and the entertainment industry teach us that you will only find satisfaction and meaningful living if you have enough money, fun and sensual pleasures.

And just in case we Christians think that this Babylon is all out there, in the bad world, it is good to remember that little Babylons operate also in our own hearts. The beast controls his followers by fear, and the prostitute seduces people by playing on their desires.

Well then, the sinful tendencies in our hearts as God's children also involve fear and desire. Why do we compromise with sin? Because we fear. We are afraid of suffering. We are afraid of being ridiculed or rejected.

We also compromise with sin because of the desires of our heart. Things like sex, wealth, fame, power, health, beauty, and you name it, are not all bad in themselves. But these can all become objects of our desires, our idols.

Babylon is the city where we all dwell, as we travel to the Promised Land. But as you make your way through it, make sure that you travel with your eyes wide open, and that you recognize the true nature of Babylon, the great prostitute, the mother, the origin of all immorality. Guard your heart. The consequences of associating with her are deadly. If she cannot seduce you, she will kill you.

John noticed that too. He saw this woman *drunk with the blood of the saints, the martyrs of Jesus,* the folks who refuse her enticing invitations, because of their faith in Jesus. The image of "drinking blood till you're drunk with blood" stands for enjoying killing without restraint. Babylon, the prostitute hates those who proclaim Jesus as the only Saviour, and who call all people to worship the living God. She revels in their violent persecution.

When you see the moral character of this woman, the true nature of Babylon, it is clear that she is ripe for God's punishment. Under the attractive and tolerant veneer hides a deeply rooted hatred towards God and his church.

The whole picture leaves John astonished. His first reaction is, "Wow…!" It almost sounds as if even the apostle John has to steel himself against the intoxicating draught that wafts from the cup that the prostitute holds.

BABYLON'S DECEPTIVE STRENGTH

Apparently the angel can see on John's face how stunned, how perplexed he is, perhaps even somewhat confused, such evil showing such grandeur. And he reacts right away in v.7. *Why do you marvel, why are you so astonished?* the angel says. But he does not wait for an answer. Immediately he continues. There is need to clarify what John is seeing in this vision.

As we have seen more often in Revelation, seeing alone can be insufficient or confusing. Appearances can be deceptive. That is why John needs the interpretive words of his guide to clarify what he sees. The angel says it several times: "what you saw... is", or: "what you saw... are".

Look at this powerful beast the woman sits on. We have recognized it already as one of the awful animals from Rev. 13, the evil, antichristian political power that claims to run the world. He seems to give the woman strong support for her promise to provide pleasure, wealth, and happiness without God. With arrogant pride she rides this monster, sitting on it as a queen on a throne, like God sits on his throne.

The antichristian cultural power of the great city not only controls, but is also carried by the antichristian political and economic power of the beast. They get along so well and rely on each other's strength. This evil duo seems invincible.

"However, when you look at it *with a mind with wisdom*," says the angel in v.9, "you will recognize how deceiving this whole impressive picture really is. You will find out how deceptive the strength is that this beast gives to the woman. And thus, how deceptive the strength of this woman is".

Such *a mind with wisdom* is a mind that relies on God's wisdom, the wisdom we get in the view from above, from heaven. Yes, the strength of this antichristian beast may look impressive from here, from below. But from above you can see that it *once was, now is not, and will come up*. The angel mentions it three times. Two times in v.8 and once in v.11.

That sounds remarkably similar to what Revelation also mentions three times as characteristic of our Holy and Almighty God, that he is the God *who is, was and is to come* (Rev.1:4,8; 4:8). Similar indeed, but at the same time so different. It exposes the beast at once as a counterfeit God. With his divine pretensions he tries to mimic God's eternal sovereign power. But he makes a poor copy. All the time this beast is trying hard to be like the eternal God, but it will never work.

Just as in Rev. 13, *the dwellers on earth* are astonished when they see the beast. He used to be strong (*he once was...*), then he was defeated through Jesus death and resurrection (*he is not....*), but his strength seems to come back (*he will come up again...*). They marvel at its resilience. But that is because they do not have a *mind with wisdom*. "Dwellers on earth" is used ten times in Revelation, and is a standard expression for people that don't believe in the living God and reject Jesus.

"But do not be deceived", the angel says to us. Look from above. Do you see the contrast? Jesus Christ died, but he rose again and will come in glory. He is coming from heaven to establish an eternal kingdom.

And this evil, antichristian monster? Oh, he looks strong. But do not be intimidated, he is coming from below, from hell, and he is destined for destruction. The antichristian political power the prostitute relies on for her seductive programs will not help her to escape God's judgment.

What about the seven heads of this ugly monster? That sounds pretty powerful and frightening. But again, here too his power is deceptive.

Interestingly, John's interpretive guide gives two different explanations. These heads represent seven hills on which the woman sits (v.9), but they also refer to seven kings (v.10), he says. So we have two metaphors to describe the same feature of the beast.

Many scholars have come up with an enormous variety of literal interpretations as to what these seven hills stand for and who these seven kings are. There are just too many options to pick from, and the one is as good or as bad as the other. All together it becomes highly speculative, and often confusing.

It seems more fitting to take these things symbolically. And since both metaphors say something about the same feature (the seven heads), it makes sense that both symbolize the same thing. As always, the number seven stands for completeness. It is all about the claim of this beast to have absolute authority and invincible strength. But we learn to look at this from two different angles.

When the prostitute Babylon sits on seven mountains, it emphasizes that the evil power she relies on, appears to be as solid, strong, stable and immovable as mountains. That sounds discouraging for God's people that live in the midst of this Babylonian culture.

But again, this strength is deceptive. There is also the image of those seven kings, of which five are gone, one is now, and one is yet to come. And that picture is full of encouragement for Christian believers in this world.

No matter how solid, stable, and never-ending it looks like, the antichristian political power, driven by Satan, is coming to an end; five of the seven kings are gone already. And the fact that the last of these kings will only be around for a short time, reinforces the good news that evil will not last, but that the end is near.

But what about this beast itself as an eighth king? Well, when the complete number of seven has failed, the number eight suggests a new beginning, with new hope that the antichristian power will be able to remain in control in this world. After all, this is the monster that makes the astonishing comeback, remember? (Rev.13:3) A frightening perspective!

But do not worry. God's fierce enemy will fail miserably. Since he belongs to the seven, he will face the same future as the others. He will not escape his destruction. Indeed, from whichever angle you look at it, this woman and her beast are ripening for God's judgment, and Jesus is going to win!

This comes out again in the last detail of the beast's appearance, the ten horns. What do we make of that? We hear that these ten horns represent ten kings, who are going to operate in this world all at the same time. Again, scholars have come up with various explanations as to who these kings are or what they stand for. But here again, let us forget confusing speculations, and focus on the symbolic meaning.

Under the image of a powerful political and military coalition we see the total of all earthly opposition to God Almighty coming together. They join forces under God's fiercest enemy, the monstrous beast we have seen before, as "commander-in-chief". Their power will not last long, but long enough to launch a massive attack on the Lamb Jesus Christ and his church. However, it will not get them anywhere.

Satan pulls out all the stops in a violent outburst of hatred towards Jesus Christ. But even the strength of all these hostile powers combined is deceptive. The war they start is futile. Jesus' superior power as Lord of lords and King of kings defeats them easily. Rev. 16:14-16 alluded to this already.

And we will hear more details about this great battle and victory in Rev. 19:11–21.

According to v.14 Jesus' faithful followers will share in his victory. This makes it an urgent question for everyone. Where are you in this battle? Do not be mistaken. In this spiritual war there is no neutral position, no sitting on the fence. You are either with the Lamb or with the beast.

Are you afraid for the strength of the beast, sometimes? Do not be deceived, he is ripening for God's judgment and his ruin is unavoidable. Remain faithful to the Lamb Jesus Christ when the final battle rages in your struggle of faith, every day.

BABYLON'S SURPRISING END

Backed up by the seemingly impressive strength of the beast she rides, Babylon the great, the prostitute, enjoys her worldwide corrupting influence (v.15). With her immorality and depravity, she infects and intoxicates people everywhere in this world *peoples and multitudes and nations and languages*.

We see it all around us. The world as the centre of political persecution (= the beast) and the world as the centre of the antichristian culture (= the prostitute) seem to make a strong and successful couple, unified in their hatred and opposition toward God and his church.

But, as we saw, her strength is deceptive, because the power that supports her is on its way to destruction. It makes for a pathetic picture.

In the v.16 and 17 the angel who has been talking to John, shows us from above, how unreliable the whole set up actually is. This evil, antichristian cultural power, this impressive prostitute, she will find her end, because she can no longer rely on the strength and support of her political counterpart, the beast.

In the beginning we saw the woman sitting on the beast, self-confident, proud, triumphant. But in the end it throws her off, turns around, and attacks her.

It is a surprising turn of events. The beast and his ten horns, the collective political, antichristian opposition here on earth against Almighty God, turns against Babylon, against the prostitute, against the antichristian culture in this world. They hate her, because her immoral, evil influence did not bring the happiness she promised. In the end the world without God is not going to be a better place. The pleasures of sin leave people empty, miserable, angry and frustrated.

The final scene of this chapter is full of graphically violent images. They will ruin her and rip away her expensive clothes, her gold and jewelry. They will strip her naked leaving her with no dignity whatsoever. It is a striking image of the completely impoverished, deeply embarrassing and shameful end of a culture without God.

It also says that *they will devour her flesh,* a barbaric demonstration of bitter and deeply rooted loathing. It reflects the horrible feast in Rev. 19:17,18 & 21 when scavenging birds gorge themselves on the flesh of God's enemies.

And then *they will burn her up with fire.* In the end there will be nothing left of the proud and brazen prostitute, absolutely nothing. When the sinful, immoral human culture in this world is ripe for God's judgment, it will face complete annihilation.

The violent language and gruesome images are unsettling. And yet, it is the Holy God who shows John the reality of the destruction of all evil and wickedness.

Here is the judgment the angel told John he was going to see (v.1).

Today Babylon seems so powerful and so influential. It is scary. But she is ripening for destruction. That tells you, "don't be scared". It also tells you how foolish it is to compromise with the sinful world, with the dominant antichristian culture. It will all come to nothing. God's judgment will deal with it and nothing will be left.

Yes, God fulfils his plans. The course of history has no surprises for him. He knows the end from the beginning. He is the power behind Babylon's destruction. But the surprise is that God uses her own allies as tools in his hands (v.17). The end of this vision shows us the self-destructive nature of evil.

Indeed, all evil and injustice carry within themselves the seed of self-destruction. And therefore, when God gives room to the powers of evil, do not be discouraged. The seed will grow and ultimately the whole edifice crumbles and comes tumbling down.

Trust that in the end it is all God's work. Know that he is firmly in control. When his enemies work out their own plans, they accomplish his purpose, until every word of him has been fulfilled, and the victory of his grace in Jesus Christ will make all things new.

26

Revelation 18

WE WITNESS BABYLON'S FUNERAL

We find ourselves still in the middle of what is perhaps the darkest and most gloomy part of John's visions in the Book of Revelation. And so it is good to remember that in the end, all this is still about the glorious victory of Jesus Christ, about the unfolding of our history according to God's plan of salvation.

Rev. 16:19 reports briefly about the destruction of Babylon when the last one of the seven bowls of God's wrath was poured out, ushering in God's final judgment.

Then, in the next part (17–19:10), it is all about this city of Babylon, which is also called 'the great prostitute'. Through the eyes of the apostle John we see a variety of details of Babylon's disastrous future. In this way we learn to see how the holy God will deal with sin and evil, for the comfort and encouragement of his people.

Rev. 17 showed how and why Babylon is getting ready for the day of God's judgment.

26 • REVELATION 18

Here in Rev. 18 we see what is going to happen to her on that day. Next we hope to see in Rev. 19:1-10 what the effect of all this is on those who belong to God, followers of Jesus Christ and angels in heaven.

One more thing we must remember is that throughout all this, Babylon, the great prostitute, stands for the world without God; the human culture that rejects Jesus Christ; the world driven by secularism and materialism; the world obsessed with hedonism; the world were sin is the norm, so that right is wrong and evil is right; the world that hates the Christian faith, persecutes Christian believers, and has as its ultimate goal to destroy the church of Christ.

With this in mind we turn to Rev. 18, where we witness Babylon's funeral.

THE DEATH NOTICE

As the story unfolds of what is going to happen to Babylon on the Last Day, the apostle John sees in Rev. 18:1 another angel. It is not the same as the one in Rev. 17. The angel who talked to him in Rev. 17 has made clear that *Babylon the Great, the mother of prostitutes* is ripe for God's judgment. And now she has it coming!

This is a different angel, because this one comes straight from heaven. You could say that all angels come from heaven. But it is mentioned here to emphasize that this angel is a messenger directly from God. And that there should be no doubt that his message is God's own message.

You could also see this. He comes with *great authority* and *the earth was made bright with his glory*. He reflects God's power and glory in such a way that everyone can see it, and so that everyone will understand that his message comes with the absolute authority of the holy and almighty God himself.

It is clear that John is greatly impressed by what he sees. And this feeling becomes even stronger when this angel opens his mouth. *He called out with a mighty voice.* We have noticed before that Revelation is not just a picture-book, but a very noisy picture-book. Here we have it again. What this angel has to say, he shouts so loud, that it can be heard everywhere.

Everyone in this world, believers and unbelievers, must hear his announcement about the destruction of Babylon, the great prostitute, riding on the scarlet beast, as pictured in Rev. 17. Here is the breaking news headline of the Last Day of the history of our world: *Fallen! Fallen is Babylon the Great!* The absolute end of this sinful world is here.

As a matter of fact, this announcement is a repeat of what another angel had announced already in Rev. 14:8. That was a forewarning. But now is the time to paint the harrowing picture of what will happen to a world dominated by an antichristian culture, and by hostile political powers that try to eliminate God's church by violence.

To be sure, it is a vision with a prophetic message about the world in which we live today. So, it still has to happen. But it will happen! It is so certain that this angel issues a public death notice, as if it has happened already.

The powerful and wealthy city of this world, a vibrant business centre, where people from all over the world enjoy the good life, will become a barren wasteland, a collection of desolate ruins that will forever be uninhabitable. It is a graphic picture in v.2. It will be a dead ghost-town, only fit for housing unclean, detestable creatures; a haunted place, filled with evil spirits.

The description is symbolic, and stands for everything that is disgusting, repulsive, ugly and scary, awful, terrifying…..! Anyone ready to sign up for a place like that? And yet – this is the future of the world without God.

Why is this? What is wrong with this world that makes this death notice inevitable?

The angel explains (v.3). It is because of the poisonous and corruptive influence of Babylon's sexual immorality, her hostility towards God and her antichristian propaganda. The *kings of the earth* and the *merchants of the earth* stand for the political and economic powers that control the nations. And the way these politicians operate and run the economy is not determined by what God says in his Word, but by their intimate involvement in Babylon's ungodly pleasures and treasures.

Babylon tempts us to forget about God's will as holy and good, and to find our joy and happiness, the true meaning of life in her values, what is called here *the wine of the passion of her sexual immorality* and *the power of her luxurious living.*

John then hears another voice in his vision. He does not see another angel. No, this voice comes directly from heaven. So we probably have to think of the glorified Jesus Christ speaking, or perhaps even the Holy and Almighty God himself.

This voice sort of takes over, and continues to elaborate on the reason why the Day of God's judgment comes with this unavoidable death notice of Babylon.

Her sins are heaped high as heaven, the voice says (v.5). There is an element of irony here. Do you remember the story of Babel in Genesis 11? The folks in Babel were determined to build a tower that would reach to the heavens. They wanted to challenge the authority of Almighty God. But the whole endeavour was a miserable failure.

But now, here we are, at the end of our history, and look, Babylon manages to build a tower into heaven. Only, it is a tower of sin and evil. That is a metaphor for this world's massive accumulation of terrible wickedness.

And it keeps going. You watch and read the news, and sometimes it looks as if God does not care about the evil that is going on. Should he not do something about it? The sins of this world keep piling up.

But do not be mistaken! Remember Genesis 11. God will remember. This is again so certain that he can say, *God has remembered her iniquities.* Every single sin will be accounted for. None of it will be forgotten. The day is coming that she will pay for what she has done. This evil, sinful world will not get away with anything.

Some people have trouble with this idea. What we read in v.6 and the beginning of 7 sound more like an Old Testament thirst for revenge, than the New Testament message of love and forgiveness, they say. Does it not say that God so loved the world that he gave his one and only Son Jesus as the Saviour?

That is correct. But always remember that salvation is for all who believe in him, and not for those who reject him. The Lord is a God of grace and of justice. And his judgment is a fair judgment. Babylon's amount of punishment will be the exact equivalent for the wickedness of those who reject Jesus.

Look at her, as she sits there in arrogant self-glorification. The second half of v.7 gives the same picture as Rev. 17:3-6. *I am invincible. I am the queen of this world. I will rule forever.* And it seems to make sense. Do we not live in exciting times?

Sure, there is trouble in various corners of this world. At the same time: most of us enjoy prosperity and technologies as never before in history. And without God! It's impressive. Don't you feel intimidated by that, sometimes? The godless world we live in seems invincible.

But her claim to divine power is a direct assault on the holy and almighty God himself, the King of kings and Lord of lords. And therefore, she will not escape her deadly destruction. Hear the death notice! Babylon's punishment is inevitable.

God's judgment over a wicked world seems to linger. But it will come. And when it comes, it comes fast and furious! One day is enough to make this whole arrogant world-power collapse. *Her plagues will come in a single day,* says v.8. The one disaster after the other. It will not stop until she is completely consumed by God's fire.

This prospect makes the call in v.4 really urgent! God's voice from heaven calls, *Come out of her, my people, lest you take part in her sins. Abandon Babylon lest you share in her plagues.* It's like the angels urging Lot to leave Sodom: "Hurry! Get out of this place. Or you will be swept away when the city is punished" (Genesis 19:15-17).

The difference is, of course, that here Babylon is not just a place on a map, which you could literally leave by loading your family in the car and getting out of town.

No, Babylon is the human society, the culture of the world where we all live in the in-between times. God's children share the world with all other people. It is impossible to get away from it physically. As a matter of fact, even trying to do so, would be wrong.

God gives us a place here, in the midst of this antichristian world, because the church has a message for this world, for the culture we live in.

People may not like a message that challenges our modern culture and that gives God and Jesus Christ the proper place as the only source of hope and comfort. But that does not mean that we can abandon the responsibility to proclaim this counter-cultural gospel, calling people to follow Jesus Christ, and to do so loud and clear as long as we have the chance in this world.

However, when he says "Come out of her", God's voice calls for 'spiritual separation'. He warns us not to associate with the morals, values and beliefs of Babylon. Do not accept her religious, political, and economic corruption. Refuse to become comfortable with her immoral lifestyle. Distance yourselves from her attractive influence.

That is not so easy. We all like to share in the prosperity and be part of the social life of people you hang out with in this world. And if that means that you will have to compromise your faith... It's very tempting to think that you can juggle being a Christian, and at the same time living a life adapted to the pagan culture around you.

Yes, we live here, and as Christians it is hard not to get involved in economic, political and social activities that support secular, antichristian initiatives in this world. Economic grandeur and growing wealth are also attractive for Christian believers. But before you know it, you forget the death notice that has been issued for Babylon's funeral, and then her punishment will be your punishment.

The temptations can be very subtle. That is why we need to discern carefully what it means to separate yourself from the world.

How can you do this? Know God's will. Know God's Word. Don't say: "I feel that this is okay". Or: "I feel in my heart that God would not have a problem with this". Or: "If everybody talks or acts like this; it should be fine". No, let the Word of God teach you to recognize evil and wickedness for what it is.

Parents, please show your children, your teenagers, what true faith in Jesus Christ is worth, what it looks like and sounds like. Model these things. Talk about these things. Teach them, with the Word of God in your hand, heart, and mind. Help them to discern between good and evil; to reject and refuse the values and morals of this world.

Remember, the trek to the new Promised Land is a journey of ongoing dissociation from this world if you want to stay the course. It is a spiritual rebellion against the immoral and corrupt values of the Babylon we live in. God's voice warns us not to be deceived by the charms of a culture without God. Her death notice has been given.

THE LAMENT

How do the kings and merchants of the earth, the folks who are, according to v.3, so intimately connected with Babylon, the people on earth who are committed to the modern godless culture, how do they react when they get her death notice, and when they see what happens to their beloved Babylon?

John hears this in the next passage. On the day of the Last Judgment, when this world filled with sin and evil will find her end, all her lovers and friends will join in a loud funeral dirge. It will be heard all over the world. As a matter of fact, in the v.9–20 we actually hear three categories raise their voices. They all sing their heart wrenching lament from the same page in three-part harmony.

The first group are *the kings of the earth*, the mighty political leaders (v.9). "They committed sexual immorality and lived in luxury with her," it says. These are political leaders who supported and promoted the self-absorbed, hedonistic lifestyle, characteristic for the world that has rejected God. In return they were also stimulated and empowered by the modern antichristian culture to persecute the believers.

The second group are *the merchants of the earth*, the wealthy businessmen, the economic bigwigs (v.11). These are the men who have become filthy rich by delivering without scruples everything the prostitute Babylon ordered, as demanded by her excessive and evil lifestyle. Our world is driven by greed and materialism. It promises endless happiness to those who love to indulge in luxuries. And it is in the interest of these businessmen to encourage this poisonous influence.

In the v.12 and 13 we have a whole catalogue of the fancy stuff they have been selling and shipping to Babylon. There are twenty-eight items on the list, and that number is not accidental. It is the number four times the number seven, the number of the earth and the number of completeness. It represents all the luxury products of the whole world, symbolically standing for Babylon's extreme extravagance. The point is that our sinful world is never satisfied. In her never-ending search for joy and happiness she is always looking for more, for better and bigger wealth. Babylon is good for business.

We do not have to go one by one over all the items listed here, but look at the end of the list. It highlights the deep depravity of a world, a society, a culture that wants nothing to do with God. The merchants do not hesitate to even sell *slaves, that is, human souls*. And do not think only about the slave-trade of 200 years ago. It is also what we call today human trafficking: men for forced labour, women and children for the sex-trade. When evil and immorality become the standard in this world, human lives are just commodities, to be bought and sold as animals.

The third group are *the shipmasters and seafaring men,* the mariners, the sailors, the folks that make a good living of transporting the cargos Babylon is buying from those traders (v.17). They stand for the people in this world who are eager to support the views and values of our secular society, because it is a good way of making a living. It will bring more prosperity, and thus a better life, and without God!

When you see all this, Babylon with all her loyal supporters, you might think that this will go on forever. Who will be able to stop this powerful, wealthy, and popular antichristian culture? Her supporters have money and power. They are the ones who are calling the shots in our narcissistic and hedonistic godless world.

And yet, the death notice has been issued. One day it will all go up in flames.

On that day, all Babylon's friends and lovers will gather around what used to be this great city of power and wealth. And as they mourn her death, they will join the loud lament, filled with sadness. That is not because they see how foolish they were. And that is not because they repent and turn to Jesus Christ.

No, they feel sorry for themselves. They are sad that they lost her pleasures and wealth, all the things they enjoyed so much. What do we do without her? When this wealthy and powerful world without God will collapse, there will be no future left for those who have supported her and benefitted from her. Nothing!

That is why they all *weep and mourn* on that day. When Babylon burns to the ground, people will face political and economic chaos. Markets crash. Expensive luxuries become worthless. Wealth evaporates, just like that.

But they all *stand far off* because they are desperately trying to escape their own judgment. They do not dare to come close to the fire. They fear that they may also burn. Babylon's destruction may cause their own destruction. And they have good reason to think so.

They are all shocked and *terrified by her horrible torment when they see the smoke of her burning*. This is awful!

And, unified in hopeless despair, they raise their voices to lament the sudden end of Babylon, the godless and sinful worldly culture, which had looked so strong and successful. *Was there ever a city like this great city*? No, nothing in history compares with the grandeur of Babylon. And look at her now!

On the day that the glorified Christ will come with his final judgment, we will hear the somber cry echoing all around the world. *Alas! Alas! O great city! Alas! Alas! O great and mighty city! In a single hour your judgment has come, you have been ruined, and all your power, wealth, and beauty has been laid waste!*

Did you hear that? One hour. Now that is fast and furious!

The question is, where do we stand when the day comes that the whole thing goes up in smoke? Will we join the lament, because we will also miss the material wealth of our earthly life in this world? As Christian believers we are not immune for the tempting glitter of Babylon with the promise of a good life without God, or for the social pressure to be accepted by the antichristian culture in this world. But if that is your life here and now, what will you have left on the day of Babylon's funeral?

But then, in the midst of all the weeping and crying, and in sharp contrast to this gloomy earthly point of view, there is also in John's vision the viewpoint from heaven. In v. 20 God's voice calls for another song, a song of praise that will drown out the funeral dirge. He calls his church to rejoice when this wicked world goes up in flames, and they see the smoke of her burning. For God's people in heaven and on earth Babylon's death notice is reason for joyful celebration.

No, that is not a matter of malicious revenge. That is definitely not a matter of smug Christian self-complacency. But the victory of Jesus Christ will eliminate all injustice and all anti-Christian power and influence. And that is a reason for praise.

On the day of God's judgment, the time has come to set all things straight forever.

THE BURIAL

As the last sounds of the gloomy chorus of the lament on the day of Babylon's funeral fade away, we witness one more, final act in John's vision. The apostle sees how an extremely strong and powerful angel picks up a huge boulder, the size and weight of a large millstone, and hurls it away with a powerful swing of his arm into the sea, to be buried deep in the ocean-bed (v.21).

The symbolism is striking. When you throw a rock in the water, you first see waves and ripples as the effect. But it will not take long, and then such disturbance is quickly gone. Then the surface of the water is smooth again. There is no trace left. It is as if nothing has happened.

The explanation comes immediately with the act. We witness Babylon's burial. The image shows that the last judgment of Christ is indeed the permanent, absolute, irreversible, and radical end of this sinful world. All sin and evil will be buried, gone forever. Never again will the earth be polluted, poisoned, filled with the stench of Babylon's hatred, immorality, evil, injustice, and wickedness.

Babylon the great, the great prostitute, who led the world astray by the intoxicating influence of her immorality, will find her violent end, *and will be found no more.*

This becomes the deadly refrain in the v.22–23. She was a vibrant city, full of life. People went happily about their daily activities. This describes our world, today. But it will not last.

No more music, or other arts to cheer people up, no more cultural creativity, no more joyful entertainment…

> *never again.* Only deadly silence

No more craftsmen who take pleasure in their trade, no more carpenters, bricklayers, metalworkers, painters, architects, landscapers to enhance Babylon's beauty…

> *never again.* Only dreary brokenness.

No more familiar sounds of people using the hand-mill to prepare meals and baking for their families…

> *never again.* Only hopelessness.

No more lamps that light all the houses in the evening, for people to enjoy family-time and social activities…

> *never again.* Only silent darkness.

No more weddings filled with laughter and the happy voices of young people who are looking forward to the future with excitement and hopeful expectations. No more love…

> *never again.* Only despair.

As a pounding hammer the repetition of the words "no more… no more…" reinforces the finality of what is happening. It amplifies the sheer magnitude of the disaster our world will be facing on the Day of Judgment, the final, complete, and unrestrained outpouring of God's wrath over all sin and evil.

This is the inevitable end for a world that rejects Jesus Christ and is obsessed by human greatness; the end of an arrogant, pleasure-mad world, filled with brutal violence, filled with the blood of God's murdered children and other innocent victims; the end of a world filled with hatred toward God, his Word and his people.

It leaves us with a frightening picture of a dark, silent, and empty world. The world as it was before God said, "Let there be light".

But this is not the end. Our Father in heaven does not give up, even if he has to start again from scratch.

The city of death will die and be buried to make room for the city of eternal life and eternal joy, God's new city in God's new creation.

Babylon's funeral will clear the way for the Marriage Feast of the Lamb Jesus Christ.

27

Revelation 19: 1 – 10

THE DAY OF BABYLON'S FALL IS THE DAY OF GOD'S VICTORY

When we looked at Revelation 18, we noticed that we were still in the midst of the darkest and most gloomy part of John's visions in the Book of Revelation.

But the tone of the next passage, Rev.19: 1–10, is remarkably different. It is much more joyful, much happier. It leads to a wedding, and to the distribution of wedding invitations. Those are wonderful events. There is also loud singing of massive choirs, all to the praise and glory of God Almighty.

However, we are still dealing with the fall of Babylon, the destruction of the great prostitute.

The difference is that in Rev. 18 the fall of Babylon was seen from an earthly point of view. We heard weeping and mournful cries on the earth.

But in this passage we look at this event from above. And now we learn what the effect of all this is on those who belong to God, the followers of Jesus Christ and the angels in heaven.

When the news of Babylon's fall reaches heaven, we do not hear a lament (as in Rev. 18), but we hear an outburst of praise, sung by heavenly choirs.

27 • Revelation 19:1-10

We witness a heavenly liturgy to celebrate God's victory over the prostitute Babylon. There is tremendous joy, because Babylon's fall clears the way for the exciting new beginning on that same day, the day of God's victory.

The Celebration Begins

You may remember what we listened to in Rev. 18; how we heard all the weeping and lamenting that was going on in response to the horrible destruction of Babylon.

But then, right in the midst of all that was going on, we heard, unexpectedly, God's voice calling for another song. *Rejoice over her, O heaven, and you saints, apostles and prophets.* He called for a song of praise and joy! That was in Rev. 18:20.

Well, here it is – in the first part of Rev. 19. We are still looking at the impact of what happens to Babylon, the great prostitute, on the day of God's Final Judgment. Here the apostle John hears the mighty sounds of the heavenly liturgy of praise and worship in response to Babylon's fall, praise and worship to glorify God on the day of his victory. As it turns out, the day of Babylon's disastrous fall is just that, it is the day of God's victory over his enemies.

That is why on this same day the grand celebration begins! *Rejoice over her, O heaven!*

In this section of John's vision about Babylon's fall there is not much to see. John hears more than he sees. And, as we have noticed before, what we hear in Revelation gives us often the right view, the proper interpretation of what we have seen.

In this passage we hear three choirs singing. The glorious tone of what they sing is set by the four-fold use of the word *Hallelujah, Praise the Lord!* There are differences, of course, but this verbal thread ties these songs and choruses together. It makes for one, unified, joyful response to God's actions when the seven bowls of God's wrath were poured out (Rev. 16), leading to his Last Judgment and Babylon's destruction.

These three heavenly choirs form a stark and striking contrast with the other three choirs we have heard in Rev.18, the groups that were so loudly lamenting in v. 9–19: "alas…. alas…. alas….!" Here is the opposite.

We are familiar with the word "Hallelujah" in the Old Testament as the call to each and every one, to all of God's people, to praise and worship the holy and almighty God. Time and again we hear it in the Psalms. And it could often be heard in Jerusalem, as the call to worship coming from the temple.

Now we hear it from heaven and it is unique. In all of the New Testament the word "Hallelujah" only occurs here, in these songs in Rev. 19. It is a special glimpse of a powerful fragment of heavenly worship. It is different from the fragments we heard in Revelation 4, 5, 7, 11, and 15. This one tells us how close we have come to the glory of heaven on the Day of God's judgement.

The first thing that John hears is what sounds like the loud roar of a large crowd, and it comes from heaven. A great multitude of voices is shouting in unison, *Hallelujah! Salvation and glory and power belong to our God.*

We do not get any specifics to help us identify these voices, other than that John hears them shouting *in heaven*. This makes us think it is most likely an enormous choir of angels. We have a precedent of this in 5:11, where John hears the loud song of many angels, *numbering thousands upon thousands, and ten thousand times ten thousand*. It is just huge, and John hears the exuberant joy of this "Hallelujah-chorus" reverberate throughout the heavenly realm.

What's the reason for this excitement? They are full of praise for, in the fall of Babylon, the destruction of the antichristian culture of the world without God, they recognize God's salvation. They recognize God's determination to rescue his creation from perishing. They recognize God's commitment to recover the world from the power of Satan. They recognize how God's deep love delivers his people from the deadly influence of the great prostitute. They recognize how he leads his people in a new exodus, through many dark dangers, to the new Promised Land.

They are full of praise, because they see in all this, the evidence of God's power and the manifestation of his glory. Indeed, heaven rejoices in Babylon's fall, for in this fall our God shows that he is a reliable God, a God who

27 • Revelation 19:1-10

is true to his word, a God who is just in his judgments. This is our God. You can trust him. You can rely on him. Everyone can on the Day of Judgment.

Yes, he punishes sin and evil. But in doing so he does what he says. He does what he has always said as the God of the covenant, in his promises and in his threats. There is nothing unpredictable here. Your God is absolutely true and fully just, you can hold him to his Word.

The angelic choir also gives evidence of God's true justice. *He has judged the great prostitute who corrupted the earth with her immorality.* We do not have to elaborate on this again. In Rev. 18 we have already witnessed Babylon's death notice and burial, as well as the lament of her lovers and friends.

She deserves it, because of her corruptive influence. With false religious ideas and antichristian philosophies, she has led many people away from God, into the darkness. With the temptations of a secular, materialistic, hedonistic, and immoral lifestyle she has made the world a filthy, polluted place to live.

God's justice also holds her accountable for the death of many of his servants. *He has avenged their blood on her*, it says. By stimulating and promoting a hostile attitude towards Christians in the culture without God, the prostitute has orchestrated their persecution. But their God, our God, is a just God, who responds to the urgent plea of his murdered children, *the souls under the altar, who call out "How long, Sovereign Lord, holy and true, until you avenge our blood"?* (Rev. 6:10).

Wickedness is destroyed so that a just world can be re-established. It is all part of God's plan of redemption, and it gets the multitude of angels in heaven really excited.

Once more they cried out: Hallelujah! The smoke from her goes up forever and ever. Babylon's destruction is final and complete. All opposition against God's salvation has been crushed forever. The picture of smoke rising up alludes to what happened to Sodom and Gomorrah (Genesis 19:23–29). It indicates how intense, how radical this punishment is. God's righteousness guarantees that Babylon will never raise its ugly head again to destroy God's work.

The day of Babylon's fall is the day of God's victory

Then John hears other voices that echo the *Hallelujahs* of the angels. This is a much smaller choir, the *twenty-four elders and the four living creatures*... We have met them for the first time in Rev. 4 and 5 as the most prominent throne-attendants of the Holy God. They have witnessed how Jesus Christ, the Lamb of God, was given the scroll with the outline of God's plan of salvation. And they have witnessed everything that happened when this Lamb opened the seals of this scroll.

Here they appear for the last time in Revelation. It is the moment of the grand finale that wraps up the unfolding of the whole content of the scroll. When they see the victory of God Almighty they fall down in deep awe. They worship God and confirm the angels' reason for celebration with just two words: *Amen! Hallelujah!*

Then a third choir joins in. It is the response to a call from heaven, from the throne. John hears an unidentified voice (v.5). There has been some speculation as to who is calling. One of the elders? One of the living creatures? An angel? We do not know. However, what he is saying comes with the authority of God's will.

Praise our God, all you his servants, you who fear him, small and great.

The effect is just explosive! This call triggers a massive outburst of praise. A chorus of thunderous 'Hallelujahs' fills the universe.

The singing of this crowd is more powerful than anything John has heard before. It drowns out everything else. The deafening sound is so loud and overwhelming, that the apostle needs three similes in an attempt to capture what he hears: (1) it seemed to be a great multitude, (2) it was like the roar of pounding waves or a mighty waterfall, and (3) it was like booming sound of mighty peals of thunder.

And all these things at the same time. Incredible!

Who are those singers? And where are they? It is not mentioned. But one thing is clear, this crowd is larger and louder than the first one. "God's servants, who fear him" (v.5) often refers to followers of Christ. But then, angels are also called 'servants'. In other words, without getting into specifics, on the last day of our history the call is issued from God's throne for everyone,

27 • REVELATION 19:1-10

everywhere, to let the celebration of God's glorious victory begin, and to fill earth and heaven with festive praise and worship.

And all who belong to God and to Jesus Christ will be involved, both small and great, young and old, rich and poor, important and insignificant, men, women and children, whatever your rank or position is, whoever you are, come on! Join in!

Hallelujah! For the Lord, our God the Almighty reigns. Praise and glory to God Almighty. He reigns with power and majesty. God's triumph is complete. Recognize Babylon's destruction as manifestation that God's royal power is supreme and that his rule controls all things.

Are you looking forward to joining this choir? Then you better start practicing today. Sure, it is a vision, a prophetic picture. We still live in Babylon and the Day of God's final victory is not here yet. But the glorified Christ is coming. And so is God's triumph over all his enemies. It is irreversible and inevitable.

Let this trigger in us, today already, the beginning of our joyful praise, worship and celebration.

THE WEDDING IS COMING

That God's judgments are true and just is indeed a good reason to fill the universe with resounding *Hallelujahs* on the day of God's glorious victory, and to celebrate the salvation, glory, and power of God.

But there is more to celebrate. The destruction of the great prostitute, the day of Babylon's fall, signals that the time has come for the wedding of the Lamb Jesus Christ. And therefore, the countless voices of this mass-choir continue. They stir each other up and encourage each other. *Let us rejoice and exult and give him the glory, our Lord God Almighty,* who won the victory, *for the marriage of the Lamb has come, and his Bride has made herself ready.*

The metaphor of 'the wedding' pictures an image of joy. A wedding is an occasion to celebrate a happy new beginning. It is an event that is filled with hope and high and exciting expectations.

To really appreciate the metaphor, it is helpful to know a bit about wedding ceremonies in those days. From the day of the betrothal, which is sort of like our 'engagement', bridegroom and bride were legally bound to each other by the pledge of marriage, made in the presence of witnesses.

Between that day and the day of the actual wedding both partners were busy preparing for the big day. For the groom this included also paying the dowry, so that on the wedding day he could 'claim' his bride. The festivities to seal the commitment would last for at least a week, with the wedding banquet as the highlight.

The metaphor is well-known throughout the Bible. In both the Old and New Testament, scripture often compares the love-relationship between a bride and a bridegroom to the relationship between God and his people.

In the Old Testament many of the prophets use this image. They employ the language of love to describe the relationship between the LORD and Israel. This includes the negative impact on the relationship when Israel walks away from the LORD to serve other gods. The prophets describe this in terms of sexual immorality or adultery.

But then, when the people of God repent and return to the Lord, these same prophets express God's deep and intense longing to restore the relationship with the people of his love (Isaiah 54; Hosea 2).

Throughout the entire Old Testament all these metaphoric references to the relationship between the LORD and Israel announce the messianic wedding that is coming. They prophecy the marriage feast of the Lamb Jesus Christ.

But it is not only the Old Testament. In the New Testament the apostle Paul talks about the human marriage relationship here on earth as a symbolic reflection of the glory and the beauty of the relationship between Christ and his church (Ephesians 5:22-33).

And it is this relationship that, on the day of God's final victory, will culminate into the marvellous wedding feast of the Lamb, Jesus Christ glorified,

27 • Revelation 19:1-10

and his bride, the church that has remained faithful to the testimony of Jesus Christ, her bridegroom.

This bridegroom loved his bride so much, that he paid the ultimate price for his bride; he gave his life for her. He took on flesh and blood and died on the cross. That is how he paid his 'dowry', so to speak. He bought her with his precious blood. And now it is our only comfort to belong to him with body and soul, both in life and in death.

It is a lovely metaphor, this wedding image in Revelation 19. It expresses the intimacy, the love and joy between Christ and his people, and it anticipates the glorious picture of Revelation 21.

At the same time, it is also a confrontational image. This wedding on the one hand, and the immoral affair with the prostitute on the other hand, emphasize again the two choices we all have to make in our lives: you can either follow the Lamb Jesus Christ or you can choose to follow Babylon the prostitute. And remember, both choices have far reaching consequences, eternal consequences.

As church of Jesus Christ you must realize this. It says here that *the Bride of the Lamb has made herself ready*. It means that she is preparing her wedding dress: *fine linen, bright and pure*. The bride's clothing contrasts with the prostitute's outfit. Oh, this prostitute is also dressed in expensive fine linen (Rev. 18:16), but hers is not "bright and pure". It comes with dark purple and scarlet. The purity of the church exposes the impurity of the world.

But hang on, how "pure" is this bride actually, this church of sinners? Listen carefully: yes, she has made herself ready. At the same time, her wedding dress is a gift, a gift of love. *It was granted her to clothe herself with fine linen, bright and pure*. This wedding dress does not honour the one who wears it but honours the One who gives it.

This fine and pure linen the bride of Christ is wearing at the wedding is explained as a symbol. It stands for the spiritual and moral purity of God's people, the *righteous deeds of the saints,* the believers. It symbolizes your holiness.

The entire time between Jesus' ascension and his return is a time of preparation for the church, a time of getting ready for the close communion with Jesus that is coming.

But how do you do that?

Well, you have to dress yourself with "righteous deeds". Every day you have to distinguish yourself from the world by living a holy life, in persistent, thankful obedience to God. You must consistently refuse to compromise with Babylon's values and beliefs, the culture without God. It is the kind of language Paul uses in Colossians 3, *Put on your new self. Clothe yourselves with compassion, kindness, humility, meekness and patience. And above all these put on love.*

At the same time, such 'righteous deeds' are not the successful result of our own pious efforts. In the church we continue to struggle with (sometimes terrible) sins. Remember, the 'fine linen' was granted to the bride. So how can we, as God's church, living in the midst of the Babylonian temptations, maintain our purity? Only when we are empowered by God's grace and forgiveness in Jesus Christ. Then we learn to do *the good works, which God prepared for us to do* (Ephesians 2:10).

And then, at the end, the bridegroom, accompanied by his glorious angels (Matthew 25:31), will come to take his bride and bring her home. And the feast will last, not for a week, but forever. Then the purpose of all that the bridegroom has done and is doing for his bride will have been accomplished, the lovely intimacy, the everlasting fellowship, the blessed communion between the Redeemer and the redeemed, the final fulfilment of all the promises of the gospel. And we shall be with him for ever and ever.

THE INVITATIONS ARE OUT

This marvellous perspective as the result of God's victory is so important that we must remember it, all the time. We can so easily be distracted by all the things that keep us busy here. Different experiences ask our attention every day. Those are not necessarily bad things, of course. But they can all become obstacles that make us forget the big picture and the grand future in Jesus Christ.

But we simply cannot afford to forget it.

That is why the angel who is talking to John since Rev. 17:1 instructs him to write down this congratulatory note: *Blessed are those who are invited to the marriage supper of the Lamb.* Here you have it, black on white! A card on your fridge. A sticky note on your mirror. The screen saver on your computer: 'Save The Date'.

No, we do not have a date, but the wedding festivities, the abundant wedding banquet for the Lamb Jesus Christ and his church are coming. In v.7 it says that the marriage *has* come, and that the bride *has* made herself ready. This is again the strongly prophetic wording to emphasize how sure, how certain it is that it is coming. Do not doubt it for one second. That is why we hear today already, "Congratulations! Happy are you when you live in this dark world with this wedding invitation in your pocket".

We do not get a description of the menu for this supper. We could think of Isaiah 25:6 – *rich food... aged wine... the best of meats and the finest of wines.* Are we to take this literally? Who knows? But it does at least reflect the perfect, joy-filled communion between Jesus Christ and his church in the eternal kingdom of his glory.

It is coming. The invitations are out. Today already! Did you get one? Attendance at this wedding celebration on the great day of God's victory is by invitation only.

No, that does not mean that it is exclusively restricted to a small elite of spiritual celebrities. On the contrary, the doors of the banquet hall are wide open for all who hold on to the testimony of Jesus, all his faithful and loyal followers.

That is why this is also the message of the church for everyone in this world. "Would you like an invitation for this fantastic wedding supper? Repent from your sin. Believe in Jesus Christ as your Saviour. Trust God's promises in his Word. Love him. Dedicate yourself to following him. And by God's grace it is all yours."

But that is the choice you must make. If not, you will end up at another feast. This terrific meal stands in stark contrast to the other supper God is organizing, mentioned in the second part of Rev.19: 17–18. That is going to be a horrific meal, when the wild beasts and birds gorge on the corpses of the wicked (v.21). So, yes, everyone will be part of one or the other feast. The question is, will you eat or will you be eaten?

But you, with your invitation to the wedding supper of the Lamb Jesus Christ: Congratulations! And do not lose it. Hang on to it.

How do you do that? Hold to the testimony of Jesus given to you in God's Word. Let that testimony control and govern your lifestyle choices. Then you also know how to prepare yourself for the festivities that are coming. Do not try to get to the wedding banquet without wearing wedding clothes, like the man in Jesus' parable (Matthew 22:1–14). He found out that trying to get there unprepared was not a good idea. So, get ready. Live for God. Live by his grace and forgiveness. Live in love and thankfulness.

Never question the reliability of your invitation. Satan loves to help you do that; "What makes you think that you are invited? Come on, you, with your sins and many failures, with your dark thoughts and whatever else is wrong with you – really?" Those are the thoughts he will try to put in your mind. Do not believe him.

John was told to write it down. But just in case you might think, "Oh, well, that's just John", the angel adds, *these are the true words of God*. It is not junk-mail. It is not SPAM. It is real. It is genuine. It is trustworthy.

Is it not amazing? No one less than God Almighty himself guarantees your invitation. So carry it on your heart and come to the wedding. Do not hesitate.

John is so overwhelmed and excited, that he begins to worship the angel. We do not know why he did that, but he is quickly corrected. And then it becomes a teaching moment for all of us: *Worship God alone*. Always remember, God alone is worthy of all praise, honour and worship. He alone has issued the invitations for the Lamb's wedding banquet, to celebrate his victory.

And therefore, on your way to the wedding of the Lamb, echo in your own daily life the heavenly *Hallelujahs* to the glory of God.

27 • Revelation 19:1-10

And when the doors of the banquet hall swing open and you will be ushered into the New Jerusalem to celebrate the love and grace of our God and the living communion with Jesus Christ that will last forever.... *we will dance on the streets that are golden, the glorious bride and the great Son of man. From every tongue, and tribe and nation we will join in the song of the Lamb.*

28

Revelation 19: 11 – 21

JESUS RETURNS AS WARRIOR TO BEGIN HIS FINAL CLEAN-UP

As we continue to move forward through the visions of the apostle John, we find ourselves still in the midst of one decisive and exciting event, the last event of the history of our world, God's final judgement at Jesus' return in glory.

This event has two aspects, two sides to it, which occur simultaneously. We will see the coming of the New Jerusalem, the restoration of everything, the renewed creation, the new heavens and the new earth, filled with joyful praise and worship. But we will also witness the disappearance of Babylon, the destruction of God's enemies, and the punishment of Satan, his evil henchmen and his human followers.

This started in Rev. 16:17–21, when the seventh bowl of God's wrath was poured out. What follows then, in the next chapters, is all part of this one event on this one last day.

In Rev. 17 and 18 we got a detailed report of what happens to the antichristian culture that dominates our world. It is pictured in the image of the fall and destruction of Babylon, the great city, which is also called 'the great prostitute'.

28 • Revelation 19:11-21

Then, in Rev. 19:1–10, the tone changes. The *Hallelujah* choirs of heaven celebrate the day of Babylon's fall, praising God on the day of his victory. We heard about the coming wedding of the Lamb Jesus Christ, with his glorious bride, the church. We heard about the invitations for the wedding supper of the Lamb. That is fantastic!

However, with the destruction of Babylon the clean-up is not complete yet. Evil must be destroyed entirely. The end of Satan's rule is absolutely necessary to make room for the New Jerusalem. Jesus' final clean-up is one action, but John describes it in three stages: the destruction of the two beasts, the destruction of Satan himself, and the destruction of Death and Hades. The expression that links these three steps together as one act, is "the fiery lake of burning sulphur". That is where they will all end up, when the clean-up is done. We focus now on the first of these three stages.

THE GLORY OF JESUS' APPEARANCE

You may remember that in Rev. 4:1 John saw *a door standing open in heaven*. The apostle was then invited to come up and come in, to have a peek in what turned out to be God's throne room, the heart of the operational centre of the One who rules the world.

This was the start of a fascinating series of visions that gives us the view from above, from heaven, to help us understand what is going on here, in our world.

In this vision (Rev. 19:11-21) we are not following John through a door to see what is going on in heaven. No, the apostle John sees *heaven open*. Indeed, on the day of Christ's return heaven itself will open wide. Then the whole human world, everyone on earth, will be able to see, not what is going on *in* heaven, but what is coming *out* of heaven, out of God's centre of operations. And that is impressive.

What appears before John's surprised look is a horse, *a white horse*, and on it a rider who will turn out to be a fierce and powerful warrior.

And this rider is not alone, with his horse. There are more. In v.14 we read that *the armies of heaven were following him*. Behind him comes a massive stream of men on horseback, all coming out of the wide-open space of heaven, a huge army and all on white horses.

This must have been incredibly dramatic to behold. Try to imagine that. Do you remember the 'Lord of the Rings' movies? The wizard Gandalf rides a magnificent white horse, called Shadowfax. In one of the big battles, the evil forces of darkness are closing in on the good powers and are winning. The situation looks hopeless. And then, when it is getting frighteningly dark, a huge army of horsemen appears, coming down the mountainside, led by Gandalf the White on his white horse, who is standing out brightly against the dark surroundings. It is an impressive moment.

Here in John's vision the white horse symbolizes that God's victory conquers all the evil powers of darkness. The history of our world is full of wars and battles. But the great war behind all hostilities, the war that determines the course of our history, that is the ongoing battle between God and Satan, and that war is also raging in our own lives.

Well, the appearance of this glorious warrior means that the end of this battle is certain and coming soon.

This must have been such a powerful 'wow-moment' for the apostle John. Yes! There can be no doubt. This is the day. What John is seeing, and what we are allowed to see, through his eyes, is the returning Jesus Christ, ready to complete his work of salvation. And this includes the destruction of his enemies.

That is why the first thing we see of Jesus when he returns in brilliant glory, is that he comes as an awesome warrior, a fearless fighter. He enters this world for the final judgment, ready to fight the final battle in a just war for a just cause.

Several things stand out when John describes him here as a mighty warrior, things that make us stand in awe. I mean, what do you expect to see when Jesus comes back? Have you ever thought of that? Yes, it is a vision, and the description is loaded with symbolism. And yet – the marvellous glory of his appearance is so encouraging. Who can withstand our coming Saviour?

His eyes are like a flame of fire. This is a feature of the exalted Christ we have seen before. Remember how John saw him in Rev.1 as *someone like a son of man...., with eyes like a flame of fire.* His penetrating gaze goes everywhere. It reaches beyond the surface of things in this world. He sees the evil intentions of the Beast, the antichristian powers. He exposes the lies and deceptions of the false prophet, the antichristian views and ideas that distort the truth of God's Word. And he will deal with it!

For him nothing in the whole world remains hidden. And that is also true for everything in the heart of each one of us. For him, each one of us is an open book. He sees and judges what lives here. And he is not fooled by what may look and sound good in our lives. He sees right through it. He knows where you are in the great war between God and Satan. He knows how easy it is for us to be taken in by the antichristian views and ideas we are bombarded with in our culture.

John also sees that on his head this rider *has many diadems* [NIV: *crowns*]. That might look weird, but the symbolism becomes clear when we know that the word used here occurs only three times in the New Testament, and all of those in Revelation. In 12:3 Satan is pictured with seven crowns, and in 13:1 the Beast out of the sea is said to have ten.

Indeed, Satan and the Beast claim to rule the world. But the One with most crowns ("many") is the only legitimate royal authority over all things. Christ alone is our unique and universal King. Do not be intimidated by the arrogant ridicule of your Christian faith and the hostile criticism that is so fashionable in our society. Jesus is coming as the all-knowing and all-seeing Ruler Supreme.

There is also a lot of emphasis on the names of this rider, names that reinforce the glory of the warrior from heaven. In the Bible someone's 'name' tells important things about a person's character or position. Here we are alerted to this three times. That makes it urgent to pay attention to these names.

Two of these names we know. In v.13 he is called "the Word of God". John has mentioned this before. *In the beginning was the Word, and the Word was with God, and the Word was God.* That was in John's gospel, chapter 1:1. In other words, through Jesus we come to know God. To put it differently, through Jesus the Almighty God speaks and works. In his person and work Jesus displays the Holy God, and who he is.

Today people have lots of ideas about Jesus, and many deny or ignore his "role", so to speak as "the Word of God". But on the day of Christ's return, everyone will see how true this is. Then everyone will recognize in Jesus' appearance how true and just, how loving and merciful, how faithful and fair God is, and has always been.

The other name we know is the name we hear in v.16: "King of kings and Lord of lords". It is also mentioned in Rev. 17:14, and it reinforces again the universal royal power that makes him invincible as he carries out the judgments of the Almighty God.

It says that this name *is written on his robe and on his thigh*. There has been some discussion whether this refers to two different locations, or to one, like, "on his robe where it covers his thigh". But the point is that, when the glorious Christ appears, no one has to wonder who he is. Everyone can read it and knows right away.

But then there is also this mysterious name that we do not know. This Rider on his white horse *has a name written on him that no one knows but himself* (v.12). This tells us that there are also many things to know about him that are beyond our imagination. Only Christ himself can fully grasp the height and the depth, the magnitude of his own power and glory. We can only stand in awe and praise him.

There is another remarkable detail in the appearance of this impressive horseman. It says (v.13) that *he is clothed in a robe dipped in blood*. Some scholars suggest that this blood is his own blood, the blood that was shed when Jesus died on the cross for our salvation. But this vision is not about the redemption of believers. It is about the destruction of God's enemies. In v.15 John says that the mighty warrior Christ *treads the winepress of the fury of the wrath of God the Almighty*.

You may remember this from Rev. 14:20, about the grape-harvest being trampled in the winepress of God's wrath, and blood flowing out of the press. And that picture echoes what we find in Isaiah 63. The bloodstains on his garment show the destructive power of Christ's decisive victory on the day of his return.

So, look at the picture of this mighty warrior. See the great glory of his appearance. Here he is, coming out of heaven, your Saviour, your Lord and King. We know that when Jesus returns, he will usher in the new heaven and the new earth. He will bring new life and new joy, life and joy that will never end. And his power guarantees that nothing will stand in the way of his glory. He is faithful and true (v.11). Are you looking forward to this? Do you like to see this happening with your own eyes?

At the same time, it is also a frightening picture. Before this never-ending joy will be reality, the final clean-up of this world must be completed. And the Lord will do so. Look again at the glorious and awesome appearance of this warrior. He is ready for war. He is ready for the final battle against God's enemies. Are you looking forward to this as well? Do you like to see this happening with your own eyes?

But how is he going to do this? What is going to be his weapon of mass destruction? Remote controlled cruise-missiles with nuclear warheads? No, a sharp sword. And not a regular sword. It is a sword that comes out of his mouth (v.15 and 21). This is again a prop that reminds us of the picture of the exalted Christ in Rev. 1. This unusual sword is symbolic, of course. But what does it stand for?

This sharp sword is the message of God's Word. You will find this metaphor a few times in the New Testament. Now, when we talk about the message of God's Word, we look for a message of hope, encouragement, and comfort. But not here! Remember, we are talking war. This sword is used *to strike down the nations, and rule them with a rod of iron*. We heard the same about the male child in Rev. 12:5. He appears here as the anointed King who fulfills Psalm 2 by destroying all who rebel against him.

But it will not be an ordinary battle with traditional weapons. When the end comes, the warrior Jesus Christ will win his victory only by the power of God's Word. At that time, the truth of the gospel will expose the falsehoods and lies of God's enemies. And that confrontation will make them crumble and disappear.

In fact, on the day of Jesus' return everyone, followers and enemies alike, will acknowledge that the battle was won already when Jesus died on the cross and arose from the dead. With this testimony of God's Word Jesus alone wins God's victory. He carries out God's punishment all by himself. That is his glory.

This is reinforced when we have a close look at the heavenly armies that accompany him on his mission (v.14). It is an impressive sight to behold, these massive forces riding on white horses, and dressed in fine linen. But it is an unusual army. They have no weapons! And they do not have bloodstains on their white garments.

Who are they, this militia from heaven? Angels? Probably. A few times we hear Jesus talk about "the Son of Man coming in his glory, and all the angels with him". But they may not be the only ones. The believers who died before Jesus' return are probably also part of this. Their clothing is like the bride's dress (Rev. 19:8), and like the white robes of the multitude no one can count (Rev. 7:9). And, according to Rev. 14:4, they are the ones *who follow the Lamb wherever he goes.*

But here is the point. Although they are called 'armies', they do not need to fight. They play no role in the battle. No, they are only present to enhance the glorious appearance of the warrior Jesus Christ. Indeed, on that day all the focus is on him alone. Your Saviour wins the battle singlehandedly, all on his own. *Glory to the King of angels, glory to the Church's King.* The One who died on the cross and arose from the dead does not need any help in the brutal war against sin and evil. Just remember his names. Trust his great power and stand in awe.

THE DEFEAT OF JESUS' ENEMIES

Then the picture shifts in John's vision. From our view from above we are going to have a look at the battlefield of the final battle, the battle of Armageddon, as it is called in Rev. 16:16.

But remember, it is the view from above. Oh sure, it looks frightening when the evil powers in this world unite to attack God's work and assault his people. But do not be afraid. Jesus' victory is certain. He is winning hands down!

To remind us of this, the vision shows this battle within the framework of the appalling scene of hawks, eagles, and vultures, gorging on human flesh in v.18 and 21. This hideous symbolism builds on Old Testament imagery (Ezekiel 39:17-29). The defeat of Christ's enemies could not be demonstrated more obviously.

We first hear another loud cry by an angel. This angel is *standing in the sun*, it says. He attracts all the attention and from where he stands everyone can see him and hear his unusual invitation. He summons all the birds of prey to *the great supper of God*.

The word "supper" links this event with the other supper, we heard about in Rev. 19:9: "the marriage supper of the Lamb". However, this supper here is the absolute opposite. Yes, it will also be held under the auspices of God. But it is a gruesome caricature, a bizarre and repulsive parody of the joyful celebration of the union of the Lamb and his bride, the glorified Christ and his church.

Here the human guests will not enjoy a happy celebration. Here the human guests are on the menu! God's curse on those who rebel against him, will result in a great slaughter. The people in this world who continue to resist the Holy God and deny Jesus as Saviour will supply enough food for a horrific meal.

And do not be mistaken; v.18 shows that the list of human guests for this supper includes all segments of society: the small and the great, important people and insignificant folks. It says, "all people", which means all kinds and categories of people, regardless of your rank or social status. No one is exempt beforehand.

As a matter of fact, the only ones excluded here, are those mentioned in v.9, *the guests who are invited to the marriage supper of the Lamb*. So, here is what is coming: you and I and everyone else, we are all invited for supper. And it is going to be either one of these two suppers. But here is the difference you need to be aware of: either you eat or you will be eaten.

Next we see through John's eyes the enemies of God and Jesus Christ, the enemies of the church, join forces and line up for battle. They are led by two commanders, the beast and the false prophet. You may remember these monsters from other chapters and especially from Rev. 13 where we met them for the first time as "the beast out of the sea" and "the beast out of the earth".

The first one stands for the political powers of antichristian persecution. The second one is the propaganda chief of the first one, and stands for the antichristian religious, cultural, ideological, and philosophical powers that want to lure you away from trusting God and his Word. They want to impress you and promise you a good life without worshipping God; v.20 sums up the evil these gang-leaders are guilty of.

Well then, this whole world of unbelief and hatred towards the true God is coming together to attack the faithful church of Jesus Christ. And by doing so, they *make war against the rider on the horse and his army*.

However, here is the surprise, on the day that the divine warrior on his white horse appears, with his heavenly armies, we do not hear anything about a fight, not even about minor skirmishes, let alone a real battle! When facing the glory of the returning Christ, the massive concentration of enemy power simply shrivels up!

It is already over, even before it starts. The planned battle immediately becomes an execution, something we will see again in the account of the same confrontation in Rev. 20:8, 9. And this is possible, because the outcome of this battle has been decided already by the warrior with the blood-stained garment. This outcome is evidence of Jesus' victory achieved on the cross and manifest in his resurrection. Nothing can injure or damage the glory of the King.

The battle of Armageddon turns out not to be a long struggle, not even a real battle. It is a step in Jesus' final clean-up operation. By his presence alone Jesus Christ defeats his enemies, with his un-armed armies as glorious backdrop. As Paul puts it in 2 Thessalonians 2:8, *The Lord Jesus will overthrow his adversary with the breath of his mouth and destroy him by the splendour of his coming* [NIV].

Recognize the superior power by which your glorified Saviour makes room for the renewal of this ruined world. He comes to put everything into its proper place, the place where it belongs. For the enemies of God and of Jesus Christ this place is *the lake of fire that burns with sulphur*. This is the place of

God's permanent, God's definitive punishment. It is a horrible place, more horrible than you and I can ever imagine!

As the first step of Jesus' final clean-up, the two enemies that are mentioned here (v.20), the beast and the false prophet, are captured and thrown alive into this "lake of fire". This is the final abode of all evil. In Revelation it is also called "the second death" (Rev. 20:14; 21:8). This is "hell". And they end up there "alive", it says. They will experience God's unrestrained wrath, permanently. Terror beyond description.

In the next passages we will find that this "lake of fire" is also the destination of Satan (20:10), of Death and Hades (20:14), and of all whose names are not written in the book of life (20:15). And they will follow shortly, all on the same day of Jesus' return because the history of this world cannot be concluded before all evil has been utterly destroyed, never to come back again.

The rest of them were slain by the sword that came out of the mouth of him who was sitting on the horse. All who have remained loyal to those evil gang-leaders, stuck with them, until the bitter end, in fierce hatred towards God, and towards Jesus Christ as King, will find their horrible end by means of the sword of the glorious warrior.

The victory of the Returning King will leave the wicked dead for ever and ever. The bodies of the casualties are not buried, but they end up being just carrion for the vultures, who will gorge themselves on their flesh. This is a deeply humiliating end. It demonstrates how thorough, how drastic, how complete the victory of Christ is.

The whole scene is graphically described in terms of the great supper as announced by the angel in v.17, 18. Try to imagine the scenario. The battlefield, littered with dead bodies, numerous corpses everywhere, and then the huge flocks of birds-of-prey soaring above the carnage, and slowly coming down, the scavengers summoned by God himself, eager to feast on the human carcasses.

It's a grisly and sinister picture, and some of you might think, "You don't have to give such a graphic and detailed description. We do not need to hear those gruesome specifics."

And I agree, it is not a pretty picture. But, yes, we do need to hear this. We do need to be aware. We do need to realize what the horrendous consequences are when we choose to follow and worship the beast, when we go for the deceptions and believe the lies of the false prophet.

When we do not distance ourselves from everything that leads us away from the truth of the gospel and so from our only hope and comfort in Jesus Christ, there is a price to pay, a humiliating and disastrous price.

It is true, what happens to the hostile armies that join in rebellion against the Holy God, does not make for a pretty picture. But it is also a picture that makes clear that the victory of the Returning Christ is beyond dispute.

And this is what you and I must know today. The evil powers are not going to make it. They do not have a chance when the warrior Jesus begins his final clean-up.

So here is your question: Are you ready for supper?

And if so, which supper would you prefer to attend?

Do you want to eat?

Or do you want to be eaten?

29

Revelation 20: 1 – 10

JESUS RETURNS AS KING
TO CONTINUE HIS FINAL CLEAN-UP

It can be very discouraging to contemplate the disturbing reality that there is so much evil in this world. Is Jesus Christ really a King, who sits on the throne at God's right hand to govern all things? Sometimes you wonder.

But then, remember that Revelation was written to encourage suffering and persecuted Christians. The message is that Christ is indeed King, and that he will return as King, glorious and victorious. This is what we have come to recognize as the main theme of the book: *the victory of Jesus Christ and his church over every enemy.* This is the theme that appears again in the passage we look at here, the first part of Rev. 20.

It is also good to remember that the order in Rev. 17–20 is not chronological. The visions we have seen in Rev. 17, 18 and 19 show us simultaneous events that happen on the same day. We see the effects of the seventh bowl of God's wrath, poured out in Rev. 16:17–21. In Rev. 20 we are still in the middle of the events on this last day of history, the day of Jesus' second coming, the day of the final judgment.

The world is out of kilter due to the evil work of Satan and company. But the good news is that proper order will be restored. In Rev. 19 the two beasts were removed from the scene and put into their proper place, the lake of

29 • Revelation 20:1-10

fire and sulphur. Now Satan follows. The returning Christ will continue his clean-up.

This makes this a passage full of encouragement for you and me today.

Satan Restrained

At the end of Rev. 19 we witnessed, through the eyes of the apostle John, the destruction of the beast and the false prophet. *The two of them were thrown alive into the lake of fire that burns with sulphur.* When Jesus returns as warrior, the final clean-up of the evil in this world has begun.

However, this is just the beginning. The major evil power behind those two is still alive and active. That is Satan. The final clean-up on the day of Christ's return is not done yet. It continues. It must continue, for there will only be peace when the grand-master of all evil himself will be eliminated. This is what is going to happen next.

But not right away in the beginning of this passage. First, John's vision transports us back in history. In the v.1–6 we get, in a few broad strokes, the big picture of history as it unfolds on earth and in heaven, a picture that is full of encouragement for us, today. For it shows that our history leads to the unavoidable and permanent end of the fiercest enemy of God and his church.

During a symbolic period of one-thousand years before his final and absolute end, Satan will be bound. We will learn more about the implications of this restraining order, but let's remember this from the start, that, despite the terrible things you see happen in this world, despite the ruinous influence of the antichristian powers we are faced with, Jesus Christ **IS** King. And he will return as King. He will return with royal authority and power. And everything is firmly under control, all the time.

John sees *an angel coming down from heaven* (v.1). His point of departure tells us that, whatever he is going to do, he acts on behalf of Almighty God, powerful and with great, divine authority.

With him he carries two props that confirm his power and authority: a key and a heavy chain. What is he going to do with those things?

The key is *the key to the bottomless pit,* or the Abyss. We have heard about the "Abyss" before. For instance in Rev. 9:1,2. This image of an 'underworld', an awful place deep underground, symbolizes the place were dark powers, demons, evil spirits are dwelling and waiting for God's eternal punishment. Think of 'hell' before the Last Judgment. After that it is called the "fiery lake of burning sulphur".

And what about this heavy and strong chain? Apparently someone is going to be shackled and locked up.

Then John sees again the most frightening of all the horrible creatures he has seen in any of his visions so far. It is the enormous fiery red dragon. We have met this fire-breathing monster in Rev. 12. He is God's most formidable, most notorious, and absolutely irreconcilable adversary.

This shows also in his other names. It's the same list as in Rev. 12:9: *the ancient serpent,* that cunning liar from Gen.3, *the devil, Satan himself…,* just to emphasize his major role as the very root, the source of all evil under the sun.

Well then, God's angel, coming down from heaven, is so incredibly powerful, strong and big that effortlessly he grabs this enormous monster – think T. Rex, but then ten times larger and more ferocious! The verbs John is using demonstrate how overpowering this angel is. Look at the power and strength he uses.

He grabs the dragon, binds it with his chain, throws it in the Abyss, closes this dark, smoking hole with a heavy lid, locks it and seals it. Done! He will not escape.

Now remember, it is a vision. This whole impressive action has a symbolic meaning. What we are seeing in this graphic picture, is that God's fiercest enemy is being restrained. His power and influence are being restricted. In the glorified Christ, Satan found his Master. He can no longer do what he wants to do. He has no longer the freedom to reach his goal which is to undo the work of Jesus and to destroy the consequences of this work. God's power will prevent him from getting there.

All this will last for one thousand years. When it comes to the interpretation of these thousand years, also called "the millennium", Rev. 20 is the most controversial and hotly debated chapter in Revelation, perhaps in the whole Bible.[11]

This book reflects the view that is also expressed in the Reformed confessions. Since all the numbers in Revelation have a symbolic meaning, also here we should not be thinking of a literal period of a thousand years. As a cube of 10x10x10 is symbolic for completeness and perfection, so a thousand years represents not only a long, but also a perfect and complete time period.

So, yes, although we do not know the exact length, we are talking real time, with a beginning and an end. In v.2 and 3 we find out that the beginning and the end of the thousand years are marked by two events. It begins when Satan is bound, and it ends when he will be set free for a very short time.

What does it mean that Satan is 'bound' or 'restricted'? Does the Bible say other things about Satan being restricted? Yes, it does. In chapter 12:23, 31 of the Gospel of John we hear Jesus say, when he predicts his own death: *The hour has come for the Son of Man to be glorified..... Now is the judgment of this world; now will the ruler of this world be cast out.* Think also of Luke 10:18, where Jesus says *I saw Satan fall like lightning from heaven.*

In other words, Satan is bound, his power is restrained at Jesus' first coming. He is expelled, driven out, as the result of your Saviour's death, resurrection, and ascension into heaven. That's when it begins, this one thousand year time-period.

Here is the picture. Before Jesus came, only Israel was God's special people, the people of the covenant, chosen to share in God's saving grace. All other nations were in Satan's grip, covered in moral and spiritual darkness. But that would change. To Abraham God had said, *You will be the father of a multitude of nations* (Genesis 17:4-5), *and in you all the families of the earth shall be blessed* (Genesis 12:3). And God did not forget his promise: Jesus came.

---

11 There are three major millennial views, *Premillennialism, Postmillennialism and Amillennialism*. However, within each of these views there are a number of varieties. Brief descriptions are given in the introduction. For those who want to learn more about it I recommend C.P. Venema's *The Promise of the* Future, Banner of Truth Trust, 2000.

To be sure, throughout Israel's history in the Old Testament individuals from other nations have joined God's people. And there is a longing in the Old Testament for other nations to join worshipping the One True God. But only after Jesus died, arose, and went to heaven, did the Holy Spirit open up the whole world for the preaching of the gospel of God's saving grace in Christ.

Then the church began to grow and spread among Jews and Gentiles, to the ends of the earth. Satan could not stop it. And he will still not be able to stop it.

What began in the Book of Acts and continues today, is the result of the restriction of Satan's power. Despite persecution the church is everywhere and the Bible can be read and heard in many languages. The glorious majesty of Jesus our King will keep Satan from destroying the church. As a matter of fact, gnashing his teeth in fury, the devil is forced to see the work of Jesus bear fruit.

Will this go on forever? No, only *until the 1000 years were ended*. Then Satan *must be released for a little while*. In v.7–9 we will find out that this will give him a very, very short time, only to be sent to his final destruction at Jesus' return as glorious and victorious King.

That's why the thousand year period stands for the entire gospel era, between our Saviour's first and second coming. This is the exciting time we live in today. From his throne in heaven Jesus guarantees that his work continues. Satan is restrained and he can do no more damage than God's superior power allows him to.

But yes, indeed, the devil can still do a lot of damage today. Let us not forget that. Satan's restraining order does not make him entirely powerless. We are not living in, or heading for a thousand years of universal peace, a golden age of unhindered freedom and unprecedented prosperity for the Christian church before Jesus returns.

It does not say that Satan was restrained to make such a golden age possible. Nowhere does the Bible promise this.

On the contrary, as the gospel makes progress, persecution goes on too. The growth of the church triggers growing opposition, hatred, and resistance.

It is true, the devil, who *prowls around like a roaring lion, seeking someone to devour* (1 Peter 5:8) can indeed do much damage. But there is one thing he cannot do today. He cannot muster enough power to put an end to the saving work of Jesus.

This is so encouraging. Long before Jesus' return we may know already that evil is on its last legs. What happens to Satan during the thousand years tells us already how the story is going to end. Jesus can handle him, today already.

The frightening dragon will become the pathetic loser.

THE KINGDOM SECURED

Then another scene appears in John's vision (v.4-6). The apostle John was familiar with persecution. And throughout the centuries large numbers of Christians have been and are being tortured and killed. Others are being ridiculed or marginalized. Does that make the Christian faith a failure?

There are many who want you to believe this. "Do you really think that Christianity is still relevant and has a future? Do you not see that many churches are empty and that Christians only survive in the margins of our society? What do you think will be left of it a hundred years from now?"

But John turns our eyes to heaven. And the first thing he sees are *thrones, on which were seated those to whom the authority to judge was committed.* Who are they? Many scholars think of "the souls of the martyrs" mentioned in the next sentence of v.4. But it does not say so. At the end of v.4 these 'souls' of the martyrs are said to reign, not to judge.

It might be better to think of a heavenly supreme court that is called to 'judge' those martyrs, as well as other believers who die. This court declares them worthy to come to life in the first resurrection, and to reign with Christ!

John then sees *the souls of those who had been beheaded for the testimony of Jesus and for the Word of God...* the martyrs who had suffered and were killed for their faith. Then the ESV (also the NIV) continues "and who had not worshiped the beast and had not received the mark of the beast". There is a suggestion that this is an added description of those same martyrs.

But it actually says: "the souls of those martyrs and [the souls] of those who had not worshiped the beast".

In other words, the "souls" that John is seeing include others who may not have been martyred, but who died as people who refused to worship the antichristian powers in this world. That is all faithful believers.

John sees the souls of all who die in Jesus Christ *coming to life to reign (as kings) with Christ for a thousand years,* whether they died as martyrs, or died a natural death, or in any other way. That is what we believe, right? All God's children who die here will be with the Lord in heaven.

"It is true," says John, "I see them! There they are, fully alive for the full time, till the day that the thousand years are ended. The glorious day of Jesus' second coming."

This "coming to life in heaven" he calls *the first resurrection*. This means that there must also be a second resurrection. The latter is the resurrection of the bodies, which will happen when Jesus returns, on the last day of history. Here he sees "souls in heaven".

This is so full of comfort. We do not know what 'souls' look like. But we do know, when God's children die here on earth, they come to life in heaven, right away! As the Heidelberg Catechism puts it in Question and Answer 42: "for those who die in Christ, death becomes an entrance into eternal life." The first resurrection!

Do you believe this? Do you trust John's vision when you have to say farewell to your loved ones who die as God's children? We say sometimes that 'we have lost a loved one'. But that is not really true. You have lost something if you cannot find it; if you do not know where it is. I can say, for instance, "I lost my car-keys. I don't remember where I put them, and I have no idea where to find them".

But that is different with believers who have died. We can no longer see them and for a while we can no longer communicate with them. That can be hard. But it does not mean that we have lost them. We know where they are.

It is so amazing if you come to think of it. The moment of their death on earth turns out to be a glorious moment of great victory. Remember what Jesus said to Mary & Martha: *I am the resurrection and the life. He who believes in me will live, even though he dies* (John 11:25 [NIV]). And really, this is what happens today, all the time!

The souls of those who believe in the Saviour Jesus and have died in him, continue to live with him in glory, in his Kingdom. The Kingdom of God is the Kingdom of his people. And in this Kingdom the values of this world are turned upside down, now already. The oppressed find justice. The dead live. The despised rule.

Oh sure, we can ask many questions that no one can answer. What do these souls look like? What does it mean and how does that work, "to reign with Christ"?

But do not worry about those questions, says John. These souls belong completely to God, and so *they are blessed and holy,* now already. They died the first death, here on earth. But they do not have to be afraid for the second death. They are beyond its power. The second death is the eternal death, God's unrestrained wrath with no chance of parole.

No, with the first resurrection behind them, they may now look forward to the second one, when the souls will be re-united with their glorious bodies, to be ushered into the New Jerusalem.

This is such an encouraging vision. From here, the point of view from below, Satan and his evil buddies appear to be pretty successful. The church is under attack and continues to lose terrain to the powerful antichristian culture we live in. When Christians are a weak and marginalized minority, when powerful lobby-groups line up against them, is there any hope for survival, never mind victory?

To the world it looks like Christians have been defeated. Oppressing governments are powerful and getting away with murder, sometimes literally! Christian communities are being wiped out, then here, then there. And if that is not the case, much of Christianity has done a good job in making itself irrelevant in our modern culture.

Does God not care? Is he really in control? Can anything undo this depressing picture?

But the view from above, in 4–6, tells us, if you want to see the full picture, you must include heaven. There we can see that those who belong to Jesus, reign with the glory of kings and serve with dedication of priests. They experience the reality *that our present sufferings are not worth comparing with the glory that will be revealed in us* (Romans 8:18).

And what a glory it is! Ruling with Christ, communion with Christ, rejoicing with Christ, celebrating Christ's victory – now already. From above we see that God's Kingdom is secured – now already. Today, the souls of the King's people live in the presence of the Holy God and the exalted Christ.

This is such a tremendous comfort. It fills you with so much hope and courage. As it turns out, you cannot defeat Christian believers. It is impossible. Even when demonic forces ravage the church, all they are doing is putting more and more Christians in positions of real power.

John also answers, at least partly, another question that may come up when we try to wrap our head around this astounding vision. What about those who died during the thousand year period, but not in Christ? What about the folks who did worship the beast and who did have the mark of the beast? John mentions them in v.5.

Those dead do not come to life with Christ in the first resurrection. After all, they refused to live with Jesus here on earth, and this will not change after they die. Then their final destination will not be with Jesus Christ either.

No, their souls remain in the deadly grip of evil for the entire time, until the end of the thousand year era, the day of the second resurrection when also their souls will be re-united with their bodies. What this will mean for them will come later, in the last part of Rev.20.

SATAN DESTROYED

Since we believe the thousand years to be the time between Jesus' first and second coming, John's words in v.7, *when the thousand years are over*,

29 • Revelation 20:1-10

imply that Jesus' return is about to happen. This brings us, in John's visions, back to the time of all the events of Rev. 17, 18 and 19. We are back at the events that unfold on the last day, the day of the completion of Jesus' victory.

In the "flash-back", so to speak, which we have seen in the v.1–6, we were encouraged and comforted to learn that it was actually clear all along, since Jesus' first coming, that he was going to win this victory.

So, yes, when the thousand years are over, Satan is going to be released from his prison in the Abyss. His restraining order will be lifted, as announced in v.3. He will be free to go and deceive the nations; free to go and unite mankind in one antichristian front against God, against Jesus Christ, and against the Christian church. One more try. And he might succeed.

That sounds scary. But remember, we are on the last day. With royal power the returning Christ is working on his final clean-up. And God remains in control. Satan does not escape from his dungeon. He does not fight his way out of the Abyss.

No, he *will be released*. Somebody stronger than him and with authority over him has to do that. God, or perhaps the glorified Christ.

Also, his release will be at God's time and only for the short time God has set for it. In other words, Satan's "freedom" on the day of Jesus' victory only serves God's plan. It will expose the depth of his evil nature. And it will show at the same time his powerlessness, and how much he deserves what is coming.

Satan's goal has always been to wipe the church of Jesus Christ from the face of the earth. And he will hang on to that to the bitter end. He is not giving up. And when the end is near, he will be given more room to pursue this, to the point that he will manage to pull out all the stops and rally all the troops he can find.

Indeed, he will be able to unite the nations, the peoples *at the four corners of the earth* for a massive assault on the church and on the Christian faith. More and more the Christian believers have it coming from all over the world, a huge accumulation of hateful attacks, oppression, and hostilities.

In this vision it comes to us in the image of a huge army. The numbers are staggering: *like the sand of the sea*.... With the qualification *Gog and Magog* John refers to powerful enemies of God's people Israel in the Old Testament: Gog, the prince of Magog (Ezekiel 38 and 39). It is a frightening name for a strong enemy, who is filled with so much hatred, that he was almost successful in his attempts to destroy God's people.

Here the name becomes a symbol for God's most fanatic, powerful and final enemies to wage war against Christ and his church. It looks like it might even work.

Verse 9 pictures a frightening scene. It says that these enormous armies *surround the camp of the saints and the beloved city*. The word "camp" reminds of Old Testament Israel as they were travelling. They were free from slavery but had not yet arrived in the Promised Land. They were camping out in the wilderness, which made them pretty vulnerable.

Today, God's church is also travelling, freed from the power of sin, but still on its way to the new heaven and the new earth. Still camping out in the wilderness of this world. That makes us quite vulnerable, with the hostilities coming from all directions.

This passage is full of military imagery. But Satan's war comes also with religious, philosophical, cultural, social and economic attacks. Whatever works for Satan, he can use it all.

Today this whole idea of uniting people from all over the world under Satan's leadership in support of one cause is not as farfetched as it may sound. He only has to send out one message with a cool-sounding 'hashtag', and add, "Like me on Facebook, follow me on Twitter and all other social media", and it will go viral in no time! There they all come, from the four corners of the earth.

But as it turns out, all this impressive and frightening display of power only leads to Satan's final and permanent defeat. Yes, what we are seeing here, looks dark and gloomy. It is the same battle that is also mentioned in Rev. 16:14, 16; Rev. 17:14 and Rev. 19:19, 20: the great battle of Armageddon.

But it is not even a real battle. It is over before it starts. *Fire came down from heaven and consumed them*. The end is swift, sudden, and unexpected. On the last day of history, the glorified Christ appears as King and his royal power consumes the enemies. In one sweep they all go up in a puff of smoke.

Nothing and no one can stop the returning King, Jesus Christ, when he continues his final clean-up. He did away with the beast and the false prophet and now he also successfully removes Satan himself, the ultimate source of all evil.

John sees how *the devil was thrown into the lake of fire and sulphur*. He ends up where his evil cronies are, never to come out again. Here, in this most horrible place of hellish darkness and never-ending destruction and agony, all three of them will be tormented, and torment each other, for ever and ever.

Do you recognize this? Here is the complete fulfilment of what God had promised Satan in Genesis 3:15, *he will crush your head*.

Our God is true to his Word. He will reach his goal. Jesus wins!

30

Revelation 20: 11 – 15

JESUS RETURNS AS JUDGE TO COMPLETE HIS FINAL CLEAN-UP

Are you looking forward to Judgment Day? When I was still teaching young people in our church, and we talked about Lord's Day 19 or 22 of the Heidelberg Catechism, I asked that question sometimes. And then there is always an eager student, who says, "yes, of course".

But then I would say: 'Ok, you gave me the answer you thought the minister would like to hear. So, now for real, be honest: The Last Judgment, is that an event you really look forward to?"

And then someone would suggest, 'I guess we should. But it is kind of scary, this idea, that everything you say and do is going to be exposed and then judged by God, who sees and hears everything!" That is a hesitation we can all relate to, I think.

Revelation 20:11–15 gives us a closer look at this Judgment Day. We know already that the day of Jesus' return, his glorious second coming, is going to be full of dramatic events. It sees the destruction of Babylon, the antichristian culture. That was in Rev. 17 and 18. But we have also seen that this does not complete Jesus' final clean-up.

30 • Revelation 20:11-15

In 19:11–21 we heard about the destruction of the beast and the false prophet. In 20:1–10 we heard about the destruction of Satan. One more act is still required. Now it is time to strike the final balance of the history of our world. And in this one we are all personally involved.

One thing to keep in mind, when we look at the Last Judgment in John's vision in this passage, please remember again that the events in Revelation 17 - 20 do not happen in chronological order, but simultaneously.

John's description of the Last Judgment is sober, but the reality is pretty overwhelming.

The Judge

The vision John describes for us in the passage at the end of Rev. 20, highlights another element of the many things that are happening on the day of Jesus' return, the day of his second coming. This day will also be the day of the Last Judgment.

After the elimination of Satan and his evil sidekicks, the Beast and the False Prophet (Rev. 19:20 and 20:10), the final clean-up on the day of Christ's return is now almost complete. But this last action is different. This event comes close to each and every one of us. And it will affect all people directly and personally.

In the scenes that the glorified Christ has shown to his servant John, the end of our present world has now arrived. Through John's eyes we have seen, with the view from above, all that has led up to this decisive moment.

Then I saw a great white throne, and him who was seated on it.

It is not the first time that the apostle John sees this throne. The wording tells us that this is the same throne he has seen when it all started, in Rev. 4. He sees the heavenly throne of God. And when you read through that chapter, you can see how there already the emphasis is on the splendid glory, and the universal power and authority of the One who is seated on this throne.

John does not name the One on the throne, but, also in light of the connection with Rev. 4, it is clear that it must be the holy and almighty God himself.

You can also think of the glorified Christ sitting on this throne. In Matt. 25:31 Jesus says that, *when the Son of Man comes, he will sit on his glorious throne*. And in 2 Cor. 5:10 Paul speaks about *the judgment seat of Christ*.

However, this is not really a contradiction. In John 5:22 Jesus says that *the Father has given all judgment to the Son*. Jesus does not only return as Warrior (Rev.19:11) or as King (Rev. 20:4,6), but also as Judge. This is how we will meet him here in John's vision. And this is how we will all meet him one day in person.

We hear two things about this throne. It is "great" and it is "white". Its greatness has nothing to with actual measurements, but it reflects the marvellous grandeur, the immense, superior power and authority of the Judge who sits on it. The colour 'white' reflects God's glorious light, his heavenly holiness.

John's vision unfolds for us the superior power, the great splendour and dazzling holiness of him who is going to speak the very last word, the word that will bring to completion the history of our world.

The world as we know it will face the final judgment.

It is good to pause and think about this for a moment: there will be a Day of Judgment. Which means that there is a Judge. Now you and I may take this for granted but do not be mistaken, this whole idea of a Judge and a Day of Judgment is not very popular.

To begin with, many Christians have a hard time matching the thought of an eternal punishment with everything they read in the Bible about God's love. How can a God who is love, condemn people for what they are doing? Should we not tell people about God's love? "Come to God, come to Jesus. He will not judge you. He will not condemn you. He accepts you as you are. And in the end everyone is going to be saved anyway."

But, is that correct?

And then, for people who are not Christians, this idea of a Divine Judge, who will one day call everyone to account, is just bizarre. This is the prevailing view in our culture. There is no one above us. There is no one to tell us what is right or wrong. We are on our own. We are not accountable to anyone above us, not even to each other. We are only accountable to ourselves, to our own conscience.

There is no Judge. And there will be no judgment day. Everything will just go on, as it always has. This way of thinking is actually predicted in the Bible already (2 Peter 3:3,4). And that is okay, they suggest. There is nothing to worry about.

But if that is true, if there is indeed no Judge, and there is no real accountability, we have lots to worry about.

Try to imagine that there is no Judge. Some of you may have seen movies or TV shows where much of the action takes place in courtrooms. You see a courtroom filled with people: defendant, plaintiff, prosecutor, lawyers, witnesses, etc. Everyone is waiting for the judge to appear. When the judge is seated on the bench, he is supposed to apply the rule-of-law, so that justice will be done.

Now imagine that everyone is waiting, and waiting, but no one shows up. There is no judge. And no judge means 'no justice', because there is no one to apply the rule-of-law. Everybody is going home dissatisfied, for no one is held responsible for the crimes that have been committed.

What are people going to do if that would happen all the time? What do people do when the justice system fails in society? They stack up on guns and take the law in their own hands. But that is terrifying. Everyone is going to make up his own law and defend his own idea of justice. A lawless society turns into a violent and dangerous society.

Let's get back to our world, and think of it as one, huge courtroom. Yes, there are many decent people, but we all know it is a world filled with sin, evil, injustice, corruption, oppression, violent persecution, racism, hatred, gang-rape, and you name it. Do you know how many refugees there are in our world? The latest number is over 70 million. That is incredible. And then imagine, there is no Judge. There is no one on the bench. There will never be a Judgment Day.

What does that mean? It means that there is no way for the victims to find justice. There is no way that criminals and oppressors will be held accountable and be prosecuted. If there is no one to apply the rule-of-law in this world, then there is no proper way to deal with sin, evil and injustice.

And then what? Then as nations, political parties, dictators, criminal organisations, even religions, we are all going to make up and enforce our own laws that serve our own interests. This will often mean political unrest, and sometimes war or civil war. But none of that will ever guarantee that 'justice' will be done.

But the Bible assures us: do not be afraid that evil and injustice will go unpunished. There IS a Judge. That is good news. The bench in the courtroom of this world is not empty. Jesus himself says so in John 12:48: *There is a Judge for the one who rejects me and does not accept my words.* [NIV]

Indeed, we are accountable to the One who made us. We all are. He comes and will apply the rule-of-law. The rule of HIS eternal law. He comes and no injustice or suffering will ever escape him. He comes and all wrongs will be righted. He comes and those who persecute, and practice evil and injustice will not get away with it.

Yes, there is a Judge, and John saw him. He has seen his power and glory. A power and glory so majestic, so overwhelming that *earth and sky fled away and no place was found for them.* This is the same as when the Bible says elsewhere that "heaven and earth will perish, or vanish, or pass away" (Isaiah 51:6; Psalm 102; Matthew 24:35). "Earth and sky" stands for the creation corrupted by sin. When Christ appears in his glorious majesty, they disappear without leaving a trace, to make room for what is coming.

In the end all that remains in the whole universe is the great white throne and the One who is seated on it. In the end this throne stands as the only firm, immovable, reliable point, with nothing left to challenge its absolute supremacy.

When the Judge begins to speak, all obstacles between God and humanity are removed. Nothing impairs the reality of a face-to-face encounter with the heavenly Judge. We have nowhere to hide when the summons comes from God's throne: "What did you do with my world? What did you do to my people? What did you do with the life I gave you?"

THE SUMMONS

Then John also sees those who have been summoned to appear before the throne and to face the Judge. Who are they? In v.12 the apostle reports: *And I saw the dead, great and small, standing before the throne.*

Now, that sounds kind of spooky, would you not agree? John saw "the dead". Was he seeing 'dead men walking' as in the Zombie movies of some ten years ago?

No, he was not. In v.13 he explains what has happened in the meantime: *The sea gave up the dead who were in it, and death and Hades gave up the dead who were in them.* As it turns out, and that is in line with the rest of Scripture, the day of Jesus' return is also the day of the resurrection of all of mankind.

In Rev. 1:18 "Death & Hades" are also mentioned as companions that are hostile to God. There the glorified Christ assures John that he is the Living One, who holds the keys of Death and Hades. They also appear as a murderous duo when the Lamb opens the fourth seal. That is in Rev. 6:8. You could say that "death" is the power that separates body and soul, and "Hades" keeps" them separate.

In the past "Hades" was sometimes translated as 'hell', but it is not the same. Today it is sometimes translated as "the grave", but that does not quite cover it either. It is the realm where the dead are waiting for the day of the resurrection. Even believers, who come to life and reign with Christ after they die on earth, which in Rev. 20:5 is called 'the first resurrection, even they can still be said to be physically in Hades as they are still waiting for the second resurrection, the resurrection of the bodies on the day of Jesus' return.

That 'the sea' is mentioned in this context is kind of puzzling, and it is probably best to think of it as another image of the powerful hostile realm that holds the dead in its grip. Put together, we get a picture of a location where people end up after their physical death rips apart body and soul.

However, no matter how powerful and frightening that is, Death & Hades do not own these dead bodies. God has allowed them to take them. But that is temporary. He remains in control, and when he demands them back, they must give them up. All these dead bodies, the glorified Jesus Christ claims them. And here they come!

In v.12 and 13 John uses the expression "the dead" four times. It stresses that all the dead come back to life. Not one stays behind. All the tombs break open. Believers and unbelievers alike, everyone will be confronted with the coming judgment!

Perhaps you remember that "pre-millenialists" believe in two bodily resurrections: one before the (literal) thousand years reign, and one after. But the Bible does not know about two such resurrections. No, at the same time, in one massive physical resurrection on the last day, all people everywhere who have ever lived on earth will come to life when the summons is issued from God's throne.

Jesus himself has confirmed this. In Matthew 25:31, 32 he says: *When the Son of Man comes in his glory..., He will sit on his throne..., and all the nations will be gathered before him.* And in John 5:28, 29 he tells us that *an hour is coming when all who are in the tombs will hear his voice and come out...*

This is so incredibly amazing. How in the world do you visualize something like this? It is impossible. It is mind-boggling already when you stand in the middle of a large cemetery, and you try to imagine what it is like when all these tombstones start moving and all around you the people come out. But then all the dead! We are with more than seven billion on the earth right now, and no one knows the number of those who have died since the beginning, or where all these bodies are.

But this is what John is seeing. He must have been stunned. There they stand, summoned for judgment, waiting for what is coming, waiting for the final word of the Judge. All of them. All of us, *great and small.*

This means that, regardless of rank or social status, the important and the insignificant, the wealthy and the poor, the powerful and the oppressed, all of them are summoned to appear before the throne of the Great Judge. No one is exempt on that day. No one is **so** great, or powerful or wealthy that he can get away with evil and escape judgment. No one is **so** small, or insignificant that he will be overlooked.

There they all stand, deeply impressed by the glory of the Judge sitting on the great white throne. Whether it fills them with joy or with an anger that makes them gnash their teeth, they all see his glorious power and they all have to acknowledge his right to judge *each one of them according to what they have done* (13b).

So, how is all this going to unfold on that day?

Well, John also sees that *books were opened*. And that *the dead were judged by what was written in the books, according to what they had done* (12).

These "books" with the records of everyone's words and actions are not literal books. That would make for the biggest library in the universe. No, they stand for the reality that, whatever you and I and everyone else says and does, God will always know. He will always remember how your words and deeds show your spiritual loyalty either to God and Jesus Christ, or to Satan and the antichristian culture of the Beast. And he will hold you accountable for all of it.

Scripture stresses this accountability in more places. In Matthew 12:36, 37 Jesus says: *I tell you, on the day of judgment people will give account for every careless word they speak, for by your words you will be justified, and by your words you will be condemned.* And the apostle Paul warns in 2 Corinthians 5:10 that *we must all appear before the judgment seat of Christ, so that each one may receive what is due for what he has done in the body, whether good or evil.*

In Matthew 25: 31 – 46 Jesus gives us a little peek in how this is going to work.

And remember, this Judge only goes by what is on record. Privileged positions do not play a role. The image of 'books' reflects the actual presence of proven and undeniable evidence. Only the facts will speak for themselves. This makes for a fair judgment.

What everyone receives is only the result of his or her own activities, nothing more and nothing less. That is fair.

Let us make this concrete: Mr. or Mrs. X...., volume #....., page #..... And there you have it, your complete file. It is all there, the total sum of your whole life. It shows everything. And there is much more on record than you would care to remember. And it is much worse than you might have thought.

Indeed, even my Christian desire to love and obey God, to live in faith and hold on to Jesus, it was often weak, and I have often failed. It is all tainted by my sin. Altogether, it is not good news.

But John sees more. There was another book, which was also opened. It is called "the book of life". We have heard about that book a few times already in Revelation. There is something peculiar about this book.

It does not have a list of things you have done or failed to do, but it is always about people who are, or who are not, listed in it. This book does not have a list of achievements. It has a list of names, all the names of God's children. It is the register of the Redeemed.

And again, it is not a literal book, but it stands for the reality that God knows all who belong to him, and that he will not lose any of them. As Jesus says about his followers in John 10:28, *I give them eternal life, and they will never perish; no one will snatch them out of my hand.* They are the ones who have come to life spiritually already in the first resurrection, mentioned in Rev. 20:4,5.

Here is your surprise on the Day of Judgment: if your name is in the book of life, you will find the page in the other book, where all you sinful words and deeds are supposed to be, you'll find that page blank, clean, spotless. Your sins have been deleted, covered up by the blood of Jesus. And all that is left are the good things you did not even remember.

Think again of Jesus' words in Matthew 25:34–40.

How is that possible? Well, 'the book of life' is not filled by you or by me. It does not describe our achievements. It is filled by God himself. And it has a subtitle, so to speak. It says, "Saved by Grace".

The final judgment on the day of Jesus' return is based on what is written in those two books. Together they picture how God's justice and God's mercy go hand–in–hand. This is incredibly encouraging for those who know themselves to be God's children by God's grace in Jesus Christ.

But do not take it for granted. Do not just say, "If you're in the book of life you're ok as God's elect, so that it doesn't matter how you live and what you do with your life. But if your name is not in the book of life, you will be punished for all your sins."

Remember that we see John's vision of what is coming! It is not here yet. Hearing about these books with records today is not intended to make you feel smug and complacent. You have not arrived yet.

No, the picture of these books with records comes today with the most urgent call to repent. Break with sin. Embrace Jesus Christ and his saving grace. Live joyful and thankful lives out of God's love and for his glory. Show this in your attitude and in the things you say and do – every day. And share your gratitude with others.

Hearing about the 'book of life' today, comes with the urgent question: how can I be sure that my name is written in this book? And the answer is not, "you can only wait and see and hope for the best". No, no, believe with all your heart in your Saviour Jesus. Believe that the forgiveness of your sins is in him alone. Believe that his death and resurrection alone makes you share in God's mercy.

But if you treat God's gracious love in Jesus carelessly, you might lose it.

Are you ready for Judgment Day?

THE VERDICT

To underline how urgent that last question is, John also pictures for us the final outcome of the Last Judgment; the verdict of the Judge on the great white throne (v.14): *Then Death and Hades were thrown into the lake of fire. This is the second death, the lake of fire. And if anyone's name was not found written in the book of life, he was thrown into the lake of fire.*

We have heard about this lake of fire before. In Rev. 19:20 the beast and the false prophet, Satan's evil helpers, *were thrown alive into the lake of fire that burns with sulfur.* Then, in Rev. 20:10, the devil himself was thrown into this same lake, this place of horror and torment. This will now also be the destination of Death & Hades, after their prisoners have been released in the second resurrection.

Almost everything is now in its proper place. Jesus Christ's final clean-up is almost complete. The destructive powers of Death & Hades are done away with, as they join the other masters of evil where they belong, the second death, which is eternal death, eternal punishment, hell! Evil will be gone forever. Death will be powerless forever. As Paul promised in 1 Corinthians 15:26, *the last enemy to be destroyed is death*. This was actually promised in the Old Testament already. The prophet Isaiah says, *the LORD Almighty will swallow up death forever* (Isaiah 25:8).

What a comfort! Hear the triumphant song of the apostle Paul: *Death is swallowed up in victory. O death, where is your victory? O death, where is your sting?* (1 Cor. 15:54, 55). Neither on the new heaven and the new earth, nor even in hell, body and soul will ever be separated again. All cemeteries will be closed forever. And there will be no more funerals, ever! The powers that have severely damaged God's creation since the fall into sin, will be removed, and they will never rear their ugly heads again.

And anyone whose name was not in the 'book of life', because they refused to believe in Jesus, and they have resisted God's majesty and mercy, they will join God's enemies in their proper place. With them they will gnash their teeth in anger and be tormented day and night for ever and ever (20:10).

It is a horrible punishment. But no one can complain about it. It is a fair judgment. Their own deeds and their own words will condemn them. Because their deeds and words show the refusal to turn to the blood of Jesus for forgiveness and to live by God's grace alone.

And what about those whose names were written in the 'book of life'?

John does not tell us, not yet! But as he completes his final clean-up, by removing the old order of things, and by eliminating sin, evil and death, the holy God is making room for a brand-new beginning.

John's vision of the Day of Judgment shows that our journey to the new Promised Land is almost over. That is full of exciting expectations. But it also underlines how urgent it is to repent. Break with sin and turn to Jesus as long as it is still possible.

Today we are still on this journey. Funerals are still part of our experiences because the power of death is still around. But its days are numbered.

And in John's vision the glorified Christ will show us, from above, what we are heading towards, when our names are listed in God's 'book of life'.

So keep your eyes peeled for the breathtaking splendour of what is coming!

31

REVELATION 21: 1 – 8

WATCH THE DAWN OF A NEW WORLD

With Revelation 21 we come to the final and, for many, the most beautiful and exciting part of the Book of Revelation. In the visions of the apostle John we now come to the climax of the Grand Finale of our history. We will see the unfolding of the final result of God's redeeming grace in the victory of Jesus Christ.

But this Grand Finale has two sides. Jesus' victory does two things.

Let us back up a bit. The outpouring of the seventh bowl of God's wrath in Rev. 16:17 ushered in the great day of God's Last Judgment. What is happening on that day is then shown to John in the visions of Rev. 17 - 22, the whole final section of the book.

Chapters 17–20 picture God's wrath, God's punishment, and Jesus' victory over his enemies, those who are put into their proper place, the fiery lake of burning sulphur.

Chapters 21–22 picture how God renews heaven and earth, and so fulfils his commitments and promises. And because of Jesus' victory he graciously rewards those who remained faithful to him.

31 • Revelation 21:1-8

In 21:1–8 we see the first vision of the amazing new realities that are coming. Later on, in 21:9–22:5, we will get more elaborate descriptions of the New Jerusalem.

But the beginning of Rev. 21 is also connected with the previous passage, 20:11–15. Remember, we were wondering what was going to happen to those whose names were listed in the book of life. In the picture of the judgment of the wicked there is already a hint of the coming joy.

And here it is: through John's admiring eyes we watch the dawn of a new world.

THE ORIGIN

As we move with the apostle John through the last day, the day of Jesus' return, we see, through his admiring eyes, this great wonder of a new creation, the dawn of a new world. *Then I saw a new heaven and a new earth,* he tells us. The glorified Christ shows him what is coming, so that on this old earth, we may look forward to the new.

Some think of this as something that is so entirely new, that it has no connection whatsoever with the old. And, yes, it is true, John adds that *the first earth and first heaven had passed away*. In Rev. 20:11 it says that they fled from God's presence, and that there was no place for them. They had to make room for a new beginning.

And that is understandable. It is our world where Satan, the beast, the false prophet, and Babylon the great prostitute have carried out their evil schemes, as our history unfolded. That was disastrous. And so this dark world, filled with the consequences of sin, rapes, thefts, hatred, anger, revenge, hurt and pain, it cannot and should not remain. A new world must replace the old.

However, 'new' is not the same as 'another'. The Creator does not abandon the works of his hands. In his second letter the apostle Peter explains how this universe will be subjected to a purifying fire, and that out of this a new universe will be born. Everything John sees is new, but it is the redemption of the old, not its abolition.

It is the same heaven and earth, but so totally and so comprehensively renewed, redone, rejuvenated, that it looks and feels brand-new, and at the same time familiar. A glorious transformation of the old world.

It is like an old house that is such a rundown ruin that it is beyond fixing. Minor renovations will not do. It can only be demolished. But the owner loved the old house so much, that he decides to build a new one at the same location and exactly according to the architectural drawings and blueprints of the old one. And when people who used to live in the old house walk into the new one, they feel at home right away.

In the Old Testament we read about this promised transformation in language that points at continuity in the midst of changes so drastic, that it will be totally different from the world as we know it today (Isaiah 65:17–25). And now John sees how God fulfills Isaiah's words.

In the New Testament the apostle Paul pictures a groaning creation, stuck in futility and inevitable decay. But it carries the hope of freedom and renewal, as it is waiting for God's powerful and glorious re-creation (Romans 8:18–25).

As the result of sin there is much pain, suffering, damage, and brokenness in this world. We do not mind leaving those things behind. But sometimes people wonder about losing beautiful things they love in this life. And indeed, Jesus tells us to be prepared to give up everything for the sake of our loyalty to him.

But in the process we will also find that nothing that has genuine value in God's eyes will be lost. After all, God himself is the source of all that is beautiful and joyful, and you will get to live with him, in his presence. We do not know the details of what we will find back in the new world. But we do know that his presence means perfect joy. So, no, you will have no regrets and no longings that cannot be satisfied.

John also noticed that *there was no longer any sea*. There are some different opinions on this. But there is no need to think that you will not be able to sit on the beach and enjoy a beautiful ocean view. In the Bible, and in particular in Revelation, the sea is often a symbol of chaos, danger, and evil. It

31 • Revelation 21:1-8

stands for a breeding place of antichristian political and cultural powers (as in Rev.13).

In other words, the removal of the sea is symbolic for the permanent removal of every resistance against God's authority. All the powers that challenge God's rule and order will be exterminated, to make for peace and stability in the new world.

But then there is something else that catches John's attention. With this totally renewed universe as backdrop, John sees *the Holy City, the New Jerusalem.*

A city is a permanent place of residence where many people live and work together. And so this new world will have human inhabitants, who form a society where people experience communion and enjoy fellowship.

When you read this, you might wonder: why don't we hear again about the New Heaven and the New Earth after v.1? As we read on we find out that in the rest of Rev. 21 and 22 all the attention is only for the New Jerusalem. Are there not more cities, towns, or villages on the new earth?

Now you can be quite sure that the re-created world is bigger and has more to offer than just one city. But the vision zeros in on what is at the centre of this new world. Think again of the symbolism. This city symbolizes the marvellous reality that the Holy God and the new mankind will live together in a happy communion that will never end.

Let us have a closer look. We are all familiar with the name "Jerusalem". The 'old' city of Jerusalem we know as the place where God dwelled with his people Israel, first in the tabernacle and later on in the temple. Here the sacrifices of the priests gave all Israel access to God, to pray and receive forgiveness.

Later on, all this was fulfilled in Jesus Christ. Everyone who believes in him and in his one sacrifice on the cross has direct access to communion with God. And the Bible tells us that Christ sent the Holy Spirit so that the church all over the world may be this place where God dwells and allows us to come close to him.

That is why the church is called 'Jerusalem', a symbolic name that tells us that the Holy God himself is present. That is a wonderful way of looking at the church, yes, also your own church.

Today already you may look beyond the failures of people in the church, the things that annoy you, bother you and disappoint you in the church. Today already you may see in the faithful church the gathering-project of the glorified Christ.

But what you see of the church today is not the final product. It has all the weaknesses and shortcomings that come with every project in this broken and sinful world. The Jerusalem that John is seeing is called 'new' and 'holy'. It represents the final perfection of the church's communion with God and the joy in his presence. And its 'holiness' shows in its complete, unrestrained dedication to God.

And it comes *down out of heaven, from God*. Indeed, the origin of the New Jerusalem, the complete universal church, as the centre of the new earth, is God himself. It is not the result of our hard work. No, it is the product of God's craftsmanship.

The church of Jesus Christ is often dismissed in this world, as some human structure to fulfil our religious needs, something that has no future in our secular society. But the church is born from above. It is the result of the transforming work of the Holy Spirit. And this is going on today already.

Think of it! This is so encouraging, so comforting. Christian believers become strangers in an antichristian culture and society. This is not where they feel at home. But they do not become homeless. In the church they find a new home, as a foretaste of the New Jerusalem.

And on the last day of the history of this world it will be seen by everyone that God's salvation project is complete, successful, and permanent in the New Jerusalem as the perfect church. Let this future help you to resist the pressures of our idolatrous society.

Then the vision shifts from the city to *the bride adorned for her husband*. This is also a picture of the church. Think of Rev. 19:7-9 about "the wedding of the Lamb". And Rev. 21:9 speaks again about *the bride, the wife of the Lamb*. This image stresses the intimacy, the love, and the pleasure we may experience in the communion with God. And again, this may start today already, but will be perfect in the world to come.

But John not only sees things. He also hears things. This is not the first time, and, as usual in these visions, what he hears explains what he sees.

He hears *a loud voice*. That is not the first time either. It is obviously important that people everywhere will hear this news from the throne in heaven. This is God's throne (see Rev. 20:11), but apparently God is not the speaker.

God's voice we hear in v.5. So, the one who speaks here could be one of the four living creatures that stand around God's throne (Rev. 4:6), or perhaps the angel mentioned in Rev. 1:1 as John's contact person with Christ.

But the point is the message in v.3. And that is incredible! In the old order of things, determined by sin, the Holy God dwelt in heaven, while the earth was our living space. But this will change.

O yes, God dwelt with Israel in temple and tabernacle. And today he dwells with his people in Jesus Christ and by the Holy Spirit. But this is different. This is an enormous step forward.

Why is this holy city coming down from heaven? Because we see the dawn of a new world in which God is coming to live with his people. Jesus' victory means that all separation between God and us will be removed.

Listen to what John is hearing. *Behold, the dwelling place of God is with man. He will dwell with them and they will be his people, and God himself will be with them as their God.*

Notice that the expression "with them" is used three times. It stresses the significance of what is happening. This is what it is all about. This is what the New Jerusalem stands for: God will live with people. He will live among us as close as never before. And we will be worshipping him and enjoying such strong, deep, and intimate communion with him as we have never experienced before.

When the festivities begin of the eternal marriage-feast of the Lamb Jesus Christ with his glorious bride, his perfect and complete church, gathered from all nations, his Holy City will be filled with joy. And everything that disturbs our joy today will be gone.

Watch the dawn of a new world, a world from which every stain of sin, every scar of wrong, every trace of death will have been removed, never to come back! God's new world and city will be free from the corruption and the groaning that are so typical of our world today.

Today death is the enemy who fills our eyes with tears as we stand at the graveside of our loved ones. We try what we can to escape him. But on that day Death, and together with him, all the misery that comes in his wake, all grief, sadness and mourning will be gone.

Human lives get stuck in loneliness, anxiety, depression, mental illnesses, and addictions. Our lives are often damaged and broken. Our hearts are filled with pain. But one day that will all be over. The helpless and desperate cries, "O God, where are you?" will never be heard again. For he will be with us, so close that with his own hand he will wipe away every tear in deep and tender love. A stunning picture!

THE ARCHITECT

Then John hears a second voice. It is the voice of the One *who was seated on the throne*. Now the Holy and Almighty God himself is announced as the Speaker. This has happened very few times before in Revelation, in 1:8 and 16:17, and now again. It tells us that we come close to the glorious climax and the end of this book. God's plans are coming to completion. Can you imagine hearing God himself speak, directly?

So, let us listen carefully. The One on the throne said: *I am making all things new*. As it turns out, the throne of judgment we saw in Rev. 20:11–15, is also the throne of grace. In his grace our God personally guarantees the very newness and certainty of what is coming. That is his sovereign power as the Creator and Re-Creator. As in Genesis 1, God speaks and it is. God's speaking brought about all things in the beginning and it will also bring about all things new at the end.

I am making all things new. Indeed, 'all things'. Nothing will remain the same. Nothing will remain untouched. As it said in v.4, *the former things have passed away.*

He alone does that. We do not. As they have always done, people dream about ways to make this world a safe and happy place for everyone. When we keep the environment clean, provide better education, promote social justice, and a more equitable distribution of health and wealth in the world, we will get there. Eventually, we will be able to usher in a new and better era. Utopia is coming.

But it will not happen. Every human effort to bring about a better world is bound to fail. God alone can make all things new through his Holy Spirit. And this begins in the human heart. No one else can bring in a new and better world-order.

The Holy God, the Maker of all things, reveals himself as the Architect and Builder of the new world and the New Jerusalem that is coming. He is working on it already. He will complete it and present the final result when Jesus returns. Today you and I can hardly imagine that the effects of sin can ever be removed. And yet, it is going to happen, it really is! I cannot wait to see what it looks like. How about you?

To strengthen this trust and anticipation in us, John is also told to *write this down, for these words are trustworthy and true.* Who is saying this? The ESV suggests that it is God, who just continues to speak. But then it is not clear, and a bit redundant, why we need in v.5 and 6 three times the words "And he said" so close together referring to the same speaker.

It makes more sense, and gives a more lively and dynamic picture of what is happening, when speakers alternate. God first says, "I make all things new" and then someone else, perhaps John's guidance-angel (mentioned in Rev. 1:1) instructs John right away to "Write this down". And then God continues, saying, "It is done!"

In Rev. 1:11 & 19 the apostle John was given the general instruction to write down everything he was about to see and hear. But a few times he is instructed to write down particular sayings, because they are so important. That is in Rev. 14:13, 19:9 and here. It is like reading a document that has some sentences highlighted, or in bold print, so that you will always remember what it says.

In other words, we are told to never forget that what God says here is trustworthy and true. Of course, everything that God says is trustworthy and true. But we are just people. We need this reminder in a world where such announcements are often ridiculed. The promise that God will make all things new is often dismissed as the nonsense that keeps religious fanatics busy. And since we do not see the result yet, we can easily be sucked into this kind of thinking.

So let's read those highlighted words over and over again. God will really do this. We live in a broken world. But he will make all things new. We do not just dream it up. We trust God's Word that cannot be broken.

Then, in v.6 God continues and adds, *it is done*. This is the same statement that we heard in Rev. 16:17, after the seventh bowl of God's wrath was poured out. Both statements are each other's counterparts. In 16:17 it marks the completion of God's punishment, and in 21:6 it marks the realization of God's salvation.

And remember what we have seen earlier, the description of these things in Rev. 17–22 is not a chronological narrative. It is one event on the Day of Jesus' return. With the words "It is done," both Punishment and Salvation come together as effects of the seventh bowl. As the new world appears, God declares, "What I promised is now completed. It is done. Mission accomplished according to plan".

I am the Alpha and the Omega. With the first and the last letter of the Greek alphabet God presents himself as *the Beginning and the End*. He controls everything. Throughout the history of our world he has led all events to this point (see also Rev. 1:8).

He is not just present at the beginning and at the end. No, he is personally the beginning of everything, and in him personally is the end of everything. Everything began with God, everything went out from him as the source. And everything will lead to him as the final goal, and result in his glory.

This makes you wonder what life in this new world is going to be like. "Well," says God, *to the thirsty I will give from the spring of the water of life without payment*. This "water of life" is mentioned also in Rev. 22:1 and 17, and Jesus himself talks about "living water" in John 4 and John 7:37. It is an image of "eternal life".

So, when God talks about those who are thirsty, he refers to all who are looking forward in faith to eternal life, the time to enjoy life to the fullest, for ever and ever, never-ending bliss.

If that desire determines your life here and now, God will give it to you! At the end of your journey to the New Promised Land, God provides exactly what the parched pilgrims need, living water. And it comes from a "spring". There is by God's grace in Jesus Christ an endless, inexhaustible supply of water that gives life for ever.

The Architect of the New Jerusalem is also the Provider for those who live in the Holy City. And it is for free. Your eternal joy will not cost you anything, because Jesus paid for it. In the New Jerusalem God fulfils abundantly the words of Isaiah 55:1–2 *Come, all you who are thirsty, come to the waters; and you who have no money, come, buy, and eat! Come, buy wine and milk without money and without cost.* [NIV]

In the New Jerusalem God himself guarantees your life as the free gift of his love.

THE ACCESS

As God continues to speak he answers one more question: for who is all this, this promised eternal life in the presence of the Holy God and of the glorified Christ? Who will have access to this Holy City? Who will qualify to inhabit the coming new world?

The one who conquers will have this heritage. You might remember this expression "he who conquers". You will find it at the end of the letters that were written to the seven churches that were the first recipients of the Book of Revelation (see Rev. 2 and 3). Each of these letters ended with the urgent call to remain faithful and keep fighting the good fight of faith, to resist the power of Satan, to persevere in the ongoing battle with the evil powers.

Here God repeats this urgent message for everyone, for you and me. Ask yourself, do I fight in this world the good fight to remain faithful and to resist the evil powers of sin in my life? Or do I take it easy when it comes to this?

As we watch the dawn of a new world, the battle rages on in this old world and it rages on in our own lives. But listen carefully to what God is telling you. Do not get discouraged. Do not give up. Those who remain faithful and loyal to the end will have free access to his new world, to the New Jerusalem.

They will inherit what God has in store for them. The wording reminds of what Peter says in 1 Peter 1:4, 5 about *an inheritance that is imperishable, undefiled, and unfading, kept in heaven for you, who by God's power are being guarded through faith for a salvation ready to be revealed in the last time.*

When this heritage is given to you, the Holy God will say to you, "I will be your God, and you will be my son or daughter". Do you recognize the Old Testament covenant language of Genesis 17:4? In this strong, personal, and intimate father–child relationship God's love bridges the centuries and fulfils his promise to Abraham as never before. *You shall be the father of a multitude of nations.* God will give himself to you who trust in him. And you will see with awe the full reality of his glory.

God reinforces this promise of eternal bliss, by also pointing at the flipside. Those in the church who flirt with sin, or who live in sin, those who are open to the poisonous propaganda that a life without God is actually pretty attractive, and sounds like fun – if that's you, he addresses you with the same urgent message to remain faithful. *The cowardly, the faithless, the detestable, the murderers, the sexually immoral, sorcerers, idolaters, and all liars.*

With this list God does not address the pagan outsiders. Those were mentioned already in Rev. 20:15. No, no, he talks about folks in the church, who claim to be loyal to Jesus Christ, but who do not show the commitment to follow him, Christian believers who abandon their loyalty to God.

God warns you, if you think that a compromise with the wickedness of the antichristian culture is okay; if you fail to resist the temptations of lifestyle choices that ignore God's holy will; if you go for antichristian ideas or worldviews; if you make money and power your idols to trust in.

31 • Revelation 21:1-8

With v.8 God wants to shake us up and wake us up. Because if that is you, you are not "one who conquers" (7), and the consequences will be dramatic; you will be shut out of the Holy City, the New Jerusalem. You will find the same urgent warning in Rev. 21:27 and 22:15.

God is a God of justice and in his new world no sin and evil in any form or shape will ever again disturb the security and bliss of those who live there. The holiness and peace of the New Jerusalem requires the exclusion of all evil.

And therefore those who do not repent and turn to Jesus Christ will join Satan, his evil henchmen and all his followers, and find themselves *in the lake that burns with fire and sulphur,* symbol of eternal death, of horrible torment day and night for ever and ever.

Why does a beautiful vision of the dawn of a glorious new world – why does it have to end with such a terrifying picture?

So that you and I and everyone who hears it, will not be missing when it comes.

32

Revelation 21: 9 – 21

ADMIRE THE ARCHITECTURE OF THE NEW JERUSALEM

The individualistic culture of the time in which we live, makes for some real challenges for the church today. Yes, we know how important the church is in the Bible. But it can become difficult to get excited about the church.

And what we read in this part of Rev.21 does not make it easier. Sure, we read about these wonderful, glorious images. But it all sounds so strange, so foreign to us, does it not? How do we relate to a hugely oversized city of gold, decorated with jewels?

Now, let us think of the church as God's building-project in this world. For a big building project an architect often presents, with the drawings, also what is called an 'artist's impression', or 'architectural rendering'. That is a picture of what the final result is going to look like. And it looks beautiful, it looks great!

But then you go to the construction site, and all you see is a hole in the ground. It has been raining, it is muddy and messy; building material is laying everywhere. And you wonder if it is ever going to look like the 'artistic picture'.

So it is with the church. Here, in Rev.21, we have in John's final vision, the 'artist's impression' of the church. And it looks great.

But today, we are plodding along at the construction site of the church. And it does not always look that great. It can get pretty messy. Sometimes the construction guys disagree on how to move forward. Sometimes they want to change the drawings of the Architect. Sometimes a crew walks away to start from scratch elsewhere.

Is this project going anywhere?

But then, look again at the 'artist's impression' and be encouraged by what you see.

Take a step back and admire the architecture of the New Jerusalem

ITS AMAZING DESIGN

In this passage the apostle John is given the opportunity to have a closer look at what he initially saw in v.2. This is his final and most awesome vision of the whole book. The purpose is that each one of us becomes fully aware of the magnitude of what is happening on that day, the day of God's Last Judgment.

We see that an angel presents himself to John as his tour-guide. This is not for the first time, of course. But when you read v.9 and 10 does it not strike you as something we've heard before?

Here it is: *Then one of the seven angels who had the seven bowls came and said to me, "Come I will show you the judgment of the great prostitute who is seated on many waters, with whom the kings of the earth have committed sexual immorality, and with the wine of whose sexual immorality the dwellers on earth have become drunk. And he carried me away in the Spirit into a wilderness, and I saw a woman sitting on a scarlet beast that was full of blasphemous names, and it had seven heads and ten horns.*

This is Rev. 17:1-3. There is a remarkable similarity between this passage, and what we hear in 21:9-10. Both angels belong to the same category. And both issue the same invitation: "Come, I will show you... a woman". Both times these women turn out to be cities as well. And in both cases John has the same experience: He is carried away in the Spirit to have a good look.

At the same time, what seems to be so similar, is meant to expose the deepest and most dramatic contrast you can think of. Yes, it is about two women. Both adorned with gold, pearls, and precious gemstones. The one is called the great prostitute, also the city of Babylon. The other one is called the bride, the wife of the Lamb, also the holy city, the New Jerusalem.

At first sight someone might wonder whether there is really so much difference between these two ladies; between Babylon and Jerusalem. Is there really so much difference between the church and world?

But by putting these two visions close together on the day of God's judgment, introduced by identical tour-guides, the Holy God exposes the opposite. The bride of Christ is everything the prostitute is not. At the last judgment everyone will see and acknowledge that the worldly, antichristian culture of Babylon is the absolute opposite of the New Jerusalem.

And we know what happened. In Rev. 17:3 John is carried away in the Spirit into a wilderness, to witness the horrible end of Babylon the Great, the mother of prostitutes.

In this passage in Rev. 21 he is again carried away in the Spirit, this time to *a great and high mountain,* a place that gives him a good view of what God's grace is doing when the victory of Jesus Christ is being completed.

From this mountain he is shown *the Holy City, Jerusalem, coming down out of heaven, from God.* Here is no darkness. It is a scene of incredible beauty and splendour. The city is 'holy', fully dedicated to God. And it's called Jerusalem, as the place where God dwelt with his people, the old city of peace. The prophets have said marvelous things about its great future (Isaiah 54:9–17).

Interestingly, John was promised to see *the bride, the wife of the Lamb Jesus Christ*. But what he is actually seeing when he gets there, is this city. However, just as in Rev. 21:2, these are obviously two images for the same thing. Both represent the church of Jesus Christ, as it appears when Jesus returns.

Yes, you can also talk about the church today as the 'bride of Christ'. But today she is still preparing herself for the marriage feast to come. And you can also call the church today a 'holy city'. But today it is still under construction; it is an ongoing project.

However, in this vision John is shown the 'artist's impression' of what it is going to look like. He sees how the perfect fellowship of God's people is filling up God's new world. And it becomes clear that nothing in the whole universe is as glorious as this fellowship, this living relationship that people may have with God.

Indeed, we see God's artistic rendering of "the Father's house with the many rooms", as Jesus talks about it (John 14), and of the city Abraham was looking forward to (Hebrews 11:10). And when it arrives, all God's children will be there.

So then, let us have a look and admire the amazing design of the architecture John is seeing, and is trying to describe for us.

The first thing he reports is that the city has *the glory of God, its radiance like a most rare jewel*. This is what jumps out when he looks: strong radiance, a bright shine. Like, when you walk in the dark, and someone switches on a strong spotlight, right in your face! This bright radiance is the most spectacular characteristic of God's holy city.

John compares it with a rare or precious jewel, *like a jasper, clear as crystal*. There is a bit of a problem with the names of the gemstones in this chapter. We have the same in v.19 and 20. The Greek names as we have them in the New Testament time do not always refer to the same stones as we know them in English today. Today a 'jasper' is a multicolored gem, not very rare or expensive, and opaque instead of transparent or clear as crystal.

John's description gives the impression of something like a diamond, sparkling and dazzling, a fitting picture of the reflection of God's glory.

The Bible speaks often about the 'glory of God'. It is the majestic brilliance, the magnificence and awesomeness that is associated with the appearance of God, both in Old and New Testament. For instance, when Israel was at Mount Sinai, *the glory of God was like a devouring fire on the top of the mountain* (Exodus 24:17), but it was also in the cloud that filled the tabernacle (Exodus 40:34). And you will remember from Luke 2 the fear of the shepherds, when *the glory of the Lord shone around them.*

This impressive glory now appears when the holy God comes to live with people. And no longer here or there, occasionally, but permanently. John sees how God's heavenly splendour fills the New Jerusalem as evidence of God's presence.

When the Queen's Royal Standard is flown over Buckingham Palace, Londoners know, the queen is home. So John sees the glory of God shining brightly in the New Jerusalem, and knows, here God is home. The church is his residence.

Next John tells us that the New Jerusalem *has a great, high wall.* If you were to approach an ancient city, the city-wall was usually the first thing you would see.

However, why would the New Jerusalem need a wall? A wall was to keep enemies out, to protect against hostile armies. But when the New Jerusalem comes here, there will be no more enemies. No more need for protection.

That is true. But a city-wall also functions to establish the city as a defined area. It helps people to identify themselves as belonging to a particular community. Today we do not build walls for that purpose, but the idea still exists. Someone might say, "I was born and raised in Hamilton. I've lived here all my life. This is where I belong. When I've been away for a while, I'm happy when I'm back. This is my home."

In other words, the wall John is seeing around the holy city is a symbol identifying that 'the church is a unique community, eternally secure in its fellowship, its communion with the holy God'. This is not meant in a smug way, in arrogant isolation. There is nothing elitist about it.

No, no, the wall has many gates, which are all open, all the time and in all directions. There is a warm welcome for everyone who wants to become a resident of the city. But to get there, you will need to enter through one of the gates. That is the only way in.

That makes it important to have a good look at the amazing design of this wall. For then you will find out what defines the church as a unique community.

When you read v.12-14 it is clear that the whole structure is dominated by the number twelve: twelve gates, twelve foundations, twelve angels, twelve tribes and twelve apostles… So, why the number 12?

It is usually seen as the symbolic number for God's people: in the Old Testament twelve tribes, in the New Testament twelve apostles. Sometimes it comes in multiples, like the familiar 144,000.

And then we see the names of the Israelite tribes and of the apostles written on the city-wall, on the gates and on the foundations. What does that tell us?

There is a hospital in Hamilton, Ontario that has the name "Juravinski". That's because in the first decade of the 21st century Charles and Margaret Juravinski donated $43 million to healthcare in Hamilton. McMaster University, also in Hamilton, has the "Michael de Groote School of Business", named after the wealthy businessman and philanthropist who donated over $100 million to the university.

Names on buildings remind us of the people who played such an important role in establishing those institutions that we should not forget them.

So, which names are so important for the church that they should never be forgotten?

Well, the names of the twelve tribes of Israel remind us of the origin of the church. The church is the evidence of God's faithfulness to his old promises. It identifies the universal church of the New Testament as the true Israel of God.

And the names of the twelve apostles tell us that this church is being built on the preaching and teaching of the apostles (Ephesians 2:20). These names are a strong reminder of the apostolic testimony of Jesus Christ crucified as the only basis for our hope and salvation. Only this testimony will usher us into a living communion with God.

Now remember, John's vision shows us God's 'artist's impression' of a city that is today still under construction. So, what does this amazing design mean for us, here, today?

Many Christians like to emphasize that the Christian faith is first and foremost about your personal relationship with God. But when you believe in Jesus as your Saviour, when you commit yourself to serving God and following Christ you become part of something that is much bigger than a personal relationship.

You join the community of the redeemed by grace in Jesus Christ. And this design of the New Jerusalem tells you that you can only do so if you submit to what these gates represent. That is if your personal faith is the faith proclaimed by the twelve apostles.

And when you embrace this, you are grafted into the twelve tribes of God's Israel, the roots of the church, gathered from the beginning of the world to its end.

This is true for everyone. Remember that the twelve gates in the wall are wide-open in all directions. It does not matter where you come from. The great multitude that will live in the New Jerusalem is coming from every nation, from all tribes and peoples and languages. But the only way in is through the gates. By believing in Jesus Christ as your Saviour, you become part of God's fulfilment of Psalm 87. *In Jerusalem are the springs of my salvation.* Nowhere else!

And today, as the building project is still ongoing, it is our job as God's church when doing outreach, mission, and evangelism, to tell people this. To let them know that otherwise there is no salvation, no hope. Show them the 'artist's impression' of the city we are heading for and urge them to join the journey.

And you, are you looking forward to coming home where God is home?

32 • Revelation 21:9-21

Its enormous size

John then sees that his personal tour-guide has with him a measuring stick. It is not an ordinary measuring stick, like the one John himself had been given in Rev. 11:1.

After all, this is no ordinary city either. This is the holy city, the New Jerusalem. And the 'rod of gold' fits with the fact that 'gold' is the dominating building material of the holy city and the colour of heavenly glory.

And so, the angel sets out *to measure the city, its gates, and walls.*

Why is that? What is the purpose of the exercise? You can look at it as a survey to determine the exact boundaries, and so to confirm God's title, his exclusive right of ownership of the holy city as his property. That makes it symbolize God's commitment to protect his church and take care of her.

But the next verses show that these measurements are especially significant to impress on us the enormous size of this architectural miracle. And that in turn is then meant to impress on us how great, how generous, how welcoming, but also how awesome and how glorious the One is, who designed it and built it.

This going around to measure the New Jerusalem, is like walking around to count the towers and citadels of the Old Jerusalem. Psalm 48 sings about that as an activity that should not lead to pride in the city's strength or beauty, but to abundant praise of God's glory and majesty.

Well, when this angel is done measuring the city of God, the results are absolutely stunning. It is beyond belief. Which emphasizes even more the symbolic significance of these numbers.

Let us have a closer look. The city's ground-plan is laid out like a square. But it is huge, it is 12,000 stadia long and wide. That is about 2,300 km each side. In Canada this would cover an area from Winnipeg to Vancouver, and from the US border to the Arctic Circle, which is close to 5,000,000 square kilometres. That is an enormous area for a city. The largest cities in the world today are tiny villages compared to the New Jerusalem.

Remember, the number twelve stands for the church, the people of God. And now it is multiplied by one thousand, or 10 x 10 x 10, the ultimate completeness and perfection. This completed church is so incredibly large. Again, it may not look all that great when you look at the church today, but God's plan and purpose for his church are immense. We travel to the New Jerusalem as a growing multitude that no one can count.

Think of God's promise to Abraham, offspring as numerous as the sand on the beach and as the stars in the sky (Genesis 15:5 and 22:17). Indeed, your Father's house does have many rooms, many more than you and I could ever imagine (John 14:2). The purpose of God's love includes everyone who turns to him anywhere, anytime. Do not worry, no one is going to be excluded for lack of space. No one who turns to Jesus Christ will be turned away.

But there is more. This city is just as high as it is wide and long. That is also 2,300 kilometres.

To get an idea how high that is, when you fly from North America to Europe, your altitude above the Atlantic is about 10 or 11 km. The International Space Station circles the earth at an altitude between 350 and 400 km. So, 2,300 km brings you way beyond that, in space!

Most scholars picture this three-dimensional city as an enormous cube. The idea is that it reflects the Most Holy Place in the temple, which was also a cube, overlaid with gold. This is where God dwelt with his people in the Old Testament. In John's vision this Most Holy part of the temple, shaped as a cube, is then immensely expanded. Now the whole city is God's holy dwelling-place, but it still resembles the location in Israel.

However, the picture of a cube is somewhat problematic. It does not look like a city. It is a huge golden box. Where do people live in this box? One could say, of course, "That does not matter. It is a vision and it is all symbolism anyway". Okay, but in his visions John often sees things that he recognizes. Here he recognizes a city, a place where people live, a place with streets, with a river and trees.

An attractive alternative to the cube is to think of this city in the form of a pyramid. Imagine that from his high and great mountain John sees the holy city built and its inhabitants living on terraces all around on the slopes of a mountain with its top as high as its length and width, 2,300 km.

Do you want to know what this might look like, on an extremely small scale? Look at the city of Gondor in the third one of the "Lord of the Rings" movies. Or travel to Italy and see how villages and towns are built on the steep mountain-slopes of Cinque Terre or the Amalfi-coast.

What is measured next is the wall around the city. It is one hundred forty-four cubits, which is about seventy meters. Whether this is its thickness, or its height is not clear in the original, although most scholars choose 'height'. Perhaps the number one hundred forty-four is more significant as a multiple of twelve. Again, the number of the church!

But regardless how we interpret some of the details, here is our firm comfort, our great encouragement: this walled city is an eternally safe and secure place for everyone who lives there. This is what your God has in store for you.

You may wonder about that, sometimes. You and I live here, today, in a dark world where the Christian church and the Christian faith is often dismissed as irrelevant. The frustrating experience of being busy with outreach, is that the large majority in our post-modern western society seems to be simply uninterested. And then, in the well-known Hymn "The Church's One Foundation" we see the picture of a church *sorely oppressed, by schisms rent asunder, and by heresies distressed*. Does God's building-project have a future? We see so little progress at the construction site.

But God says, "I will reach my goal. Look at the 'artist's impression' I have shown you, and stand in awe! See how big, how massive it is going to be? This is how wide and long and high my love for you is in Jesus Christ."

ITS AWESOME SPLENDOUR

But there is more. What God is doing when he completes his church-project, is not only big beyond our imagination, it is also going to be incredibly beautiful. In v.11 John mentioned already the awesome, breathtaking, and dazzling splendour of the New Jerusalem. But a closer look in v.18–21 shows even more spectacular details of its unique building materials and decorations.

The wall was made of, or built with "jasper", the same crystal-clear diamond-like jewel as in v.11. Think of this 70-metre high wall, with a length of thousands of km, thickly studded with billions of huge diamonds. It is like a sparkling diamond bracelet, surrounding the city in which everything is made of pure shining gold.

Indeed, the whole city is made of pure gold, clear, transparent as glass (v.18). And so are the streets of the city (v.21). The word 'pure' or 'clean' has a deep meaning here. It is a metaphor for the moral perfection and spiritual purity of the church that fills God's new world. Think of the pure, spotless clothing of the Bride of Christ, which according to Rev. 19:8 stands for *the righteous deeds of the saints.*

And today already you may experience the beginning of this purity. Oh, I know, it is only a small beginning. But it is real. This is the life-renewing power of God's grace and love in you. As his redeemed children, purified by the blood of Jesus, the Holy Spirit enables you to begin to enjoy the pure and holy communion with your God, today!

But that is not it. John also has another look at the foundations of the city-walls. He had noticed already the names of the twelve apostles, but now he also sees that these foundations are decorated with all kinds of precious stones. In v.19-20 we get the whole list. We are again reminded that God fulfills the prophetic words in Isaiah 54.

I mentioned earlier how challenging it is to identify these jewels with current English names, because of the different names in Greek and Hebrew. So, we are not going to try that.

But here is the big idea. Reading those names, one after the other, leaves you with an overwhelming impression of the perfect beauty, the super-abundant brilliance of all these bright, sparkling colours in dazzling heavenly light. It must have been totally overwhelming to see such awesome splendour, reflecting God's glory.

And then there are the twelve gates. *Each of the gates made of one single pearl.* This is absolutely unimaginable. It is over the top. One of the largest pearls in the world has a diameter of twenty-four centimetres. And here, twelve times, the bright, sparkling shine of the diamond studded wall is interrupted by the delicate lustre of a pearly gate.

And every gate is another open door to a highway into the city, a golden city full of beautiful avenues, avenues of pure gold. It is a super-symbol of the truth that everyone coming home in God's holy city will have unlimited access to the throne of God. Here everyone will enjoy the deepest communion with Jesus Christ possible.

God's creativity in what he shows here, knows no bounds. No words can capture adequately the awesome splendour John is seeing.

The spectacular beauty of the 'artist's impression' of the New Jerusalem is so very encouraging as we find ourselves in the middle of this building-project.

But in the end it has only one purpose. In the end it is not even about the church. No, it is about the beauty, the power, and the majesty and the glory of God himself!

People dream of building a better and more glorious future for their children and grandchildren, for our society. Look at mankind's amazing achievements! We've come a long way, have we not? But it will all fail.

God alone can usher in his great future. And he will! He is the Almighty God who will single-handedly finalize his building-project to the glory of his Name.

Think again of Psalm 48:12, 13. *Walk about Zion...., number her towers, consider her ramparts, go through her citadels.* But the point of the Psalm is not: "Wow, look what an awesome city we have". No, no, it is: "Wow, look what an awesome God we have!"

The same thing is true here. The point of admiring the architecture of the New Jerusalem is not: "Look how awesome we are going to be as church". But it is: "Look at the majesty and glory of our awesome God!"

But this 'artist's impression' of the future is at the same time our challenge today. What do we see as we walk around at the construction site? Do we look with the eyes of faith? Do we already see some of God's glory in Jesus Christ?

And how do we reflect God's glory as church today?

Is this even our goal as his church in the world in which we live?

And how do we do this? Have you ever asked yourself this question: How am I going to reflect God's glory in what I say and do today?

That's not a bad question to begin with when you get up in the morning.

33

Revelation 21: 22 – 22: 5

LIVE THE GOOD LIFE IN THE NEW JERUSALEM

It has been a long journey through the Book of Revelation. As we are approaching the end of John's visions, it is good to recall what it is all about.

It is about the church's voyage toward the final victory of Jesus Christ over all God's enemies. A victory that opens up the glorious future of all who believe in Jesus and who have, by God's grace, persevered during the journey to God's new creation, God's new world.

Revelation was written, not only to assure us of God's final purpose, the glorious victory of Jesus Christ, but also to increase our longing for the realization and completion of this purpose. This assurance and the prospect of the great joy that is coming, comforts us in times of suffering and persecution.

Revelation directs our desires to God and to his glory. And when we focus on that, we will also recognize this world for what it is. It may look great sometimes. But it is marred by sin and evil. That is why it has no future apart from the love and grace of God Almighty and the sacrifice of the Lamb Jesus Christ.

Therefore, we turn again to Revelation's picture of the New Jerusalem, God's holy church. As we saw before, today God's church is his building project in

33 • Revelation 21:22-22:5

this world. And at the construction site it often does not look very impressive. But in John's visions we see the marvellous artistic impression of the church of Jesus Christ as it will appear on the last day.

So far we followed the apostle John, as he admired the architecture of the holy city, described in Rev. 21:9–21. In this next section John and his guide take us on a tour inside the city-walls, to show us the unique character of the good life in the inner city.

This will then complete the portrait of the New Jerusalem.

It will also complete the description of Christ's final victory on the last day of our history.

We reach the end of John's visions.

Mankind Redeemed

In the first part of John's tour of the New Jerusalem, he admired the impressive architecture of the city: the wall, the twelve gates and foundations with their splendid decorations. But the angel, his tour-guide, is not done yet. There is much more to see in the artist's impression of God's completed church. Next we are going to see through John's eyes, in a virtual tour, what life in the holy city is all about.

So, perhaps John is still standing on this high mountain, mentioned in Rev. 21:10, but you can also imagine that, still in the Spirit (v.10) he enters through one of the gates. And as he looks around, he is missing something: he does not see a temple anywhere in the city.

He sounds a bit surprised. Apparently this was something he did not expect. If anywhere, you would expect to see in a holy city, called "New Jerusalem", a beautiful temple as a symbol of God's presence. After all, in Ezekiel's Old Testament prophecies of the new city of God, the temple has a prominent place (Ezekiel 40 – 44). It is the very heart of everything.

But then John remembers the loud voice that said in v.3, that God will now dwell with man. In other words, the majesty and glory of the Holy God fills the entire city, it is everywhere, not just at one, separate, designated location. The presence of God Almighty and the Lamb Jesus Christ turns the whole city into one, huge temple. And that, of course, defeats the purpose of having a separate temple.

What a breathtaking picture this is. Throughout the New Jerusalem, which is God's holy and perfect church, our fellowship and communion with the living God is direct and everywhere. Every barrier, every obstacle for such direct fellowship with God, because of our sins, has been removed by Jesus Christ.

In fact, this is true today already, though not yet perfect. But this is our reality: Today already we do not need a special location to meet God, a place separate from where we live and meet each other every day, a temple!

Sure, Christians get together for corporate worship at particular times and special locations, most of the time in churches. But this can be done anywhere, despite the fact that over time large and magnificent churches and cathedrals have been built. And we often call our place of worship a 'sanctuary'. But the reality is that in Jesus, the Almighty God is with us, anywhere and everywhere.

Think about this: in Jesus, your Saviour, you are constantly in God's immediate presence wherever you are and regardless of what's going on in your life. What does this do to you? Is it encouraging? Is it exciting? How does it make you feel: Joyful? Happy? Safe and secure? And how does that impact your life? This focus makes your whole life a matter of 'worship', does it not?

Well then, this communion with God will be your absolute perfect reality in the New Jerusalem, in the glorious future when God will live with his people, with you and me, as never before. Now that will be heaven on earth!

And since this presence of God will fill the New Jerusalem with the radiance of his glory, as described in v.11, there is no more need for sunlight during the day and moonlight at night. For millennia sun and moon gave light to sustain life in God's old creation. And yes, sometimes we see glimpses of God's glory in this world.

But there is still so much darkness. It can be hard for us to recognize the glory of the Holy God in our broken and suffering lives, in a world filled with hatred and violence. But when Jesus returns to usher in a new heaven and a new earth, all this will change. Then God's children may live 24/7 in the most powerful light ever, the intense brilliance of the glory of God and of the Lamb Jesus Christ (see Isaiah 60:19–20).

John reinforces this, by identifying "the lamp of the holy city" as the One who says, *I am the light of the world*, the Lamb Jesus Christ. He came here to drive out the darkness of sin and evil (John 1:4,5,9). In him the light of God's glorious grace shines in the church. Yes, today already, wherever the church is faithfully following her Saviour.

We admit that today this is far from perfect. But we are looking forward to see the full brightness of this light, when the New Jerusalem will be filled with it from the one end to the other, without any obstruction. Then the light of sun and moon will be redundant.

This light of God's glory will be so powerful, says John, that it attracts even "the nations and kings of the earth". *They will walk by the light of the holy city*.

That is an unexpected change. In Revelation 'nations' and 'kings' are usually the enemies of God's people. They represent the hostile world-powers, the antichristian culture of Babylon, the great prostitute (see Rev. 17 & 18). They hate and persecute the followers of the Lamb Jesus Christ, the believers.

But here is the surprise. As it turns out, when the New Jerusalem appears, nations and kings have repented. They have broken the shackles that bound them to Satan and his evil helpers, the beast and the false prophet. In faith they have given themselves to Jesus Christ and now they follow him to the new Promised Land.

This is what we will see in the end, we will see the international, multicultural population of the New Jerusalem, God's United Nations. We will see believers, converted from all nations, including political leaders and powers-that-be. They come to enter the gates of the holy city, to walk in the glorious light of God's love and grace in Jesus.

We will see the fullness of the complete church of Christ as we cannot imagine it today. We will see the final results of centuries of world-mission.

We all know how important that is, mission, evangelism, and church-planting. But sometimes you wonder about the impact of those efforts.

When you train for mission or evangelism, they will tell you to be prepared for dead-end roads and frustrations. You will run into resistance and other obstacles. When, after many years of hard work, you count converts, you may be disappointed.

And yet, the faithful church cannot but remain faithful to the Great Commission given to her: *Go, and make disciples of all nations*.

It is true, today we will not be able to measure the final results. It is fragmented at best. Remember, today God's church-building project is still a messy and muddy construction site. John's vision is the artist's impression of what it is going to be like. And that is beautiful. Then we will see God's mission accomplished. When the pilgrims arrive in the new Promised Land no one will be missing. From all nations they will come to live the eternal good life of God's redeemed people.

Indeed, we will see mankind redeemed in all its colourful and multicultural diversity. There is no reason to believe that the gospel will wipe out the cultural distinctions and differences between the nations. The gospel will redeem those distinctions and make them useful to glorify God.

That may sound nice, but how is that going to work?

Well, says John, all this is going to serve the glory of God, and so enrich his holy city, the church. Look, and see that these kings and nations will not enter the New Jerusalem with empty hands. In v.24 it says that *the kings of the earth will bring their glory (or: splendour) into it*. And in v.26 that *they will bring into it the glory and honour of the nations*.

From all directions these kings and nations come with wedding-presents. Yes, that's right, wedding-gifts! We get a picture of a constant stream of contributions for the celebration of the marriage feast of the Lamb, Jesus Christ, with his lovely bride, the holy city, the New Jerusalem from heaven, the church.

But what kind of gifts are we talking about? Many see this 'glory' or 'splendour' as liturgical honour. They bring their worship, praise, and glorifica-

33 • Revelation 21:22-22:5

tion. The apostle Paul talks about the time *when at the name of Jesus every knee shall bow and every tongue confess that Jesus Christ is Lord, to the glory of God the Father* (Philippians 2:10–11).

This is, of course, fantastic. But is it everything? God the Creator gave mankind so many different talents and gifts when he told them to develop our human culture to his glory. This is what has been going on. To be sure, today all human activities are tainted by sin, often driven by evil intentions, and used for the wrong purposes.

And yet, in spite of this, even today we see a rich diversity of beautiful and precious cultural achievements that serve the glory and honour of the Creator, whether they are material, artistic, technical or scientific achievements.

And all this needs to be redeemed and purified, but not necessarily destroyed. Just as the wise men from the east came with material gifts to worship the new-born King, so, in line with the words of the prophet Isaiah (Isaiah 60:3–6), kings will come from everywhere. And they will bring into the new world, what was glorifying God already in this old world.

John emphasizes the significance of this ongoing influx into the city. He assures us that the twelve gates (mentioned already in v.12,13) *will never be shut*.

In ancient cities the gates were bolted when it got dark. With criminals and enemies lurking outside the city-gates, it was too dangerous to leave them open. But on the new earth we do not have to worry about hostile attacks. There will be no more enemies. And it will never get dark. The gates will be left open, all the time (Isaiah 60:11).

Jesus came to drive out the darkness of sin, evil and misery. Believe in him. Trust in him, and you will see how this begins today already, in your own life, in his church. He died on the cross and arose from the grave to conquer God's enemies. He clears you from all guilt. He protects you against the dark powers around you.

It is still a battle. But one day the battle will be over. Hostilities will have ceased. Freely enjoy the good life with all of God's redeemed mankind, because God's New Jerusalem will be absolutely and perfectly safe.

So yes, those wide-open gates are inviting. They give abundant opportunities to enter God's holy city as a welcoming place. That feels good. But let us be careful not to make a mistake. It does not mean that everyone and everything is welcome and free to enter. John makes it abundantly clear who does, and who does not have access. Always remember that the holy city is a society dedicated to God and to Jesus Christ.

As such, n*othing unclean (or impure) will enter the city, ever* (v.27). Nothing that is sinful, nothing that would even in the slightest form offend, grieve, or anger the most holy God. There is absolutely no place for those things. And this means that there is also no place in the New Jerusalem for people who persist in doing those things.

John talks about folks *who do what is detestable or false.* That covers anyone who leads a morally shameful life, but also anyone who rejects the truth of God's Word and who resists his grace in Jesus Christ.

Yes, access to the city of God, joining the redeemed mankind is free. But only for *those whose names are written in the Lamb's book of life,* those who repent and are registered as belonging to the Saviour Jesus Christ.

Perhaps you wonder, by that time, when the New Jerusalem comes down from heaven, will there be any people left that might try to get in, but need to be refused? Is that what is behind v.27?

The answer is 'no'; v.27 does not picture a last-minute final selection at the gate. Like something that can happen when you are about to board a plane. You are already in the line-up for the gate, and your name is announced. You go to the counter and an official tells you, "Sir, you're not boarding. Your ticket is not valid."

No, v.27 is a warning, a very urgent and serious warning for us today. Here and now, you and I must remember that no one will be able to live the good and eternal life in God's holy city, just because he happens to be white, or wealthy, or a westerner… or the opposite of all those things. Or just because we happen to think about him or her as a good and nice person, or whatever.

No, no, there is only one criterion. And that is the same for everyone, whoever you are; wherever you come from; whatever you look like; whatever has been going on in your life. Here is the decisive question: Are you clean or are you unclean?

Are you registered in the Lamb's book of life, or are you not?

And always keep in mind that this is not about your own achievements or qualities. You can only become 'clean' through the blood of Jesus (Rev. 22:14). And this too, is the same for everyone. There is no exception. Jesus' sacrifice for the forgiveness of sins is the only sure way to be registered in the book-of-life.

PARADISE RESTORED

There is more to see within the walls of the New Jerusalem. John's tour-guide continues to show him other aspects of life inside the holy city, aspects that make for a really good life. And what is then brought into view before John's eyes, and through him before our eyes, is truly amazing. What a fantastic picture this is. Powerful symbols to explain what we cannot imagine!

..... the river of the water of life, bright as crystal, flowing from the throne of God and of the Lamb through the middle of the street of the city....

Do you remember the enormous size of the holy city John was seeing (Rev. 21:15–17), and then the street of the city, made of pure gold, transparent as glass (21:21)?

Well, now John also sees a river. This word 'river' highlights the connection with other rivers mentioned in the Old Testament (see Genesis 2:10; Ezekiel 47 and Psalm 46:4). This one flows through the middle of the street. Technically, that would make for two streets already. This helps us to recognize that the singular 'street', 'river', and later on also 'tree', are used as collectives. They stand for many streets, rivers, and trees, all over this huge metropolis.

So yes, this makes for a spectacular view: rivers of crystal clear water, flowing down through the New Jerusalem, alongside streets of pure gold.

And then this water, called *the water of life,* is water that makes alive, gives life, and sustains life. And it can do so, because it is absolutely pure, totally unpolluted. The metaphor is simple, but clear. This water is a symbol of eternal life and spiritually pure life, eternal salvation.

Think of Jesus, who in John 4 and 7 speaks about himself as the source, the well-spring of living water. In him God fulfills what we read in Ezekiel 47: *Everything will live where the water goes*. In Ezekiel's vision the river streams towards the Dead Sea. It goes where death rules. But wherever the river goes, death disappears, and life begins to flourish.

Ezekiel sees the river flowing from the temple. John sees it flowing *from the throne of God and of the Lamb*. But it tells the same truth; God Almighty is in Jesus Christ the abundant source of real life. From him alone comes the never-ending supply of living water, life that is stronger than death. And only in the intimate fellowship with the living God, through Jesus, will we ever overcome death and live the life that is truly the never-ending good and perfect life.

And there is still more. John's final vision is full of great pictures of life in God's glorious future. There is also *the tree of life*. We hear about such a tree in the Old Testament as well (Genesis 2 and 3). Here, in line with Ezekiel 47, it sounds like there are many trees. The rivers and streets of the New Jerusalem are lined with rows of trees, trees of life. It is a picture of a garden, a park with tree-lined avenues.

We see Paradise restored, but then in a way that goes far beyond the bounds of the first paradise. God's new creation is a marvellous orchard of trees-of-life in the midst of a huge city that fills the new world.

Indeed, that is what it is, an orchard. These are all fruit trees. But these are the most miraculous fruit trees you have ever seen; twelve times per year they produce an abundant crop of fruit, and twelve kinds of fruit (see also Ezekiel 47:12).

What an incredibly encouraging image of God's loving care as he ushers his church into eternal life. When Christ returns, his completed church will be there, gathered from all over the world as the New Jerusalem; a huge city with a multitude of inhabitants, too many to count. And no one will get hungry or thirsty, ever!

33 • Revelation 21:22-22:5

These amazing fruit trees are the permanent source of nourishment that sustains all the folks in the holy city for ever and ever. It is a symbol. And it shows us that in Jesus, God himself will sustain the good life of his children in ways beyond our wildest dreams and imagination.

But these trees not only provide food. *The leaves were for the healing of the nations.*

We know that God's new creation will be free from all misery. In that sense, strictly speaking, the nations, the people that inhabit the New Jerusalem, do not need healing.

But in this way John's final vision reinforces again the deep contrast between the world as we know it today, filled with suffering, pain and death with the future world filled with the fullness of life. The fullness of eternal life God has in store for us will take care of everything we struggle with today. He will remove the scars. He guarantees your physical and spiritual wholeness.

So, step by step, we get this grandiose picture of the good life that is coming when God completes his building project, his church, and brings us all together in his new world.

And here is the deep meaning of all this. Look at 22:3a. Here is what makes this grand project of Paradise Restored possible. *No longer will there be anything accursed…*

Do you remember God's devastating curse that struck the world after we fell into sin? Because of the sacrifice of Jesus Christ, it has been abolished. Gone forever! Recognize the superabundant character of your salvation in Christ; Genesis 3:14–19 will be totally reversed. Man's exile from paradise will be entirely undone. No one in the New Jerusalem will ever be on his way to death and destruction.

Are you still with this? Your God promises you a new world, a world which he shows you as a huge city, which is at the same time a most beautiful and lush garden that sustains life abundantly. It is a city that is totally different from all the cities we know. Our inner cities are often dark and depressing places but not gardens.

Live the good life in the New Jerusalem

Here is the question: What makes this city so entirely different; a place where huge crowds live the good life in paradise restored?

Here is your answer: in the very centre of the holy city, the new heaven and the new earth is *the throne of God and the Lamb*. It is the grand throne of Rev. 4. This throne, evidence of God's Majesty, Authority and Power will be the heart of the New Jerusalem.

Everything and everyone in the city, and that means everything and everyone in the glorified church, depends on the sovereign power of God's deep love in Jesus. He gives life. He sustains life. He brings about the beauty of his new creation. He distributes the blessings of his grace.

What does that mean for those who will live in the New Jerusalem, those who will live the good life in paradise restored? What is that going to mean for you and me, when we enter the holy city, where the throne of God and the Lamb is in the centre?

John lists five things.

1. *His servants will worship him* [3b]. The sole purpose, the ultimate goal of the servants of God and of the Lamb Jesus Christ, that is you and me and all believers, will be nothing more and nothing less than serving, worshipping God Almighty and the exalted Christ for ever and ever. How? Always, everywhere and in whatever you do. It is going to be your joy that his desire is going to be your deepest desire. You are going to fill the New Jerusalem with never-ending praise and worship to the glory of God's name. And if that is what we are going to do, we better start practicing today.

2. *They*, the believers, *will see his face* [4a]. In a most intimate relationship, you will enjoy God's love; you will experience his goodness and gracious presence; and you will know him as never before. This is a magnificent promise. The full awareness of direct and personal communion with God will be yours. Here is what the good life in the New Jerusalem is really all about. It will not get more awesome than that.

3. *His name will be on their foreheads* [4b]. It will be abundantly clear that he claims you for himself. He expects you to be fully dedicated to him at all times in whatever it is you will be busy with.

4. *The Lord God will be their light* [5b]. Twenty-four hours a day, seven days a week, you will walk in the bright light of God's glory, and you will never tire of it. For it means that the frightening darkness of today will be gone forever. And you will not need any other light to find your way in life.

5. *And they will reign forever and ever* [5c]. Yes, indeed, you will share in his royal glory and power as kings and queens in your Father's new creation.

Do you not feel overwhelmed when you try to fathom the depth of your Father's love and grace in your Saviour Jesus Christ? Try to imagine what all this will be like. Oh – to see him face to face…!

34

Revelation 22: 6 – 21

REMEMBER CHRIST'S URGENT MESSAGE: I AM COMING SOON

We have come to the end of the Book of Revelation. Rev.22:5 marks the end of John's visions on this remarkable Lord's Day on the island of Patmos. What did we all see and hear? And what do we do with this? Let us have a quick look at the big picture.

The Bible tells us the story that begins with the Tree-of-life in Paradise, and that ends with the Tree-of-life in the New Jerusalem. From a literary viewpoint you can picture it in a U-shaped form. After paradise, the corruption of sin and evil sends everything down toward disaster and destruction.

But Jesus Christ comes, and through his messianic restoration God reverses this, as he had promised right away. By his grace, the course of history goes upward again, toward a new heaven and a new earth. And as this goes on, people in this world are called to break with Satan, the Beasts, to repent from the values and beliefs of Babylon (the world that resists God and his plans), and to follow the Lamb Jesus Christ in the new exodus to the new Promised Land.

Revelation has given us the view from above on the final episode of this journey to God's renewed creation. Then all evil will be removed, the damaged universe will be completely repaired, and God and man will live together in eternal joy and harmony. All that is now needed is for Jesus Christ to come again.

The passage we look at here, is some sort of epilogue to all this. It is a final opportunity to reinforce the message of John's visions. And the whole passage is dominated by Jesus' final promise that he is coming soon. He repeats it three times. That makes it an important reminder.

Trust the promise

After he has taken him on a tour around New Jerusalem, explaining here and there what he was seeing, the angel of Rev. 21:9 assures the apostle John in 22:6 that what he has seen and heard is *trustworthy and true*.

He talks, of course, about what he has shown and explained to John about God's holy city (Rev. 21 and 22). But it is more than that. He confirms all of Revelation as 'true and trustworthy', the whole content of this book.

How do we know that? Listen to what he says next: *God has sent his angel to show his servants what must soon take place*. We have come full circle. This is the same expression the apostle uses in Rev. 1:1 when he starts recording all his visions. And in line with Jesus' instruction to John in Rev. 1:11, 'write what you see in a book', we now have this 'trustworthy and true' book.

Now here is an interesting observation: in this passage the expression "this book" is used seven times (v.7, 9, 10, 18[twice] and 19 [twice]). That tells us that we are at the end of John's visions. This is the closing paragraph that wraps up the whole book, and all the speakers here talk about everything God has revealed in those visions.

As we journeyed through the Book of Revelation we have seen and heard many different things. And not everything was always so easily accessible. But the message is reliable. All these events make clear one thing: Jesus Christ is coming. He will punish God's enemies and win the final victory over all sin, evil and wickedness. And that promise you can trust.

But how do you know for sure? Throughout history many people have tried to predict the future. So why are the things we have found here true and reliable? Well, this book comes from him, who is called *the God of the spirits of the prophets.*

In the Old Testament, God authorized men like Isaiah, Ezekiel, Zechariah and many others to bring his message to his people. The spirit of these prophets were under his constant guidance and control. This separated them from false prophets.

The same God is the driving force here. He is the source of all the things we have seen and heard throughout Revelation. The Holy God himself is the author of this book. And that makes it true and absolutely trustworthy.

But this angel is not the only witness. Suddenly we hear the voice of a second witness, the glorified Christ himself (v.7). And he reinforces the words of the angel, indeed, the book of Revelation is true and trustworthy.

Behold, I am coming soon, he says. He will repeat this announcement two more times, with increasing emphasis (v.12 and 20). "Behold", please, pay attention! That is how urgent it is to remember what this book is all about.

Sometimes we struggle a bit with the word "soon". This promise was made about 2000 years ago. What do you mean, 'soon'? But the point is not that we should be able to put it on a human timetable. Revelation speaks about things that are already in process today. Since Jesus' resurrection and ascension into heaven we are in the final stage of the history of God's redemption. There is one more event to come and wrap up everything. But you and I, we do not know when he will return. So, we better be watchful, all the time!

But he **is** coming! This is so trustworthy that Jesus calls you "blessed" if you keep these words. The glorified Christ qualifies the book of Revelation as "prophecy". We hear again that this is God's own message. Trust his promise and be blessed.

Realize that *keeping the words of the prophecy of this book* is not just a matter of keeping them on a bookshelf, or just listening. Take these words to heart. Apply them in your life and live by them, every day. Keep them alive so that the promise of Jesus' return determines your choices and actions, your hope and perspective. Think of the words of the apostle Peter. *Since all these things are thus to be dissolved, what sort of people ought you to be in lives of holiness and godliness…, since you are waiting for these things, be diligent to be found by him without spot or blemish, and at peace* (2 Peter 3:11–14). If you do that, you are blessed; you are to be congratulated. Your future is secure.

And then the third witness takes the stand. In v.8 the apostle John himself speaks up to confirm what both the angel and Jesus have said. He has seen a lot of spectacular visions. He has heard many powerful words. And now he testifies that the words of this book are trustworthy and true indeed, because it is an accurate record of everything I saw and heard.

The book of Revelation is not made up by a man with a bizarre fantasy. It has not been assembled from ancient religious mythology. It is not the brainchild of a man whose imagination has spun out of control. No, no, it is a trustworthy report of reliable ear- and eyewitnesses, three of them!

When God wants to assure us that his message is absolutely trustworthy, he pulls out all the stops, so to speak. He calls three witnesses: his angel, his Son, and his apostle. And they all say the same things. They all confirm, they all guarantee the truth and the reliability of what we have seen and heard in John's visions.

And as all these events unfold, during our journey through the centuries toward the return of Jesus Christ, we can trust that the prophecy of this last book of the Bible is a reliable guide. It is so reliable that we can have absolute certainty in the trustworthiness of God's promise.

Yes, the storms are raging in this world. Watch a bit of TV news for a week, and you see it come by on your screen: wickedness, evil, hatred, violence, cruelty, war, terrorism, infectious diseases, political uncertainty, and economic instability, etc. No wonder many people live in fear. But in this world full of insecurity, always remember, God's promise is sure.

Jesus Christ is coming, and he will right all wrongs. He will make straight what is crooked. He will heal what is broken.

It is overwhelming when you come to think of it; as it was for John. He tells us that he was so totally perplexed, that he makes the same mistake as in Rev. 19. He goes down on his knees to worship the angel who is still with him. But this angel was only his tour-guide, just a fellow-servant. "Stop that," he says. "No one is worthy of worship but God alone. You and I, we only testify to the truth of his Word."

HEED THE WARNING

In that role the angel continues. Yes, in the v.10–15 the three witnesses speak again. God's promises are so reliable, you can trust them always. But that makes it also important to emphasize the warning not to ignore or reject what you find in the book of Revelation. And so God's angel, God's Son and God's apostle are coming again, now to urge us to heed this warning. There is much at stake.

As the angel continues, he wants to make sure that we all remember how urgent it is to keep alive the prophetic words of this book. We cannot afford putting off responding to what God shows and tells us in Revelation. God's message claims the central place in our lives. And we have to give it that place, now.

That is why the angel instructs John clearly: *Do not seal up the words of the prophecy of this book.* Here is a remarkable connection with the Old Testament. The prophet Daniel was told the opposite: "close up and seal the words you have heard till the time of the end" (Daniel 12:4; see also 12:8-9). Daniel had heard things about a distant future; things that would still be a long time in coming.

But that is different here, since the coming of Jesus Christ. He was worthy to open the scroll and break its seals to unfold God's plan of salvation (Rev. 5). And therefore, "what you have seen and heard, John, should not be kept secret. It must be proclaimed everywhere." The message of Revelation is urgent and should be heard by as many people as possible.

Why? Because now *the time is near*. It must soon take place. Yes, even as we are talking, God's prophecies are being fulfilled. John's visions are being realized, as we are moving closer to the day of Jesus' return.

This makes the message of Revelation utterly relevant for the church in these last days, the days between Jesus' ascension and his promised return, to be proclaimed, to be studied and explained during the journey to the New Jerusalem.

Everyone needs to know that now is the time to make choices. Now is the time to show your allegiance to God and to commit yourself to following Jesus Christ. Whose side are you on? You can no longer ignore it. Time is running out.

This is serious business. The angel underlines this with v.11: *Let the evildoer still do evil, and the filthy still be filthy, and the righteous still do right, and the holy still be holy.*

Now it almost sounds as if, when you make a choice between listening or not listening to God's Word, you will be stuck with the dramatic consequences. As if in this life no one can repent. You make your bed, you lay in it.

But that is not the point. On the contrary, you can repent. You can turn away from a dead-end road. In fact, these words are an urgent appeal to do just that, to repent from sin and evil, and turn to Jesus Christ when you still have the opportunity. Otherwise things may go from bad to worse in your life.

This is such a stark warning to keep away from evil because there is no standing still on the way of sin. Realize, if you persistently refuse to listen to the message of God's Word, if you continue to ignore it and defile yourself, if that is what you want, you can keep going. No one is going to stop you by force.

But then be aware of this: if hearing God's Word does not make you change the course of your life, it will do the opposite. It will fix you more firmly and deeper in the course you have chosen. And if that continues, then the moment will come that God himself will say, 'let him be.' Then it will indeed be too late. And if you pass that point of no return, there will not be a second chance! So, heed the warning, now!

With what he says about "the righteous" and "the holy", the angel is urging those who believe in Jesus Christ to remain strong and faithful. Under oppression God's children can easily lose heart and be tempted to compromise. But do not be distracted, he warns. Do not give in when the going gets tough. Do not flirt with sin and evil, but persevere in doing what you are doing by God's grace and the power of the Holy Spirit. Trust in God to give you strength for the journey.

So, yes, heed the warning, and do it now. Your Saviour is coming soon. Do not postpone the choices God wants you to make. In the book of Revelation, he puts these choices right in front of us. What do we do? In a world in which many do not care so much about God's Word, but rather go by what they feel, to this world God says that there are only two ways and two destinations.

And then we hear again the voice of the glorified Christ. He repeats with even more emphasis his urgent message: *Behold,* please, pay attention. *I am coming soon.* And to confirm the serious warning of the angel, he adds: *bringing my recompense with me, to repay everyone for what he has done.*

"Remember," says Jesus, "the whole book of Revelation tells you that my coming is real and close. And when I arrive, I will arrive with my rewards. On that same day, the great day of the last Judgment, these will be distributed right away. Everyone will then receive in accordance with his or her works, eternal punishment or eternal life".

No, that does not mean that you are saved by what you are doing. The Bible is clear on that. Sinners are saved only by God's grace in Jesus Christ. But sinners are not saved in order to continue to live in sin. No, in this life already you may begin to live a holy life in thankfulness. It will not give you a basis for eternal joy, but it does show the genuineness of your faith.

Do you live by grace in gratitude? That is what God is looking for. And in his mercy he is pleased to reward that. And yes, today there will be remaining imperfections and sinful inclinations that make God's children stumble. Turn to Jesus every day, and all this will be covered by his blood.

But the point is that your and my choices today will have eternal consequences. And the day of reckoning is rapidly approaching. Then there will be no more delay. Then justice will be done, and grace will be shown in Jesus Christ.

That is why Jesus wants to convince us: "Do not harden yourself in unbelief," he says. All the promises and punishments you have been confronted with in Revelation, take them seriously. Heed my warning words. They have eternal significance.

Why is that? "Well," says Jesus, *I am the Alpha and the Omega, the first and the last, the beginning and the end*. In Revelation you will find these words also in 1:8 and 21:6, both times as titles of God Almighty. But here Jesus assures us with his claims that "I have the same power, the same glory, the same majesty and authority. I am God Almighty!"

Indeed, that's your Saviour Jesus Christ. He is the beginning and the final goal of everything. He was before everything and he will be there when everything is gone. He survives everything and everyone. "And I will see you soon," he says.

Therefore, heed the warning! Do not ignore him who is on his way, with his rewards with him. Your access to the New Jerusalem is at stake.

And the apostle John, the third witness, who responds again to the voice of Christ (v.14, 15), can only reinforce this. "Always remember," he says, "there are only two ways and only two destinations."

Here is the one (v14): *Blessed are those who wash their robes*. "Robes" stands for your life as it is affected by what you think, say, and do. Now your "robe" is naturally dirty, filthy, stained by sin. You will find the same image in the Old Testament (Zechariah 3:3).

And in this world nothing can clean it, absolutely nothing.

Only God provides the remedy. "Washing your robe" means turning to Jesus Christ, and the cleansing power of his blood. Only his sacrifice removes all my sin and guilt.

Note here that John does not talk about those "who *have* washed...", but "those who wash..." – present tense! Let it be an ongoing action-item in your life. Tap into God's forgiving grace in Jesus, day after day as we journey to the new Promised Land. And you will be blessed when you enter God's New Jerusalem by the open gates.

And here is the other one (v.15): But *outside are the dogs*... For us dogs are popular pets; 'Man's best friend'. But in the ancient Middle East the many stray dogs were not only a nuisance, they were also filthy carrion-eaters that live at the garbage-dump. Do not touch them, they carry diseases.

And so in the Bible the word 'dog' became an abusive characteristic for wicked folk who reject God, and who show utter disdain for his word. And then John gives a list of people who do just that. They refuse to heed Christ's urgent warning, and they live as if his impending coming is nothing but a fairy-tale.

SPREAD THE WORD

What do <u>we</u> do with all these things, this urgent message of Christ: *I am coming soon*? What does God want us to do with it?

In v.16 the glorified Christ speaks again, this time to remind us of his intention with all this: *I, Jesus, have sent my angel to testify to you about these things for the churches.*

Here is the goal, the purpose: Jesus had the churches in mind when he showed John all these visions, had them explained by an angel, and then recorded in a book.

Revelation is a testimony for the churches.

When we hear this, we immediately think of the seven churches in Asia Minor. They are listed in Rev. 1 and are separately addressed in Rev. 2 and 3. They were the first recipients.

But that is not where it stops. All the churches of Christ, of all places and all times, need to hear this grand news of Jesus' final victory, and his urgent message *I am coming soon*. And so it comes to us today.

Isn't it amazing when you think of that? Jesus says to you and to me: "my dear friends in…… [*fill in where you live*] ………, in all the things you have seen and heard in this book of Revelation, I was thinking of you and of your future. And I am coming soon to be with you!"

"Trust me, for I am the promised King from the ancient royal house of David. *I am the bright morning star*". When the light of other stars is fading at the break of dawn, the morning star is the last one to shine brightly.

When you see it, you know the night is almost over, a new day is near.

The world as we know it, is coming to its end. But in Jesus a new era is arriving. The day of his complete victory and full salvation is near. This makes it such an urgent message, not just for the church, but for this whole world: *Behold, I am coming soon!*

All this makes it urgent for the churches that have been given these prophetic words of Revelation, to spread the Word that Jesus is coming.

Indeed, as church of Jesus Christ, driven by the Holy Spirit, together with everyone who hears this grand message, we must never stop issuing this call: "Come."

In v.17 the Bride (which is the well-known image of the Church), and the Spirit (which is the Holy Spirit, who dwells **in** the Church), together with those who heard the message, are pictured as calling out with one voice, "Come."

Quite often this is seen as a prayer for Jesus' return. And that is not impossible of course. But then we have a surprise twist in the second part of v.17: *let the one who is thirsty come*. This third "come" is clearly a call to come to Jesus and be saved. However, nowhere does v.17 indicate this as a switch from calling for Jesus to come again to calling people to come to faith.

And so it makes more sense to read 'come' all three times in the same way. Driven by the Holy Spirit, the church of Jesus Christ has this message for the world: 'Come! Come to faith and follow Jesus. Come and join us on our journey to the new Promised Land. Break with Satan and his evil henchmen. Break with the culture of the day that ignores or hates God's prophetic words. Trust his promise, the promise of a bright future in the kingdom of Jesus Christ. He is coming soon to usher in his new heaven and new earth, his New Jerusalem.'

As long as you have the opportunity, let people know that everyone who is thirsty for hope and longing for salvation may come and take and drink *the water of life without price.* We have read about the 'water of life' before. It stands for the abundance of God's grace and love in Jesus. The New Jerusalem is filled with it (Rev. 22:1).

And yes, it is for free (compare Isaiah 55:1-2). It costs you nothing because Jesus Christ paid for it. In him you will find your joy, your happiness, your life and salvation by grace alone. Do you hear the deep and tender love of your God calling? "Are you thirsty for this? Come, do not hesitate." Do you meet people who are thirsty for this? Bring them to the water of life.

If it is so important to spread this Word, if it is so important to let people know about God's glorious future in Jesus, if it is so urgent to get the message of Revelation out that Jesus is winning and that he is coming soon, then you also understand the warning in v.18 and 19 to leave the words of this book intact as it was given.

Tampering with the things God has made known to us will make the message powerless. So, let no one add to it or take away from it. God's Word does not need to be updated or improved. Do not believe people who claim to have received new revelations. Do not trust folks who question or deny the trustworthiness of this book, or those who distort or twist its message, because they do not like what it says.

The consequences for people who do this will be disastrous. You will not share in the promised blessings, but you will experience the promised punishments.

So yes, spread the Word as it has been given to us. And let us remind each other of the urgent Biblical message as it finds its culmination point in Revelation: "Jesus is coming. And he is coming soon!"

Christ himself assures us of this for the third and now the very last time (v.20): *Surely, I am coming soon.* I promise to make haste to come and get here.

We are coming to the end of Revelation, which is the end of the Bible. When you close the book let it ring in your ears and echo in your heart, loud and clear: "Jesus my Lord is coming soon. And I will see him, face to face"

Then you will also join John in his response on behalf of the churches, on behalf of everyone who hears these words, who reads this book, on behalf of you and me, a response filled with joy, hope and longing: *Amen! Come, Lord Jesus...*

"We are on our way to your wedding banquet, Lord; on our way to your holy city.

And we cannot wait to get there and see you in your glory on the day that you will rent the sky asunder, appearing on the clouds of heaven".

Is this your deep longing today? Or is it often fading in the background because of everything else you are so busy with?

Keep it alive. March on from day to day, carried by the grace of the Lord Jesus, with the prayer in your heart and on your lips: *Maranatha – Come, Lord Jesus.*

BIBLIOGRAPHY

There is an enormous amount of literature about the Book of Revelation. This list is only a very small part of it. The reader will notice that the majority of these resources are in Dutch. This may not be helpful for most readers. However, I received my training for the ministry in Kampen, The Netherlands at the Theological College (now University) of the Reformed Churches (liberated) in The Netherlands and then served two congregations in that country. After this we immigrated to Canada to serve another two congregations. This journey is reflected in my library, and thus in this bibliography.

Aune, David E., *Revelation. Series Word Biblical Commentary.* Nashville: Thomas Nelson Publishers. Vol.1: 1997; Vol.2 & 3: 1998.

Bavinck, J. H., *En voort wentelen de eeuwen. Gedachten over het boek der Openbaring van Johannes.* Wageningen: N.V. Gebr. Zomer en Keuning Uitgeversmaatschappij, (1952).

Beale, G. K., *The Book of Revelation. A Commentary on the Greek Text, series NIGTC.* Grand Rapids MI / Cambridge UK: William B. Eerdmans Publ. Comp., 1999.

Boersma, Tj., *Middenin De Eindstrijd. Een practische uitleg van Openbaring.* Barneveld: De Vuurbaak, 1992.

Bremmer, R. H., *Visioenen op Patmos. Beknopte Bijbelstudies.* Groningen: De Vuurbaak, 1982.

Greijdanus, S., *De Openbaring des Heeren aan Johannes. Serie Kommentaar op het Nieuwe Testament.* Amsterdam: H.A. van Bottenburg, 1925.

Gunning J.Hz, J. H., *Het Boek der Toekomst. De Openbaring van Johannes voor de Gemeente des Heeren toegelicht.* Utrecht: Kemink & Zoon, 1900.

Hartog, A. H. de, *Openbaring van Johannes.* Amsterdam: Uitgeversmaatschapppij Holland, 1935.

Hendriksen, William, *More than Conquerors. An interpretation of the Book of Revelation*. Grand Rapids MI: Baker Book House, 1992.

Kamp, H. R. van de, *Israel in Openbaring*. Kampen: J.H. Kok, 1990.

Kamp, H. R. van de, *Openbaring. Profetie vanaf Patmos. Serie Commentaar op het Nieuwe Testament*. Kampen: Uitgeverij Kok, 2000.

Miskotte, Dr. K. H., *Hoofdsom der Historie*. Nijkerk: C.F. Callenbach N.V., 1944/1945.

Moor, J. C. de, *De Hemel Geopend*. Kampen: J. H. Kok, 1926.

Mounce, Robert. H., *The Book of Revelation. Series NICNT*. Grand Rapids MI: William B. Eerdmans Publishing Co., 1977

Poythress, Vern S., *The Returning King. A guide to the Book of Revelation*. Philipsburg, NJ: P&R Publishing, 2000.

Resseguie, James L., *The Revelation of John. A Narrative commentary*. Grand Rapids MI: Baker Academic, 2009.

Ringnalda, A, *De Openbaring van Johannes*. Kampen: J.H. Kok N.V., 1962.

Thomas, D., *Let's Study Revelation*. The Banner of Truth Trust, 2008.

Venema, Cornelis P., *The Promise of the Future*. The Banner of Truth Trust, 2000.

Visser, A. J., *De Openbaring van Johannes. Serie De Prediking van het Nieuwe Testament*. Nijkerk: C.F Callenbach N.V., Uitgever, 1965.

Vuyst, J. de, *De structuur van de apokalyps*. Kampen: J.H. Kok, 1968.

Waal, C. van der, *Oudtestamentische Priesterlijke Motieven in de Apocalyps*. Goes: Oosterbaan & Le Cointre N.V., 1956.

Waal, C. van der, *Openbaring van Jesus Christus, Inleiding en Vertaling*. Groningen: De Vuurbaak, 1971.

Walfoort, John F., *The Revelation of Jesus Christ*. Chicago: Moody Press, 1966.

STUDY SUGGESTIONS AND QUESTIONS

Due to the size it can be a bit daunting to use this book as a study-guide for a Bible Study Group. There are others. In *Let's Study Revelation* Derek Thomas gives a scheme for studying Revelation (with the help of his book) that covers 13 weeks. This is convenient for one study season, but then there is much material to deal with in each session, which can also become overwhelming. Using for this purpose the book you have in your hands is not impossible, and to facilitate this somewhat I have added to every chapter four questions.

A helpful study pattern could be:

- Pray for the Spirit's guidance.
- Read at home the Bible passage to be studied before turning to the chapter in this book, or other literature.
- Write down questions and/or comments that come to mind when reading the passage.
- After this read the chapter in this book, and write down questions and/or comments.
- In this way your study group will most likely have more to discuss than just the four questions given.

Chapter 1 – Revelation 1:1-8

1. In many ways Revelation is a unique book in the New Testament. Despite the many references to other parts, it is unlike any other writing in Scripture. Describe what sets it apart from, let's say a gospel or a letter from Paul, in what it presents in those graphic pictures?

2. Verse 1 speaks about *the things that must soon take place*. What are the implications of the word 'must'? What does that tell us about what is happening in the world today as what appears to be the result of political decisions, economic planning, military strategy, or of just human wisdom or foolishness in general?

3. Do you really believe that *the time is near*, as it says in verse 3? How does this affect your priorities in life today, but also your activities with a long-term focus, for instance your education, your career or raising your children?
4. In v.4 and 5 God greets the churches. Quite often the same words are used to greet you and welcome you in church every Sunday. It implies that God himself is greeting you and welcoming you with these words when you come to worship. Explain why this is significant and discuss how this affects you.

Chapter 2 – Revelation 1:9-20

1. In v.9 we hear the word *tribulation*. It reflects that in the last days, the days between Jesus' 1st and 2nd coming, the world is often a hostile place for those who believe in Jesus Christ. Find passages elsewhere in the New Testament that illustrate and affirm this.
2. How are you comforted and encouraged in what is going on in your life and in this world by the various details of the vision of the glorified Christ as John describes those in the verses 12 – 16?
3. John's vision of the glorified Christ causes him to *fall at his feet as though dead*. Christ then lays his hand on him and says, *fear not* (v.17). Explain what this tells you about how we should experience our relationship with Christ, and how we should worship him.
4. What makes 'golden lampstands' (v.12 and 20) a fitting image for churches? And why the plural and not just one golden lampstand as image of the one universal church?

Chapter 3 – Revelation 2:1-7

1. Are there any aspects of the church-life in Ephesus Christ is pointing at, either negative or positive, that you can also identify in the church you belong to? If so, discuss what they are and how you should deal with these.
2. Can you, and dare you, identify what drives you, either personally or as congregation, in your Christian life and in your activities in the church, but also as church?

3. Sometimes Christians make a contrast between defending and promoting purity of doctrine, rejecting false teaching and applying discipline on the one hand, and being a church where love and social compassion are in the centre of everything we do. It is often seen as traditional, conservative versus contemporary and outreach-minded. Is it correct to contrast those things? Explain why or why not. Can you appeal to this letter to Ephesus for this?

4. Seven times we read in Revelation that John was *in the Spirit* and that he saw and heard things *in the Spirit*. What do you think it means "to be in the Spirit"? Discuss the question whether God might use the same experience today to communicate with people.

Chapter 4 – Revelation 2:8-11

1. Are there any aspects of the church-life in Smyrna Christ is pointing at, either negative or positive, that you can also identify in the church you belong to? If so, discuss what they are and how you should deal with these.

2. In Smyrna, the Christians were facing severe persecution. This is a significant aspect of the Christian life throughout history, and is still the case in many parts of the world. What do you think is the secret of believers who remain steadfast and strong in their faith under serious threats? Think of the story of Polycarp.

3. Have you ever experienced negative reactions to your Christian faith and/or Christian life? How did you or would you handle that and deal with it? What makes it hard not to compromise your faith?

4. In the political and economic situations we find ourselves in, here in North America, we enjoy much prosperity, as well as freedom to worship and serve the Lord. Does the call of Christ: *Be faithful unto death...* mean anything for us? Can we do anything with it today?

Chapter 5 – Revelation 2:12-17

1. Are there any aspects of the church-life in Pergamum Christ is pointing at, either negative or positive, that you can also identify in the church you belong to? If so, discuss what they are and how you should deal with these.

2. Satan is described as sitting on a throne. He claims to rule and to be in control, opposing God's rule and authority. He wants us to be loyal to him. How does he do this in the world today? And what does he do to back up his claim? What does Christ's ascension into heaven teach us about his claim?
3. Where else in the New Testament do you find warnings against a compromising attitude towards the world? Why is the purity of the church, when it comes to doctrine and Christian life, also important for each of you personally?
4. Where else in the New Testament do you find a reference to a *two-edged sword*? How does this verse help you understand what Christ is saying here in the verses 12 and 16 to the believers in Pergamum and to believers today?

Chapter 6 – Revelation 2:18-29

1. Are there any aspects of the church-life in Thyatira Christ is pointing at, either negative or positive, that you can also identify in the church you belong to? If so, discuss what they are and how you should deal with these.
2. What does it look like today, in our time, to face the dilemma: if I want my business to be successful I should actually make decisions and do things that meet the requirements or expectations of our culture, but may be contrary to God's Word. How do you handle such situations? Does the New Testament have anything to say about this?
3. Do we still have prophets or prophetesses today through whom God gives us new revelations? If someone claims this, should we believe him or her? Why or why not?
4. Read Acts 5:1-11. Why were Ananias and Sapphira killed in the church in Jerusalem? And what was God's intention by doing this? How should we apply this today?

Chapter 7 – Revelation 3:1-6

1. Are there any aspects of the church-life in Sardis Christ is pointing at, either negative or positive, that you can also identify in the

church you belong to? If so, discuss what they are and how you should deal with these.
2. How can a dead church become alive again? Describe the differences between a dead church and a church that is alive. How do you find out?
3. Some interpretations of the Book of Revelation (and other passages in the New Testament that speak about Jesus' return) talk about 'the rapture'. This is the view that Jesus will come to take the true believers up to heaven, before 'the hour of trial', also called 'the great tribulation', after which he will return to judge. What do you think about this idea, and how would this impact our faith life?
4. How can the Book of Revelation help us today to apply, in our lives, passages like Ephesians 6:10-18; Matt. 25:1-13; John 17; Colossians. 1:15-23; 1 Thess. 5:1-11?

Chapter 8 – Revelation 3:7-13

1. Are there any aspects of the church-life in Philadelphia Christ is pointing at, either negative or positive, that you can also identify in the church you belong to? If so, discuss what they are and how you should deal with these.
2. Compare the promise in Revelation 3:9 with what the apostle Paul writes in Romans 11. Some Christians believe that the Jews still have a privileged position as God's Old Testament covenant people, and that there is a special promise of a general conversion of the Jewish people. Discuss.
3. When the church is facing opposition in this world – something we are seeing and hearing more and more – Christian believers need to be reassured and encouraged. What are the ways in which the glorified Christ is doing this here in this passage?
4. How does the letter to the church in Philadelphia encourage us to be actively involved in mission and evangelism?

Chapter 9 – Revelation 3:14-22

1. Are there any aspects of the church-life in Laodicea Christ is pointing at, either negative or positive, that you can also identify in the

church you belong to? If so, discuss what they are and who you should deal with these.

2. What does it mean to be *lukewarm*? And how can we help each other to avoid a lukewarm attitude toward God, toward the church and toward each other?

3. What is the wrong thinking behind the use of Revelation 3:20 to stimulate evangelism activities in the church?

4. In all these seven letters we hear close to the end or right at the end the words *he who has an ear, let him hear what the Spirit says to the churches.* What is the intention of this phrase, which is apparently important enough to stress this to all the churches?

Chapter 10 – Revelation 4

1. At the end of all seven letters the glorified Christ promises various blessings to *the one who conquers*. What does he mean by that? And what or who are we to conquer? And how are we supposed to do this?

2. John's vision in Revelation 4 is pretty amazing. What does it mean for us and how should it impact us that God is supremely holy? How should the worship in heaven we read about, impact the manner in which we worship this holy God?

3. When the 24 elders represent the church in God's presence (verse 4), what does that tell us about the place and the role of the church in the last days (the time between Jesus' 1st and 2nd coming)? Does the fact that the church is represented by 'elders' teach us anything about the office of 'elder' in the church today?

4. Read Isaiah 6:1-3 and Ezekiel 1:4-28 and compare those descriptions with the description of the four living creatures in Revelation 4:6-8.

Chapter 11 – Revelation 5

1. How do we come to know God in Revelation 4 and 5? And what does 'worship' mean in the light of this chapter?

2. We read here about abundant worship: the 4 creatures, the 24 elders, myriads of angels, and joined by all God's earthly creatures. Is

there a connection, and if so, what kind of connection between this universal choir and how we worship God and sing to the praise of his glory?
3. The content of the scroll in Revelation 5 is an outline of God's judgment and salvation as these unfold in the last days, the time between Jesus' 1st and 2nd coming. In the visions of the rest of the book Christ is opening the seals one by one, and every time new things are happening. Can we look at current events in the world today and determine at which one of the seals (or trumpets or bowls) we are right now? Why or why not?
4. Why can we say that Revelation 5 is the key to understanding the whole book?

Chapter 12 – Revelation 6

1. What is the best way to explain the things we (and all people throughout the world) experience in light of what we read about the impact of the four horsemen and their activities in the verses 2 – 8? And what is the double purpose of those activities?
2. When the apostle John is given these visions he is *in the Spirit* and he can see and hear things he could not have seen and heard normally, with his physical eyes and ears. Does that mean that what he sees and hears is not real? Is there a difference – and if so, what would be the difference – between a dream and a vision?
3. People have different ideas as to what heaven looks like and how they imagine the souls of believers live on together with Christ in heaven. How does what we read in verses 10 and 11 help you to form an idea about this?
4. Verse 12 mentions *a great earthquake*. Where else in Scripture do you find references to great earthquakes as manifestation of God acting as Judge?

Chapter 13 – Revelation 7:1 – 8:5

1. Read Ezekiel 9. What would be the connection between this chapter and what we read in Revelation 7 about *sealing the servants of God on their foreheads*?

2. The list of the twelve tribes of Israel in the verses 5 – 8 is different from the list(s) in the Old Testament (like in Genesis 49). Find the differences and explain what you think the reason might be for those differences.
3. If *the prayers of the saints* (meaning: the believers or the church) are going to have such a major impact on what is going to happen on earth, what do you think was the content of these prayers? What did the believers pray for?
4. When we pray – either personally, as family or as church – we pray that God may bless mission, evangelism, and that the Holy Spirit may open hearts and minds for the gospel of Jesus Christ. Do we also pray for justice and righteousness? For Jesus' return and the coming of God's kingdom? For the Last Judgment? What should we pray for?

Chapter 14 – Revelation 8:6-13

1. Can we recognize the disasters, triggered by the first four trumpets, in the time in which we live? How does God want us to respond to these disasters?
2. How does Revelation 8 help us to respond to people that say: 'If God is responsible for, or even involved in all the terrible things that are happening in the world, I cannot believe in a cruel God like that'....?
3. Read Romans 8:18-25. How can this passage help us to understand what is happening in Revelation 8:6-13?
4. The disasters following the trumpet-blasts in Revelation 8:6-13 are at least partly the results of *the prayers of the saints*, the church (Revelation 8:3-5). What does this teach us about what the church should be praying for?

Chapter 15 – Revelation 9

1. What does Revelation 9:6 mean? What is the only way out of the human misery?
2. In verse 13 we hear about *a voice from the four horns of the golden altar before God*. In Revelation 6:9 this same altar was connected with the voices of the martyrs, and in 8:3,4 it is connected with the

prayers of the saints. What kind of connection could there be between the voice coming from this altar and the frightening and violent destruction that is unleashed by this voice here in Revelation 9? Can Christians pray for God's judgment over evil and wickedness?
3. How does God's love for the world and the joyful message of the Gospel, the good news of salvation in Jesus Christ – how does that fit with the picture of a God who inflicts the horrible terror of ruthless warfare on this world. What does this imply for the message of the church today?
4. Can we recognize what we read in the verses 20 and 21, as something that is happening in our society today? Should this stop us from reaching out in our society with the gospel of Jesus Christ? Why or why not?

Chapter 16 – Revelation 10

1. What is the purpose of the interlude in Revelation 10 and 11, between the blowing of the 6th and the 7th trumpet?
2. What is the meaning of the oath of the angel (see the verses 6-7) for us? Think of expressions like: *there will be no more delay*, and: *at the 7th trumpet call the mystery of God will be fulfilled.*
3. What does the symbolism of eating the scroll, as John is told to do in verse 9, mean for us? Read also Ezekiel 2:1 – 3:11.
4. Eating the scroll (verses 9 and 10) comes with the message that it will taste as sweet as honey, but that it will make John's stomach bitter. What does that tell us about the sweet and bitter things we will experience when the church will faithfully reach out into this world with the message of salvation by grace alone, the gospel of Jesus Christ?

Chapter 17 – Revelation 11:1-14

1. Read Zechariah 4. Why was this an encouraging vision for Israel after the exile? And how does it help us to see the encouragement for the church today in the vision of the two witnesses in Revelation 11?
2. In what way do the two witnesses resemble Moses and Elijah (see the verses 5 and 6)? Where else in the New Testament are these

names mentioned? Why are these names significant for the future of the church?
3. Read Revelation 11:13. In what way is this verse encouraging for the believers not to give up doing what…..?
4. The Christian church is a community of 'witnesses'. What does it mean to be a 'witness'? What is characteristic for 'witnessing' in the New Testament?

Chapter 18 – Revelation 11:15-19

1. In verse 18 we read about the effect of the fact that God Almighty, with the Glorified Christ, rules as King, and that the time has come for rewards and for judgments. How does (or how should) this affect your life today?
2. Is fact that Almighty God governs the whole world and everything that happens, including the things that are going on in our lives, comforting for you, or encouraging, or unsettling, or scary, or upsetting? Discuss God's sovereignty.
3. As Christians we have a deep desire for others to be saved by turning to Jesus Christ. At the same time there is also a strong longing for justice, for evil to be punished. How does the Book of Revelation help us to hold on to both?
4. When we reach out to people outside the church, do we make it clear that the Christian message is not only the good and happy news of salvation, but do we also share that it includes that the judgment of unrepentant wicked and evildoers is unavoidable?

Chapter 19 – Revelation 12

1. After Jesus' ascension into heaven (verse 5b) and the war mentioned in v. 7 and 8, it says in verse 8 that *there was no longer any place for them* [meaning: Satan and his angels] *in heaven*. Can you find indications in the Old Testament that this was still the case before this moment?
2. How do believers become conquerors of the power of Satan, as mentioned in verse 11? Look at the three ways given, and discuss how we can apply these in our lives as Christians.

3. In verse 16 it says that *the earth came to the help of the woman*. How does God use the earth, his creation to protect or sustain his church?
4. When the dragon [Satan] cannot destroy the church, he turns to the believers individually and personally (verse 17): *those who keep the commandments of God and hold to the testimony of Jesus*. See also 1 Peter 5: 8, 9. How can we personally protect ourselves against those attacks of Satan?

Chapter 20 – Revelation 13

1. The beast from the sea represents the evil, antichristian political powers, inspired by Satan to resist God's authority and driven by the desire to destroy God's work and God's people. How does this square with the words of the apostle Paul in Romans 13:1-7?
2. Imagine that the efforts of the two beasts will be successful, in the sense that they will be able to create a world without war, without poverty and hunger, without racism and other social injustice. Would that make the church, faith in God and in Jesus Christ, as well as Christian living superfluous? If you think so, why? If not, why not?
3. Read 2 Thessalonians 2:3-12 and 1 John 4:1-6. How do these passages help us better understand Revelation 13?
4. The ultimate difference between Christians and non-Christians is a difference in worldview. What is a worldview and what makes a Christian worldview different from other worldviews? In the big picture of God's plan and providence, what was the purpose of the coming of Jesus Christ in the world? How does this affect your worldview? And how does your worldview affect you personally?

Chapter 21 – Revelation 14:1-13

1. In reference to the beginning of this chapter (the story of Ryan Bell), what difference does God make in your life?
2. The 144,000, mentioned in Rev. 14, are called (v.4) *redeemed from mankind as firstfruits for God and the Lamb*. In the O.T. 'firstfruits' represent the whole harvest still to come (see Leviticus 23:9-14). Would this suggest that the 144,000 are only a fraction of the whole,

as Paul uses this expression in 1 Corinthians 15:20, where he calls Christ *the firstfruits of all the redeemed*? Would this imply that in the end all of mankind will be saved? Earlier (see Rev.7) we identified the 144,000 as all the redeemed. What is then here the meaning of the term 'firstfruits'? Compare James 1:18

3. What does it tell you about the world we live in, when Revelation emphasizes the contrast between "those who follow the beast" (13:3) and "those who follow the Lamb wherever he goes" (14:4)?

4. Could or should Rev. 14:7 be used as a theme for an evangelism or outreach campaign? Why or why not?

Chapter 22 – Revelation 14:14-20

1. The vision in this passage shows a separating harvest: the grain harvest leads to eternal joy, whereas the grape harvest leads to eternal wrath. What is the connection with Jesus' words in Matthew 25:31-46? This triggers difficult questions. What does it mean to follow Jesus Christ as Saviour, to live faithfully and obediently as he calls us to do? See also James 1:27. Explain the term 'social gospel'.

2. In Matthew 22:37-39 Jesus indicates that at the heart of Christian living is: loving God with all your heart, soul and mind, and next to this, loving your neighbour as yourself. What about all the people who do not believe in God and do not follow Jesus as Saviour, but who do live according to good Christian values (helping the poor and hungry, caring for refugees, homeless, victims of disasters, etc.). They may not love God, but they do love their neighbour. Can we emphasize the 2nd of these two commandments [love your neighbour] at the cost of the 1st one [love God]?

3. What is the task of the church? Changing the circumstances in people's lives or giving people hope for the future? If you think it's both, should one have priority over the other? If so, which one and why? How does Rev. 14:14-20 help you to answer this question?

4. How do we see God's patience, God's long-suffering in Rev. 14:14-20? Compare 2 Peter 3.

Chapter 23 – Revelation 15

1. In God's judgments, God's wrath, God answers the prayers of the martyrs (Rev. 6:9-11; Rev. 8:1-5) and the saints/believers for vengeance upon his enemies and upon those who persecute the church. How does Rev. 15 assure us that God is fair when he does this?
2. What is the different perspective between the seven seals and the seven trumpets on the one hand, and the seven bowls on the other hand?
3. How can you sing about God's wrath (as in Rev.15)?
4. Many Christians like to have Bible texts on the walls in their homes that speak about God's love and grace. But there is more to say about God. What does the song in Rev. 15:3-4 teach us about God?

Chapter 24 – Revelation 16

1. How do you defend your faith as a Christian, when you hear people say: 'How can you believe in a God who controls everything and who allows all the suffering and misery in the world to go on? For me that's evidence that there is no God!'?
2. In what is called "the battle of Armageddon" the Christian church is facing the hostile power of Satan. This can be in the form of violent persecution, but your faith can also be under attack in a much more subtle way. Have you read C. S. Lewis' *Screwtape Letters*? What should Christians watch out for?
3. The plagues in Egypt, described in Exodus 7 – 11, are in many ways similar to the plagues we hear about in Revelation. What is the connection?
4. How should we apply/put into practice what the glorified Christ urges Christian believers to do in Rev. 16:15? Look at Matthew 25:1-13; 1 Timothy 4:7b-8; Titus 2:11-13.

Chapter 25 – Revelation 17

1. The name Babel or Babylon we know from Genesis 11 and from Daniel 4. But the name is mentioned more often in the Bible, especially by the prophets. Consult a concordance to find out where.

How do these references help you to understand the symbolism of the use of this name in Revelation 17?

2. In this chapter Babylon is seen as the influential antichristian culture that lures people away from God and from Jesus Christ by controlling their moral choices. Discuss examples of how today's culture will try to do this.
3. Some see the woman or Babylon as a religious power, the apostate church that persecutes (or supports persecution of) the faithful church. There is an element of truth in this. Why?
4. What does it mean when this chapter wants us to remember that "little Babylons" operate also in our own heart?

Chapter 26 – Revelation 18

1. In v.4 the voice from heaven urgently calls the believers: *Come out of Babylon, my people, lest you take part in her sins, lest you share in her plagues.* What does this mean for Christian believers today, and how do you put this into practice?
2. Someone summarized the intention of v.4 in this way: "The church is in the world, but the world must never be in the church." Explain this statement.
3. How does Rev.18, so full of wrath, revenge, and destruction fit with the Christian message of love and forgiveness? How does v.20 fit here? Does it mean that Christians are called to malicious pleasure at the misfortunes of unbelievers?
4. Read Ezekiel 27 and 28. In Ezekiel's time Tyre was a wealthy and powerful city that was hostile towards Israel. What are aspects of the lament and prophecy Tyre that come back in Rev.18?

Chapter 27 – Revelation 19:1-10

1. Would those who live in heavenly glory with Christ be aware of the terrible fate of the wicked? And if that is the case, how can they rejoice when they see the horrors of God's judgments (v.3 and Rev. 18:20)? What is the key expression in this connection (v.2)?
2. We can have a hard time with the idea that heaven rejoices when God's wrath destroys the world. What does that tell us about our-

selves and about our perception of the biblical testimony to the character of God?

3. According to v.8 the Bride's wedding dress is made of 'fine linen', described as 'the righteous deeds of the saints'. At the same time it says that this dress is given to her. How does this help you understand what Paul writes in Philippians 2:12-13?

4. What difference does it make for your daily life if you either do, or do not believe in heaven or in a life after this earthly life?

Chapter 28 – Revelation 19:11-21

1. The Rider on the white horse is Christ and he is called "the Word of God". How does this help you to understand John 1:1-5 and 14?

2. Christ, the rider on the white horse, is called "The Word of God" and has a sharp sword coming out of his mouth. How does Hebrews 4:12 help you to understand what this part of the vision tells us about how Christ operates?

3. We like to stress how important it is to have a personal relationship with Jesus, who is full of compassion. We teach our children to love Jesus, because he loves them. We sing 'what a friend we have in Jesus'. Here we meet Jesus as a fierce warrior in a robe, stained with the blood of his enemies, master of the horrifying scene in v.21. What does that do to your relationship with him?

4. In Rev. 19 and 20 we read four times about "the lake of fire" (and sulphur). What is this lake of fire? Should we think of it as a literal fire? What are other images that the Bible uses to describe this place?

Chapter 29 – Revelation 20:1-10

1. Few parts of Scripture have been so hotly debated as what we read in Rev. 20 about the 1000 years that Satan is bound and that Christ reigns, joined by the souls of believers who have died. Many evangelical Christians in North America hold to the premillennial or postmillennial view of these events. Explain these views and discuss what the implications are for our expectations of the end time?

2. Read Matthew 12:22-30 [in particular v.29], and also Luke 10:17-18, and John 12:31-32. Could there be a possible link between Rev. 20:2 and these passages? How would that help you to understand the 1000 years period?
3. How can we see that today we live in this period of a thousand years and that Satan's power is indeed restrained?
4. What does this passage mean with: the 1st resurrection; the 2nd resurrection; the 1st death and the 2nd death?

Chapter 30 – Revelation 20:11-15

1. How do passages like Matthew 25:31-46, Romans 2:6-10 and 2 Corinthians 5:10 connect with Rev. 20:11-15?
2. In Rev. 19 and 20 we read how all the enemies of Christ are systematically eliminated. What is the significance of this for us today and for the future?
3. Today the reality of 'hell' as a place of never-ending punishment is not only rejected by those who do not believe in God or in an afterlife, but it is also heavily disputed by many Christians. How can a loving God punish eternally? What about the view that in the end everyone is going to be okay?
4. Those who do not believe that hell is a place of eternal punishment have sometimes turned to the idea of *annihilation* or to *universalism*. What do these terms mean and why are they consistent or inconsistent with Biblical teaching?

Chapter 31 – Revelation 21:1-8

1. The new heaven, the new earth, the new Jerusalem are obviously the very opposite of the old heaven, the old earth and the old Jerusalem. Explain the differences between the 'old' and the 'new', and also how the 'new' versions relate to the 'old' ones.
2. What kind of connection do you see between Rev. 21:1 and Genesis 1:1?
3. The saying *I am the Alpha and the Omega* is also found in Rev. 1:8. What does this tell us about the Book of Revelation and about the visions in this book?

4. Christians are looking forward to going to heaven when they die and be with Jesus. In Matthew 5:5 Jesus says that *the meek shall inherit the earth.* What is the significance of this beatitude for the expectation Christian believers should have about the future, in light of Rev. 21?

Chapter 32 – Revelation 21:9-21

1. This passage speaks a few times about God's glory in the New Jerusalem. How do we reflect God's glory as church today?
2. How should you reflect God's glory in what you say and do, today?
3. How does this passage of Revelation show the continuity between the Old Testament and the New Testament, and what does this mean for our view of the church?
4. What are going to be the most important differences between life as we know it now, and living on the new earth, based on the description in Rev. 21?

Chapter 33 – Revelation 21:22 - 22:5

1. Several visions in the book of Revelation offer us a glimpse of 'heaven'. Some claim that 'heaven' is not real, as in a particular location, but that it is a 'state-of-mind' or a 'spiritual experience'. Can you find other passages in Scripture that talk about 'heaven'? What do we learn from those?
2. Living in God's immediate presence and our direct communion with Him will be perfect in the New Jerusalem, but it is reality today already in Jesus Christ. How does that make you feel? And how does this impact your life?
3. In 1 Corinthians 15:24 we read about Jesus' return: *Then comes the end when he delivers the kingdom to God the Father after destroying every rule and every authority and power.* Does this mean that after the Last Day Jesus Christ will no longer be King? Compare this with Rev. 11:15; 19:16 and 20:4. See also Luke 1:33, as well as what the Nicene Creed says about Christ.

4. How can you be sure that your name is written in the Lamb's Book of Life, so that you will not be thrown into the lake of fire and sulphur (21:8 and 27, see also Rev. 20:15)?

Chapter 34 – Revelation 22:6-21

1. This last section of Revelation mentions seven times "this book", and stresses the reliability, the trustworthiness of this book, and therefore the urgent need to "keep this book" or "the prophecy of this book". Why is this so important and how do you do that?
2. In this closing section of Revelation the glorified Christ stresses three times: *I am coming soon*. Does that strengthen you in your faith? How? Compare 2 Peter 3:1-9 and 1 Corinthians 15:58. And what does this mean for the task of the church in this world? See the whole of v.7 and v.12.
3. What does it mean to be "thirsty for the water of life"?
4. How does it show in the way you live your life, and how should it show in the life of the church, that we are longing for the return of the Lord Jesus?

LITURGICAL SUGGESTIONS

The chapters in this book were originally presented as sermons. They have been somewhat adapted and questions were added to make the material also suitable for group Bible study and personal devotional reading. However, if so desired, it is still possible to use these chapters as sermons to read in worship services. To facilitate this, liturgical suggestions for additional Scripture readings and songs are given below. About half of the songs are psalms, which can be chosen from any Psalter. Hymns have been selected from the Book of Praise of the Canadian Reformed Churches, edition 2014, and from the Trinity Psalter Hymnal of the Orthodox Presbyterian Church and the United Reformed Churches in N.A., edition 2018.

1. Scripture reading: Revelation 1:1–8 and 22:6–21
   Suggested songs: Ps.99; Ps.65; Ps.2; *Give to our God immortal praise; Glory be to God the Father; Let Us Love and Sing and Wonder; All Praise to Christ.*

2. Scripture reading: Ezekiel 1: 22 – 2:2 and Daniel 10:1–11
   Suggested songs: Ps.46; Ps.32; Ps.46; *Rejoice the Lord is King; Christ shall have dominion.*

3. Scripture reading: Acts 19:8–12 and 21–41
   Suggested songs: Ps.115, Ps.139; Ps.16; Ps.133; *Praise God from whom all blessings flow; I'm not Ashamed to Own My Lord.*

4. Scripture reading: 1 Peter 4:7–19
   Suggested songs: Ps.27; Ps.33; Ps.140; *O God, our help in ages past; The hope of faith shall not deceive us; For All the Saints.*

5. Scripture reading: John 6:32–58
   Suggested songs: Ps.93; Ps.93; Ps.37; *O faithful is this well-known word; What is in life and death my only aid; Great King of Nations; Hear Our Prayer.*

6. Scripture reading: Psalm 2
   Suggested songs: Ps.8; Ps.65; Ps.110; *A mighty fortress is our God; Now blessed be the Lord our God; In Doubt and Temptation.*

7. Scripture reading: Luke 12:35–56
   Suggested songs: Ps.71; Ps.143; Ps.56; *The Church's One Foundation; Come, Lord Jesus! Maranatha! Kind and Merciful God, We Have Sinned.*

8. Scripture reading: Isaiah 22:15 –25
   Suggested songs: Ps.84; Ps.130; Ps.27; *Christ shall have dominion; Behold the amazing gift of love; My Hope is Built on Nothing Less.*

9. Scripture reading: Isaiah 55
   Suggested songs: Ps.19; Ps.111; *Lo, what a glorious sight appeared; Glory be to God the Father; O Lord, How Shall I Meet You.*

10. Scripture reading: Ezekiel 1:1–11 and 22–28
    Suggested songs: Ps.99; *Holy, Holy, Holy, Lord God Almighty; Praise to the Lord, the Almighty; By the Sea of Crystal; Holy God, We Praise Your Name.*

11. Scripture reading: Daniel 12:1–10 and 1 Corinthians 1:18–25
    Suggested songs: Ps.66; Ps.96; *Now blessed be the Lord our God; Sing Choirs of New Jerusalem; Mighty God, While Angels Bless You; Crown Him with Many Crowns.*

12. Scripture reading: Zechariah 1:7–13 and Luke 21:8–28
    Suggested songs: Ps.46; Ps.25; Ps.94; Ps.35; *O God, we praise you, we acknowledge you as Lord; The Church's One Foundation; When this Passing World is Done.*

13. Scripture reading: Revelation 7 – 8:5
    Suggested songs: Ps.18; Ps.68; Ps.89; *Lo, round the throne a glorious band; Ye Servants of God, Your Master Proclaim; Here from All Nations; Who are these like Stars Appearing.*

14. Scripture reading: Exodus 7:14–21, 9:13–25 and 10:21–23
    Suggested songs: Ps.148; Ps.103; Ps.78; Ps.106; Ps.46; *O Father, You are Sovereign.*

15. Scripture reading: Exodus 10:12–20 and Joel 2:1–11
    Suggested songs: Ps.43; Ps.93; Ps.72; *A mighty fortress is our God; Who trusts in God, a strong abode.*

16. Scripture reading: Ezekiel 2:1 – 3:11
    Suggested songs: Ps.35; Ps.29; *Christ shall have dominion; Alleluia! Alleluia!; More than Conquerors.*

17. Scripture reading: Zechariah 4
    Suggested songs: Ps.26; Ps.79; Ps.48; *The Prayer of Habakkuk; Who trusts in God, a strong abode; Though Troubles Assail Us.*

18. Scripture reading: Exodus 25:10–22
    Suggested songs: Ps.97; *Rejoice, the Lord is King; Christ, above all glory seated; All Hail the Power of Jesus' Name.*

19. Scripture reading: Revelation 12
    Suggested songs: Ps.68; Ps.32; Ps.62; Ps.18; *A mighty fortress is our God; The Son of God Goes Forth to War.*

20. Scripture reading: Daniel 7:1–7 and 15–18
    Suggested songs: Ps.97; Ps.2; Ps.68; *What is in life and death my only aid; Lord, Keep Us Steadfast in Your Word.*

21. Scripture reading: Genesis 19:23–29, Isaiah 21:1–9 and Matthew 13:49–50
    Suggested songs: Ps.33; Ps.29; Ps.96; *Day of judgement! Day of wonders! For All The Saints.*

22. Scripture reading: Joel 3:1–16 and Isaiah 63:1–6
    Suggested songs: Ps.84; Ps.40; *Thank the Lord and come with praise; Jesus shall reign; Now blessed be the Lord, our God; It Is Well with My Soul.*

23. Scripture reading: Exodus: 15:1–21
    Suggested songs: Ps.18; Ps.130; Ps.74; *Holy, Holy, Holy; Lord God Almighty; Who trusts in God, a strong abode; O God, We Praise Thee.*

24. Scripture reading: Revelation 16.
    Suggested songs: Ps.97; Ps.86; Ps.18; Ps.105; Ps.94; *In Christ Alone*

25. Scripture Reading: Revelation 17
    Suggested songs: Ps.2; Ps.57; Ps.109; *What is in life and death my only aid?; Hope of the World; He leadeth Me: O Blessed Thought.*

26. Scripture reading: Revelation 18
    Suggested songs: Ps.111; Ps.46; Ps.68; *Comfort, comfort now my people; Jesus Lives and So Shall I.*

27. Scripture reading: Isaiah 54:1–8 and Hosea 2:16–20
    Suggested songs: Ps.135; Ps.148; *The church's one foundation; Ye servants of God; Glory be to God the Father; Soul, Adorn Yourself with Gladness.*

28. Scripture reading: Isaiah 63:1–6 and Ezekiel 39:17–29
    Suggested songs: Ps.110; Ps.1; Ps.2; Ps.68; *Rejoice, the Lord is King; Look, Ye Saints, the Sight is Glorious.*

29. Scripture reading: John 12:23–32 and Ezekiel 38:1–9 & 39:1–8
    Suggested songs: Ps.97; Ps.56; *Rejoice, the Lord is King; The church's one foundation; Let All Mortal Flesh Keep Silence.*

30. Scripture reading: 2 Peter 3:1–13.
    Suggested songs: Ps.47; Ps.51; Ps.98; *Come, Lord Jesus! Maranatha!; Day of judgment, Day of wonders; Great God What Do I See And Hear.*

31. Scripture reading: Isaiah 65:17–25 and Romans 8:18–25
    Suggested songs: Ps.57; Ps.25; *Lo, what a glorious sight appeared; The church's one foundation; Now thank we all our God; Be Thou My Vision.*

32. Scripture reading: Isaiah 54:9–17
    Suggested songs: Ps.122; Ps.87; Ps.48; *The Spirit, sent from heaven above; The God and Father of our Lord; Jerusalem The Golden.*

33. Scripture reading: Isaiah 60:1–3, 10–14, 19–22 and Ezekiel 47:1–12.
    Suggested songs: Ps.46; Ps.56; Ps.42; *Behold the amazing gift of love; Holy, Holy, Holy, Lord God Almighty; The Sands of Time Are Sinking; Come to the Waters.*

34. Scripture reading: Daniel 12:1–10 and 2 Peter 3: 11–14
    Suggested songs: Ps.126; *Alleluia! Alleluia! ; Thank the Lord and come with praise; Come, Lord Jesus! Maranatha! Wake, Awake for Night is Flying; Lo, He Comes with Clouds Descending; Christ is Coming.*